THE RESISTANCE AND ME

ISBN: 978-0-578-62052-7

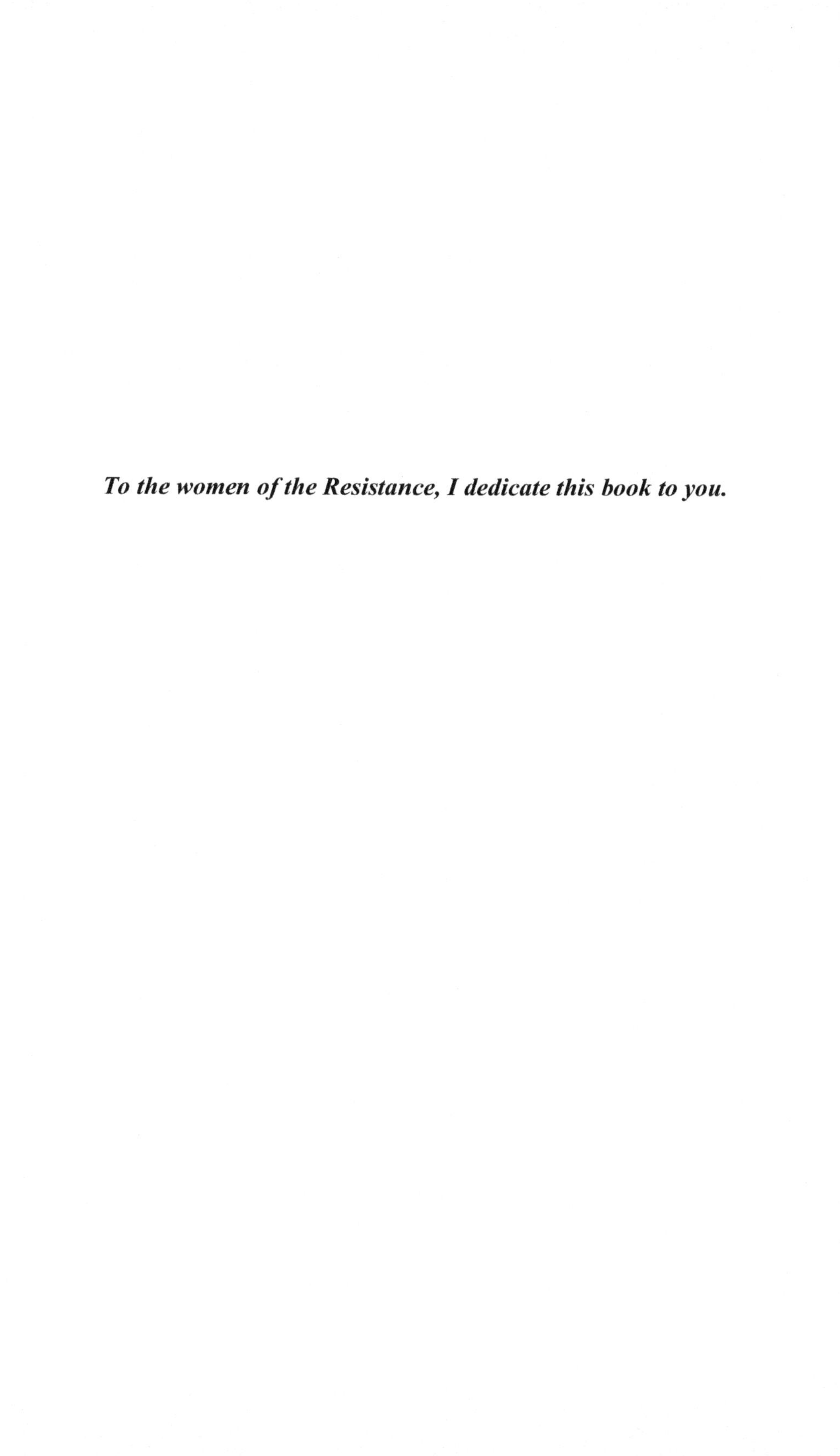

To the women of the Resistance, I dedicate this book to you.

Table of Contents

Acknowledgements

This is a story about women. Women, like me, who said, "Enough is enough," after Trump was elected. Women who refused to sit on the sidelines and silently allow Donald Trump and his Republican enablers to define what it means to be an American. Women who were busy protesting, registering voters or running campaigns but also spent hours with me in countless interviews. So to all of these women who were so generous with their time and agreed to be interviewed on the record, I can never thank them enough. Their cooperation, honesty and insights made this book possible.

Some warrant special mention, such as the leadership committee of East End Action Network - Sharon Adams, Patricia Callan, Rebecca Dolber, Syma Gerard, Cindy Salwen and Wendy Turkington – and the vice chairs of the Southampton Town Democratic Committee, Andrea Klausner and Robin Long. Without all of them, I would have been lost, as an activist and as an author. Words cannot describe how much I appreciate their inspiration and friendship.

While this book is primarily about women, there were many men who offered invaluable assistance. Two of them are Southampton Town Democratic Committee Chairman Gordon Herr and former Chairman Michael Anthony, who helped me understand and navigate the world of local politics, of which I was woefully ignorant.

I would also like to thank the six 2018 Democratic primary candidates who took time out from campaigning to participate in this project. I could not have written a book about the midterm election without their assistance.

In addition, I am grateful to my two talented editors, my niece, Elyse Hennes Sheehan and my son, Matthew Floyd, who each brought skills to the project beyond my own editing of the manuscript. Elyse studied the publication tools available to us and learned how to transform a manuscript into a book. A newly-minted attorney and married mother of two young children, she still carved out time to edit, design and format the entire book. This Herculean job took more than four months and I could not have done any of it without her. Matthew, who is a narrative story designer, edited the book for story continuity. His notes and suggestions substantially strengthened the story I wanted to tell. To paraphrase Hillary Clinton, it takes a family to self-publish a book.

It also takes a family to sustain this kind of personal and professional journey. Along with being my editor, Elyse attended the Women's Marches with me. On the book cover, we are standing next to my sister, Nanci Hennes, and my best friend, Victoria Aspinwall, at the 2017 Women's March. They never stopped marching with me, from the darkest, earliest days of the Trump administration to the present. In fact, it was Nanci's suggestion that I put my reporter's hat on and chronicle the work we were doing. In Resistance and in life, they are always standing beside me, part of the foundation of my life.

Separate from his help with the book, Matthew, along with my husband, Eugene Floyd and my father, Jack Weber, form the cornerstone of that foundation. Their encouragement picked me up each time the news or my own doubts knocked me down, never allowing me to give in to despair or give up on this project. The unconditional love from these three exceptional men emboldened me to believe that I could write a book about so many extraordinary women.

Finally, to all my family and friends, too numerous to mention, thank you for the support you have always shown me, not just in this project but throughout my life. I am very blessed.

Prologue

On September 24th, 2019, the Trump presidency was forever changed. Speaker of the House Nancy Pelosi announced a formal impeachment inquiry into the allegations that Donald Trump had abused the power of the presidency to try to extort Ukraine into digging up dirt on his potential Democratic opponent, Joe Biden. If this day marked the end of Trump's unchecked corruption and possibly the end of his presidency, it is because on January 21st, 2017, millions of women began a journey that started with a March and ended with a blue wave, resulting in the largest midterm election turnout in 40 years and the Democrats taking control of the House. Without that journey, Pelosi is not the Speaker and Trump would not be headed to impeachment.

Driven to marching on Pennsylvania Avenue the day after Trump's inauguration by a desire to show the world that we did not approve of such a manifestly unfit person ascending to the presidency, Trump was the reason we began this journey. But this memoir is about much more than Trump. We started in reaction to the Trump agenda, organizing protests against the Muslim Ban and to save the ACA, but as we became more connected to our own district we learned a secret: the foundation of democracy begins with our own neighborhood.

Who are we, these ordinary women who joined hands at the Women's March, created what came to be called the Resistance, knocked on thousands of doors and helped elect progressive Democrats up and down the ballot through the power of the blue wave? What propelled us to struggle with the often-monumental task of integrating activism into our daily lives? Why would we, the retired, senior citizens of the suburbs, trade in our book clubs for postcard writing parties and voter registration drives?

I am one of these women, but I am also a journalist and I began a diary of the work we were doing in 2018, chronicling in real time our fight to flip our district in the midterm election. This book puts you, the reader, alongside us as we organized our protests, registered people to vote and worked to get our candidates elected. By following our story, I also created a case study about my district that can be seen as a microcosm for other suburban districts similar to mine. Hopefully this study will impart lessons learned to take forward into the 2020 election and beyond.

I had no way of knowing throughout 2018 what the outcome might be but it was my hypothesis that should Democrats take back the House and make inroads into state and local governments, it would be because of the on-the-ground efforts of the women of the Resistance.

The book is organized into four parts, with chapters within. Part I is a look back at how this all began in 2017 and introduces the key people who shared this journey with me. It also includes three lengthy interviews with Rebecca Dolber, Robin Long and Andrea Klausner, three women who were mentors for me and who represent the different life stories of people who were pushing the blue wave forward in our district. Parts II and III contain the diary. Not every entry in the diary ended up in the final draft of the book. For example, we spent months knocking on doors speaking to voters in a process called canvassing. I often went out canvassing every day. Not all of these experiences are included. The handful that are described in detail illustrate something essential about the experience of canvassing or something essential about the voters. Part IV contains post-election analysis.

While the book is a memoir of my journey, the spine of the story is the mosaic of thoughts, insights, fears, joys and conflicts of the people I met and worked with along the way. Their generosity and honesty are what turned an idea into a book. My interviews with them were conducted on the record, in person or by phone or in written responses to emailed questions specifically earmarked to be used in the book. Their Facebook posts, text messages and emails are reprinted with permission from the authors. All photos included in the book are included with permission from each individual whose image is featured. All campaign emails, speeches and Facebook posts are reprinted with permission from the candidates. Newspaper articles and photos are reprinted by permission from the news organization and/or the news photographer.

A note about paragraph formatting: because the body of the book contains so many different types of content, block paragraphs have been chosen to make the book easier to read, rather than the traditional indented format used in the Acknowledgements, Prologue and Epilogue.

While impeachment swirls around us and we are possibly witnessing the end of the Trump presidency, this book takes you back to the beginning. There is much to be learned from looking back, about the trajectory of the Trump presidency and about ourselves. It is important to look back and remember so that as we gaze towards the future, we never take our eyes off our democracy again.

Barbara Weber-Floyd
November, 2019

PART I
LOOKING BACK AT THE BEGINNING: 2017

Chapter 1

From the 2016 Election to the 2017 Women's March

"Waking up after the election in 2016, that feeling, oh God, I was going out of my mind. I needed to do something, a need for support, like needing a grief group after someone died."

Sharon Adams, East End Action Network (EEAN)

The 2016 Election

During the 2016 presidential campaign, I looked to the future with excitement because I was sure that the election of the first woman president – something I had been dreaming about for over 40 years – would usher in a new women's movement. This movement would inspire women running for political office which would in turn create a new, more unified and centrist view of what we always referred to as women's issues, such as paid maternity leave, on-site day care, universal pre-K, equal pay for equal work, insurance-covered women's health care for all. In truth, these issues have never really been women's issues, they are family issues. It is not that these issues were not popular. Most polling had the majority of the country supporting them but they were still trapped in the culture wars and not an accepted part of the fabric of our lives, as they are in other Western countries. It was troubling that the young women of today still did not have a basic support system they needed to be working mothers, similar to my own experience when I was the mother of a young child. The three words "President Hillary Clinton" gave me hope that this dynamic might begin to change. It was also crucially important to me to protect the policies of the Obama administration, on everything from civil rights to global warming to immigration to healthcare. And, as a country, we needed to repudiate the ugly, divisive rhetoric of Donald Trump, to send such racist, xenophobic, sexist, anti-facts, anti-science beliefs to the dustbin of history. They had no place in the global 21st Century world.

As a reporter in New York City for many years, I sometimes had to cover a Trump press conference. I was familiar with his toxic brand of braggadocio uncoupled from reality. When he bought the Plaza Hotel in Manhattan in 1988, reporters at the press announcement I attended whispered to each other wondering how long it would take for him to run it into the ground. He had overpaid for it and within a few years, it was in debt and sold, part of the bank restructuring that kept him out of personal bankruptcy. I also remembered the press articles about "The Donald" from the 80's and 90's, the tabloid war covering his affairs and divorces, the New York Magazine article about his ties to the Italian mob, his casino collapse in Atlantic City. I told anyone who would listen that Trump was a con man and not to be trusted. And that he was uniquely unqualified, by experience, temperament – he was a chronic liar and thin-skinned narcissist – and political views, to be president. And he was promoting a message of hate. My family told me not to worry. My friends told me not to worry. All the polls told me not to worry. But I was worried. Throughout history, stoking fear against the "other" has been a powerful, mobilizing message.

Like the good Democrat I am, I made phone calls for the Clinton campaign in the fall, just as I had for every Democratic nominee for the presidency since I first volunteered for Walter Mondale in 1980. But these calls were not reassuring me. The Clinton campaign had us calling into Ohio and Pennsylvania, just as I had for Obama in 2008 and 2012, but Democrats were often hanging up on me or saying disparaging things about Clinton. Something seemed wrong.

Julie Sheehan, Southampton Town Democratic Committee (SHDems)

"I was volunteering for the Clinton campaign, and the conventional wisdom, you'll remember, was ground game, she has a great ground game. As a volunteer, I got called three times and asked if I would be willing to host a house party for Hillary, and I said, 'Yes. What's the next step?' 'Someone else will contact you.' Then click. That happened to me three times. I never held a house party for Hillary because I could never get to step two. So, on the ground, something was wrong... And the call lists were inaccurate and I couldn't correct the list, I couldn't add to the data. You know, just little things like that were alarming to me. Especially since those little things make a huge difference with what was supposed to be her ace in the hole... And I just remember the last weekend before the election, I was in the car and the news was on the radio, and they did those little plugs about the candidates – 'Donald Trump is in Wisconsin, Michigan, and Pennsylvania today. Hillary Clinton's at a fundraiser in Seattle.' It was two days before the election. I said to myself, 'Stop raising money, you don't need more money, you need to get voters, because in the end, voters win elections.'

Rebecca Dolber, East End Action Network (EEAN)

"When Hillary won the primary, and towards the end of the election, right before, I knew that things weren't really going well. And I said I have to do everything I can. It was just out of necessity; there was no

> question in my mind that I needed to be more involved. So, I went to Maine and I campaigned for her up in Portland, Maine for a week."

I watched all three debates and there was no question that she won all three. Yet the media focused almost exclusively afterwards on Trump. The more outrageous he behaved, the more he consumed all the political oxygen. I continued to worry. Then came the Comey letter and my worry became panic. I obsessively read the polls and Nate Silver's blog and while the race was tightening, every poll still had Clinton ahead. So when I walked up the steps of the firehouse to vote, along with my son, Matthew Floyd, I was cautiously optimistic that we were going to see the first woman president elected.

This was our first time voting together in a presidential election. In 2012, he was away at college and voted by absentee ballot. He is not very political though he believes in the policies of the Democratic Party and was an enthusiastic Obama supporter. That moment when Obama was declared the winner in 2008 had resonated so much with him that he chose to write about it for his college essay. We joked around on the way to the firehouse. Afterward, I bought us white wine and lots of our favorite snacks for our viewing party for what we expected to be the historic moment of the election of the first woman president. It would also mark the end of Trump and his ugly, divisive campaign. So, despite warning signs, based on the polls, based on what the media was saying, we had every reason to believe we were going to have a great night.

Robin Long, SHDems

> "We got to the Jacob Javits Convention Center in New York City and I was so grateful I was given credentials. We walked in with our credentials hanging around our necks and I thought, 'Oh, man, I have hit political nirvana. This is heaven.' I thought the Democratic Convention in the summer was good, but this was going to be the jewel in the crown. It was very hard to get in. There were lines and security. We finally got in, and we got there very early. As we were walking in and you had different color passes, and you had to go to different spots. There were these three elegant black women in front of me. They were from Southern states. They were absolutely magnificent looking women, women of great pride. I'm not talking about model beauty. I'm talking about women of dignity. There was a beauty that shines from within. She turned to me and she said, 'You know it's over.' I looked at her, and I said, 'It's only 6:30, or 7 o'clock.' She said, 'There were results from certain Southern districts that had come in.' She looked at me at 6:30, and her eyes welled up with tears, and she said, 'I'm so sorry. It's over.' I looked at her, and I said, 'No, no, no. The polls didn't close.' She said,

> 'It's over.' I lost her in the crowd, but her words just stuck with me. I said, 'Son of bitch.' Later that night my daughter called me from Seattle and said, 'Your hair looks great, but you look like shit.' I said, 'What are you talking about my hair looks great?' She said to me, 'You're a meme, Mom.' All her friends were calling saying, 'Isn't that your mother? We're watching the election. That looks just like your mother.' There were two or three memes of me floating out there that night."

By 10:00 PM, I turned off the television. I could see the handwriting on the wall and the most unimaginable outcome was becoming reality. I was stunned. I wanted to reach out to my family, particularly my sister, who I knew was also feeling crushed. But it would have to wait. My immediate concern was my son.

We instituted a news blackout. No media at all, no television, computer, smartphone. So instead of watching Trump's victory speech and Hillary's concession speech, we stayed up talking about what we could do that would help him feel safe in what was now a world turned upside down. I told him the only answer to such an atrocity was to fight back. My predominant feeling was one of anger and I was thinking of ways to challenge what I knew would be a catastrophic assault on our rights.

"That might work for you," he told me. "But I can't live in a place where every day is dominated by fighting for basic rights. Nothing changes in this country. The economy collapses in 2008, the country elects Obama to correct it, which fuels a racist backlash that then elects Trump. You have spent your life fighting these issues. I can't do that."

"I understand," I said. I also knew that the threats to healthcare were on his mind, as they were on mine. In his twenties, he was still on our health insurance thanks to the Affordable Care Act (otherwise known as Obamacare or the ACA).. Trump and the GOP had campaigned on gutting the healthcare safety net. At that moment we had to assume that the ACA and protections for pre-existing conditions were in grave danger. "What can we do right now that would make you feel whole, make you feel safe?"

He thought about it. "I think I need to know if I can live in another country where I won't have to spend my whole life fighting for these basic rights, like healthcare," he said.

"What country do you imagine you could live in?" I asked. I expected him to say France, since he had studied French in high school and visited France on a school trip.

Without hesitation, he said, "Canada. They seem like the nicest people. They don't keep fighting over the same things, like healthcare." He thought some more. "And they have baseball."

So, we spent the rest of the night online, investigating Canada. We went to the country's government website to find out how an American can get a visa to live and work there. He took their test and found out that he could accrue enough points – college degree majoring in engineering, fluent French speaker – to live in Canada. He first needed work experience in his field which would give him even more points.

We then studied what it would be like to live in Toronto. He said he could happily be a Blue Jays fan. We looked at the prices of apartments as well as the job market. We did not speak of the election and instead formulated a plan that would give him some hope going forward. He finally went to sleep as the sun came up.

But I couldn't sleep. I hid from him just how frightened I was. I also hid the intensity of my rage, at Trump and at the people who had just elected him. What did Trump's election say about this country?

Julie Sheehan, SHDems

> "Trump rallied a group of voters who care about keeping brown-skinned people in their place and in prison or in poverty or whatever, and people who care about, 'I'm going to get my graft and everybody else can follow the laws. That's for the little people.' He put together a coalition. So, the despair was also about the nature of the electorate. Like, how could this electorate that had given us Barack Obama, as he put it, a skinny black guy with a funny name, two-time winner with decisive popular vote majorities, then turn around and give us Trump… At the time, it felt like the electorate was this unknowable mass. Who are you people? That's not who you are. You just voted four years ago in a very different way. And, of course, it was a different electorate. A lot of people who don't vote voted for Trump."

If I had felt proud of the progress the country had made on equal rights by the election of Barack Obama in 2008, I felt equally ashamed of what it said about America that it had just elected a narcissistic, pathological liar with no governing experience, who used blatant racism, sexism and anti-immigrant bigotry to win the presidency. What did it say about how entrenched misogyny is in America that people would vote against Hillary Clinton, believing every far-fetched bizarre right-wing conspiracy about her, but ignore the accusations of sexual assault, the Access Hollywood audio tape, the cozying up to Putin, the constant lying and the lack of any qualifications for office in order to elect Trump?

The next day, on almost no sleep, I finally looked at the news on my phone for the first time. I felt physically ill.

Andrea Klausner, SHDems

"Oh God, I will never forget election night. I remember as the returns started coming in and everybody's jubilation started turning to anxiety and then to downright depression. People just started leaving without even saying goodbye. People just started trickling out. And I remember going home and I couldn't put on the TV. And I woke up in the morning and turned on the TV and saw that he was president and I was in shock. And I remember one of my daughters calling me because they had heard me rant and rave throughout the election and she was in tears saying, 'Mom, I'm really scared. What's going to happen to our country? What's going to happen to us with all the anti-Semitism and the racism?' And she said I'm really scared about what our country is going to turn into. And this is a child who is never political, who only recently became knowledgeable about politics. And I said we'll be okay, not knowing if we would be but I said we'll survive. It's one election. We'll vote him out."

But any hope of voting him out in 2020 seemed like a pipe dream. Republicans held all the levers of power in Washington as well as most state houses. The Democratic Party was decimated. And the Hillary/Bernie rift from the campaign was an open, oozing wound that, at that moment, seemed too deep to ever heal.

Rebecca Dolber, EEAN

"My biggest gripe during that 2016 election was not the Trump supporter. I understood their racism. I didn't agree with it, but I understood where it was, I understood the misconception. I understood the lies that they were being fed and why they believed them. But what I could never wrap my head around, were Democrats, who hated Hillary Clinton so much, that they couldn't bring themselves to vote for her and instead voted for a third party or didn't vote."

Wendy Turkington, EEAN

"It started for me during the election… I had some friends on Facebook, the Bernie bros, posting some very vile stuff. I was amazed at the nastiness. And a turning point for me was joining Pantsuit Nation, an online Hillary group. It was great. I liked every post on it."

Kyle Cranston, EEAN

"What stoked the Bernie campaign, I think, is because he was so authentic. I didn't vote for Clinton or Trump. I thought that they were both wrong, and both bad. A critical part of the problem is that we have these two political parties that are corporate, both of them, corporate-owned and domineering. And both of them are basically just vying for power and position, and one is marketing themselves to one segment of the market and the other one to the other segment of the market. And they basically just divide it up, and that keeps us divided and it keeps them in power."

Kathryn Szoka, Progressive East End Reformers (PEER)

"We created a group called the Bernie East End Supporters (BEES) and the group morphed into the Progressive East End Reformers (PEER) after Bernie lost the nomination. Some people in the group canvassed and worked for Hillary; some people didn't and continued to be disappointed. I was sort of in the middle. I didn't canvas for Hillary, but I knew that if Trump won it would be a disaster of epic proportions. So, I encouraged people to vote for Hillary - she may not have been my candidate, but she was a thousand times better than Trump."

Rather than repudiate Trump's brand of white nationalist fear-mongering, his election elevated it. And I feared for the country as a whole, in truth the world, because the Republicans had the White House, the Senate and the House of Representatives. There were no checks on the GOP agenda – repeal the ACA on "Day One," gut federal agencies, weaken consumer protections, weaken civil rights, promote fossil fuels, pull out of the Paris Accords on climate change, institute a Muslim Ban on immigration, defund Planned Parenthood, appoint pro-life judges, overturn Roe vs. Wade, etc., etc. The outlook looked very bleak. What we were feeling resembled mourning, with the acute pain that comes from a deep and personal sense of loss.

The day after the election was my husband's birthday. He had been away on business in the days leading up to, and including, the election, which is why he wasn't with us at the firehouse but voted by absentee ballot. He returned that Wednesday. We had planned on a dual celebration for that day, the election and his birthday and now a day for our family meant to be happy was turning into a funeral. I spent the day in what I can only describe as a daze, mindlessly looking up articles on the internet thinking "this can't be happening."

Still, it was good to be together. And in the end, we were able to take some solace in that. I noticed Matt's mood improved once Eugene returned, and mine did as well. We sang, ate chocolate cake, and spiritually held hands. Things felt okay that evening for us, but I knew that there were families out there that were not as lucky.

Looking back at my emails after the election, the first one is from my Dad, Dr. Jack Weber, who was 92 years old at the time, the day after the election. As a Democratic donor, an enthusiastic Obama and Clinton supporter, he had received the concession email that Hillary Clinton sent to her supporters and he forwarded it to our family along with a note:

> *Kids, I cannot ever recall being as angry, disappointed, or just plain mad at any political event as this election result. In case you didn't see this email from H it has helped me a bit. Love, Dad*

I wrote back:

> *Thanks, Dad. Like all of us, I am shattered and hurting. Hillary and Obama are nicer people than I am. I am not there yet. It was a horrible night, one of the worst I can ever remember. Like a death in the family. There have been times in my life that I have hated this country and this is one of them. It is going to be a long time before that can change.*

The 2017 Women's March

Either that day or within the next few days, I saw the first Facebook posting about a protest for and by women, a Women's March on Washington D.C. to protest the Trump agenda. I might have seen the first posting on Pantsuit Nation, which I had joined during the campaign. I responded immediately that I was in. I didn't know any details about it but that didn't matter. I knew I would be there. I was 64 years old and had not marched since the Vietnam War. I didn't even know if I could physically march on Washington or anywhere else. It did not matter. I would be there. For my son, knowing that he could live in Canada helped him recover from the pain of the election results. For me, I needed to find a way to fight back. The March gave me that opportunity.

At the same time, emails went back and forth with my family because we were trying to arrange our annual visit to the cemetery on the anniversary of my mother's passing. We had planned to gather there after the election and then go out and celebrate Hillary's winning.

On November 12th, my Dad wrote:

> *Kids, I know we are all depressed and angry post-election and what we thought would be a victory celebration together on Sunday will not come to pass. But I think it will be therapeutic to be together to lift each other up, if possible. What is the time frame to meet at the cemetery? Love, Dad*

My sister, Nanci Hennes, was the first to write back:

> *I know all too well that even though I feel like staying in bed and pulling the covers over my head, I can't succumb to those feelings. We will hopefully get to the cemetery by 12:30.*

Hillary's loss was particularly hard on my sister because she had lost her husband, Richard Hennes, just two years before to brain cancer. That loss was still raw. She, her daughters and her granddaughters went to vote together and planned on celebrating with pink champagne that night. The champagne stayed in the refrigerator and I found out from her later that she too had gone to bed early.

We did gather together that Sunday, November 13th, and we did go out to eat after the cemetery, though not for a celebration. We tried not talking about the election. My older brother, David, did not want to hear anything about Trump. He had been convinced throughout the campaign that the American public would never elect someone as grossly unfit for office as Trump. He told me later that he hadn't been this disappointed in the United States since the Vietnam War.

But just as my very wise father had surmised, it was cathartic to be together. And when inevitably the election came up, I told them not to despair, that the country would fight back. I predicted that there would be a resistance to Trump and all he stood for, even though I had no evidence at that time that this would be true.

The next day, on November 14th, I received a posting on Facebook from The Women's March. This was less than a week after the election. It was seen by 3.8 thousand Facebook members.

On November 18th I emailed my entire family with information about the Women's March:

> *I am continuing to struggle every day trying to cope with the new world order where the words President Trump are the reality. The pain is still there and like all mourning, is going to take time to move from severe,*

acute pain to a dull, constant ache, which will be there for the next 4 years (please Lord, not for any longer than that). Everything about the transition and the picks so far for the cabinet confirm all the worst fears. I have bought my Megabus tickets to go to DC for the Million Woman March, so if anyone else is interested in going, let me know. If a bunch of us want to go together and take other transportation, I can easily change my tickets to another trip to DC. And if anyone wants to join me on the Megabus, let me know. For me, the only way I can cope is to actively participate in the fight.

In response to my email, a family dialogue about the Women's March began. My sister, Nanci, wrote:

Dear Babs, Please buy me a ticket. I want to be standing right next to you on Jan. 21st. Love, Your sister.

My sister-in-law, Heidi Pressley Weber, who lives in upstate New York, wrote:

I am planning to take Rose (her daughter) and our new roommate to DC for this. We have never been and would love to join you. Let me know what we need to do. I can totally relate. I can't sleep, cry at the drop of a hat, have lost 8 pounds, am addicted to coverage of this horrible nightmare, feel like I will have to get a little pill, have joined the resistance, have signed more petitions and donated more money in the last 8 days than in the entirety of my life, combined. I need this episode of the Twilight Zone to be over soon. Help!

My step-mother, Pearl Glassman, who was then 89 years old and had been the first Democrat elected to her local Town Board in 1984, wrote:

Dear Babs and Nanci, How great you are to take such an active role in this demonstration. I wish I could join you. So, march for me and for all other American women and for our great country. Love you, Pearl

And I answered all of them:

We are truly stronger together and we are Sisters in Resistance! Do not lose hope!

My first email from the New York City organizers of the Women's March was December 12th, 2016. I had signed up on both Facebook pages, for the national organization and the NYC organizers. This email was about organizing buses to go to the March. My first email from the national organizers of the Women's March was on January 1st. In the meantime, we all started making plans. Heidi and many of my friends decided to attend the Women's March in New York City.

New York City is a lot closer, a day trip rather than a weekend one, but we decided to go to D.C. As Nanci explained to me, she wanted to be part of the sea of women that would greet Trump on his first day when he looked out the window of the White House. Nanci's youngest daughter, Elyse, and Elyse's three-year-old daughter Mackenzie were also on board with a road trip to D.C. Rounding out our merry band of protesters was one of my dearest friends, Victoria Aspinwall. We have been friends since we were twelve years old. We would all be staying with her daughter, Mimi, who ironically, is Elyse's best friend. They have carried the friendship into the next generation and have been friends their whole lives. Both raised on Long Island, both college graduates, both in their mid-twenties, Mimi was living and working in Washington, D.C. Elyse was in law school at Hofstra University on Long Island. Because we weren't sure just what the March would be like, Mimi offered to take Mackenzie to the Washington, D.C. zoo while we attended the March.

I bought Women's March NYC T-shirts from the NYC organizers for all of us, including for Mimi and Mackenzie. Along with our travel plans, we discussed what we wanted our posters to say. We thought of the many anti-Trump messages we could choose or of the pro-Hillary messages that meant the most to us, like "Stronger Together" and "We're With Her." After much deliberation, we chose a quote from Michelle Obama, from the last speech she gave as First Lady on January 6th, 2017. Below is an excerpt from that speech.

> ***So that's my final message to young people as First Lady. It is simple. I want our young people to know that they matter, that they belong. So don't be afraid — you hear me, young people? Don't be afraid. Be focused. Be determined. Be hopeful. Be empowered. Empower yourselves with a good education, then get out there and use that education to build a country worthy of your boundless promise. Lead by example with hope, never fear. And know that I will be with you, rooting for you and working to support you for the rest of my life.***
>
> ***And that is true I know for every person who are here — is here today, and for educators and advocates all across this nation who get up every day and work their hearts out to lift up our young people. And I am so grateful to all of you for your passion***

> ***and your dedication and all the hard work on behalf of our next generation. And I can think of no better way to end my time as First Lady than celebrating with all of you.***

We took the four messages from her speech, "Be Focused, Be Determined, Be Hopeful and Be Empowered" and put them on our four posters. We wanted to be uplifting and to honor Michelle Obama. I bought all the art materials and one evening a week before the March, I played with Mackenzie while Elyse designed and created our posters.

Late Friday afternoon, I met up with Nanci, Elyse and Mackenzie and together we drove to Vicky's in Nanci's van. It was close to 6:00 PM when we got to Vicky's since we could not start out until everyone had finished work and school for the day. While I have been semi-retired as a freelance journalist for several years, my sister and Vicky still work full time, Nanci as a teacher and Vicky as a college research librarian. We were in buoyant spirits. Into the back of the van we piled our suitcases, coats, rain slickers, boots and our four posters.

Our first glimpse of the enormity of the March was the traffic on the New Jersey Turnpike heading south. When we stopped at the first rest stop on the Turnpike we had to circle the parking lot several times to find a parking space. When we went inside, the building was almost wall to wall people, almost all women, most of them wearing pink pussy hats. There were long lines to use the bathroom and to buy food but even waiting on line was uplifting as we smiled and chatted to the women next to us. Everyone said hello to Mackenzie. The mood was joyous. The drive, usually five hours, took much longer because the traffic was so intense. But we knew that the traffic represented women like us who were headed to D.C. to make their voices heard.

My only regret at that point was that I had missed out on getting us all pink hats, never imagining that they would become an important symbol of the Resistance. I had seen the patterns for knitting them distributed on Facebook and hadn't thought much about it, especially because I don't know how to knit. Instead I had bought us all T-shirts but at that moment, I wished I had gotten us all hats to go with our shirts.

We got into D.C. after midnight. Mimi had her studio apartment all ready for us, with blowup beds and the sofa made up with sheets and blankets. Elyse carried a sleeping Mackenzie into the apartment and put her to bed. Too excited to go to sleep, we sat up talking until finally we all collapsed into bed. It was late and we had to be up early and I worried that I would be too tired to walk the length of the March.

But we managed to get ourselves awake early, made breakfast and headed out of the apartment to the bus station near Mimi's building. We were a little behind schedule, but not that much. Our plan was to take the bus to the Metro station and take the Metro to Union Station, while Mimi took the Metro to the zoo with Mackenzie. Mimi took a selfie of all of us at the bus stop.

We all wore our NYC organizers T-shirts with the Statue of Liberty and the Women's March logo on the front. (Logos reprinted with permission from the New York Women's March Alliance). We had worried about cold weather, after all it was January, but it was an unusually warm day. We had been able to leave our boots and parkas in the car. Wonderfully fitting that it was far nicer weather than the day before had been for the Inauguration.

When the bus came, it was so packed with women in pink hats carrying signs that we almost couldn't get on. But we did and even found seats in the back. Elyse sat with Mackenzie on her lap. A woman, about my age, sitting next to us commented on our shirts and we commented on her pink hat. She told us she had knit hats for herself and all her friends who were with her on the bus. She then reached into her handbag and pulled out a hat she handed to Elyse explaining she had made it for a friend who couldn't make it and she wanted Elyse to have it. We hugged her and thanked her and all laughed as Elyse donned her pink pussy hat! At least one member of our little group now was anointed with the symbol of the March. (I had a pink wool hat I had bought for the March, but it was not a pussy hat. Ironically, when I look at the pictures, it kind of looks like it is.)

We transferred from the bus to the Metro station. Long lines of pink-hatted women streamed down the escalators to the Metro. We waited for a train but the trains were so crowded that they did not stop and let any more passengers on. We were headed for Union Station and would walk to the beginning staging area of the March from there. But we couldn't get on a train to get downtown. There were empty trains heading uptown, so we got on one going back to the beginning of the line to then take the train back downtown. That worked.

At the first stop on the line, we got on and very quickly the train was too crowded to let any passengers get on as it headed downtown. Mackenzie and Mimi got off for the zoo and everyone in the car waved goodbye to them. No one else was getting off. Finally, we got to Judiciary Square, the stop right before Union Station, but that was as far as we could go. The transit officials stopped the train, had us all get off but it was not a problem.

We exited the Metro station and joined the sea of bobbing pink heads, signs, laughter and song. We were not sure what direction to go in so we joined in with the massive crowd walking away from the station. It truly was a sea of people, far more than anything we had ever seen before in our lives and seemingly far more than had been anticipated.

We were never able to get close to the rally but it did not matter. We found a wall to sit on and wait, found port-o-potties and just when the word went out that the marching part had to be cancelled because the route was too crowded for anyone to move, we saw the crowd beginning to walk down the street that was closest to us so we jumped in with them. Turns out the police had opened up more roads. We marched, we sang, we chanted, we held our posters high. And then our road emptied onto Pennsylvania Avenue.

The walk on Pennsylvania Avenue was astonishing. All along the sides of Pennsylvania Avenue, bleachers set up for the inauguration the day before were filled with cheering, chanting people, many of them probably D.C. residents but many also marchers who had arrived there long before us. We held up our signs, they pointed at them and cheered, signaling thumbs up with our message that quoted Michelle Obama. The chants continued and we were lifted along in a joyous parade. We walked six miles that day.

We had no way of knowing when we made our plans to attend that it would be one of the biggest protest marches in U.S. history. That night we watched the news coverage in Mimi's apartment and marveled at the many marches around the world. Mackenzie was fascinated with the images of all the marchers.

We got a picture of her at Mimi's in front of our signs. At one point, she picked up one of the signs and marched around the room chanting, "We will not go away."

That night, Nanci posted about the March on Facebook. Along with her message, she included the photo of the four of us that is on the cover of this book:

> *I will remember this day, marching on Washington with my daughter, sister, and good friend, as one of the best days of my life. Everyone was so upbeat and kind and energized. I feel empowered to go forward, and try to make a difference, standing up for the things that I believe are important in order to have a compassionate world to live in.*
>
> *Thanks to my Sweet Elyse Hennes for making these signs which quote Michelle Obama's advice to the younger generation in her farewell address:*
>
> *Be focused.*
> *Be determined.*
> *Be hopeful.*
> *Be empowered.*
>
> *I feel ALL of those things today...thanks to the hundreds of thousands of people that I physically marched with as well as the millions around the world who marched by my side in spirit! We are NOT going to go away!*

For many, the Resistance to Trump began on election night when he won. But for my sister and me and so many other women, Jan. 21st was the day it was truly born, the day we found our voices.

Julie Sheehan, SHDems

"It was just so heartening to see a really diverse crowd, young women and older women. I ended up staying with a friend who was way at the end of the bus line and took a bus in. And we were the first stop for the bus, basically, and it was almost full by the time it left the first stop. Everyone was talking to each other and it was really joyful. That phrase 'happy warrior' came back to me with the Women's March. People had a sense of humor. People had a lightness and a joyfulness. And that's what combats fear and combats that kind of frozen, there's nothing we can do feeling of despair. It's really important and it's been great to see groups having a sense of humor and the protests themselves being inventive and that has carried forward and I think it's really an important element. Plus, it drives Trump crazy because he's like mirthless."

Andrea Klausner, SHDems

"I marched with some friends from Westchester (in New York) and one of my daughters and some of her friends. We started out as a bigger group but it was hard to stay together... But I still remember my daughter before the March saying 'Mom, please don't make any signs or wear any funny hats. I'm going to feel embarrassed.' And so, we didn't. But then, after the March she said, 'Mom, we should have had signs and hats'... And I knit, so I could have made our own hats! It was honestly one of the most moving and empowering experiences of my life. I had marched for different causes before. Seeing all of these people join together from all backgrounds, all fighting for the same thing, all saying we don't accept this. And it went further than women's rights... Because women are also the half of society that cares more about nurturing and cares more about healthcare and education, all those things. And so, I felt like the women's rights march was all about all of the quality of life things that we're talking about, all the compassionate social issues. And it was just breathtaking."

Patricia Callan, EEAN

"The Women's March was one of the best days of my life, and also one of the worst. I was in a ten-year relationship that ended because I went to the Women's March. He broke up with me while I was on the bus at the Women's March in Washington... At eight o'clock in the morning, we're rolling into Washington, we're finally there, exhausted, but so excited. Everybody's so pumped, the whole bus is excited to be there, we have our signs, and we're all set. And I get a text and I'm like, 'Oh, I have a message, I have a messenger,' so I looked at it, and he said that he was disgusted that I went to the Women's March, he can't believe I actually went, and that I turned his stomach by not supporting his president.

But you know what? Now we're rolling into the depot, we're all getting ready, everybody's getting off the bus with their signs, and I'm like, 'I'm just going to have a good time, because what else can I do? He's dumped me. But I'm going to march, to do what I came here for; I came here for a reason.' And I had the best day. I put it aside, I had women and men all around me, supportive, like-minded, nobody saying I turned their stomach, everybody's saying kumbaya. It was so nice, it was so much better. And I walked around, and every now and then I would think of him, and I would have a moment of disbelief, shock, and horror, and then I would just go, 'Nope, not going to do it right now, because look at that sign.' And I walked over and took a picture of something, and I distracted myself, and I got through the day. And I met some really, really good friends that I'm still friends with today. In fact, Becca's mom was on the bus.

After the Women's March, I mean, I'm not going to say I wasn't heartbroken, I spent a lot of time eating ice cream and pickles, as if I was drowning every sorrow I had with salt and sugar. And I muddled through. I mean, it's been a year and a half and I'm still single. I don't know if I'm fully over it yet."

Robin Long, SHDems

"As soon as the Facebook post came out, I said, 'I have to be there to ruin his inauguration, because he did not win the popular vote. He cannot believe that the country is behind him.' I have to ruin that day."

Chapter 2

Finding My Way and Joining a Huddle

> ***"After the election, I was sitting there enraged and there wasn't anybody I could talk to. I have a husband who says he loves Trump. So, we try not to even talk about it because when we start talking, it just tears at us. After my first EEAN meeting, I came home that night aglow. I called all my friends in Denver and told them that I found all these people that I can talk to."***
>
> Syma Gerard, EEAN

We were not marching for any political party, for any candidate or for any one issue. The unifying theme was a determination to be heard, to voice the message that the bigotry of Trump and Trumpism did not reflect our values.

After the March, women came home and decided that the March was not the end but the beginning. That was when it changed from a protest to the Resistance. It cannot be emphasized enough just how unique this was to those of us who were living it. I had protested before, I had volunteered for candidates before, I had marched before. But at no other time in my life did I make the decision to turn my life upside down and inside out and to devote my free time to political activism.

But I felt I had no choice. Trump was moving forward, aggressively, to institute his hateful agenda. On January 25th, the GOP in Congress announced their goal to repeal the ACA by the spring. On January 27th, Trump issued the first of his travel bans against citizens from seven Muslim majority countries. On January 28th, there were protests at airports around the country. Throughout January and February, blatantly unqualified people were being confirmed by the Senate for Trump's cabinet, to oversee agencies that they were committed to gutting.

It helped that my son had stopped talking about moving to Canada (for now). His focus turned to graduate school, first applying and then, once he was accepted to Carnegie Mellon University, on making plans to move to Pittsburgh that fall. While he still did not want to speak about politics, he encouraged and supported my quest to find ways to contribute to the Resistance.

I started my Resistance work with a group called Rise Stronger (https://www.risestronger.org). Started by former Obama national security staffer Andy Kim, Rise is a national policy-based grassroots group that was organizing against the Trump agenda.

You had to be recommended for the group and Elliot Hecht (the son of my dear friend Catherine), who was working as a policy aide at a non-profit in D.C., had recommended me. Interesting that in 2018, Andy made the decision to run for Congress in New Jersey.

The goal of Rise was to bring together volunteers doing research about the issues, organized in policy working groups, and to then disseminate that information for the grassroots through the Rise newsletter. Because the issue I was most concerned about was the repeal of the ACA, I joined the healthcare policy working group.

At our first conference call, the leader said that our goal was "to weaken the resolve of the GOP and to strengthen the spines of the Democrats" in order to save the ACA. And to keep insisting that there could be no repeal without a replacement plan and since the Republicans had no plan, this could help prevent the ACA from being repealed.

My first assignment from Rise was to create a pdf graphic with information about the impact of repealing the ACA without a replacement that could then be distributed to grassroots groups around the country to use in their protests against their Member of Congress (MOC). I found a template online, researched what the data would be, created the graphic and uploaded it to Rise so it could be used across the grassroots. Finishing this graphic helped me to feel like I was fighting back against the GOP mission to gut the ACA.

But on our next conference call, it was suggested that I go in a different direction. Instead of focusing on national statistics, the group advised me to focus exclusively on my district. Because I have a Trump-supporting GOP Congressman in my district, they felt I could be even more effective if I focused all my efforts on organizing my district to persuade him not to vote to repeal. We would do this by challenging him at a town hall meeting in front of his constituents and exposing how many people in this district would be hurt by repealing the ACA. They told me to write Letters to the Editor for my local newspaper, reach out to other grassroots groups and healthcare organizations and try to organize a coalition to fight against repeal.

To help me understand this kind of local activism, it was also suggested that I download and read the Indivisible guide – the free guide from two Obama White House staffers – with guidance about how to resist in your own district.

Indivisible was growing quickly, with chapters opening in every congressional district across the country. I downloaded the free guide and read about the kinds of activities and protests that might be effective in my district.

Along with learning about the forms of activism that might work in my district, I realized I needed to learn more about the district itself. Like so many voters, I knew woefully little about the political make-up of my own congressional district.

I live in Congressional District (CD) #1 in New York (also referred to as CD1, NY01, or NY#1).

Geographically it is a large district, encompassing almost all of Suffolk County on Long Island, in the state of New York. Some parts of Suffolk County are carved out and are part of CD#2 and CD#3, but it is the majority of Suffolk County. It is made up of different townships. I live in Southampton Township, often referred to as part of the East End of Long Island.

The 2012 congressional map of CD1 from the New York State Legislative Task Force on Demographic Research and Reapportionment shows where Southampton Township is located within the district.

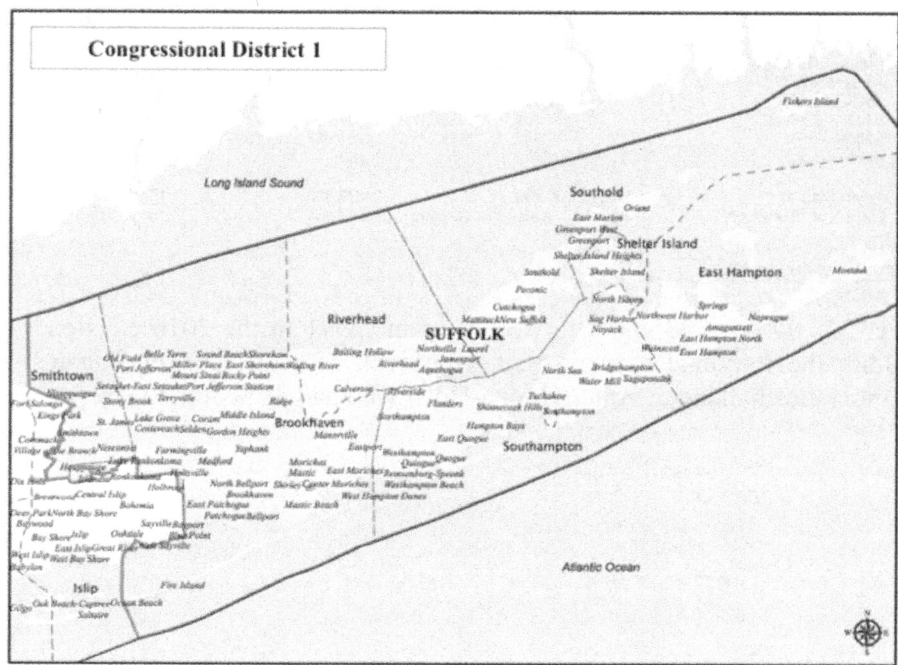

Source: New York State Legislative Task Force on Demographic Research and Reapportionment[1]

The following table contains basic demographic information about CD1 in comparison to New York State and the United States. The 2018 data is from the Census Bureau.

NY Congressional District 1

	CD 1		New York State		United States	
Sex						
Female	361,680	50.3%	10,050,896	51.4%	166,049,288	50.8%
Male	357,046	49.7%	9,491,313	48.6%	161,118,151	49.2%
Total	718,726		19,542,209		327,167,439	
Age						
Under 18	152,056	21.2%	4,064,685	20.8%	73,352,242	22.4%
18 to 64	437,666	60.9%	12,265,459	62.8%	201,392,083	61.6%
65 and over	129,004	17.9%	3,212,065	16.4%	52,423,114	16.0%
18 and over	566,670	78.8%	15,477,524	79.2%	253,815,197	77.6%
Median age	42.3		39.0		38.2	
Race						
White	616,452	85.8%	12,375,601	63.3%	236,173,020	72.2%
Black or African American	41,995	5.8%	3,069,259	15.7%	41,617,764	12.7%
Asian	32,067	4.5%	1,666,113	8.5%	18,415,198	5.6%
Other	12,001	1.7%	1,783,581	9.1%	19,681,426	6.0%
Two or More	16,211	2.3%	647,655	3.3%	11,280,031	3.4%
	718,726		19,542,209		327,167,439	
Ethnicity						
Hispanic or Latino (of any race)	114,404	15.9%	3,752,523	19.2%	59,763,631	18.3%
Not Hispanic or Latino	604,322	84.1%	15,789,686	80.8%	267,403,808	81.7%
Education						
Less than high school	40,709	8.1%	1,757,364	12.9%	26,044,163	11.7%
High school	138,655	27.6%	3,546,789	25.9%	59,961,893	26.9%
Some college	138,080	27.5%	3,276,724	24.0%	64,402,330	28.9%
Bachelor's degree	101,843	20.3%	2,846,770	20.8%	44,599,186	20.0%
Graduate or professional degree	82,752	16.5%	2,244,696	16.4%	28,151,275	12.6%
Household Income						
Under $50K	64,683	25.8%	2,842,526	38.6%	49,618,733	40.8%
$50K - $100K	64,259	25.6%	2,001,789	27.2%	36,352,818	29.9%
$100K - $200K	83,959	33.5%	1,737,778	23.6%	26,268,260	21.6%
$200K +	37,969	15.1%	784,922	10.7%	9,280,369	7.6%
Median	$97,149		$67,844		$61,937	
Veteran Status	30,250		678,833		17,964,242	
Percent of 18 and over	5.3%		4.4%		7.1%	

Source: Census Bureau [2]

Over 320,000 people voted for Congress in CD#1 in the 2016 election. Lee Zeldin, the Republican incumbent, won with 58% of the vote, against the Democratic challenger, Anna Throne-Holst who had 41% of the vote.

Congressional District 1 – Congressional Representative 2016
Election Districts: 473
Votes Cast: 323,777 out of 469,641 (68.94%)

CANDIDATE	PARTY	VOTES	SHARE
Zeldin, Lee M.	Republican	158,409	48.93%
	Conservative	23,327	7.20%
	Independence	5,920	1.83%
	Reform	843	0.26%
	TOTAL	188,499	58.22%
Throne-Holst, Anna E.	Democratic	126,635	39.11%
	Working Families	6,147	1.90%
	Women's Equality	2,496	0.77%
	TOTAL	135,278	41.78%

Source: Suffolk County Board of Elections[3]

Suffolk County - President & Vice President 2016
Election Districts: 1,052
Votes Cast: 677,167 out of 954,622 (70.94%)

CANDIDATE	PARTY	VOTES	SHARE
Trump / Pence	Republican	314,639	46.46%
	Conservative	35,931	5.31%
	TOTAL	350,570	51.77%
Clinton / Kaine	Democratic	292,720	43.23%
	Working Families	8,001	1.18%
	Women's Equality	3,230	0.48%
	TOTAL	303,951	44.89%
Johnson / Weld	Independence	9,169	1.35%
	Libertarian	4,747	0.70%
	TOTAL	13,916	2.06%
Stein / Baraka	Green	8,099	1.20%
Others	Write-In	631	0.09%

Source: Suffolk County Board of Elections[4]

He did better than Trump, who won all of Suffolk County with 51% of the vote, to Clinton's 44%. New York went for Clinton, thanks primarily to the strength of Democratic support in New York City.

I had been shocked at the large margins of Zeldin and Trump. Zeldin had first been elected in 2014 as a Tea Party Republican, beating the Democratic incumbent Tim Bishop, coming into Congress in a Republican wave that year. Rep. Bishop had voted for the ACA and paid a price for that vote. 2016 was Zeldin's first reelection. I did not expect it to be such a blowout. His lopsided win was going to make unseating him difficult. How that came to be after having a Democratic Congressman for 12 years was something that, at that time, I did not understand.

Zeldin is slick, well financed and plays from the Trump playbook, winning elections by dividing people rather than uniting them. Immediately after the election, the word among Democrats in our district was that we would have a hard time getting financial support to take on Zeldin in 2018 from the national Democratic Congressional Campaign Committee (DCCC) because our district was now considered solidly Republican. Zeldin's big reelection added insult to the injury of Trump being elected in 2016.

While I moved forward with Rise and continued to try to learn about my district, I also participated in the Women's March "10 Actions for the First 100 Days." The first actions involved mailing postcards to members of Congress which I downloaded from the March site. The postcards said, "Hear Our Voice" and in the evening, while watching the news, I filled out my cards. Zeldin received a series of cards from me on different issues, from the ACA to the Muslim Ban. I was less focused on our two Democratic Senators, Senator Charles Schumer and Senator Kirsten Gillibrand. I also mailed cards to Trump.

The next action asked us to find and join a "huddle," a group of other activists in our own district. I reached out to a couple of groups I found online that had in-person meetings but they were too far away. I was striking out finding my huddle so for the moment, I put that aside.

I continued to write Letters to the Editor to my local newspaper. Finally, in February, after several tries, *The Southampton Press* published my first letter. It was in response to Zeldin issuing a press release about his "local priorities." I found his press release disingenuous because it tried to obscure his support for the Trump policies that would thwart these priorities.

Reprinted with permission from *The Southampton Press* [5]

February 23rd, 2017
Letters to the Editor: "Wrong Agenda"

U.S. Representative Lee Zeldin's press release of February 9 states: "Our security, economy, veterans and law enforcement are some of the highest priorities to focus our local efforts on in 2017 and beyond." The article is full of generalities and platitudes while purposely ignoring how the radical Trump agenda will undercut these priorities.

Security: If allowed, the Muslim travel ban will make us less safe by inflaming the jihadists against us.

Economic: Mr. Zeldin points to the GOP REINS Act as instrumental to help grow the middle class. But this act is part of repealing Dodd-Frank, the financial regulations put into place after the "Great Recession" wiped out thousands of jobs, savings and homeownership. Repealing these regulations will not increase growth or jobs. The opposite is true; returning to an unfettered Wall Street will be detrimental to the economy of Main Street.

Veterans: We must "ensure every veteran has a roof over their head" is a worthy sentiment, yet Rep. Zeldin has been silent on President Donald Trump's executive order to freeze federal hiring. Is he unaware that the federal hiring system, which is a points system, applies a veteran's preference of additional points, which helps many veterans attain employment? This freeze, which will do nothing to balance the budget, will disproportionately hurt veterans, because there is no veteran's preference in private-sector hiring.

Law enforcement: How can the congressman square a desire to help law enforcement officials with voting to repeal a law that prevented people with a history of mental illness from purchasing guns? What could be more dangerous to our first responders than unstable people with weapons?

But the most disingenuous aspect is the omission of any mention of health care. Mr. Trump and the GOP have stated that their most important legislative priority is to "repeal and replace" the Affordable Care Act. Tens of thousands of us depend on the ACA, either from the health care exchange or the Medicaid expansion, and from the ACA laws that protect everyone (including those with employer-based insurance)—laws that keep us from being discriminated against for pre-existing conditions, remove lifetime caps that used to cause bankruptcy, allow our dependents to stay on our insurance until age 26, cover wellness visits and birth control at 100 percent, and so much more. In addition, our district includes large health care organizations and hospitals that rely on the federal funding from the ACA. Tampering with this funding would create a major economic crisis.

The press release is Part 1, with a Part 2 yet to come. I would hope that in the follow-up article, Rep. Zeldin will answer why he supports an agenda that will nullify the very priorities he claims to care about.

It was the publication of this letter that brought me to my huddle. A friend of mine, who I had not corresponded with in a while, sent me a Facebook message congratulating me on the letter:

> *Wonderful letter. Would you be interested in joining East End Action Network? They are working on making our voices heard ....especially about Lee Zeldin. This group is part of the Indivisible framework. If so, I will send you an invite. There is a meeting this Friday.*

I went with her to my first meeting of East End Action Network (EEAN) on February 24th. The meeting was held on a cold winter evening, with lots of snow still on the ground. I was grateful she was driving. Having lived in New York City for 25 years and relying on public transportation before moving to the East End in 2001, I was still somewhat driving phobic and these roads were icy.

We drove to Manorville to a family home. I was surprised how many people were in attendance. There was a hunger among all of us to connect that reminded me of being at the Women's March. It was predominantly women, with some men, mostly women my age with a smattering of younger women. While this was my first meeting, I didn't know at the time that this was one of the early meetings of the group, a first meeting for most of the people there, and a much larger crowd than had been anticipated.

The meeting was moderated by a young woman named Rebecca Dolber, who I would come to learn later was the founder of EEAN. It was a bitter cold night and she wore a wool hat over her dark hair, making her look more like a college student than the leader of a Resistance group.

Rebecca told us about having met face to face with Lee Zeldin, in a meeting that EEAN secured by placing numerous phone requests with his office, and how she quietly but firmly confronted him about his record. Listening to Rebecca speak about Zeldin was riveting. Up until then, Zeldin was just a name to me and Rebecca had sat across from him and confronted him directly.

She then explained her idea for how to organize the group, with different issue-oriented policy working groups and the aims for the organization. She was completely calm, as if she had been doing this kind of work forever. As I got to know her better over the next two years, I learned how new this kind of leadership was for her, that she had never done anything like this before.

I volunteered for the healthcare policy working group since it was in line with what I was already doing for Rise. We were given an agenda of suggested actions to follow up on before the next meeting. I came home from my first huddle energized.

While my friend dropped out of EEAN shortly after this meeting, I could not have known on that February day how significant this meeting would become in my life.

Sharon Adams, EEAN

> "A group of us went to the March, and then we reached out and heard about a meeting at Melinda's house. I was on board, immediately from that first meeting… The friendships are the biggest thing but also a personal feeling that I'm doing something good."

Wendy Turkington, EEAN

> "So, when I heard about EEAN and I thought, 'Okay, well if it's like Pantsuit Nation, then I can find a place that feels safe.'"

Patricia Callan, EEAN

> "I probably would've fallen into a deep depression. I would right now be deeply troubled, and depressed. But because I had something to focus on that was positive, and I had a great network of people like Becca, and Deb, and everybody from the group, it helped to prevent that... Everybody's so nice, and like-minded, it's like you don't have to argue with them over everything, it's so nice."

Lisa Fliny, EEAN

> "Being part of EEAN has helped me turn my rage and disappointment into action. Although I am very busy working part-time as a teacher assistant and running a household with three kids, I find time to act. In 2017, I protested for my very first time. I admit our nation's proclivity for gun violence made me hesitate to join the Women's March in NYC, but I did find the courage and some friends to help me march in Port Jefferson on Long Island. It was inspiring and energizing, once I got over my initial fear."

Kyle Cranston, EEAN

“What we're doing now with these action groups, I'm hoping we will wake up and realize that everything that's happening right now is our own doing, either because of our actions or our inaction, which is the good news because that puts all the power in our hands. And that's what I tell people.”

Here is the initial description of EEAN on the closed Facebook page:

Welcome to the East End Action Network (EEAN). We are constituents of New York's 1st District who believe the next four years depend on citizens across the country standing indivisible against the many items in the Trump agenda that do not model the American values of inclusion, tolerance, and fairness.

Donald Trump is the biggest popular vote loser in history to ever call himself President. He has no mandate. The EEAN is opposed to any attempt made by his administration to use his congressional majority to reshape America in his own racist, authoritarian, and corrupt image. We must stand opposed to him and any members of Congress who would do his bidding.

Our strategy is a simple one:

1) Members of Congress hold local Town Halls and public listening sessions throughout our district. We will use these events to both directly pressure out Congressional members and attract the media to our cause.

2) In addition to town halls, members of Congress regularly attend public events for other purposes--parades, infrastructure groundbreakings, etc. Like town halls, we will use these opportunities to get face time and make sure they're hearing about our concerns while simultaneously changing the news story that gets written.

3) Our members of Congress have multiple public district offices that are open for anybody to visit, no appointment needed. The EEAN will take advantage of this to force impromptu town hall meetings. It is much harder for staff to turn away a group than a single constituent, even without an appointment.

4) Mass office calling is a light lift, but can actually have an impact. We will hold events with prepared questions on specific, current issues that EEAN members can call our Congressional members with.

You have been invited to this group because an existing EEAN member felt you'd be interested in participating. In addition to the strategies listed above, we encourage all members to roll up their sleeves and volunteer for various groups and administrative roles. This could include offering your home as a meeting place, taking meeting minutes, recording events, helping to track a Congressional office's schedule, writing op-eds for local papers, taking pictures of our efforts and engaging on social media. We are a participatory democracy and the EEAN encourages everyone to take on a role, however big or small.

"Change will not come if we wait for some other person or some other time. We are the ones we've been waiting for. We are the change that we seek." -President Barack Obama

Thank you for joining the cause and we look forward to meeting you at our next event.

Most of the members of EEAN live in Brookhaven Township, which is in the western part of the district, but there are a few of us in Southampton Township and most of the meetings were close enough that I could drive to them. EEAN also maintained an online monthly calendar for not only our events but all grassroots events for the Resistance in our district.

By the beginning of 2018, I decided to increase my involvement with the group by joining the leadership committee, a smaller group that planned the group's activities and helped to set the agenda. Much of my experience in the Resistance came from my work with the leadership committee, which for most of this period was made up of seven women, including myself. The bonds between us only grew with time. They also gave me invaluable time and insights for the book project, so much so that they came to form a core focus group for the project. We are different, with different backgrounds, different life stories, but the through line that connects us all is the experience of being women in a male-dominated world and how something was triggered inside each of us when Trump was elected.

These six women are the backbone of my Resistance community. Their insights, their work, their voices are crucial to this journey and to this project. By way of introducing them to the reader, here are short biographies that each of them submitted to me along with a photograph.

Sharon Adams isn't originally from Long Island, having grown up in Scottsville, New York and attended undergraduate school at Hiram College in Ohio. Her college being located near Kent State University, Sharon became the activist she is following the massacre on May 4, 1970 and during the Vietnam War. Sharon taught elementary school upstate and then on eastern Long Island for 36 years. She is enjoying her retirement on the East End and devotes much of her free time to volunteer work and local grassroots activism. Sharon has been married to her avid sailor husband for 38 years. She's very proud of her adult daughter who founded The Feminist Bird Club and is the Advocacy and Outreach Manager for NYC Audubon.

Patricia Callan is from Queens, New York and moved to the East End in 1992. A single parent, she raised her two sons here. She has a business degree from SUNY Empire State College and works as a Licensed Realtor in project management. She would like to continue her education in the near future. She enjoys writing children's books and poetry in her spare time and loves living near the water since she is an avid kayaker. For her, saving the environment is a big priority. After the first Women's March in D.C., she joined Rebecca Dolber to form East End Action Network. Meeting so many like-minded people gave her hope and helped her to keep her PTSD as a survivor of gun violence at bay. She became an activist to show her grown sons that we have to stand up to racism and bigotry. Though she lost many close relationships by standing up to the Trump agenda, a few of them have become stronger.

Rebecca Dolber grew up here on the East End. After earning a BA in Communications and Film from Manhattanville College, she continued her studies in screenwriting at The New York Film Academy. She spent her twenties living and working in New York City, coordinating various productions for Iron Films and NBC Universal. She moved back to the district to build her own business, a wholesale jewelry and design firm of her own name, Rebecca Dolber | R.E.D. http://www.rebeccadolber.com/ Rebecca's studio is located within the historic Silly Lily Fishing Station, and her jewelry can be found in surf shops and yoga studios from Moriches to Montauk. She currently resides on the East End with her wife, Sarah and Boston terrier, Luca Bean.

Syma Gerard, originally from Denver, Colorado, remarried in 1990 and moved to Long Island. Divorced for twenty years, she had been operating a small real estate firm in Denver and had three adult children. It was a difficult transition though it did provide an opportunity to finish her education, adding an MS and MFA to her BA. In 1994, she discovered the Peconic Land Trust's efforts to conserve farmland and opened a new business consulting with them and selling land and farms, primarily those already preserved or which the purchasers wished to protect. She also learned the art of getting along with her predominantly conservative clients. This came in handy in her marriage to her husband Lloyd, a native of the East End who is an antique gun collector and lifetime right wing Conservative. They managed to carve out a successful second marriage because Lloyd is also kind and charming with a quirky sense of humor. Unfortunately, these bonds have been strained since Trump got elected since Lloyd is an avid Trump supporter. Now in her eighties, surrounded by Trump supporters at home and at work, Syma made the choice to retire.

Cindy Salwen (behind Rebecca and Patty)

Cindy Salwen was born and raised in Teaneck, New Jersey, 15 minutes from the George Washington Bridge. She is the third of six children in a politically active family. Her parents were involved in the mission to integrate the Teaneck schools as well as Teaneck Fair Housing. Cindy attended civil rights marches in Newark and anti-Vietnam War protests in Washington D.C. with her parents. After graduating early from high school Cindy went to Barnard College where she proceeded to study abroad in England and then drop-out. While living in the East Village in New York City for eight years she worked as a computer operator and field engineer before returning to college. She graduated from Stevens Institute of Technology with a degree in electrical engineering and moved to eastern Long Island with her partner in the mid-eighties where she has worked as an engineer and raised two children, whom she homeschooled. She was delighted to have her children move out and now lives with her husband of 30 years and their two cats. She spends her free time playing the flute, avoiding cleaning her house, and reading too many newspapers and too few romances.

Wendy Turkington grew up on Long Island. After earning a BA in English Literature from St. Lawrence University/Dowling College, she married and had two sons. After a divorce required her to find a career that would support her family, she returned to school for her Master's in Library Science from Long Island University. She remarried and added a daughter to the family. After her sons had graduated from high school and her daughter was in 4th grade she ran for, and served, twelve years on her local school board. She is now retired from a satisfying career as a high school librarian first in Kinnelon, New Jersey, then on Long Island. She currently resides on the East End and stays active in her retirement by volunteering at her church's Food Pantry, Westhampton Beach Performing Arts Center, and for political campaigns.

Since I did not start this project until 2018, I sat down with this group and asked them to look back at 2017 and at their own beginnings with the movement. I wanted it to be more of a conversation than an interview and it was. On April 25th, 2018 we gathered at my house for a fascinating, freewheeling discussion, filled with honesty, laughter, and lots of wine. The only negative is that Patty, who was with her elderly mother in the emergency room, was unable to attend.

Below are lightly edited and condensed excerpts from our conversation with my question prompts in bold.

A friend brought me to my first EEAN meeting in February. How did it start and then how did you all hear about it?

Rebecca: So, I went to the Women's March and they gave us instructions and said, "Go home and found a small group and I was like, "Oh, okay." And then it was also Indivisible. So, I started it, I invited eight people. Nancy Rose, my mom, Patty Callan, Loretta Privett, people who I knew went to the March as well.

Sharon: Melinda (Novak).

Syma: And then people just added people. Melinda invited me.

Cindy: Yeah, she brought me.

Rebecca: And then we started meeting in person because Florence, who my mom knows from being a teacher, said, "I'm having a meeting at my house for people who just need to get together and talk." I was at that meeting and I wrote an agenda, saying "Here are the things that I need to talk about." And people just kept showing up.

Cindy: I found the group on the Indivisible list.

Rebecca: I had registered the group.

Cindy: I felt like Trump is a real threat. My point of view about activism is that I don't want to have to be that. My family's very political. I think if politics are important, they're not just politics. It's a moral question. It's not what I was interested in but I felt it was important to get involved. And so, I figured, it's a lot easier to get involved if you've got a group.

I went to the Women's March in Washington with my sister and my niece and one of my good friends. And it was a phenomenal experience.

Wendy: It really was.

Syma: It really was.

Sharon: It was perfect because then when you came back, the day of the March, by that afternoon, they told you what you are going to do in the next hundred days and you're going to have ten things to do. And boom, boom, boom. It was great. They had it all lined up.

Cindy: The March pissed me off because they didn't emphasize voting enough.

Sharon: But that was just the beginning of everything else.

Cindy: Well no, but they really didn't until the very end.

Wendy: I think they need to emphasize that more, they really do.

Cindy: I do, I mean they're talking about that now.

Sharon: Now, it's power to the polls.

Rebecca: How did you hear about the group?

Sharon: I think it was somebody else that went to Washington with me. That was my first huddle. And it was also my book club.

Rebecca: Because you started your own huddle after Washington, correct?

Sharon: I've started two huddles. The first one was the people I went to Washington with and most of those people were my book club. I've got great pictures of the whole dining room table covered with Dump Trump postcards; writing postcards to Trump was the first big thing. And I tried to keep that going, but I was the only retired person and it fell apart. And that really broke my heart that that fell apart. But I do bring postcards to book club now and they do them. And I send them information whenever anything's going on.

Syma I was so out of the loop that it didn't even occur to me to look for a group. I just sat there and was enraged and there wasn't anybody that I could talk to.

Do you think there's something about being women and what happened to Hillary that was the biggest motivating factor for getting involved in all this?

Rebecca: I think if she had maybe lost to somebody else I wouldn't be here right now. I think it was more Trump. Not just that she lost to him, the whole election and his behavior and the reactions of other people supporting him and agreeing with him.

Wendy: I think I would've been here if Ted Cruz had won and Rubio too!

Sharon: I can't imagine anybody making such a mess of the government as this guy, though.

Wendy: Cruz could definitely have. I think that's where it's really important to separate the personality from the governance because Trump has done nothing, really, that Republicans haven't bought into. They wanted tax reform, they wanted to gut Obamacare, that's not new to the game. He has simply been the flaming show, fronting this with all these stupid Tweets and his disgusting behavior.

Syma: It's in the language that they know and love. "He talks like us, he works like us, he thinks like us, he's brave enough to say all the things we feel" but they don't have the courage to say in public.

Wendy: Who knew anybody wanted to be that rude, right?

Sharon: There was a need for support. I was going out of my mind, I needed to do something.

Rebecca: Without the group, I think I would be catatonic.

When you first joined East End Action Network or another huddle, at that time did you have any sense that this would be a long-term mission for you? Any idea that a year and a half later, you would still be doing this?

Wendy: I knew that I was hanging in until the midterm elections. And I've said to my husband a few times, "If we don't win, if America doesn't turn around, then I'm quitting."

Rebecca: I've thought about this too, and if the midterms don't go the way we're talking, I don't know ... And you can't think about the future.

Wendy: You can't but-

Rebecca: I don't know what I will do.

Wendy: Right. At times I've just been so discouraged by things and I'm like, "Okay, I am going to fight tooth and nail for two years to try and turn this around, to really try to find like- minded people who we can really work with towards this end." But if America chooses not to, then I think it's going to break my heart for the final time and I don't know what I'm going to do after that.

Syma: I had no sense of what I was in for. But I was so devastated and I honestly did not believe this man would be in office for more than a few months. I knew that within a very short time he was going to be gone because he was nuts!

Wendy: I think we all had that initial feeling.

Syma: So, there was no thought in my mind that this was going to be a long-term haul and that a year and a half later I'm still dealing with the same craziness.

Sharon: And even more craziness. It got worse in certain ways.

Syma: I have a husband who says he loves this man.

Wendy: Nothing has changed his mind? Still? No qualms at all?

Syma: He is so closed out. He picks up the local paper and we get both *Newsday* and the *Times*. And he never even looks at the *Times* anymore. He looks through the local paper to see what's going on, mostly locally.

Barbara: He has no objection to you being part of the group?

Syma: Not only does he have no objection, but he overdoes it to embrace it!

Sharon: Like telling you, "Don't you have a meeting to go to?"

Syma: Yes! So, we try not to even talk about politics but sometimes a question about something else will lead to Trump. It's still very, very difficult. And he is really a gracious, courteous man who's got a great sense of humor. He's a charming man.

Sharon: I don't think I thought about a long haul. I really don't. It was just, "What do I have to do before the next meeting." It was kind of a step by step by step and then the long term was the 2018 election. That's pretty much as far as I was thinking.

Cindy: I think too that I don't want it to be a long-term thing, not that I don't enjoy the group.

Wendy: This has been the best thing about the work.

Sharon: We could still get together if there was no Trump.

Cindy: We could. But I think that from my point of view, it's longer than this because even if we win in 2018, there's going to be a long rebuilding time.

Wendy: And there are still the 2020 elections.

Cindy: Right, there's 2020 and even beyond that.

Rebecca: I think it evolves, you know. I think it evolves individually and maybe the group itself evolves. I don't know that I would see myself doing the grassroots thing for years and years, but maybe potentially I could be doing something that's more hands on, more of an active role within government or something.

Barbara: Would you run for office?

Rebecca: Never... I would love to be part of either a campaign or an administration and have influence over a candidate. I think I could be helpful in terms of helping them read audiences or situations. Crafting messages, outside of that, I'm not really sure.

Was there ever a previous time in any of your lives that you felt motivated to become an activist? I know when I was at the Women's March, I was talking to a stranger I was marching next to and I said the last time I did this was against the Vietnam War. Seriously, it was the 1970s.

Cindy: My family was very involved, I went to the March in Washington for the Vietnam War, drove down with one of my sisters and my father. My family was right there. I remember marching in ... Newark or something like that.

Sharon: I was tear-gassed in Columbus for the Vietnam War because that's where I was in school. I was in Ohio when Kent State happened. I was 20 minutes away from Kent State. Tanks would drive through my campus every morning.

Rebecca: In 7th grade, they let the boys use bigger basketballs, we had different size basketballs, like the girls had to use these small basketballs and the boys used the big ones and I was so outraged, that I came to school with a poster. I said, "We have the same size hands in 7th grade so why are the boys using a bigger ball than the girls? This is stupid." That's something silly but I think it was the first time I was really motivated to do anything. Then in college, I saw The Vagina Monologues and the whole V-Day Movement happened my freshman year in college. I brought that whole movement to Manhattanville College and they're still doing the play there to this day. We did the play all four years.

Wendy: Bush and the Iraq War did it for me. Not as much as this but my sons were in college and I went to a march. I said, "I have two sons and this is war." Then when we went to Iraq and that it was so manipulated ... Once we had a president who said we have nothing to fear but fear itself in the middle of a World War and the Great Depression and now we have this man who's manipulating alerts, "Oh, it's an orange alert, a red alert…" Playing on people's fears for political power and monetary gain. Many of the people who are in positions of power now started with the Bushes. They can act as saintly as they want now and people want to put a shine on it now but they were vile people.

Cindy: The danger now is that they are doing stuff that's very long-lasting, like in the national parks.

Wendy: Bush cut lots of money to the national parks and allowed logging and different things.

Cindy: Still, the level is different.

Wendy: I don't know. Some of it is, some of it isn't. But yes, Trump is different.

Cindy: Trump's definitely different.

Do you ever think of quitting? Do you ever think of saying to yourself, "I have got to walk away from this?"

Syma: Yes.

Rebecca: It's sort of like being in AA though. Not the therapy part of it but the part of learning to take it day by day. There are times when I'm like, "Enough already. I can't anymore." But you just get past that and then it's the next day and you just keep going.

Sharon: You have to also focus on self-care.

Rebecca: You also have to say no sometimes.

Sharon: Yes. Rebecca reminds me of that.

Rebecca: How to say no to stuff is crucial.

Barbara: Do you think you would feel worse about the state of where the world is if you weren't doing all this?

Wendy: Absolutely. I was brought up to feel that you could make a difference, that you have to work and try to make a difference, so yes, I couldn't not do things. My mother would tell us all the time, "You don't need me, everybody else does." As kids you feel your mother should want to be with you and that you need them. And my mother was always there for everybody else. And when she went back to work as a social worker, forget it. It was like, "Okay that's it. I have to go save the world for everybody and you guys know what you're doing." It's a very tough thing. And then it's funny because I have recreated it by being on the school board for all those years. Some school board members will say, it's my kid's birthday, I can't come. But I was always like, "Well let's celebrate your birthday tomorrow." And so, it's choices. And I have found over the years that some people will never make the choice of, "I'm doing this rather than my kid's birthday." It's just whatever drives you. I think that's why some of us stick to this and some of us don't.

Sharon: It's hard work.

Cindy: It is work.

Wendy: A lot of people just aren't interested. I would be eating, living, breathing school business and other people would barely know there's an election coming up or that there was a budget being prepared.

Cindy: But people dismiss it. It's back to the, "Oh it's just politics," or something like that.

Syma: And letting someone else take care of it, saying, "I don't need to worry about it."

Cindy: But it's not that somebody else is taking care of it, it's that politics doesn't affect us. It's ignoring the fact that politics decides whether we have...

Sharon: Whether we have clean water...

Wendy: Or not getting a good education.

Cindy: Or having good parks.

Wendy: To too many people, it doesn't feel that personal.

Cindy: Yeah, it's like it's not a moral issue, that's "just" politics. And so, I think that's how they can dismiss it.

Sharon: With these changes that are happening since Trump was elected, though, I can't see anybody that hasn't been touched by one thing at least. Because the list is so long and regulations have been taken away. I can't shut it off.

Wendy: But for too many people, their day-to-day life hasn't changed. They have a point saying that it doesn't affect them, because they don't see it all the time.

Cindy: Because they're privileged.

Wendy: Yes, absolutely.

Cindy: Because if you're an immigrant, it's affected you.

Rebecca: Or black, or a woman or a gun massacre survivor.

Sharon: So much has happened that somebody's got just a few degrees away from somebody that has been in a shooting.

Rebecca: This is why the gun safety is such a way in for people who would never normally be political. Because I can't help but think that, regardless of your political affiliation, if a gunman comes into your child's school or you're seeing it come into another child's school and you have a child, then you need to be involved because you care about your kids.

Has there been anything about this experience that has changed you in a personal way? Not so much in terms of becoming politically involved, but more personally.

Cindy: I feel like the election affected me personally because it made me crazy, you keep going over it, over and over, in your head and what could we have done? But I think I just felt that it wasn't going to get better until I started actually doing something instead of just being in my head.

Wendy: I think in an odd kind of way, I'm less angry. I think that being with this group and feeling like we are on the same page and supportive of each other and we commiserate has helped. I've always been very political, like when Bush was president and so is my family, but with many friends, I always felt like my interest in politics bored the vast majority of them. So, you adjusted and didn't talk about it. But now being in a group where this is our common interest, I finally feel like I found a group that shares my interest because really for me this has been a lifelong interest. And I realize that over the years I have muffled it because so many people don't find it interesting at all.

Syma: I hadn't thought about that part of it, but when you said that I realized that when I first came home I said to my husband, "I found a group of people who I can be friends with." Because one of the things that have been very hard for me is that I used to have a whole bunch of friends in Colorado, in Denver, but out here I don't have any friends. And I also think because I found something that I was really intrigued by and people with whom I could comfortably and easily interact, I could talk to them. We made sense to each other.

Sharon: The friendship is definitely the biggest thing. I mean, everybody here.

Syma: I really feel like you're all my friends.

Wendy: And the personal satisfaction of doing something good.

Sharon: And I'm recognized for it by family members and friends. And particularly in that other huddle because they said they never would have been doing anything if it wasn't for me. It's a good feeling.

Rebecca: The friendships. I've always, especially since moving back to where I grew up, longed for a group of women specifically because in college I really had that. And also longed to be plugged in politically to something, which was completely lacking from my life for the past 15 years.... I knew how much I would enjoy it because I wanted to do it so badly. And whenever I want to do something, that's how I know I am onto something. And another thing has changed. Before this I would never consider myself gregarious in any way. I'm intrigued by people but I don't particularly want be around them. I really struggle with authoritative people who tend to find themselves in charge. I'm not combative, I just disengage. So, I haven't been able to really do anything but work for myself. And thank God it's working and who really succeeds at selling jewelry, and somehow, it's happened. I've been connected with people more and I've been around people more with this movement and that's surprisingly been enjoyable, not 100% of the time, but most of the time.

Wendy: You meet a lot of people.

Rebecca: It's hard, you know. But I am enjoying it, so that's definitely been a change. And then just to speak to that, it's really what I wanted for everybody in the group is to not tell people what to do, but to say, "What are you good at and how can that apply to what needs to get done." That's been my hope for everybody that comes to the East End Action Network.

Chapter 3

Rebecca Dolber – The Outsider

"It's hard when other people don't vote. I mean, you don't have to be part of the Resistance, but you have to at least vote; it's part of your responsibility as a citizen. I do think it's a pendulum, and the question is can we swing far enough to undo what's been done? Have people had enough already? Personally, I don't think people have. I don't think there will be an undoing in the next election. It's going to take much longer."

Rebecca Dolber, EEAN

When you meet Rebecca, nothing about her seems very "political." She is in her late thirties, moderate height and build, slender, dark black hair against pale even-toned skin. She is striking and attractive in a quiet understated way. She dresses casually for comfort, cotton loosely fitting tops and jeans, good shoes or sneakers; nothing showy or ostentatious, nothing dramatic, nothing radical.

At present, her profession is as a jeweler and her work is displayed on her website, http://www.rebeccadolber.com/ [6]

Rebecca Dolber's jewelry studio, located within the Silly Lily Fishing Station on Moriches Bay.

In my visits to her studio, where we sat for several interviews, I noticed that her work space reflects her. It is organized, practical, everything in its place but with a flare of color, like the yellow chairs, and tools and necklaces on hooks on the walls. The studio is rustic, with weathered wood, lots of light, a high ceiling and no air conditioner for the summer or heat for the winter. There is something basic, artistic and honest about the space, reflecting qualities that are inherent to Rebecca. The studio has no frills but has a "Gestalt" that reflects the integrity of the work and of the artist who works there.

As I thought about her jewelry and how it reflects who she is, I realized that to be a jeweler is to be creative and artistic but also a manual worker, stringing beads, weaving threads, taking simple, colorful items and turning them into wearable art. Jewelry is practical art. The beads in her bracelets and necklaces are organic, from the earth, not trendy, with soothing designs or deep, dark colors. Her beaded bracelets for the 4th of July are red, white and blue with small charms attached.

At first it would seem that these two parts, art and practicality, might be incompatible. But they live side by side within Rebecca. This ethos gets applied to her activism as well. Idealism tempered by reality.

In large planning sessions attended by representatives from many grassroots groups, for events that EEAN was participating in, there were often activists who were louder, more assertive, more aggressive, more monopolizing of the time and the meeting. But in the end, the decision would often bend in the direction that Rebecca pointed towards, and the group moved there quietly, not through any edict or show of force, but guided by a quiet strength that would steer the group towards consensus. Meetings rarely went as well when Rebecca wasn't there.

At the group interview for the EEAN leadership, this was a point that everyone agreed on. Syma summed up everyone's feelings when she turned to Rebecca and told her, "One of the ways in which you were really crucial was you are accepting. And it came up when I first got involved and brought up a good idea, but it was also a crazy idea and we didn't have enough time to do it. But you immediately supported me and immediately found ways how we can make it work. And you were just so open and welcoming and kind and that's what pulled me in. It was the fact of being able to work with someone like you. In other words, you have been important for this group, but we have been able to share the value of who you are with a wider group, and they have become the same kind of fans."

Rebecca says she always felt like an outsider, someone who always seemed to be swimming against the current, someone who is different. Maybe from being a girl playing competitive ice hockey with the boys; or from being a strong feminist at an early age; or from coming out as gay in her twenties. While she says that she did not become actively political until after Trump was elected, those seeds had been planted throughout her life.

Below is the lightly edited and condensed transcript of my interviews with Rebecca.

You sent me some writings of yours about your background and in reading them, what runs through is a theme of being exceptional, like playing competitive hockey when there was no girl's hockey and then how that went on to be such a big part of your life. Being different from the girls around you, I had a sense that that informs a lot of your political awareness.
It's not so much the being different, I think that feeling different is just who I am. It's funny because a roommate once had a psychic party and the psychic said to me, "You've never felt like you fit in your whole life." I was like, "True." But that's never been a bother to me, so I don't want that to be put out there like it's a negative thing. I actually enjoy not fitting in.

Did you ever feel discriminated against for feeling different?
It's funny, of all the things that people could use to discriminate against me, you know, being gay or being a feminist, the thing I've felt people have been most critical of has been my parents' affluence. I've always felt that I've had to overcome other's perceptions of that, felt that maybe the things I did in my life weren't really taken as seriously, or they were pushed aside as not important because I had a leg up. There's no denying that I've been afforded countless advantages because of financial access and because of race. I have an awareness surrounding that and that understanding only grows as I get older and venture outside of my own experiences. I'm lucky, too, that my dad, while wealthy, has always valued and modeled community involvement. He doesn't just give money, he gives time and attention. He too steps outside of his own comforts and into worlds that aren't his. He's been an example for me that way.

Was your family very political when you were growing up?
They were always paying attention. My mom was always a Democrat and my dad always a Republican, that is, until the 2000 election. My dad has voted Democrat ever since and although he still considers himself a Republican, I know he grapples with what has happened to his party.

You were an active volunteer for Hillary's campaign. Tell me a little about what you were doing on Election Day.

On Election Day, I worked for the Board of Elections and I was at the polling place all day. There's no news there, you can't put it on. So, I had no idea what was happening. I came home with a bottle of champagne at 9:15 PM and when I walked in the door and saw my wife's face, I thought, this is not good. And when he won that election, well, the most honest thing that I could say was I was radicalized. I just changed as a human being. It was a point of no return.

It's really just the most honest thing I can say. I don't know who I was before this election. There's no choice for me, being part of this Resistance. If I don't do this, then I'm not being true to who I am and what I know needs to happen. It's like breathing. We're going to go to the meetings, to the protests. We're going to try to expand democracy, get people to vote, because that's our responsibility, that's my responsibility. There's no other reason for me to really be here, as I see it. This is the most pressing thing that we need to be doing right now.

You've mentioned that it was more Trump winning than Hillary losing that motivated you. Can you elaborate on that?

It was totally about being a woman, more than anything else. It was this man, this sexual assaulter, and I just couldn't stand it. Everything just came rushing to the forefront, and this mama bear came out of me, and I was like, I need to protect women. I need to make sure that everyone knows this is not okay… I just reacted.

There's nothing about being a woman that isn't political. The very nature of our biology is politicized by our government. Add to our anatomy, the socialization of our gender and all the oppressive, limiting ways we're placed in boxes from day one. Navigating those terms in a way that feels honest leaves me no choice but to be political. When your very being is at odds with the law and the widely-accepted social structure around you, how can you not find yourself bumping up against it? Or very literally, it bumping up against you.

You have talked about how being female is part of the foundation of your activism. Does being gay also play a part?

My coming out was painfully ordinary, but it was a brick in my political foundation. I don't think I was my full-self before being honest about my sexuality—and like being a woman, being a gay woman is innately political. I'm still not totally comfortable with the term, "gay". In my heart, I believe sexuality is a spectrum, and the only reason the labels exist is because we're at a stage of human evolution where everything is still super binary. I'm hopeful that we'll continue to evolve to a place where we don't need black and white answers, absolute yeses and nos. That instead we can be more fluid and open to the moment, without fear of change or loss of identity.

I've said before that I often forget that I'm gay—and isn't that a privilege! I think that's because there's nothing terribly different about the day-to-day on-goings of my relationship than any other. I've been out just shy of 15 years. It took me a road trip across America and thousands of miles between me and my past to finally accept how I really felt. I think part of this was because I had a fear that my identity would be wrapped solely around being gay. I was and am, a multifaceted, multidimensional young person and coming out—which you never do just once, you do over and over and over in your life—seemed to put me in a box that felt limiting. We're so much more than our sexuality. With that said, I love being part of the LGBTQ community and consider being out and open a form of activism, a duty I have to those who couldn't and still can't. It wasn't a road I picked, but one I go down proudly—and in the wake of this recent administration, I know now more than ever the importance of being visible and an ambassador to my community. I don't want that to be my whole identity, but it has all informed who I am now.

I was surprised to find out that you were a hockey player. It doesn't seem at all like you.
It's not! Hockey is such a male-driven sport, which is not me at all, I don't even like sports! I can barely even watch hockey, or football, or any of it. I'm like this sensitive, quiet, person, not really built for athletics. But, the way that it all started, was that we had a pond in the backyard, and I would play hockey with the boys back there. My brother played on an actual team, and one day he was sick, and my dad was like, "You want to dress? You want to go in?" That was exciting for me and I wanted to try that. One thing just led to another because of all the opportunity with Title IX. He really pushed me to keep playing, even though I didn't have a passion for it.

What was it like playing a competitive sport with boys?
There was no girl's hockey in high schools on Long Island, so I played for the boys' teams. There were issues, as you can imagine, and the girls who wanted to play were left to navigate gray areas, like, where we would dress before a game or how we would conduct ourselves in the face of overt sexism. There's no hitting in girl's hockey either, but with the boys, all bets were off and we fielded more than our share of physical encounters and verbal insults. I was pinned to the boards and asked what my cunt smelled like. I was hooked with sticks between my legs while trying to defend our goalie in front of the net. This was all normal, expected, and not something to complain about. I choose to be there, so the attitude was, as it always is, I asked for it.

Everybody knew, but it's what you had to deal with if you wanted to play. It wasn't perceived that what the boys were doing was wrong, they were just "being boys," I mean, isn't that always the way that it is? Boys will be boys. So, if I expected to be let in and to compete, I had to deal with it. And that's just that.

It sounds brutal. Why didn't you stop?
If we're being honest, it wasn't really my choice. I played on multiple teams. I was flown to Syracuse to play on the best team in the state. When I wasn't skating, I was working out with personal trainers. I drank protein shakes to put weight and muscle on. I tried out for the Olympics my junior year in high school. I tried out a few years, but I think it was my junior year that I made it past the first round and got a second look. There were moments that were exciting, but it was my dad who really loved it. He loved the parents, talking the talk, traveling for games and tryouts. He never played sports, he was a city kid… So, I think he was living a little vicariously.

You even played hockey in college, how did that come about?
The ice hockey coach at Manhattanville saw me skate at the national tournament in D.C., and after one of the games, approached my dad and me. He said he was building a team, wanted me as one of the captains and could give me a great scholarship to attend. It was my dad's dream to see me play hockey in college, let alone captain a team. Once the door opened, I walked through it.

But then you did finally stop after three semesters at Manhattanville.
I had a coach who was just an insane human being. There was a lot of physical, verbal stuff going on with him. He would monitor what we ate, look over us at the gym, and call some of us stupid. He accused me of causing divisions within the team because I was vocal and resisted his behavior, and as a result, he stripped the word captain from my jersey. When I went back during my sophomore year, I wasn't a captain anymore. He would punish the team for things that I would speak out about. There was one practice he made the whole team skate suicides because of something I said. It was bad. And there I was, my freshman year of college, not even wanting to play hockey to begin with, having to deal with this maniac. It wasn't just him either, it was all of the dynamics that go along with having a coach like this and how it reverberates throughout a team. Fear. Peer pressure. Etc.

I think many of the girls I played with would argue that we had a great coach and a supportive school, and that I was the black sheep, the one in the wrong place. They wouldn't be wrong about the latter. I never really wanted to play hockey in college. But, it is also true that a few years after he left Manhattanville, our coach was hired and then fired from the Quinnipiac women's hockey team and banned from coaching in the NCAA after a number of girls reported allegations against him, which gives insight into what we experienced at Manhattanville. While our school was complicit in ignoring his behavior, and the concerns of me and my teammates, Quinnipiac finally put their foot down. For what it's worth, in the wake of that scandal, he left the country to coach the Chinese Women's National team.

I saw through the mind games and knew what he was doing was wrong. So, I quit and it was then that I finally felt like I took the reins of my life. Ultimately, what my three semesters on the women's ice hockey team taught me was to speak up, to air my inner voice even when everyone else is silent.

My dad was devastated. He ultimately understood but he still says to this day it was the thing that broke his heart the most. But, he healed and so did I.

At our EEAN group interview, you mentioned The Vagina Monologues and what that play meant to you in college and how it helped form your political foundation.

Eve Ensler, her play The Vagina Monologues, and the whole V-Day movement was a force that transformed me. I left the hockey team at the end of my third semester and with my newfound time, as a Valentine's gift to myself, I staged a performance of The Vagina Monologues at the college in conjunction with the worldwide V-Day movement. Connecting with students from other colleges, workshopping monologues, and throwing myself into an immersive project empowered me to channel my own experiences into activism. It placed everything that came before into a context that was no longer unspeakable and instead tangible. Everything that led up to that point came rushing out in the form of art—and once it did, there was no looking back. It was like my heart, which had been a clenched fist, opened into a world of possibility and change. The way of women saved me—and what I learned was if they could do that for me, then we could do that for the whole world.

I continued with the tradition of V-Day through my senior year, each time bringing more women into the process; professors, administrators and students from neighboring SUNY Purchase. In addition to raising thousands of dollars for various women's charities, we made *The New York Times* for plastering the word "vagina" all over Westchester![7] I even attempted to double major in Women's Studies but fell short by a few credits. The Vagina Monologues is still performed every year at Manhattanville College, and one year, some of the students dedicated the show to me—a single gesture that reaffirmed my belief that we're always exactly where we need to be.

Do you think the line that connects so many of us in the Resistance is the experience of being a woman in a male world?
A gay man said to me recently, "I understand the #metoo movement and I know that women need to tell their stories, but isn't it enough already? Don't we already know?" And I said, you don't even know! You need to just take a seat and let it be because this is a reckoning and it is going to take time. It is going to take years.

In the end, the world has to change because patriarchy is not sustainable. The way we live, the way we pollute, the machines that we create, the stuff that we throw into our water and put into our atmosphere, the threat of nuclear war... The whole reason that's happening is because men were in a room and decided to do these things. So, now it's time for change, and women will be that change. We have to change the structure entirely. From a very young age, I felt the consequences of patriarchy, of a system that's just not working for us. So where does that leave us? To be part of the grassroots. I have no choice but to speak up, because if I don't, then what is there?

Rebecca Dolber with her wife, Sarah Ray

Chapter 4

The Democratic Party

"The most important thing, which is the most basic, is getting out the vote. We tend to hurt ourselves in that respect because while Democrats often take very strong, passionate positions, they don't actually translate that passion into going and voting. If they're not excited about their candidate, like what happened with Bernie and Hillary, they may just not vote. So, the message we have to work on is that every vote counts. And that whoever our candidate is will be better for our communities, our county, and our country, if we vote. Mobilize and elect a Democrat. It all comes down to voting."

Andrea Klausner, SHDems

In the fall of 1984, at a table on the corner of 96th Street and Broadway on the Upper West Side of Manhattan, I handed out flyers, campaign buttons and bumper stickers with the words "Mondale/Ferraro" on them and the campaign slogan, "America Needs a Change." Key issues for me in that campaign were the GOP economic policies, nuclear proliferation and women's rights and I believed that former Vice President Mondale would make a great president. I was even more energized because Rep. Geraldine Ferraro, from New York, was the first woman on any major political party's presidential ticket. Every weekend, I manned that table right up until the election. I would come home and tell my husband that based on the crowds and enthusiasm and how many people lined up to get a button or a bumper sticker, it looked to me that Mondale was about to win in a landslide.

The night of the election, as I watched the returns on our very tiny color television in our small apartment on West End Avenue, I learned an important lesson about the demographics of an individual district. Not only had Mondale lost, but he lost in one of the worst beatings in U.S. history. Reagan took every state except Mondale's home state of Minnesota and Washington, D.C. The Upper West Side voted overwhelmingly for Mondale but as arguably the most liberal district in the country, it clearly was not representative of the United States. In my years living there, I was first represented by Ted Weiss and then Gerald Nadler, who is still the representative for that district today.

As I watched the coverage and the enormity of the landslide for Reagan, I thought how unfair it was to Mr. Mondale that this would be how history would remember him. If I felt hurt by this I could only imagine what he was feeling. I felt the need to let him know that he deserved better than this, that I believed history would be kind to him and what his campaign had represented. So, I wrote him a long handwritten letter then fell asleep on the couch. In the morning, I looked at the letter and thought it a bit embarrassing and debated throwing it away. But I decided to put it in an envelope, address it to the campaign headquarters in Minnesota and put it in the mail. Embarrassing it might be but it was from the heart. I had no idea if it would reach Mr. Mondale.

Several months later, I received an equally heartfelt letter in the mail from the vice president. It so specifically referenced what I had said in my letter that it seemed likely to me that it was not a form letter. He thanked me for reaching out to him at one of the lowest points in his life and said he hoped that I was correct and that history would remember him as an honorable man.

Mondale's was not the last electoral loss to break my heart, though he is the only candidate who has ever written to me. I am a Democrat and always have been. I believe deeply in the Democratic platform and values and have been a reliable Democratic voter and sometimes a volunteer for presidential campaigns. Growing up my father was a moderate Republican and my mother a Democrat and she would joke how their votes cancelled each other out. Politics was often discussed in our household, sometimes loudly, among my parents and their five children, and was particularly painful during the Vietnam War years. But slowly, the impact of Nixon, Watergate and the Reagan economic policies pushed my father towards the Democratic Party.

After college, I left Long Island and moved to Manhattan in the early 1970s. I met my husband there and we lived in the small apartment for 25 years. I began working as a journalist in New York City in the late 1980s and early 1990s, first for magazines and then as a broadcast journalist for television. During this period, I was very careful to keep my political beliefs to myself. I did not attend protest rallies or volunteer for campaigns. It was important to me to not only appear to be impartial but to truly be impartial. The last show I produced was for the national PBS business news show, Adam Smith's Money World, and it was a comparison of the economic policies of President H.W. Bush and Governor Clinton in 1992. My son was born shortly after that.

We moved from Manhattan to the East End of Long Island in 2001, several months before 9/11, so that the ocean air would help heal the allergic condition my son was born with. It worked, making it the best decision we ever made. Working from home, I moved from television news to freelance research and writing for clients, usually for websites and business plans. Since my work no longer had to do with the news, I became more politically active during the George W. Bush years against the war in Iraq. In 2008, after the economic collapse, I was an active member of Organizing for Action (OFA) for the Obama campaign, including going to canvas in Pennsylvania. I then repeated my campaign canvassing for Obama in 2012. But during all of these periods of Democratic involvement, I was never a committee member for the Democratic Party. That was about to change.

As I continued doing research for Rise and working with EEAN, I was not having much luck trying to organize the coalition to save the ACA in my district. I contacted local hospitals, nursing homes and other healthcare organizations and kept having the same result. Either no one returned my calls or I was told that they could not engage in anything political.

If forming a coalition was proving difficult, confronting Zeldin was impossible. He refused to hold a town hall and met instead in small, managed settings or on telephone conference calls. I joined one of his telephone town halls and I got the feeling that the callers were screened because most of the callers who got to speak said glowing things about the Congressman. Not one single healthcare question got through.

On the next conference call for Rise, I relayed my frustration and it was suggested that I reach out to my local Democratic Committee for help. For me, living in Southampton Township, that was the Southampton Town Democratic Committee, known as the SHDems.

I had a few contacts from OFA that I reached out to and they connected me, by email, to three SHDems members, Gordon Herr, Chairman of the Committee, Julie Sheehan and Joyce Flynn. I emailed the three of them and told them a little about the coalition I was trying to form to protest the GOP effort to repeal and replace the ACA and asked for their advice and help in bringing the Democratic Party into this effort in our district.

All three of them got back to me right away. Each of their responses was different. I could not know then how much work I would later do with each of them and just like with the women of EEAN, I did not know at those first contacts, how instrumental they would be to my journey as an activist. Given that, I sat down with each of them in 2018 to learn more about their backgrounds.

In that first email, Julie sent me a list of local grassroots groups who were already working on protesting Zeldin that I could connect with, groups like Progressive East End Reformers (PEER) and Let's Visit Lee Zeldin (LVLZ). Julie was connected to the grassroots but she was also a SHDems member, having joined the party in 2016. Her commitment to bringing together the grassroots and the Democratic Party aligned with mine.

As I got to know Julie, I learned that she had not been particularly politically oriented until the economic collapse in 2008 and Obama's campaign. Born and raised in Iowa, Julie says her family were not very political, even though her grandfather on her father's side was a "big Democrat, the sort of party, back room, with cigars and that kind of stuff" party leader. She is a published poet and a professor of poetry at the Stony Brook Southampton campus. She is divorced and lives with her teenage son on the East End.

While she was motivated to join the SHDems because of the danger of Trump, she is equally motivated to push the Democratic Party in a more progressive direction. Addressing the economic inequities in the country are a big part of her mission. Educated at Yale University as an undergraduate and Columbia University for graduate school, she lived in Washington, D.C. and New York City and after working for years for a consulting firm, she came to see the business environment as a fraud. She tries to live a life balanced in both economic and environmental terms. Her poetry and her activism are an outgrowth of her way of living.

"I was horrified to discover how this vaunted business sector worked," she said. "I found it immoral. Hence my sort of faux Thoreauvian, you know, anti-materialist life. So, activism is only one step from trying to live it. And I still try to live it, hence sweltering without any air conditioning, but my house is no bigger than it needs to be."

Her goal as a committee member was to focus on opening up the workings of the committee and making it more transparent and democratic. She said when she first started in 2016 it was hard to understand how the committee and the requirements of being a committee member worked.

"You don't understand it. It's a whole thicket and there's an old guard who's been doing it for a long time and it doesn't occur to them to explain stuff because it's totally obvious to them. It's just not obvious to a newbie how all of this works."

Working with the grassroots was part of her effort to expand the Democratic Party.

"For me, I am focused on the long-term health of the Democratic Party, which I believe will come neighbor by neighbor, from talking to each other. I'm not lecturing them on being more liberal, I don't like to lecture anyone, but we are talking, and then at the same time, we could agree to support someone who's looking to push us towards a more equitable healthcare system."

Joyce, who is president of the J. P. Spata Southampton Democratic Club, the social arm of the SHDems, invited me to join the Club in her first email to me and gave me a list of upcoming events.

The club, founded in 1987 is named for its first president, John P. Spata. As explained on the Club website, "The mission of the John P. Spata Southampton Democratic Club is to offer social gatherings for Southampton Town Democrats in order to: provide a forum for discussion of issues of concern to Club members and educate Club members about these and other Southampton Town issues; increase the number of active Democrats in Southampton; and support local Democratic candidates and elected officials."[8]

Like with Julie, this brief introduction would lead to us working together on countless initiatives, including my becoming a member of the Club's advisory board. Unlike with Julie, Joy's reasons for being a committee member had less to do with wanting to see long-term changes in the Democratic Party. In many ways, the two of them represented a dichotomy of women who were working within the SHDems when I joined.

Joyce also stands out for me for another reason. The nickname she prefers is Joy and I have never met a person who so perfectly is reflected in their name. Like many of the women I worked with on this journey, Joy is a doer who takes charge and gets things done. But unlike many of us, including me, she approaches every assignment calmly and greets everybody with a smile that truly brings joy to those around her.

A cheerleader at Syosset High School, Joy grew up on Long Island with parents who were moderate Republicans in a family that was not particularly political. She attended Cornell University for college where she majored in home economics. Later she would attend Michigan State for her Masters, get her administrative license at C.W. Post College, here on Long Island, and her doctorate in instructional leadership at St. John's University in New York City. She was the Assistant Superintendent for a school district on Long Island for ten years, retiring in 2002 after 33 years in education. After retirement, with a real estate license, she started working with her husband Dan in his real estate office. She met Dan on Long Island in 1968 in between Cornell and Michigan State. Both athletic, they compete in seniors athletic competitions in swimming and track.

They moved to the East End in 2005. After joining the Democratic Club, Joy then joined the SHDems in 2006 and Dan joined a few years ago. The environment is a priority for them both. She is also part of the leadership of the Quogue Garden Club and is an active member of Planned Parenthood. Surprisingly, she says she was fairly right-wing when she entered college. While there she even dated a member of the Coors family.

"A very conservative right-wing family from Colorado, and it was the time people were burning flags and I was horrified by that. And I guess I was vociferous enough that they asked me to become the secretary of the conservative club and I said, no, I was too busy studying. I couldn't possibly do anything else."

Her brief foray into the right-wing was short lived. She quickly switched to the Democratic Party and has been an active Democrat ever since. She thinks of herself as a moderate or centrist Democrat.

"I think people from the progressive end of things would look at me as not progressive, and I always thought I was very progressive, but when I see how they are so rabid about things, I go, 'Yeah, I guess I much more centrist.'"

As I got to know Joy, it was no surprise that her first outreach to me was to come participate in the social events of the Club.

"I do social things well, that's what I do. I was a home economics teacher, and I like entertaining, and so the Club is like another party that I am throwing every month. I like making people feel welcome, don't ask me to give a lecture on what's going on in D.C. today, just I'll set it up and I'll bring in the experts, and I really value smart people, so I have no problem having the smart people around me and doing whatever I can do well. For me, I can't say I joined the SHDems to change the world in any way, it was a little bit of social and a little bit of wanting to be with like-minded folks, not having to worry about what we were saying."

But the most surprising response came from Gordon. Along with directing me to some useful links for information regarding the Resistance, he invited me to join the SHDems.

Dear Barbara

I've been following your emails and I'm delighted that you want to get more involved with the Democratic Party. If you are interested in becoming a member of the Southampton Town Democratic Committee, I have attached a questionnaire for your use. Kindly complete and email it back to me as an attachment.

As far as become active in the movement to oppose the Trump agenda, here are a few useful links:

www.indivisibleguide.com

https://5calls.org/ (Note, that you can change the representatives you're calling, by changing the zip code in the upper left-hand side bar.)

Kindest regards
Gordon

-
Gordon Herr
Chairman
Southampton Town Democratic Committee
www.shdems.org

I was surprised and a bit flattered but I did not jump at the invitation. In fact, I was quite hesitant. The work I was doing in the grassroots in 2017 was different than party politics. The Women's March was different. Rise was different. EEAN was different. We were fighting to save healthcare, protect immigrants, retain environmental regulations and consumer protections. There was a sort of purity to the activism and the protests that I liked; the issues felt bigger than partisan politics. Could I also be a party member and continue to do the work I was doing? Could I wear both hats?

In early 2017, there was still a lot of anti-Democratic Party sentiment flowing through the grassroots segment of the Resistance. And from rumors I heard, this was mutual, with many in the party leery of the grassroots. And whether in the grassroots or the party, Democrats still glared at each other across both the Hillary/Bernie divide and the liberal vs. moderate divide, with each blaming the other for the election of Trump and the GOP now holding all the levers of power. It is not an overstatement to point out while the anti-Trump fervor in 2017, as evidenced by the protest marches and town halls around the country, was embraced across the Democratic Party spectrum, this uniformity of anti-Trump anger only papered over the deep divisions within the party and between the grassroots and the party. Those divisions did not disappear just because there was unanimous agreement about the danger of Trump and his policies.

Given that, did I really want to become a "card carrying" party member? I wasn't sure. At that time, resisting through the grassroots, uncoupled from electoral politics, felt more valid to me. But it became clearer every day that protests alone would not stop the destruction being caused by Trump. The only viable avenue to putting a brake on the Trump agenda was for Democrats to take back Congress in 2018. The Republicans in Congress were a rubber stamp for Trump. They refused to conduct any oversight. Given that this was the most corrupt administration in my lifetime, never was oversight needed more than now and despite the passion of the rallies, I did not feel that we were winning in our battle to preserve the norms and civil rights in our country. To effectuate that change, we needed the Democratic Party. And we needed the Democratic Party to win. To do that, we had to find a way for all branches of the party to work together.

It took me a few days to decide but, in the end, I filled out the questionnaire and sent it back to Gordon with my resume. Almost as soon as Gordon got these documents from me, my phone rang. "Why haven't I heard of you before?" he said. "Why are you not yet on this committee?" I thanked him and said I hoped that I would be a valuable member but that my main reason for joining was to work at bringing together the grassroots and the party, fighting to save the ACA and taking back Congress in 2018.

For my subcommittee assignment, I chose the outreach committee. I felt this was the best avenue to reaching out to the grassroots. I also had some experience with outreach at PBS, coordinating the ancillary outreach of PBS documentaries via teaching materials and websites.

Gordon connected me to Michael Anthony, outreach chair, who was presently in Florida for the winter. This is the email response I got from Mike:

> *Hi Gordon,*
>
> *Based on Barbara's resume she probably knows a lot more about outreach than I do. Looking forward to meeting with you, Barbara, when I return from Fla. Thanks for joining the Committee.*
>
> *Best,*
> *Mike*

There were no Southampton Town Democratic Committee meetings in the winter so I did not attend my first general committee meeting until March 8th when I would, for the first time, meet my fellow committee members in person.

I was nervous about attending. I am not particularly shy but walking into a large room filled with people and not knowing even one of them was daunting. The meeting was held at a restaurant in Hampton Bays. The dining room, surrounded by windows with a beautiful view of the bay, was filled with tables that each seated about eight people. There was a cash bar in the front along with a coat rack. People were getting drinks and mingling around, chatting and laughing together. There would be a buffet dinner first and then the meeting.

As I stood in the vestibule, feeling terribly out of place, a short man with a shock of grey hair, an accent I could not place and a wide smile, walked up to me and asked me if I was Barbara. I said yes and he introduced himself as Gordon. He shook my hand and welcomed me and told me he would be introducing me during the meeting along with several other new members.

Two other members introduced themselves to me, Robin Long, vice chair of the committee and David Dubow, head of the search subcommittee. Robin, a real estate attorney with a practice in Southampton, was welcoming and friendly. Tiny in stature, she is a powerhouse presence and a dedicated Democratic political operative. David, tall and courtly, told me that if I knew anyone who wished to run for office in Southampton to let him know since that was his job with the search committee. David introduced me to his wife, who was not a committee member and we immediately recognized each other from volunteering together on the Obama campaign.

People sat down, had dinner, and afterwards the meeting was called to order. Very different than EEAN, since it was more formal and followed the rules of order. I don't remember much about this first meeting. There were explanations about the requirements of being a committee member, which mostly had to do with getting signatures on petitions to get Democratic candidates on the ballot and for getting out the vote in your election district (ED). I was assigned to ED 19. It all went over my head and I didn't really understand what they were talking about. It was also hard for me to shake a level of nervousness that came from feeling like an outsider. While people were friendly, it was also clear that there were strong relationships in place and sitting there as a newcomer was awkward. It was like they were speaking a language I did not understand.

When it came time to introduce the new members, and there were several of us, Gordon asked each of us to stand and say a little bit about ourselves. I have no memory what I said but I think the common denominator for all of us was the urgency of fighting back against Trump. Once we were all standing, we got a round of enthusiastic applause which made me smile. That moment elevated the evening for me. I would learn later that the applause was a thank you because, thanks to Trump and the desire of Democrats like me to fight back, this committee was at full strength for probably the first time in its history.

When I later spoke with Gordon about this history, he emphasized that the committee I was joining in 2017 bore little resemblance to when he had joined ten years earlier.

"The Democratic Party was a mess," said Gordon. "As you probably know, we had much fewer Democratic voters. We were the laughing stock of the town. We sometimes had people who we put up to run and then they dropped out halfway through the process. But then in 2007 we had a full slate of people and Anna Throne-Holst was one of the people running for Town Council and we got her elected, the first Democrat."

Gordon was born and raised in Zambia, formerly called Rhodesia, which explained his interesting accent. He came to the United States in 1980 and lived in New York City for 27 years before moving to the East End in 2006. He joined the SHDems in 2007 and became chairman in 2009. Divorced, with grown children, Gordon works at the Suffolk County Board of Elections. By the time I came on board in 2017, he told me that the Party was no longer a laughing stock.

It all sounded like Greek to me. It was clear just how much I had to learn about local politics and my own committee. This was different than the grassroots. These political committees are chartered by the state and have certain requirements so that many dates of events, such as the nominating conventions, are set state wide. As a committee member we are responsible for choosing and endorsing candidates to run for local elections as Democrats. This is the backbone of the work we do and it includes knocking on doors in the spring to get petitions signed for these candidates – every candidate needs to get a certain percentage of signatures to be eligible to have their name on the ballot either in a primary or general election – and then canvassing in the fall to get out the vote for these candidates. If we want our local government to represent the values we prize as Democrats, then we need to get Democrats elected. All of us are volunteers and all the leadership positions are also volunteers so it seemed like a big commitment for a non-paid position.

I am not sure how I would have navigated all this in the beginning without Mike Anthony's help. He and his wife Ann had returned from Florida and he took me under his wing, because he was the outreach chair but mainly because he is just an all-around great guy. Since I was such a novice at getting petitions signed, Mike went out canvassing with me to ED 19, the election district that I was now responsible for. Those first few times I just stood back and watched as he knocked on doors and spoke with residents. I was as uncomfortable with this process as he was at ease with it. Without him, I probably would have bailed as a committee member that first year.

In our canvassing times together, I asked Mike a lot of questions about the history of the SHDems. I learned that Mike had been chairman before Gordon. In fact, Gordon had worked closely with Mike for two years before the torch was passed. Mike was still a member of the executive committee along with being the outreach chair.

He knew a lot of the institutional history. Fifteen years ago, this area was so solidly Republican that the GOP held all the seats on the Town Board, most of the appointed boards and had Republican representatives to the State Senate and State Assembly. The GOP ruled through patronage and had held power forever. Mike also knew the district well because he had grown up here.

"I grew up in a staunchly Republican family: the elephant reigned supreme: grandparents, parents, uncles, aunts, cousins – if they weren't registered Republicans they were registered Conservatives. My first political recollection was seeing graffiti extolling Dwight Eisenhower for president – "I Like Ike," adorned the window of a local business. It wasn't until I went away to college, during the 1960s, that I woke up to a whole new world of protest and alternative values that I became a Democrat."

His father was the "head bartender" which meant "ordering the liquor, training the bar boys and other bartenders and pouring a million drinks in his career" at a popular bar/restaurant in Southampton. His mother was a court officer. Mike met his future wife Ann here. He attended a Catholic high school here and went away to a Catholic college. But when they both got jobs with the Health and Hospital Corporation in New York City, they moved to New Jersey where they raised their one daughter and where Mike became involved in local Democratic politics. He even ran for office and served one term as Town Councilman.

"At the age of 34, I was elected to Town Council in the village of Palisades Park, NJ, near Fort Lee. It was a lot of fun, and I learned a lot. The local party was mostly old-guard Democrats. I first met them when I was a town coordinator for the George McGovern campaign and got myself invited to one of their Democratic meetings. Not too welcoming, they all supported Hubert Humphrey.

But they saw something they liked and asked me to join the committee and later to run for council in 1983. I was the top vote getter, defeating an incumbent Republican and a former Chief of Police. I learned then that hard work and mobilizing a constituency can pay huge dividends, no matter who you face."

When it came time to retire, they came back to their roots on the East End. Wanting to continue their work with the Democratic Party, they both joined the SHDems. Mike learned that there were not enough members to field a full committee, with 2 members in each of the 42 election districts (EDs), and often there weren't enough members at a meeting to have a quorum. Being such a diminished party made it extremely difficult to get people to join and even harder to get candidates to run for office. Mike became chairman in 2007.

"Becoming chair of the SHDems was just a case of being at the right place at the right time. The committee was in a bad place, and it seemed to me that internal division was gobbling up a lot of time and effort that should have been directed at defeating Republicans. By way of my activity in the 2004 presidential race, I met some local Democrats, and one introduction led to the next, and soon the idea of me running for chair, a fresh face as it were, seemed viable. A cadre of supporters hell bent on righting the ship was decisive; their patience, advice and know-how got local Democrats pointed in the right direction. I think the turning point for the Southampton Democratic Committee came when we threw a summer party and Gordon Herr, my successor, was instrumental in conceptualizing the party and finding top rate entertainment. We looked like we knew what we were doing and that brought a lot of bonhomie and energy to the party. The goodwill generated brought us the empathy and sympathy needed to overlook or forgive mistakes so we could get on with party development. Candidate recruitment got easier so really fine people like Anna Throne-Holst, Bridget Fleming, Sally Pope and Andrea Schiavoni ran and won their races. The GOP spell was broken when Anna Throne-Holst won a Council seat in 2007. Success begets success."

From what everyone on the committee has since told me, Mike was being too modest about his contribution to turning the Party around.

In May, Mike picked me up and we drove to my first outreach subcommittee meeting at a member's home in Hampton Bays. It was at this meeting that I got a chance to sit down and speak with Robin, who I had met at the general membership meeting. I listened that evening as she described the campaigns she was putting in place for the local candidates and the outreach initiatives we needed to focus on – like improving the website, having an active Facebook page, etc. – that could help boost those campaigns as well as improve our outreach to younger voters. Like Mike, the amount of knowledge that Robin possessed about local politics was astonishing.

As I got to know Robin, who was as fervently anti-Trump as any member of EEAN, I learned that my original view of the Resistance as only the grassroots was too narrow. Women standing up to the Trump agenda ran the gamut from outside activists to party insiders.

Chapter 5

Robin Long – The Party Insider

> ***"I feel guilty every day that I wake up, that I drink wine, put on my jewelry, put on my nice clothes, and 2,000 children are in limbo. Four thousand parents don't know where their children are, and I function. How dare I do this? What makes me any better than the Poles that sat around the killing fields, hearing the machine guns going off, and closed their shutters not to hear it? What makes me better than them? I am not better than them. I should be shutting down my life until those 2,000 children are back with their parents. Every person of social conscience, who gives themselves an excuse and doesn't hold themselves to that level of scrutiny, of hypocrisy, that's where the lie sits."***
>
> Robin Long, SHDems

Robin is a real estate attorney in the Hamptons where some of the wealthiest summer homes in the country reside. For those of us in the middle class who live here year-round, we like the small towns, the good schools and the strong sense of community. But what funds this year-round lifestyle is the revenue the wealthy contribute during the summer resort season, Memorial Day to Labor Day. Unlike many other resort areas, like Miami or Hawaii, there are no hotels lining the beaches in the Hamptons and it is specifically zoned to keep it that way. There are some inns and bed and breakfasts but if you want to spend the summer on some of the most beautiful beaches in the world, you either own a summer home or rent for the season. For the one percent who work on Wall Street and live in New York City, spending their summers here makes real estate one of the top industries for our district.

Her office is in Southampton with a conference room that is decorated with light colors, soft designs and wicker chairs that reflect the beach community we live in. It is a law office that also reflects a woman's sensibilities. There is no dark paneling or heavy, dark wood chairs. It is a room that reflects confidence but with a more feminine style.

Even when Robin isn't there, her legal secretary greets us at the front desk and opens the conference room to our meetings. When Robin is there, her two small dogs join us in the meeting, making the rounds from chair to chair, with wagging tails, looking for a lap to sit on or a treat to be had.

Robin has never been part of the outside, the grassroots part of the political system. She is very much an insider, a political appointee, a political operative, as she is quick to describe herself, "a party hack." I met no one, in my journey through 2017 and 2018, who knew more about the Democratic Party, about how to win elections, about the different factions in the Party than Robin. Her official titles are: first vice chair and campaign chair of the SHDems, first vice chair of the Suffolk County Democratic Committee and first vice chair of the New York State Democratic Committee.

When one hears the phrase "party hack," one expects to meet someone who views politics through the prism of a game, or a power struggle with winners and losers, and when one listens to party pundits about national politics on cable news, this is the impression you get. The press even covers politics with the language of sports, something that was particularly problematic in the 2016 campaign. While Robin may view politics with a clear-eyed practicality of what it takes to win elections - "you need one more vote than the other side" - this is no game to her, especially now in the age of Trump. She viewed Trump as an existential threat to our democracy during the campaign and everything about the way he has governed has confirmed that fear. And she is frustrated that there is still a split in the Democratic Party, not recognizing the larger picture and the greater danger the country is facing.

Tiny, mitigated only slightly by her spike heels that coordinate with her classic suits, Robin's shoulder length blonde hair is a classic style, as are her glasses and jewelry. One assumes that the wealthy homeowners-to-be who sit in her office signing real estate contracts take comfort from a style that speaks to understated financial comfort.

This is one side of Robin. But on some level, it is a mirage, carefully constructed for the business she is in, because at the heart of who Robin is, what is her guiding star throughout her life, is the question of ethics. Not what one would expect from a real estate attorney who is a self-described party hack. I learn from Robin that she started her legal career in matrimonial law. Real estate law came later, in the need to have steady income as she raised her son and daughter as a single parent. In her descriptions of her grown children - her daughter who is a military doctor, married with a new baby and her son who is a principal planner for a major developer for affordable housing - it is clear how much she passed on a strong, moral compass to them.

Robin's constant, internal questioning about ethical dilemmas is the through line to her life. And a key to understanding just how much it has guided her can be found in a decision she made early in her professional career, a decision that took away promotions and advancement due to the fear of how the course she was on might inevitably lead to compromising her ethics.

Raised in a working-class family in Queens, New York, Robin attended York College, part of the City University of New York, majoring in political science. As she described it, "I got an internship with a city councilman and said, 'Wow. Government's cool.' And that was it. I was bitten by the bug."

She then went to work for the Queens Democratic Party as a liaison to the Mayor's office - under John Lindsey, Abe Beame and then Ed Koch. She also met Senator Charles Schumer in Albany when he was in the Assembly.

"I met Chuck Schumer when he was in the Assembly and he was studying for law school. I had to go up to Albany and tell him, 'Chuck, we need you for a vote.' And he had to put his books down and I would take him downstairs for a vote. I don't think he would remember me. I was nobody. So, I met people beyond my power. Twenty-five years old, and I was playing with the most powerful men and women in the state and learning how power brokers actually work and how hard it is sometimes to make a concession when it is needed for the greater good. I saw some people that were borderline corrupt who actually did not make a decision that was in the best interest of the people, the corrupt ones patted their pockets at the same time. But I never saw what I'm seeing now."

She was such a rising star within the party, that her mentors pushed her to go to law school, since they knew that a woman wouldn't get far climbing the government ladder unless she had more credentials. They were grooming her to be a leader in the Democratic Party. While working full time, she went to St. John's University School of Law in Queens at night, a program that would take four years to complete. At age 28, close to completing her law degree and studying for the bar, she decided to leave politics. It was a decision that made her boss and the Mayor very unhappy.

"I was studying for the bar and it was all done. I went in to see my immediate boss and I told him, 'I am quitting. I'm resigning.' And he said, 'What? Now that you have a law degree, you could become a commissioner. You could have your choice of what you want. What are you doing? I don't understand.' And I said to him, 'I have to leave. Because if your livelihood depends on this, on politics, not government, on politics, then your ethics can be questioned.' And he said, 'I'm not going into the Mayor and telling him you're leaving.' And the Mayor never came to my farewell party."

There was no particular event that triggered her unease.

"For some of us, there's an instinct. I can't tie it to this person told me this, this person told me that. But you start to get a feeling in a government when you're inside, if things are going wrong. When people are making decisions or are apt to make decisions that aren't crossing the line, but getting so close to the line that the little guy inside of you, that moral compass that you're raised with, starts saying something's wrong. And I knew that bad decisions are made when you can't make a living outside of the government. You've got to be able to go out and make a living. And if you want to be in politics, that's fine, but you can't have it tied to your living that much because then there is the potential for corruption."

After leaving Queens, she moved to Suffolk County and worked as a public defender. Years later, she moved even further east, became a real estate attorney and went back to politics as a Democratic committee member around 2007.

Her unease about corruption in the early 1980s when she left Queens proved to be prescient. In 1986 the city was confronted by a scandal so large that it rocked the Democratic Party and the Koch administration. A 1987 *New York Times* article entitled, "Tangled Strands: Anatomy of the New York City Scandal" displayed the multiple layers of corruption that began with the Parking Violations Bureau and grew to encompass city, state and federal officials.[9] Many were indicted and went to jail. Queens Borough President and Democratic leader Donald Manes committed suicide.

I sat down with Robin for a one-on-one interview in the summer of 2018, after the news broke of the Trump family separation policy. Below is a transcript of my wide-ranging interview with Robin, lightly edited and condensed for clarity. I started by asking her about the Parking Violations Bureau (PVB) scandal.

I am old enough, and lived in NYC in the 1980s, that I remember very well what a huge news story the PVB scandal was, especially the suicide of Donald Manes. How did it make you feel when that scandal hit?
It confirmed my greatest fear, and it also was sad because a lot of good people made bad moral decisions and excused going over the line. And when you cross the line once, you keep crossing it. It doesn't stop. Some of them were bad people and I'm not going to mention who, but some of them were "good people" who just made excuses for themselves for making bad decisions.

Donald was one of my leaders. Donald killed himself. A lot of people I knew were going to jail, friends of mine going to jail. I'm not making value judgments. Whether they should've gone to jail or not, whether they took graft, whether they didn't take graft, they made decisions they shouldn't have made but I don't sit in anybody else's seat. I don't sit in judgment of people. I kept myself out of doing that my whole life. But I do know to judge myself. I had told myself years earlier that if I can't practice law because I don't know how to go into court, I don't know how to plead the case, I do not know how to do a closing, I'm going to be dependent on politics and if I'm dependent on politics to feed my family, then I can be corrupted. If I want to go back into government, I can go back in but I can go back in then and keep my ethics.

I had walked away from a really powerful place that could've been my life. I was at the seat, I was at the table, politically, government wise, job wise. But I knew that ethics was everything. I saw these people twisted. And the minute you start twisting, you can't stop.

Remarkable for one so young to make a career decision based on ethics. What do you think is the foundation for such a strong moral compass?
From family, in particular my uncle. From what I understood, my uncle, my mother's brother, was a communist or a socialist in the Ladies' Garment Workers' Union. He used to say to me, "The value of a Jew is not going to Temple. It's that you've given back more than you've taken. And if you can't say that, you're not a good Jew." And he didn't want me to go into the military. He said, "Always mistrust the military." He would sit and read adult books to me when I was three or four years old, five years old, I just have faint memories of him, but he was a Zionist. Big time Zionist and a socialist. His daughter ended up in Israel and never came back here. Married. She left in 1955 I guess it was. I remember going on the boat and seeing her leave. And I remember the rest of my childhood sending my cousin my used clothes because she had daughters. You couldn't send new stuff to Israel because there was a terrible tax. But you could send used so we would crumple up clothes, we wouldn't iron it and sending the stuff and getting letters back from her about the bomb shelters, about one of her daughter's fiancées who was killed in one of the wars.

So, part of it is my uncle, saying that you have to be true to yourself, you have to be honest with yourself, and part of it is Judaism. I'm not religious but just the ethics of it.

What do you remember as your first foray into making your voice heard, taking a stand?
In high school, we had to strike to be able to wear pants, and that was my first bit of activism and I learned that I had to stand up for myself as a woman. When I went on the Women's March, and I even had this fight with my daughter, I said, "Do you realize, my little darling, that you would not be a major in the Army and a doctor if I had not been pissed on by every freaking judge in Suffolk

County to get equal respect as an attorney that the men had?" I said, "You don't realize what women before you went through because when you got there, the door was open." But what we did to get that door opened, that should have been the focus for every liberal, every left-thinking person, and they should have carried Hillary on their shoulders to have a woman break this ceiling. They never equated what Obama did for African-Americans with what Hillary was doing for women.

I know how invested you were in Hillary breaking that glass ceiling. You were a key organizer for Hillary's campaign.
I felt it at the convention that the unity that we needed, the power that we needed, the strength that we needed, the feeling that, here was a woman breaking the ceiling, was not there. Instead they were stamping on her, especially the Bernie people. They took no joy. They didn't understand.

I was at the convention, in the cheap seats. The Party did me a favor, I had credentials and while I was in the back, I was happy to be there.

So, I am sitting in the cheap seats with the people who were just there and when Michelle Obama spoke, the Bernie supporters were booing her, because of her stand on the Trans Pacific Partnership (TPP). And I said to myself, "Son of a bitch, Trump is going to win." I had a sinking feeling in my stomach. We couldn't get the Bernie people to stop. They were so intent.

Robin Long at the 2016 Democratic Convention

You have said that you saw Trump as an existential threat to the country and it sounds like you were frustrated that many other Democrats were not seeing it that way.
We were going down to Philadelphia to do canvassing for Hillary. I gave a speech on the bus and the crux of my speech was the fact that we were going to lose checks and balances if Trump won. What bothers me with these super left, which is the same as the super right, is they don't see the forest through the trees. They can't get out of the weeds long enough to understand that right now and I don't want to be overly dramatic, but to me it seems like we're in 1939 in Germany.

Veracity, truth, and ethics have already been washed away. They're gone. You can have a press conference where the press secretary actually lies. We have people now who lie. There is not just one root to rectifying this. It's going to take many people pulling together because we didn't get here overnight. This has been years of simmering horrible feelings because maybe we've been too elitist. Maybe we haven't listened to what's happening around us.

We are losing the checks and balances. We're going to lose the Supreme Court. We've already lost the Senate, and we've lost the House. We don't have much more to lose. And the majority of our country doesn't care. It's because life is hard. People struggle every day, they get up, they raise their children, it is hard and so there are only a small percentage of the public that feels a need to defend or to be involved politically. It's not for everybody.

So, it is not going to help to attack our own. If we choose to eat our own, they are going to love this.

Tell me more about your experience at the Jacob Javits Center the night of the election and about the next day.
I had doubts during the day, but we stood there and stood there, and I started seeing results come back, and I said, "I don't believe this. It's sliding away." The AP reporter who took those pictures that became the meme of me online kept saying, "Relax, relax. Michigan's not in. This is not in. That's not in. This is not in." There was a young girl in the picture who's standing next to me. She was in one of Hillary's advertisements. She just wouldn't talk to her mother. She just attached to me. She was about 15, and she got to about 1:30 AM, and it was over and she said, "I can't leave because if Hillary comes out and concedes, I want to be here." She didn't want to go home, and her mother looks at me and says to me, "Will you tell my daughter to go home?" It still makes me cry because it was just so sad.

I looked at her. Now, I had been standing on my feet for seven hours because we couldn't leave that spot. She said to me, "What happened?" She was crying and I said to her, "Understand something. You've got to believe me." I said, "I might not live to see a woman be president, but you can live to become president. You're 15. You're young. You could be president. I might not see you get elected, but it could happen." Then, I think, Michigan came in, and the whole thing started. Podesta came out, and I turned, and she was gone. She had just disappeared into the crowd, and so we left.

Now we're walking the streets trying to get back to the hotel, and we had been standing for seven or eight hours and we were starving. I said, "Look, let's go get a drink because I need a drink. Let's go get a drink, and let's just get something to eat." We could not find a bar where there weren't Trump supporters, loud and boisterous. I said, "We're going to be hungry."

The next morning just to show you what went on, we got called to come to Hillary's concession speech, and I said, "You want to know something? I'm as beat up as I can be. I'm going home. I'm getting on the Hampton Jitney, and I'm going home. I need to go home. I haven't slept. Right now, I can't figure this out." I go to the Jitney stop, and I've got my phone. I'm talking to Gordon on the phone. You know the Jitney stop at 40th Street? I'm sitting on the little bench there. We had, a bunch of us, unbeknownst to each other, had gone into the Shake Shack to watch Hillary's concession speech. We were watching for the bus and going back and forth, so it was like three people who were Hillary supporters and were outside with me.

I was sitting on the bench, on the phone with Gordon, and a man walks by, and you can ask Gordon because he heard the screaming. He didn't know what the hell was going on, but he heard the screaming. This man must have overheard me talking to Gordon. I don't think I was talking very loud because I was very sad, and he said, "You lost. Get over it." It was the last straw for me. I jumped out of my seat and said, "This is what our country is coming to. You are proud that you're eavesdropping on a private conversation. You're attacking a woman on the streets, and this is it. This is what we have to look forward to." And he said to me, "Get over it. You've lost, and you're going to feel it." And I lost it. I went to jump him. These other two people grabbed me and said, "No, that's what he wants you to do. You're going to get arrested." Gordon's yelling, "Robin, what's going on?" He doesn't even know what the hell is going on, but I just sat down, and I started to cry. I wasn't crying for Hillary, and I wasn't crying for this 15-year-old girl. I was crying for our nation because you could tell the tone of our country had changed in a matter of hours.

You have just returned from a trip to Israel and Poland where you visited one of the Nazi concentration camps in Poland. When we spoke on the phone, you said even though you have been back in the U.S. for about a month, you are still haunted by your experience.
Let's go to something that's very unsexy, which is the concept of human nature. What makes certain people have a social conscience, and what makes other people not, and it's not a value judgment. I was at a camp called Majdanek, outside of Lublin, Poland. Because they couldn't get the train tracks to go to the camp, the Jews that were gassed and exterminated at that camp had to march through the town. The train would come in; they would march through the town.

And I look at this on a personal level. Here you are. You live in Southampton. The train comes in at the Southampton station. You're going to Starbucks to get your coffee, and you look to your right, and this is less than 70 years ago, here comes the train and it's a commercial cattle car, and they open it up and out falls hundreds of people in clothes that you don't quite recognize, because they're not locals. Women and children and men, and they're being marched through your village and you're holding your Starbucks in your hand.

And here's the social question. There will be some that get them water. Maybe you couldn't save any of them, but for two seconds, you showed a tad of kindness, of compassion. Maybe somebody's last thought was not the Nazi that whipped them, but was maybe this sign of compassion, or were you the person, and I'm not making a value judgment, who said, "I have to get to work. This is not my problem. This is not my thing. I didn't do this. I didn't put them in a cattle car. I don't know where they're going. I don't know what that camp is down the road a mile and a half away. I have children who have to be in school. Jimmy, my son has been acting up in school, the teacher wants to see me today. My boss doesn't like me."

Something changes one person to give someone marching through their village a glass of water. Something changes one person to say, and I'm not making a value judgment, understand this, there is no judgment in my voice, I'm just saying that there's something that makes somebody want to fix it, and somebody who can't find the wherewithal inside them, or the need to do this. Then there's somebody who grabs a child off the line and hides the child. There are degrees of participation in ignorance and there are degrees of participation in fixing.

Majdanek, by the way, could be fully operational in less than a day. The Russians liberated the camp and the gas chambers were not destroyed, so you can walk through them. You could see the nail marks on the walls where people scratched and tried to get oxygen. You could see these crematoriums are still intact and there is a center memorial that has the ashes of three hundred thousand people under a tent.

Some people say, "Oh, why are you bringing up the concentration camps? That will never happen again, you're an extremist and you're diminishing the impact of the Holocaust and you're insulting." But I have to bring it up because it's a point of reference.

For you, how does this connect you to this moment in history today?
The point of reference is if we don't learn from history, we are going to repeat it. And we'll repeat it in a different form. So, you had the Armenians, a million and a half, and Hitler knew he could get away with killing the Jews because nobody cared about the Armenians. And then they killed six million Jews and nobody cared about that so we're going to repeat this. But the lesson that I want to bring out to even localize this, what makes a person make a decision to either get active in local politics or not vote? I mean you can't even get people to care enough to come out and vote.

So now, the question is, what do we say to people, right now, to try to get them to understand that we're in a very unique time period? And I believe this is 1938, 1939 again. Not because I believe we're going to have concentration camps opening up next week, but we have holding camps for women and children. This is the first time. So, this isn't a thing of Republicans against Democrats, it's not liberals against conservatives; it is not any of the standard guides that we ever had before. This is not McCain, this is not Bush, this is not Reagan, this isn't even Nixon. These men, though I didn't agree with some of their policies, believed in our country with checks and balances as the basis of our democracy. We are at a crossroads right now.

This is saving our democracy. You cannot attack the press the way he has. You cannot attack the judges, the judiciary the way he has. You cannot be constantly attacking the minority party which is a Democratic Party because all you're doing is undermining our country. We do not have due process at the border because those people do not have rights. That's what they said about Jews. That was the beginning, they passed laws and the judges could say, "I am just enforcing the laws."

What do you see as the difference between being an activist in the grassroots and working within the Party?
People have to realize that there are roles and positions for everybody in the system. There are activists, people that keep the organizations on the straight narrow. They are so important; an activist keeps pushing people a little to the

left, a little to the right, a little bit this way, a little bit that way. A good activist is a conscience. A good activist can be pure and a good activist doesn't have to compromise, they can take a position, hold on to the position and push everybody with that position. They have an important role in the system. Then there are people who work within the system. They have to be different. They can't be taking their position and pushing and pulling, because they have to be able to compromise. They have to be able to see everybody's side, including all the activist positions, because it's the activists pushing/pulling in all ways. You want people in government who can listen to all sides and find a compromise position. Maybe not too left, not too right, not too center, not too hot, not too cold. A good politician or a good government person is somebody who represents a little bit of everybody and a lot of everyone. You want the people to all feel a part of the system. You might not get everything you want, but at least you get an involvement.

An activist should be outside the system, poking the system to keep it moving. But if you belong to an organization that you don't believe in, that you don't believe in the structure, that you don't understand what it has to do, and then come in and want to break it… I don't understand destruction. The one thing that the person on the inside must have is integrity and ethics. They should be able to listen to all sides of issues, and then make a fair, ethical, and sound decision as to their vote. That's the difference. You should not be able to predict if I am a legislator, how I'm going to vote, except to say that I'm going to be ethical and I'm going to show integrity. And I'm going to listen to my constituents as to what they need, and then vote with integrity.

What impact do you see all the grassroots activism having in the midterm election?

Unfortunately, and this is probably going to make me the most unpopular person right now, but I think the grassroots have absolutely no effect. I think they're ineffectual now and I think they will continue to be ineffectual because party organization, unions, traditional campaigning win elections. Why do I think they are ineffectual? Because it is so hard to win an election and they don't know how to do it. Do you know the decision making that goes into campaigns, the hour by hour decision making, the writing of literature, the setting up of campaign offices? You've got to have a campaign schedule, you've got to know when every piece of literature is going to drop, when the press release is going to be there and you have to be able to react on a dime, to anything that's happening. It is hard work, it's not easy. When you have to reach the general public regarding political issues, you've got to be very pointed in how you're doing it so that it relates to something that they need. It's touching the electorate, being able to sense where the nerve is of the electorate, touching that nerve, and being authentic. You've got to be authentic. They can smell a phony. This is what makes me laugh about the grassroots because they don't seem to understand this or understand that we do know what we're doing. Give us a tad of respect.

What's your sense of the kind of campaign Zeldin will wage against our nominee?
I think that the Zeldin people are going to play the way Zeldin always plays. They're going to photo bomb photographs, they're going to misrepresent who they are and they are going to play dirty.

If you could confront Lee Zeldin right now, what would you say to him?
"Mr. Zeldin, this has nothing to do with your votes in the House, this is because you are in bed with Trump." And we've got to tell him, "You call yourself a veteran? A soldier? You are not defending our country. Our country is the Bill of Rights. You took an oath to defend that freedom of the press, freedom of religion, not Trump." Trump doesn't understand how beautiful our democracy is, how precious it is, how incredible it is.

It sounds like, for you, opposing Zeldin is your stand against what Trump is doing to the country.
I need to beat Zeldin on a local level. I can do nothing else about anything else that's happening. I could give up my practice. I could close my doors, sell my stocks, sell my bonds, sell my jewelry, and go I don't know where, because I don't know what to do. Or I could say, I can stand here and say, "This is my stand. I am going to give that glass of water." And maybe I'm not making a change, but I am showing that I believe in democracy, that I'm showing some compassion. Maybe a glass of water is all I can do. Maybe I can be the zookeeper's wife and just hide a couple of Jews in the basement. And maybe that's all I can do.

Robin Long in Jerusalem, Israel in 2017

Chapter 6
The Progressive Caucus

"Are we Americans who believe in the democracy that our founding fathers gave us? Or are we going to be Americans who are now defined by Trump? There is a revolution happening in our country. There is a coup d'état without guns. He is taking over our country and watching us as fools fight each other."

Robin Long, SHDems

As I struggled to learn and understand what my responsibilities were as a SHDems member, my work with Rise and EEAN was ongoing and I never stopped focusing my time and effort on trying to save the ACA. While I had very little luck trying to organize a coalition of healthcare organizations, I did work on coordinating with other grassroots groups to organize protests against Zeldin on the issue of repeal and replace. I followed up on Julie's advice and reached out to two of the larger groups, Let's Visit Lee Zeldin (LVLZ) and Progressive East End Reformers (PEER). Over time, I also got to know the two women who founded these organizations. They, too, represented important voices of the Resistance in my district and I would spend a great deal of time working with them on joint initiatives that EEAN would participate in with LVLZ and with PEER.

Let's Visit Lee Zeldin was founded by Eileen Duffy. Unlike with Rebecca's founding of EEAN, which followed guidelines from Indivisible, Eileen had founded her group very early, about a week after the 2016 election.

"I canvassed for Anna (Throne-Holst, who ran against Zeldin in 2016) and then Trump won and I cried for 10 days; I knew from my days working as a reporter that politicians only care if you show up or write a letter. So, I thought we have to start visiting. It was around November 16th that I started LVLZ."

She was introduced to Kathleen Casey Quigley in December and together they started organizing a rally for January 3rd, when Zeldin would be sworn in to the 115th Congress. Though devastated by Trump's win, she stayed focused on Zeldin, because she felt she could have a more direct effect on Zeldin.

"I thought, what would be the closest thing for me to have an achievable goal? I'm not going to be able to get rid of Trump in two years but I can make sure everybody votes against Lee Zeldin," she said.

She had instinctively followed the Indivisible playbook of focusing on your own Member of Congress (MOC) before the rest of us had even thought of it. She said the group then really took off after the Women's March. Today there are almost 4,000 online LVLZ members.

Never particularly political but always interested in issues of discrimination and injustice, founding a grassroots group was a new experience for Eileen. Born in Jacksonville, Florida, on a naval air base, Eileen is the middle of three children. Her mother was a homemaker and later in her life sold real estate. Her father, a graduate of the United States Naval Academy, was a career officer in the Marine Corps, who went to work on Wall Street after he retired. This was in the 1980s and when the '80s financial crash came, when she was in fifth grade, they moved to the East Bay of San Francisco. She majored in English, with a French minor, at Johns Hopkins University in Baltimore and earned a master's degree in English at New York University.

While working as a waitress in New York City, she met a restaurant manager who was moving out to the Hamptons and asked her to come along and manage a restaurant. Her parents had come back to the East Coast and had a house on the East End so she made the move and then stayed. Working in restaurants, she also was the editor of local newspapers and Edible East End, a food and wine magazine. After two years of study, she finished Level 4 class for the Wine and Spirit Education Trust. She is a partner in a wine shop in Westhampton Beach and in 2015 published a book about Long Island wine, *Behind the Bottle* (Cider Mill Press).

Like me, Eileen wore two hats. She started with the grassroots but also became a SHDems member. At our committee meetings, Eileen and I often gave an update on grassroots initiatives.

Kathryn Szoka, co-chair of PEER, had been actively involved in local civic organizations for many years, including the League of Women Voters and Long Island Progressive Coalition (LIPC). In 2018, she received an award from the Anti-Bias Task Force of Southampton for her community advocacy work.

She explained to me that PEER, Progressive East End Reformers, grew out of the 2015 group, the BEES: Bernie East End Supporters; changing its name after the Democratic Convention in August, 2016. PEER then became a chapter of the New York Progressive Action Network (NYPAN).

Kathryn is a photographer who lives in Sag Harbor. She grew up in Maryland. Her Catholic parents had a strong belief in the American system though they were not politically active. Her father was a Republican and her mother was a Democrat. Kathryn was involved with issues of social justice from an early age.

Interested in photography all her life, it did not become her vocation until she moved to the East End. Kathryn majored in Math at the University of Maryland, and studied statistics for her Master's degree at George Washington University, as part of The National Oceanic and Atmospheric Administration (NOAA) scholarship program. Afterwards she worked at NOAA in computer graphics. She lived in California and then New York City before putting down roots on the East End. She is co-owner of Canio's Books, a hub of the community, sponsoring readings and events. It also has an educational nonprofit, Canio's Cultural Cafe.

When Trump won, Kathryn organized a vigil-rally the next day in Bridgehampton. PEER's meeting attendance skyrocketed, with 100+ attending in the immediate aftermath. PEER had decided before the election to organize around issues its members were passionate about, including Immigration, Environment, Affordable Housing, Social Justice, and more. That organization made it easier to move the many who showed up immediately into advocacy. PEER Environmental group had its first meeting with Congressman Zeldin's representative shortly afterwards.

"I believe if people are really passionate about an issue, they're going to stay engaged," she said. "So, we asked people what issues mean the most to them and out of that discussion, we came up with about eight different issues, and they became PEER's committees. Two of them are directly focused on electoral politics, Zeldin Watch and Progressive Elections. Obviously, Zeldin Watch is focused on Zeldin and CD1 elections, but by association also with Trump. Progressive Elections is focused on election reform and getting progressives elected."

Since one of their committees was on healthcare, that was our initial intersection in those early months as I continued to focus my efforts on the fight to save the ACA. I started contributing information to these three groups, so that if I posted information on our EEAN Facebook page, I also posted it on LVLZ and PEER.

At the same time, I was attending SHDems meetings. Our outreach committee investigated companies who might take on the website and Mike volunteered to take charge of the Facebook page. Along with an outreach plan to younger voters, we discussed plans for outreach to newly registered Democratic voters as well as minority voters. We discussed coordinating more with the Democratic Club and using those breakfasts to reach out to other communities in the district.

At one of the meetings, I brought up my desire to find a way to reach out to the grassroots. As I was coordinating our ACA protests and actions across three grassroots groups, I had a growing concern that there was not enough connection and coordination between the grassroots and the Democratic Party that would impact our district beyond the fight over the ACA. In what was considered a GOP district, if we could bring in the army of passionate women in the grassroots to help in the local election that fall and the 2018 midterm election that might make the difference in electing more Democrats to the Town Board and in unseating Zeldin. It also might make the difference in challenging Trump in 2020.

Robin and Julie agreed as did Andrea (Andi) Klausner, another outreach member who I met for the first time at one of our meetings. Like Julie, Andi had never been involved in party politics before joining the SHDems. She was a civil rights attorney who focused on a wide range of issues from discrimination to fair housing and she was now retired. In 2014, she and her husband Ron moved to the East End from Chappaqua, New York, where they had lived and raised their four children, who were now all grown. Now she was forced to watch the Trump administration dismantling her life's work in civil rights.

"I knew from the start from what I'd learned during the campaign that I found him a real threat. I took him seriously," said Andi. "A lot of people said well let's wait and see. It's campaign bluster. I said no. I think it goes deeper. I see fascist underpinnings. I see authoritarian philosophy. I see threats to our democratic institutions. There's no reason why we should assume that our democracy, which has been a grand experiment, is going to necessarily survive this. There were democracies in Europe that thought they would survive and didn't. Democracies all over the world that didn't survive. So, we can't take it for granted. And I took it very, very seriously. The hatred, bigotry, his whole anti-government, anti-law, anti-rule-of- law... It terrified me."

Everyone agreed that getting the SHDems and the grassroots on the same page should be a priority. Robin, Andi, Julie and I set up a follow-up meeting for the four of us to discuss how to move forward on this idea. At that meeting, I believe it was Robin and Andi who put forth the idea of the SHDems hosting a meet and greet event, with members of the committee and representatives from different grassroots groups, to present a tutorial on local politics as well as a brainstorming session on how we might create an infrastructure to work together going forward.

Robin named the event "Politics 101." It would be divided into two parts. The first part would be a forum to educate everyone about how local government worked, with speeches by the local elected officials and the second part would be a brainstorming session to come up with an answer on how to move forward. Andi suggested employing the classic business technique called SWOT analysis - Strengths, Weaknesses, Opportunities and Threats - to help us break down the issues. We would divide the room into four sections and each of us would be the moderator for our SWOT section. Then at the end, we would put together the data and see the result.

Together we organized, planned and hosted "Politics 101: Southampton Edition, A Two-Part Forum for Progressives Who Vote in Southampton Township." It was scheduled to be held at the Stony Brook Southampton campus, which Julie was able to arrange for us. We reached out to different grassroots groups to attend the event and offered them a chance to introduce their organizations and their missions to a room full of Democrats by having a grassroots fair during the lunch period between the two sessions. Each group would have a table with a sign and their representatives could answer questions about their missions and sign up new members as well as hand out materials. Sharon and Syma agreed to be in charge of the EEAN table.

Julie was also a member of the CD#1 leadership committee, a steering committee with representatives from grassroots groups in all of CD#1 – Rebecca was the EEAN representative- and she had the contact information for the groups that had Southampton members. Robin invited all the local Democratic elected officials in Southampton as well as candidates for the 2017 election to speak on a panel discussion about the town politics. She even asked me if I would sit at the dais and give a short speech about bringing together the grassroots and the Democratic Party. Gordon invited all the SHDems.

Not all of the grassroots groups who were invited were available that day but we did get enough of a response to be able to go forward with the grassroots fair. The following groups sent a representative and hosted a table:

Action Together Long Island (ATLI)
East End Action Network (EEAN)
Indivisible Riverhead
Let's Visit Lee Zeldin (LVLZ)
Long Island Progressive Coalition (LIPC)
Neighbors in Support of Immigrants (NISI)
Organización Latino-Americana (OLA)
Organize Plan Act (OPA)
Progressive East End Reformers (PEER)
Red-to-Blue
Southampton Town Democratic Committee

We originally thought 40 people might attend but twice that many registered and showed up. The morning session went smoothly and during the lunch portion, when we brought in pizza and soft drinks, people walked around and visited the different tables with the grassroots groups, signing up with them and learning about what issues they were focusing on.

During the afternoon SWOT brainstorming session, a lot was aired about the potential difficulties that might hinder working together (i.e. splintering over issues, progressive vs. moderate divide, territoriality issues) but the tremendous upside if we could achieve it (i.e. more energy, more engagement, expanding the base). Each group then outlined goals and actions based on the results of the SWOT analysis. Standing in front of four large boards, Andi wrote down all the goals and actions from each group and then we saw where there was overlap and on a separate board, wrote the shared goals and actions. These shared ideas became the basis for what we would do going forward.

Shared GOALS and ACTIONS
GOALS 1. Better communication & integration between groups (internal & external) 2. Elect & appoint progressive candidates at all levels 3. Expand & empower a diverse constituency **ACTIONS** 1. Create a steering committee 2. Major voter registration drive 3. Monthly meeting

Julie Sheehan, Barbara Weber-Floyd, Andrea Klausner, Robin Long at the Politics 101 forum in 2018.

The next step was to put these shared goals and actions into place. To do that, we went back to the grassroots groups who attended the Politics 101 as well as those who had been invited but couldn't attend and asked them to send representatives from their group to a new committee being formed, a steering committee, to meet once a month with representatives from the SHDems. This steering committee would be charged with finding ways to collaborate and work together towards the shared goal of electing progressive Democrats to local, state and federal positions in New York.

The forum had been a success and I was proud of the work we did to put it into place. After months of activism, I had finally been able to help create an avenue for the grassroots and the Democratic Party to work together.

The first meeting of the new steering committee took place on Wednesday, July 26th at Robin's office in Southampton. At that first meeting, we had representatives from many of the groups that attended the Politics 101 and we continued to reach out to all grassroots groups in Southampton to grow the committee. Robin, Andi and Julie represented the SHDems.

Several of us wore two hats because like me, many grassroots members were also now SHDems members. I represented EEAN and the SHDems, Eileen was LVLZ and the SHDems and Laura Leever was PEER and the SHDems. Sharon and Syma, who were not SHDems members, were there representing EEAN.

At that first meeting Robin laid out the approach that she hoped to take, that the SHDems were here to listen and to help, not to dictate. After much discussion, we agreed that the first shared goals were to work on voter registration and educate the public about the Democratic candidates running in the local election this fall.

As part of our voter registration mission that summer, we agreed to collaborate with a group out of Brooklyn called Red to Blue, in a Second Home Voter Registration Project. We would reach out to people who have second homes in Southampton Township, and there are many of them in the Hamptons, to switch their registration to vote in the CD#1 district. This would be part of our overall mission to register people to vote Democratic, introduce our local candidates and the progressive issues they support, and then get-out-the-vote (GOTV) for the election in November 2017.

This was not only important for our local issues – a supermajority on our Town Board could move forward with more progressive policies – but it would show the national Democratic Party that our congressional district could be a swing district in 2018. This would ensure resources, funding and help to take on Zeldin in 2018. These initiatives that summer and fall would also teach us how to coordinate and work together in preparation for 2018.

That summer, in shorts and sandals with a large hat and sunscreen, I partnered with SHDems member Lulu Bouvier and we walked along Dune Road in

Westhampton, our assigned area for the Second Home Voter Registration Project. Lulu, who is also the wife of Town Council member John Bouvier, would become my ED19 partner in 2018 and we would spend many hours canvassing together.

Lulu and John Bouvier at the Southampton Inn prior to a SHDems meeting.

That day, at some of the most expensive homes in the world, we knocked on doors, left flyers about voter registration and occasionally got a chance to speak to a homeowner and discuss why they might want to switch their voting to where their summer home is rather than their primary residence in New York City, which is where most of them were from. Those we got a chance to speak to were very receptive to the idea. I was struck how often people wanted to speak with us about the horror that is Trump.

At meetings that summer, we gave our steering committee a new name - the Southampton Progressive Caucus (SPC), and a new Facebook page was created, with a logo and a mission statement:

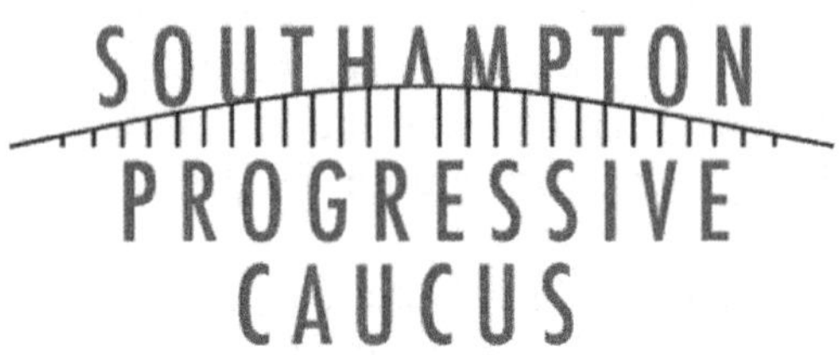

The Southampton Progressive Caucus (SPC) is an alliance of grassroots activists and the Southampton Town Democratic Committee. It was formed in 2017 to advocate for social justice, advance progressive values and elect progressive Democrats in Southampton Town, Suffolk County, New York State and New York's First Congressional District.

The logo is reprinted here with permission from the designer, Robert W. Wilson, former art director of *The Southampton Press* for 11 years. "I have been designing progressive political material for years including anti-Trump / Zeldin memes for Facebook and Twitter," he emailed to me. "I thought the Ponquogue Bridge would be a good visual symbol for Southampton Town."

I agreed and loved the design. I hoped that the creation of this committee would accomplish our shared goal of finding ways to bridge the divides and achieve success in putting forth progressive values and electing progressive Democrats. Those of us who assisted in the creation of the SPC were feeling optimistic that it would be helpful in the election battles ahead.

"I believe that we have made each other stronger. We have made the grassroots stronger by giving them help and assistance and I know damn well that they made me stronger," said Robin. "We are at mutual respect."

Chapter 7

Andrea Klausner – Career Activist

> ***"I remember saying to a number of members of the leadership of the Southampton Democratic Committee, including Gordon, that I was looking for ways to get more involved because I didn't just want to be showing up at meetings or parties and everybody patting themselves on the back and not doing anything. I told Robin that I wanted to be on the platform committee. I wanted to do substantive work. And I never got a response. So, I was very frustrated."***
>
> Andrea Klausner, SHDems

As I got to know Andi, I learned that her journey as an activist was different from Rebecca or Robin. She had been neither grassroots outsider nor Party insider. Instead she had made activism her life's work as a career civil rights attorney. Politics had only recently come into her life and was not at all what she had planned as her retirement.

Working with Andi on the Politics 101 and then the creation of the SPC, I learned that she was a relatively new committee member – she joined in 2015 - and that she had almost dropped off the SHDems shortly after joining out of frustration. While never particularly politically active, when she made the decision to become a committee member she approached it with the same sense of purpose that had driven her career – how to have an impact, how to help people. She had little interest in joining the SHDems to participate in social events. And I was surprised to learn that she had been requesting an educational forum to help the public as well as committee members understand more about local politics and to also help bring the different wings of the Democratic Party together. The divisive rhetoric among Democrats throughout the 2016 campaign had worried her. So, her push for a Politics 101 event with the SWOT analysis was two-fold. "I said we need to have people understand the process better so they know what they're doing and why they're doing it, and how important these steps are, that it's all about the vote, it's about getting people to vote. We also need to stop fighting each other and we need to bring everyone together. And so, I suggested the SWOT analysis. I said we're our own worst enemies, the Democrats. We need to draw together and work together on what we can agree on. We're not going to agree on everything but we have common goals. We want to see people elected that reflect our points of view. We may not agree exactly but we do agree, I think, that we want a Democrat versus a Republican."

But she did not find the SHDems particularly receptive. She felt the committee was a closed group that she did not feel was open to new ideas. By the beginning of 2017, with the rise of the grassroots Resistance groups in our district, she began to look outside the SHDems as an avenue for her activism.

"I met people who were also involved in grassroots groups and were expressing dissatisfaction with the Democratic Committee. They had a lot of negative things to say about the Democratic Party and how it was a closed club and you couldn't break in and you had to do things their way. I said this is not right and this is not helpful. And so honestly, what happened is that after attempting to get more involved in the Democratic Committee, I was feeling like I might just drop out."

But after attending a Zeldin Town Hall in 2017, where she sat not with the SHDems but with many people from the grassroots, she said things changed.

"Robin saw me at this meeting with this group. After that town hall meeting she came up to me and said I'd like to get you more involved with the Democratic Committee. So, we got together and had a meeting and I said to her, yes, I would like to get more involved. And here are some of the things that I think we ought to be doing. You want us to be more involved in the election process. Well frankly, I've always been involved in civil rights but I don't know that much about the election process. I think we should have some sessions on what it all means, on how the election process works, what you're asking of us, the terminology, why we do what we do, and give us an education so we better understand what it means when you call us and tell us to go canvassing or it's time to get out the vote or petitioning. I want to know how the whole process works because I don't know it. She mentioned that they had done this a number of years ago but maybe it was time to do it again, like a Politics 101. I said precisely."

So, while I was coming to the table with this idea from EEAN, Andi had been pushing for something similar from the year before. We had come from different directions but arrived at the same spot, with a belief that the different factions of the Democratic Party and the Resistance needed to work together.

"I was very happy when we finally did the Politics 101 in 2017 and to Robin's credit, she listened. I felt that this was really important both to educate our committee members and to make the work of the subcommittees more public. You need to get everybody involved in a sub-committee. And we need to work together with the grassroots. That was my agenda. And so, I was very happy that I was finally being heard."

Andi and her husband Ron have four grown children. Their retirement plans changed because of the 2016 election. Andi explains the change on her blog, http://www.thiswomansworkk.com/.[10]

> *I have always been passionate about photography, and I thought that once I retired, I would devote my time to travel photography and writing. What I discovered is my work was not done.*
>
> *In the field of civil rights, we always like to say that our mission is to put ourselves out of business. But it seems that the quest for social justice and equality is further from reach today than it was yesterday. And so, my work will continue. I renounce my retirement! I will continue to fight against bigotry and hatred through social and political activism. I will also use my artistry and love of travel to relay my message and realize my commitment to human rights.*
>
> *As Henry Miller observed, "One's destination is never a place but a new way of seeing things." If more people traveled, they might understand better that diversity is to be celebrated, not feared.*
>
> *"Travel is fatal to prejudice, bigotry and narrow-mindedness," said Mark Twain. I hope to use my travel photography to bring the world to those who cannot see it first-hand in order to foster appreciation, understanding and respect.*
>
> *Andrea lives in Southampton and Manhattan with her husband Ron and dog Mojito. Her four grown children, daughter-in-love and son-in-love, and her two new grandchildren, are frequent guests to the beach house, where they enjoy farm-to-table cooking and walks on the beach.*
>
> *Andrea is a member of the Southampton Democratic Committee, the Southampton Progressive Caucus, the Southampton Anti-Bias Task Force, the Southampton Housing Authority, and Neighbors in Support of Immigrants (NISI). Andrea also sits on the Board of the JP Spata Southampton*

Democratic Club, and chairs the Social Action Committee of Temple Adas Israel.

Along with her blog posts, visitors to her site can view her beautiful photography.

Their retirement plans also included looking forward to being grandparents. When I visited their home in Remsenburg in 2018 to sit down for our interview, Andi showed me knitted sweaters and hats she had made for her two expected grandchildren, one from her daughter and son-in-law and another from her son and daughter-in-law.

Retirement also included plans for a new house. The day I was there for our interview, much of the house was being packed by movers because in two days, she and her husband Ron were moving further east. They would still be in the district and planned to remain members of the SHDems but they wanted more land and moving further east would provide that. Andi also introduced me to one of her daughters who was visiting.

Andi, who is medium height and slender, has piercing eyes and a compassionate smile. Though new to electoral politics, her commitment to social justice has been life-long. Like Robin, she said it begins for her with being Jewish.

"We certainly lost relatives in the Holocaust and I always grew up with a strong sense that my duty as a Jew was to make the world a better place. Although we are not strongly practicing Jews, we are reformists and that's a big part of my identity, the obligation to help fix the world. That's always been a part of me."

In Hebrew it is called *tikkun olam* and it is the idea that we all bear responsibility for what kind of world we live in, not just towards the Jewish community, but for all communities. For Andi, that would mean searching for a career that helped other people. She considered social work and medicine until reading a novel about civil rights inspired her to look in a different direction.

"To Kill A Mockingbird made such a strong impression on me that I said I want to be a civil rights lawyer. I want to help people. I want to help them defend their rights. And I want to see justice done. I think especially with my history as a Jew and learning about the Holocaust, I said we have to make sure we protect the rights of minorities. The best way to protect everyone's rights is to protect every group's rights. We protect ourselves by advocating for everybody. And so, I was on a straight and narrow path. And I went to law school."

Born and raised on Long Island, Andi attended New York University School of Law with a dream of fighting against discrimination and a career in civil rights. But like most lawyers who are chosen for Law Review and graduate at the top of their class, she was steered towards a position in a top corporate law firm in New York City.

Below are excerpts of my interview with Andi, lightly edited and condensed.

Corporate law seems like the antithesis of the world of Atticus Finch. What was the motivation for taking that job and how did you end up doing civil rights law?
I was solicited by the big firms and seduced by the money. I did that for a couple years and I hated it. And so, I left to go become the in-house counsel for the American Jewish Committee and that was really my introduction to civil rights law because I wore two hats. One was just to do the in-house legal work. But the other was to head up the national affairs division. And so, the work was really First Amendment freedoms. We worked in coalition with other groups whether it was African American, Hispanic, Christian groups. We worked with immigration groups. We did everything from women's rights to church/state separation, religious freedom, freedom of speech, really across the board First Amendment. I wrote amicus briefs. I did public speaking. I published a quarterly legal journal of case law developments and formed coalition networks to work together to make bonds between the different groups to find commonalities.

This was in the 1980s, during the Reagan years, another period in our history that was challenging to civil rights. During this time, did you ever think of working within the Democratic Party or even running for office?
Before and during law school I considered whether I might want to get involved in politics. I also had a dream that perhaps I would try to become the first female Supreme Court justice. But then, that opportunity was taken away from me and I decided to give up that dream. And then honestly, I got so fed up with politics that I said this is not the best use of my time. I am fed up with the games, gamesmanship and the whole culture of politics; the ugliness of it. I had the heart for it, but not the stomach.

So, you stayed as a civil rights attorney in New York City but then you left that career. What motivated that change?
It was enough of a juggle once I had children, living in Westchester, just to go into the city. After a few times of my housekeeper not showing up to get the kids off the bus or forgetting that an art class ended and the kids were dropped off at a place where it was closed and they couldn't get home and I was in the city, I said I can't do this anymore. So, I started my own business with a partner

called Grantworks. It was a grant writing and consulting business to assist nonprofits with their fundraising. We were on retainer and did this for eight to ten years because it gave us the flexibility to work from home but continue to do good. We covered advocacy to LGBT rights to healthcare, hospitals, local nonprofit theater, a disability rights organization, it was pretty much across the board. In a sense, writing grant proposals is no different than writing legal briefs. They are all advocacy pieces.

Once our children were grown, we closed up the grant writing business and both went into different pursuits. I became the Fair Housing and then the Deputy Director of Westchester Residential Opportunities which was a Fair Housing agency. We worked to promote equal and affordable housing opportunities and to fight for fair housing, to fight discrimination in housing and lending practices.

So, the Trump administration is literally gutting everything you spent a lifetime in your career working on.
Literally, everything. When Trump started campaigning and then ultimately became president, I saw everything I had done over the past 20 years just going down the toilet.

I didn't realize you also worked on fair housing. As you say, literally every issue you worked on, including grants for the arts and for the disabled, was across the board being gutted.
We worked on across the board First Amendment issues. You name it, we were involved with it: separation of church and state, religious freedom, women's rights, freedom of the press, freedom of speech, immigrant rights, refugee asylum, LGBTQ rights; we were in favor of marriage equality. I didn't do fourth amendment work so what is happening now with immigration detention and deportation is new to me.

But people don't realize that housing is one of the core issues that affects all aspects of your life. It affects the kind of educational opportunities you have and all quality of life issues, job opportunities, transportation, social networking, health access. So, when you talk about fair housing it's important on so many levels that you be able to live where you want to live. Where you live also determines the people you are exposed to. Think how important networking is in life. Meeting people who may help your kids get jobs or help you get jobs, or having access to good doctors and healthcare, having access to good schools. I mean, it's tied up in so many quality of life issues.

Along with your career, you were also on the board of several nonprofits, including in Chappaqua where you lived. Tell me a little about the

Chappaqua School Foundation and how you came to meet Hillary Clinton through this Foundation.

I was president of the Foundation, a nonprofit that raises money to support the schools, because 97%, 98% of the budget of schools is already fixed for salaries and other programs. So, it's very difficult for schools to get the seed money to try new programs that will enhance education. Things like smart boards, or robotics programs, or other arts programs, or cultural programs. Hillary had moved to Chappaqua and we asked her to be the first recipient of our newly created “It Takes a Village Award,” named for her book. She accepted.

I got to sit next to her during dinner, as the president who welcomed her. I have to say, that's when I really became so impressed by her because she could've been there mainly to try to score points with big donors. There were a lot of affluent people there, but that's not why she was there. She was there to talk to the teachers and the students. We had the teachers and the students showing off some of the things that had been funded from the year before. She went around and talked to all of them. When she got up to speak, she spoke for 30 minutes without her notes. Not even sticking to what she was originally going to talk about, referring by name to the teachers and students that she met. And talking about the importance of education, and community, and families. She was so articulate, and so genuine, and so warm. I would hear people complain, "Oh, she's so cold, and she's shrill, and she's this and that." But in that setting, surrounded by children and families, and talking about the things that matter to her, what she devoted her life to, I saw a genuine person who really cared about people. She would've made an incredible president.

Ronald Klausner, Hillary Clinton and Andrea Klausner (reprinted with permission from the press office of Secretary of State Clinton)

I love the picture of you and your husband Ron with Hillary. No wonder the tone of the 2016 campaign was so disturbing to you. It wasn't just Trump, it was the way Hillary was being portrayed.
I was very worried during the campaign. I spent Election Day making phone calls with Ron at Robin's office with my dog on my lap wearing a pin on his collar, an ode to Hillary. I had some phone calls with people saying I would never vote for Hillary, I don't like Trump but I'm voting against Hillary. It was very disturbing. As strongly as I feel about Hillary - I did think she would make a great president - she also had her faults, her weaknesses, and shortcomings. She's not perfect, but who is? But she was held to a much higher standard than any man running for office has been held to. So obviously, I was very disappointed that she didn't win, but the fact that she lost to such a morally bankrupt, unqualified, unfit white male, was a real slap in the face.

You joined the SHDems before Trump won. After a lifetime of not being politically involved, what motivated you to become a Democratic Party member?
We moved here in 2014 and I was warned not to talk politics with people because it was very sensitive and people had strong feelings. While Westchester is also a Republican stronghold, Chappaqua is very liberal, very intellectual. I remember during the 2016 campaign when all these Trump signs started popping up around my neighborhood, I said to Ron, "What have we done?" We met Sally Pope, who was a member of the committee, and her husband Michael, who were our neighbors around the corner and we hit it off immediately. And I was very

taken with her and the fact that she had been a lawyer and that she was involved in local politics. We had a lot in common. And it was like, "I met someone who's liberal, who's a kindred spirit," and I really enjoyed them, enjoyed speaking with them. And so, when Sally approached me and said would you be interested in joining the Southampton Democratic Committee, I said yes. Ron and I both joined and we ran and became ED leaders.

What is your sense of the split in the Democratic Party?
I consider myself to be very progressive but I'm not ultra-progressive. I'm a staunch civil rights supporter. But maybe economically I am more on the moderate side. I'm not a Bernie Sanders socialist. I worry about Democrats hurting themselves by going to the extreme and pushing away some Democrats. Take immigration. There was a move at one of our town committees to declare this a sanctuary city. And I said no. We can be welcoming and fight to protect civil rights and uphold the law but we should not be advocating breaking the law. You have to have that balance between law and order, between enforcing the law and treating nonviolent immigrant families humanely and with compassion. After all, we are a nation of immigrants. But the talk is going so far to one side that people are getting turned off. They think we are advocating for gangs and violent criminals to be protected here. The far-left progressives are not making a distinction anymore. It makes it sound like we are arguing that all undocumented immigrants should be protected from deportation and we should have completely open borders, which is not our position. And I think that's going to turn off voters.

What other stumbling blocks do you see us coming up against in 2018?
My other concern is that people are feeling Trump fatigue. His constant lying is taking root. People are so fatigued that they either don't care anymore or they just don't bother to find the facts. People are tired of it. It's calculated to exhaust us, to deflect us, and it has been working. If people don't see the truth behind this public relations campaign, and the lies and deception, then I feel very pessimistic.

You and Ron travel a great deal. What were people saying about the United States during the 2016 campaign?
People were saying what's going on in your country? We were meeting people from Europe and Asia, and meeting Muslims and Buddhists. And I'm thinking oh my God, this person, this misogynistic xenophobic person, is am embarrassment. We are a global community. I remember being in Uzbekistan. We went for my son's graduation from the Kennedy School and we were invited to the home of a Muslim family for dinner. It was the family of our travel agent. And it was so lovely. Three generations of their family were there and they were

teaching us to cook chicken pilaf. They opened their home to us. After dinner, the children performed local dances for us, and then we all danced together and it was like we are brothers and sisters of another mother. And that was right around the time when Trump was saying we need to keep all Muslims out of our country. And I said I am so embarrassed to be American right now. You're welcoming us into your home. I don't even know if I could welcome you into our home because I don't even know if you'll be allowed into our country.

In your travels now that Trump is President, do people blame you, being American, for his policies?
We were in Africa when Trump made his "shithole" statement about African countries. Fortunately, most people understand that citizens aren't necessarily synonymous with the government. The same way that many of them don't like their governments or find fault with their governments and don't want to be associated with their actions. To some extent, we should be judged for our government because we elect them but they understood that we weren't necessarily representative of our government, that we shouldn't be judged by Trump's actions. And we made sure that we told everybody that we can't stand Trump, just to get the elephant out of the room and we told them that we are doing everything we can legally to get him out of office.

Where do you see yourself and your own political activism after the 2018 election?
I think at this point in my life it's more likely that I will stay motivated and continue to stay involved if there is a blue wave. Because I will feel that there is some hope, and I will feel optimistic. If we don't, I think I may just feel like I hate this country. If this is what the majority of people want, then I don't know if I can continue to live in this country. We have nobody but ourselves to blame when we elect leaders because we vote them in. If the majority of people can't see through what's happening, and this is who they want to run the country, run Congress, run the Senate, run the Presidency, then I feel like, what am I doing? This is not what I thought our country was about. I don't know how much more I will want to do. You'd think the opposite; the stakes are too high to give up but it's just so hard. I hope that everybody doesn't feel this way because we need people to keep fighting. Even if it's incremental steps, we need to keep fighting and we will win back a lot of what we lost. But I almost feel like at this point, it's time for the next generation to take over. I'm tired.

What would you do instead?
I may just retire into the country and do my photography and my knitting, and help take care of my grandchildren and travel around the world. One of the problems I see in this country is that not enough people outside of the two coasts

travel and meet people from different backgrounds. That feeds a lot of the fear. When you travel and when you understand that people are all just people, and we all basically want the same things, then you don't fear people who are different than you are. I'm beginning to see how provincial most of our country is. I mean nationalism to me is not only anti-education, it's anti-democratic. If this is what most of the country wants, then we're in big trouble.

Chapter 8
The Rest of 2017

"In the early part of 2017, you have news reports about how this (the Resistance) is the flavor of the week and it's all going to go away. People are going to lose their wind, because they don't feel they can accomplish things. From my perspective, I haven't seen that happen."

Angela Devito, Indivisible Northfork

While the creation of the Southampton Progressive Caucus (SPC) and the work to bring the grassroots and the Democratic Party together may have been the most important event for me in 2017, there were other events during the year that are worth going back and remembering before moving on to 2018.

The battle to save the Affordable Care Act continued. Throughout the year, I provided research across the grassroots and also uploaded my research to Rise. Key information was the specific implications for our district of repealing the ACA. With access to a large number of grassroots groups' Facebook pages, as well as the SHDems and the Healthcare Education Project, I continued to push what actions we all needed to take to try to protect the ACA, such as phone calls, writing postcards and attending rallies. We held several Save Our Healthcare protest rallies in front of Zeldin's Patchogue office.

I personally called Zeldin's office so often that I could almost hear their groans that I was on the phone again. During one of these calls, one of his staffers assured me that Zeldin would never vote for the repeal bill, that he had personally assured her of that because she was a cancer survivor and she would suffer if the ACA was repealed.

I also continued the letter writing campaign to our local newspapers about the ACA. The following letter focused on Part 2 of Zeldin's agenda, and was published in March in *The Southampton Press*:

Reprinted with permission from *The Southampton Press* [11]

March 9th, 2017
Letters to the Editor: "What He's Hiding"

In Congressman Zeldin's Part 1 press release he outlined his local priorities but did not address healthcare. He addresses it in Part 2:

"Obamacare has been nothing short of a disaster for countless hardworking families and our economy. This flawed law has resulted in higher deductibles, higher premiums, cancelled policies, less choices and lost doctors, among many other challenges. We must repeal and replace Obamacare with a new reality that will work better and make healthcare more affordable for Long Islanders, while continuing to cover those with pre-existing conditions and allowing children to stay on their parent's policy."

Here are the facts: the ACA has NOT been a disaster for the vast majority of Americans, it has NOT resulted in "higher deductibles, higher premiums, cancelled policies, less choices and lost doctors" for tens of millions of Americans and there is nothing in any of the GOP replacement plans that will work better and "make healthcare more affordable for Long Islanders." The truth is that every GOP replacement plan reduces the Medicaid expansion and reduces the subsidies which will inevitably reduce the number of people who can afford insurance. A CBO report from January, based on the 2015 GOP repeal with no replacement bill, estimated that under that bill, 18 million Americans would lose their coverage the first year. This would include thousands of people in our district. As to people with pre-existing conditions, these plans create high risk pools which would have higher premiums, in essence penalizing and ghettoizing people with serious health conditions. One quarter of Americans have a pre-existing condition. And this is not a static statistic; when it comes to health, this can change in a heartbeat. Nobody expects to get cancer. Thank you for conceding that our dependents will stay on our policies until age 26, as they do now, thanks to the ACA, but what about our dependents with pre-existing conditions?

The ACA is not perfect. But it can be fixed with 2 simple moves: reinstate the subsidies for the insurance companies that were designed to help cushion the first few years when newly insured people, who have never had insurance, are sicker than the average person and raise the income cap for those who earn too much for Medicaid or the subsidies but do not earn enough to afford the premiums. No repeal and replace necessary. But what Rep. Zeldin doesn't want you to know, what he is hiding in his fog of rhetoric, is the real reason he and the GOP want to repeal the ACA: to remove the tax on wealthy Americans that pays for the Medicaid expansion and the subsidies. He is not interested in improving the lives of his constituents. It is the bottom line of his wealthy donors that interests him.

In April, I took a break from healthcare and my district to travel into New York City with my sister Nanci to attend a Tax Day protest. We had participated in local rallies against Zeldin but this was our first large march since the Women's March a few months before. It was organized by a group called Tax March New York City and the purpose was to protest Trump refusing to release his taxes. On April 15th, while the rest of us pay our taxes, the protest was a way to highlight that Trump, unlike other presidents and other presidential candidates, was still hiding his.[12]

Rather than drive, we took the train into the city and walked from Penn Station to the starting place of the march in Bryant Park, between Fifth and Sixth Avenues and 40th and 42nd Streets in Manhattan. There we met up with my dear friends, Mary Copeland, her significant other, Bob Spatafora, her daughter Joanna Levinger and her 92-year-old mother, Marge. We sat in Bryant Park, a lovely park next to the main library in NYC, and listened to the speeches at the rally before the march began. It was our first time seeing the inflatable Trump Chicken up close.

It was a beautiful, warm spring day and walking up Sixth Avenue, with the streets lined with cheering New Yorkers, was quite an experience. As we passed Trump Tower the whole crowd booed and cried out, "Shame." Joanna took a selfie of our group, with our signs that I downloaded from the Tax March website.

The chants of "This is what democracy looks like" and "We're not going to go away" were just as inspiring as at the Women's March a few months before. I was surprised that there were pockets of Trump supporters on the sidelines along the route, something we certainly didn't see in D.C. At one point one of these groups of MAGA-hat-wearing Trumpsters started screaming out a bunch of really nasty comments, so much so that Bob couldn't help himself and he walked over to the barricades at the side of the street to yell back at them. We pulled him back into the march with us. It was not worth engaging these people and we certainly didn't want any violence.

After the march, we went to a Mexican restaurant in midtown that was filled with other marchers and together we toasted the Resistance with margaritas.

But while the marching boosted our spirits, it was not stopping the destruction being caused by the Trump administration. The horrors out of Washington continued each day. And there were so many urgent issues, from the Muslim travel ban, to the destruction of the EPA, to gutting regulations, to the threats to defund Planned Parenthood.

Rebecca Dolber and Sophie McHeffey

Sharon Adams

Syma Gerard

Pat Falk, Sharon Adams, Rebecca Dolber, Wendy Turkington, Cindy Salwen, Deb Dolber and Art Turkington

So, I tried to stay focused on healthcare and the fight to save the ACA and on Zeldin. With the congressional spring recess coming up, we were advised by Indivisible and the Women's March to focus on pushing our representatives to hold a town hall and answer our questions, particularly on the ACA.

Zeldin was refusing to hold a town hall. We pushed back. Along with the regular rallies held in front of his office, we also posted flyers of his face on a milk carton as "missing." Whether it was in response to pressure, he finally announced one town hall during the recess, to be held at the Suffolk County Community College campus in Riverhead, in the end of April. Luckily, it was a location I could drive to. I got there early, parked and joined Sharon, Syma, Wendy, Rebecca and several other EEAN members on a long line to get into the building. We were told we could not bring our purses or our phones but had to bring our wallets to show ID to get in. I went back to my car, locked up my purse, and got back in line. A row of policemen were in front of the building. The area where we stood on line was roped off to one side, with a separate section for Zeldin's supporters. There were very few people on that line while there were hundreds of people on our side. Many men, many younger voters, but the vast majority was older women like us.

Once we got into the building, we had to show our ID and were then given index cards and told if we wanted to ask a question, to write it on the card. We found seats in a large auditorium and wrote our questions on the cards. We were told that no one would be allowed to stand up and ask a question. Instead the cards were passed to the front of the stage and read by a member of Zeldin's staff.

Once everyone was seated, the lights in the audience were dimmed, which would clearly make it more difficult for anyone to take pictures or videos.

The room was packed, with people standing along the walls. Zeldin arrived and the moderator who was organizing the cards told us that while many of the cards had questions about healthcare, Zeldin would only answer one question about healthcare and the ACA. A few people booed when hearing that. Then when Zeldin answered with his usual talking points about how bad the ACA was, it seemed like the entire auditorium erupted in one, giant sustained "boo."

In the midst of the commotion, one woman broke through the scripted and controlled event and shouted a question to Zeldin. She was standing along the wall. She wanted to know if he was going to protect coverage for substance abuse because her son was suffering from opioid addiction. Zeldin worked hard to avoid her and he never answered the question, to the dismay of everyone in the audience. It was captured on video and reported on in the local press and went viral on social media.[13]

This was the only time Zeldin faced his constituents and our concerns about what the GOP planned to do to our healthcare. Then, despite all of our protests, despite the assurances from Zeldin's staffer, despite all the phone calls and postcards, on May 4th, the House passed their repeal bill, the American Health Care Act (AHCA) and Zeldin voted for it. Afterwards, they celebrated with Trump in front of the White House.

I felt complete panic. I could not watch the celebration in the Rose Garden. But I also knew enough about how a bill becomes a law to know that there was nothing really yet to celebrate. This was only the first step.

And so now our focus turned to the Senate. I studied the Senate bills, had conference calls with the Rise healthcare policy group, posted all my research on all the grassroots Facebook pages and presented updates at our EEAN meetings so our members would be armed with information when they called into Senate offices.

There were several votes in the Senate, the first one to open debate passed, then the comprehensive repeal failed. All that was left was a vote on the "skinny repeal" a pared down ACA repeal bill with no replacement. The night of this vote in the Senate, I was so sure it would pass that I could not watch but I also could not sleep. My sense of anxiety was almost unbearable. I remember insurance companies discriminating against people with pre-existing conditions, either denying coverage or charging exorbitant amounts. I never wanted to return to that.

In the early morning, I looked online, preparing myself for the news that the bill had passed and the glee from the GOP as it just awaited Trump's signature. I went to *The New York Times* website and read, "Senate Rejects Slimmed-Down Obamacare Repeal as McCain Votes No." To my great surprise, I learned how Senator McCain had defeated the repeal of the ACA with a "thumbs down" vote.[14]

For now, the ACA seemed safe. Sadly, we would learn later that while the overall structure of the Affordable Care Act had been saved, including the protection for people with pre-existing conditions, Trump and the GOP were still finding ways, through executive orders, through the tax bill, through the courts, to damage healthcare in this country. The ACA was saved but healthcare was not. Still, that moment when the horrific GOP repeal bill went down in flames was a moment that made all the meetings, protests, letter writing and phone calls worthwhile.

But there was little time to savor saving the ACA. It seemed that every day brought some new outrage, especially as we learned more and more about the Russia probe. By the fall, I was busy knocking on doors, canvassing for our Democratic candidates in our local Southampton Township election. If I had not stayed busy, despair would have set in.

The next worry was what damage the GOP tax bill would inflict on us. In October they moved closer to moving their bill through the House by passing a budget resolution. Many Republicans from blue states voted against it, because it was known that repealing the state and local tax deduction (SALT) was going to be included in the bill. SALT is an important deduction for higher income, high-tax districts like ours. Yet Zeldin voted yes on this first resolution. All arguments he would offer later that he tried to save this deduction, that he knew it would hurt our district, were hollow. He could have stopped this in its tracks on October 5th.

As we got closer to November, I felt increasingly nervous about how we would fare in the 2017 election. This was the first vote since Trump was elected. It would signal if the Resistance was real, if it could translate to real change, if it could elect progressives. If we failed in this local election, we would not be strengthening the resolve of Democrats and weakening the resolve of Trump and the Republicans. It would mean the opposite. Big losses in these local elections would trigger headlines that Trump's hold on the country was solid. I approached the local election with great trepidation because the destructive power of Trump and his enablers continued day after day.

And despite some wins, such as the defeat of the healthcare repeal and replace bill, overall Trump was winning. Institutions of democracy – the free press, federal agencies, regulations that protect consumers, public health and safety, the environment – were being dismantled. Cabinet officers were confirmed to run the very agencies they had dedicated their careers to tearing apart. The year had been tumultuous - Trump had fired F.B.I. Director James Comey, which triggered an investigation by the Special Counsel Robert Mueller, but it was going to take time for this investigation to finish and issue a report. This would not save us any time soon from this dismantling of our federal government. Only electing Democrats would be a check on this destruction.

During the fall, I continued attending EEAN meetings as well as the SHDems and the new SPC. It was busy, gratifying but also stressful. Election Day 2017 finally arrived. I experienced what I can only label as PTSD going to the firehouse to vote, with powerful flashbacks from a year ago. My level of anxiety literally made my hand shake as I filled out the ballot. If the results today confirmed Trump's hold on the country, then all the work that I and so many others had engaged in all year was really for nothing if it did not translate into electoral success. This would be devastating and could signal an end to so much citizen activism before we even got close to the midterm election of 2018.

For the first time in my life, I attended an election eve party for a local election. It was hosted by the SHDems and scheduled for 9:30 PM at a restaurant called Buckleys Inn Between in Hampton Bays. It was a very rainy evening and I was tired from knocking on doors earlier in the week with Lulu but I decided to go anyway. Mike and another SHDems member, Katey Moran, picked me up. Katey has been an active Democrat for a long time. She said she started canvassing for the 2008 Obama campaign and then became involved in the SHDems after that. She is the rep for ED10.

In the car, Mike told us that the early returns he was seeing on our district from the afternoon did not look encouraging. Could the rain have kept many people away? That increased my sense of anxiety.

The room was crowded. All of the local candidates were there. Gordon and Robin were there. Ron was there but Andi was not, she wasn't feeling well. I recognized many people from the committee meetings. Before the returns came in we discussed what the results might be - will our Democratic candidates be successful in Southampton Town, could we achieve something Democrats had never done before, which is have a supermajority on the Town Council? Will we see an increase in turnout from all of our GOTV efforts all year?

Most of the people at the election night gathering had been there last year so it was even harder for them because they had collectively endured that painful election night together. They told me they were cautiously optimistic. They talked about how this night would be different, how there were now, thanks to all of our efforts, more registered Democrats in this district, how that in itself was historic for a district that had always been majority Republican.

As the night went on, we watched national returns on a big screen. We learned about the large Democratic turnout in Virginia and New Jersey for those governor and state races. We learned that the Constitutional Convention question on the New York Ballot had been voted down and that was a relief due to a concern that it was a trap to open up the state Constitution to then delete many union benefits and rights.

And then the results came in. Not only had we achieved a supermajority on the Town Council but for the first time in over 200 years, Southampton had a woman elected as Town Trustee.

This is how our local newspaper described the results, reprinted with permission from *The Southampton Press*. Permission for the photograph is from Dana Shaw/The Press News Group.

Reprinted with permission from *The Southampton Press* [15]

November 9th, 2017

Democrats Sweep In Southampton Town Elections

Photo credit: Dana Shaw/ The Press News Group

Nov 8, 2017 12:27 PM

By Amanda Bernocco

Four Democrats will serve on the five-member Southampton Town Board—for the first time in history—after Tuesday's elections.

Supervisor Jay Schneiderman, an Independence Party member—his recent switch to Democratic Party registration will take effect next week—easily won with 8,172 votes, or roughly 62 percent of all ballots cast for the town's top post, during his first bid for reelection, defeating challenger Ray Overton, a Republican and a former Town Trustee, who received 4,872 votes.

Councilwoman Julie Lofstad, a Democrat, also kept her seat, bringing in 7,843 votes, or about 31 percent of the votes cast for Town Council. She will be joined at the dais by newcomer Tommy John Schiavoni, also a Democrat, who defeated incumbent Councilman Stan Glinka, a Republican. Democrat nominee Alex Gregor, the incumbent highway superintendent, also won reelection on Tuesday.

"I feel honored to be reelected," Ms. Lofstad said on Tuesday night. "I am so looking forward to representing the people of Southampton for four years."

Ms. Lofstad was first voted into office in January 2016 in a special election to complete the unfinished term of former board member Brad Bender, who resigned after he was arrested for selling prescription painkillers. Starting in January 2018, she will be serving her first full four-year term.

"I feel a little numb—I'm so happy," Ms. Lofstad said as the night started coming to a close. "But I better get to bed soon, because I have a lot of work to do over these next four years."

Mr. Schiavoni—who received 6,848 votes, and will be taking Mr. Glinka's seat—shot his fist in the air in excitement when he realized he had secured a seat on the Town Board.

"I feel so honored. And so proud—I couldn't have done it alone," Mr. Schiavoni said. "This is a big statement, that the voters responded to what we ran on. I answered every question that was asked of me, and we ran a strong, clean race. I am just so honored."

Mr. Schneiderman added to that sentiment.

"It's hard work, but tonight it shows," he said. "We have an extraordinary group of candidates to lead Southampton into the future."

A little more than a third of registered voters in Southampton Town cast votes, up from 2015, the last "off year" election, when turnout was 29 percent, according to the Suffolk County Board of Elections.

Some suggested that this year's Town Board election could be something of a referendum on a proposed golf resort in East Quogue, "The Hills at Southampton," as the Democratic candidates for Town Council both voiced clear opposition during the campaign.

In the three election districts that include the East Quogue area, turnout was generally higher than the townwide average: 46 percent in ED 35, 41.8 percent in ED 18, and 32 percent in ED 27. In those districts, the vote was mostly split, but the Republican candidates had the edge: 738 votes for Mr. Glinka and 611 for Ms. Dombrowski-Fry, compared to 550 for Mr. Schiavoni and 506 for Ms. Lofstad.

Gordon Herr, chairman of the Southampton Town Democratic Party, said he was proud on Tuesday night.

"I'm ecstatic, obviously," Mr. Herr said at Buckley's Inn Between in Hampton Bays as he watched the results roll in. "We ran very strong candidates and had a very unified party. And now we have a true majority in the Town Hall."

While Mr. Herr speculated that some of the Democratic success could have come from the national upswing in Democratic votes, he was quick to note that there were a lot of strong Democrats on the ballot in the local races, and no national issues on the ballot.

"We had great support from organizations which have not been involved in local politics before but have been galvanized by the national situation," Mr. Herr said, referring to the high number of Democratic wins across the country on Tuesday that some interpreted as a repudiation of President Donald Trump. "We also emphasized strongly that we needed to have a solid local victory in order to have an enthusiastic base to help defeat [U.S. Representative Lee] Zeldin next year."

Overall, Mr. Herr credited the candidates, however, giving a special nod to Mr. Schiavoni "The fact that a first-time candidate, like Tommy John Schiavoni was able to unseat a Republican incumbent speaks volumes."

Mr. Schiavoni, a resident of Sag Harbor, had a strong showing in the western half of town, where he collected 46.9 percent of his votes—though that was still far behind his running mate, Ms. Lofstad, a resident of Hampton Bays, whose vote total included 52.4 percent from west of the Shinnecock Canal.

The Republicans' election night party, held less than two miles west, at Centro Trattoria & Bar in Hampton Bays, was more somber. GOP Chair Dave Betts stood on a fireplace hearth in the restaurant and called everyone's attention to the news of the big Democratic win. "It's been a difficult night," he said.

Mr. Glinka, a Republican, lost in his first reelection bid, bringing in 6,017 votes. His running mate Thea Dombrowski-Fry, also a Republican, had 4,528 votes.

"I'm shocked," Mr. Glinka said. "It's amazing, because the outpouring of support that I had throughout the entire day, throughout the entire campaign, was giving me indications. Obviously, the voters proved me wrong tonight, and I congratulate the two winners."

Also disappointed with the outcome, Ms. Dombrowski-Fry said she is going to continue to work to make the town the best it can be. "It was hard—I had one line," she said, referring to the GOP line on the ballot. "I did my best, and I met a lot of great people, and I'll try it again, I think."

Mr. Overton added to that sentiment.

"I'm disappointed—obviously, I thought it would have been a closer race," he said. "But, like I said, we identified a number of issues that are affecting the community—especially west of the canal—and we've been promised by the opposition that they are going to be dealt with. And they need to be. There needs to be progress over the next few years. And if there's not, they need to be held accountable."

The Republicans also faced a loss in the race for highway superintendent.

Incumbent Alex Gregor, a member of the Independence Party who was cross-endorsed by the Democrats, won a third four-year term at the head of his department, bringing in 7,485 votes, or more than 57 percent. He defeated his challenger, Lance Aldrich, a Republican, who collected 5,580 votes.

Mr. Aldrich worked under Mr. Gregor as a general supervisor until the highway superintendent eliminated his position in 2015. Still, Mr. Aldrich prided himself on running an amicable campaign.

"I have no regrets. I had a good run—I had a clean run. I made a statement when I was nominated that I would keep it clean and focus on the issues. The outcome, I'm disappointed with—but, of course, I would be. The people decided what they wanted, and I have to respect that."

Additionally, a number of incumbents in uncontested races kept their seats in Tuesday's election.

Longtime Southampton Town Clerk Sundy Schermeyer, a Republican who was been cross-endorsed by Democrats, earned her fourth four-year term of office. Ms. Schermeyer, who lives in Westhampton Beach and has held her seat since 2006, makes $109,242 annually.

Finally, both incumbent Southampton Town justices, Deborah Kooperstein and Barbara Wilson, were reelected. Each earns $72,207 annually and serves a four-year term.

The results were even bigger than I had been able to glean at the election party. Waves of women were elected to the statehouse in Virginia, along with electing a Democratic Governor even though Trump had campaigned against him. The news broadcasts reported how women had mobilized after the 2016 election, beginning with the Women's March and the results were now seen up and down the ballot, from statehouses to city councils and school boards.[16]

There was one clear headline, from our local race to races across the country, that the Resistance had made an impact. After a year of rallies, letters, huddles, phone calls, postcards, we were on the right track. It gave me a feeling of validation that I didn't realize I had needed until I saw the election results.

Shortly after the election, I made the decision to start this book project, to keep a diary from this election until the midterm election. These turnout results indicated to me that the Resistance could be the big story in 2018. If that was the case, then chronicling my journey in my district in real time might provide a window into how the blue wave was created, making our district a microcosm for the Resistance work across the country.

I reached out to EEAN and asked them if they would participate in the project. They agreed. I informed Gordon and Robin and Mike and they were enthusiastically supportive. And on November 13th, at our first SPC meeting since the election, I told the group about the book project and asked if I could put our meetings on the record. They also agreed.

At the SPC meeting, we discussed and dissected the election results. I learned that while Southampton Democrats had a big night, Brookhaven was not so lucky and with the bulk of the population in the congressional district in Brookhaven, that meant that we had our work cut out for us if we were going to unseat Zeldin. We wondered if it might be possible to bring our formula of creating a steering committee between the grassroots and the Democratic Committee to other parts of NY01.

"It is going to be harder to duplicate the process in certain areas without certain cooperation," said Robin. "In Southampton, we attribute to the grassroots groups the work they've done, they are equal partners at our table, we thank them at every committee meeting, they speak at my town committee meetings, they have a spokesperson who gives an update of this group, they are an equal partner. I do not believe that is the case with the other townships."

As if we needed reminding just how important our work was, this is what was going on in the news on that same day: a new accuser had come forward towards Alabama GOP Senate candidate Roy Moore; evidence of Donald Trump Jr. and Wikileaks during the 2016 campaign; Sessions testifies before Congress; the GOP add the removal of the ACA individual mandate to their tax bill. Removing this pillar of funding from the ACA will weaken it and cause all of our premiums to rise.

The month of December was a mixed bag for activism and for me personally. I was sick a lot of the month. Lying on the couch, off the activist grid while nursing health problems, I had to turn off the news. It was too distressing. Watching Congress pass and Trump sign into law the GOP tax bill was a gut punch. At several points, I considered stopping the activist work and stopping the book project before it even started. I continued to wonder if being immersed in the chaos caused daily by Trump was injurious to my health. The victorious election night, just a month before, now seemed like a distant memory.

What did boost my spirits was the election of Doug Jones to the Senate in Alabama on December 13th. Imagine, a Democrat winning in Alabama. It was almost unbelievable. True, his opponent was the accused child abuser Roy Moore, but this was after all, Alabama. The race was close. All night watching the returns, it seemed that Moore would win. But African Americans, younger women, younger voters, came out in record numbers and turned the tide. Also, so many GOP voters wrote in other names, rather than vote for Moore or Jones. And it was women, older women, black women, organizing on the ground for Jones. Was this another sign of a Democratic wave next year? Could it be that what we are doing in our district will also result in ousting Zeldin? The Jones victory brought me back from the brink of giving up.

By the end of the year, six Democrats had announced running in the primary next year to become the Democratic nominee to oppose Zeldin. That is a large slate of Democrats. Was this a good sign of the enthusiasm in the district or a potential circular firing squad? That is something Democrats historically tend to do.

At the next EEAN meeting, we discussed what our role should be with the candidates. Should we choose one to endorse? That idea was voted down, to my relief. How would we ever decide who to endorse without upsetting some members? Instead, we decided that our mission will be on voter education. Towards that end, we agreed that we will invite all the candidates to come for a one-on-one interview with Rebecca as the moderator followed by questions from the audience. We will arrange to host these interviews at our local library, in their meeting room. Kyle agreed to record each interview and put them on our YouTube page for a larger audience to see. Before the year's end, we held our first interview, with Kate Browning. Rebecca did an incredible job and meeting Kate was interesting.

Zeldin attended a fundraiser in Manhattan hosted by Steve Bannon. Bend the Arc, a Jewish grassroots group, organized a protest in front of the event. I didn't attend because of my health but I did sign the petition to protest Zeldin's association with a white nationalist. The petition got 5000 signatures and was delivered to Zeldin's office in Patchogue. He continued to smear us, labeling anyone who disagreed with him as "liberal obstructionists." On his Facebook page, his supporters hurled slurs at us, and despite our continued protests, he still raised a lot of money for his reelection campaign. After the one town hall, he never held another one.

I ended 2017 feeling weary but not defeated. And I had no illusions. While I was proud of the work we had done - we saw tangible results in our district, and there were signs from across the country that 2018 could be a wave year – there was no denying that despite a year of historic grassroots activism, we had slowed down the Trump agenda but we had not stopped it. Only taking back the House in 2018 could achieve that.

PART II
GETTING TO WORK:
January – September 2018

Chapter 9

Democratic Primary Candidates

"We have got to stop saying that we are just here to defeat Zeldin. I am a Democrat, I am a union person, I am a hack, I am part of the machine, whatever words one wants to use for my involvement in politics, I am proud of all these things. We have to start being proud of who we are again. We can't just be anti-Trump or anti-Zeldin, we have to represent something."

Robin Long, SHDems

This part of the book begins the diary but before jumping into January, it will be helpful to first introduce the candidates since they figure prominently in all of our work in 2018. With the midterm election looming and the importance of creating the blue wave, our work shifted from protest to doing everything we could to get a Democrat elected.

Our primary candidates were a varied group: three men, three women, with different backgrounds and experiences. Two had been county legislators for the term-limited 12 years and coincidentally were both immigrants, one had staff New York City Council experience, one is a scientist, one is a finance real estate businessman, and one a popular local bartender with a political science background. For a short time there was a seventh but he dropped out quickly.

Through candidate forums, debates, meet-and-greets, fundraisers, Facebook live streams and numerous other events, the residents of CD#1 got an opportunity to get to know them. Being a geographically large district, it wasn't easy for them to get back and forth from the western part of the district to the eastern to meet as many potential constituents as they could, but they did it. They all attended the Democratic Committee meetings or sent a representative. They did the same with meetings of many of the grassroots organizations across the district. EEAN interviewed all of them.

In the fall of 2017 many Democrats expressed concern at the prospect of such a large field running in a primary. The fear was the candidates would wound each other and the last one standing would go into the general election as a weakened nominee. There was good reason to worry. We are Democrats. Which means we have a long history of, what Robin describes as, "eating our own."

At the SPC meeting, we agreed to organize and host three events with the candidates, the first a forum in January and then two debates, both to be held in May before the primary. All of these are covered in detail in real time in the diary, in the month they took place.

During this time, Zeldin moved further and further to the right, aligning himself ever more firmly with Trump. Was it to forestall a primary? If so, it worked, he avoided a primary and would sail into the general election with his funding intact. But as he kept moving right - standing with the NRA, promoting a concealed carry reciprocity bill in the House - it would seem that he was moving further to the right than the district.

Below are photographs provided to me by the candidates as well as short biographies based on information the campaigns gave to us for our forums and debates.

Kate Browning served in the Suffolk County Legislature for 12 years, representing the 3rd District. Before taking office, Kate worked as a school bus driver for the William Floyd School District. Her husband Steve is a detective in the NYPD and retired from the Army National Guard in 2006. They have three sons, two who are serving in the military, and three grandchildren.

Photo credit: Karen Curtiss

Elaine DiMasi spent 21 years as a federal contractor and project manager at the Brookhaven National Lab, delivering world-leading solutions in energy, environment and health. Combining engineering and biological expertise, Elaine developed new ways of seeing synthetic and biological materials at Brookhaven National Laboratory.

Perry Gershon is a successful businessman. At the age of 23, he founded one of New York's first sports bars. He then spent more than 25 years in commercial real estate finance. Perry co-founded a firm during the Great Recession to offer alternatives to traditional lending sources that had dried up, providing much-needed capital for finance-starved real estate projects and preventing defaults and foreclosure. Perry oversaw Hurricane Sandy relief efforts for his synagogue as chair of its Social Action Committee. He and his wife Lisa, a working mom, live on the South Fork. Their two sons are in college.

Photo credit: Kristen Asher O'Rourke

Brendon Henry was born and raised on the East End in a working family and is the first in his family to graduate from college. He attended Long Island University (LIU) where he studied political science, history and education. He and his wife are raising their son on the East End. He is a longtime bartender at the Southampton Publick House and Buckley's Inn Between. He is also the co-founder of the Cabin Fever Music Festival, an annual event.

Photo credit: Scott Burns

David Pechefsky was Valedictorian at Patchogue Medford High School. He then earned his BA from Hunter College and a Masters in International Development at American University. A longtime staffer for the New York City Council he also worked for the Metropolitan Transportation Authority and the Mayor's Office of Appointments. As a consultant for the National Democratic Institute (NDI) from 2010 to 2013, he worked to establish a legislative budget office to serve the Congress of Liberia. He is on leave from his current position as a senior advisor with Generation Citizen, a national nonprofit that trains college students to be "democracy coaches." He and his wife, an ER doctor, have two daughters.

Vivian Viloria–Fisher taught English and Spanish at the Middle Country School District from 1969 to 1990. In 1990 the Three Village School District recruited her to teach AP Spanish at Ward Melville High School. She retired in 2002 after having served as chair of the Department of Foreign Languages. She was elected to the Suffolk County Legislature on January 19, 1999 in a special election. She went on to serve 13 years as a legislator and served as deputy presiding officer for six years.

I reached out to the candidates and explained about the project, a memoir in real time about the Resistance and our mission to flip our district from red to blue in 2018 and that it would not be published until after the election. They all agreed to be interviewed and were generous with their insights and their time. We scheduled the interviews over the phone, given their very busy schedules and my driving challenges. I recorded the interviews in order to have accurate quotes but assured them that whatever they told me was embargoed until after the election.

Due to scheduling conflicts, I was never able to interview Brendon but he did email me answers to my questions. My questions to all of them focused on the major themes of this project, the rise of the grassroots, the intersection of the grassroots and the Democratic Committees in NY01, and the midterm election. Their answers are organized under topic headings and where possible, are in alphabetical order by their last names.

The first question I asked each of them had to do with their own back story about how the 2016 election, the 2017 Women's March and the rise of the Resistance connected with their decisions to run for office.

FROM THE RESISTANCE TO BEING A CANDIDATE

Kate said that while she participated in the march, and was outraged by both Zeldin's reelection and the election of Trump, the Resistance was not the reason she decided to run. "I have known Lee Zeldin since he was in elementary school and was never impressed by him. And I had dealt with Zeldin while in the country legislature, when he didn't support a sewer project I worked on and he put out a lot of misinformation and turned a good project into something negative. I had been approached about running in 2016 when Dave and Anna were running and I said that I wanted to finish my 12-year term in the county legislature, that there were issues I was working on and I wanted to finish out my term, and also I had a great relationship with Anna and a lot of respect for Dave so I wasn't going to jump into that race. I watched Zeldin's attacks on Anna, that she was from the Hamptons, and I felt that being from Brookhaven, where the majority of the voters are, and knowing the district, that I know how to win in this district."

"I really sat myself down and said, 'you have a nice job at the lab, but can you sit here and watch the bottom fall out as the administration assaults science?' " said Elaine. "I thought maybe I should be an activist, and then I thought of following in the footsteps of other scientists who have served in Congress. I had heard Dr. Verner Ehlers speak, he was representing Michigan, one of three physicists in Congress, and he said that the problem-solving method that we scientists use and our capabilities, how we have to look at all the data, can be applied to solving political problems. I watched how Congress could not pass a budget and the impact that could have on laboratories like at the Brookhaven Labs, so I sought out an organization that trains scientists to run for office while at the same time joining with the Resistance and the activist groups at the rallies, the healthcare rallies, and the March for Science. And then made the decision to leave my job and run for office. My focus is on clean energy and clean water and the need to save our environment."

"It is a tricky question. On the one hand, it had a huge impact," said Perry. "And it was before the Women's March. I was sleep walking from the Wednesday after the election to Saturday. But then that Saturday I joined a spontaneous protest in front of Trump Tower in New York City and for the first time since the election, I smiled as I joined the group protesting and then I did the same thing the following weekend and then leading to the Women's March. I just could not live with Donald Trump, who he is, what it said about the country and I resolved that I was going to find something to do to fight back. But I wasn't thinking at that time of running for office. I had a successful business and I thought of using my business skills at a think tank or NGO. Then I was at a fundraiser for Senator Kirsten Gillibrand (Democrat - NY) and someone in the crowd asked her what we can do for the Resistance and she said, many of you live in districts with Republican representatives and she told us to go challenge them and run for office. I told my wife and sons that I was thinking of doing just that and they had seen how depressed I had been and they thought it was great. So, I met with Tim Bishop, former Democratic Congressman from our district and he looked at my resume and my background and perceived that I can raise substantial sums of money and in a district like ours, that is so spread out but with a super expensive media market, this is what you need to win."

"While all of those events played a role, my main concern and decision for running was our current state of representation," said Brendon. "We have millionaires pretending to understand the plight of the working, middle class, and poor people of our nation, all the while they are more concerned with lining up donations and keeping those donors happy. I am a firm believer in equality for all, and we don't have that right now, and we need people without baggage to fight to ensure everyone has it. We cannot cherry-pick equality; it is everyone's right as humans. Our current representative doesn't even pretend to care about us, well until election time comes. He is the definition of a party-first politician. I had been approached by people for years, but after months of planning and my family's support, I made a formal announcement in June of 2017."

"I would say it was not the Resistance, per se, that influenced me to run but it was the overall political climate that our government was being taken over by people incompetent and corrupt," said David. "I am someone who started in politics and been in government all my life and could bring this experience to the race. And the person with the support of the grassroots has the potential to unify the party and I have stood for progressive values and issues my whole life."

"I had been to all the marches, I joined my daughter for the Women's March in New York City and I knew many people from Planned Parenthood who were attending, but that was not the reason I chose to run. I did not immediately decide to run myself," said Vivian. "I called Kara Hahn and asked her to run, and then I called Dave Calone and asked him to run. I was particularly concerned about the impact on healthcare and the repeal of the ACA. So, I went to Washington D.C. to meet with Zeldin to ask him if he was aware of the negative impact on the elderly in our district if the ACA is repealed. By the time seniors are ready for Medicare, they will be much sicker and poorer and his only answer was that NY could apply for a grant. I couldn't believe how he could be saying those things, to throw the elderly into the bureaucratic nightmare of HHS. I left his office and went over to the Smithsonian Museum and while looking at artists from the WPA, it brought tears to my eyes and I thought of Trump and all the ugliness and lies, and I called up my husband and told him that I was thinking of running against Zeldin and he said, I'm not surprised."

WHAT IMPACT THE GRASSROOTS ANTI-TRUMP MOVEMENT MIGHT HAVE ON THE ELECTION?

"I think the grassroots is always important, especially with voter turnout. This district is still more Republican than Democratic, but the hope is that the groundswell from the grassroots activism will increase Democratic turnout," said Kate.

"I think we should see this as movement building," said Elaine. "I'm astonished by my volunteers, the amount of energy they put into this campaign, even knowing they still have their real lives going on."

"The process of reaching out to get signatures really showed the power of grassroots support, and I think it surprised a lot of people," said Perry.

"I have had the pleasure of speaking and meeting many of our grassroots organizations during this campaign," said Brendon. "They are focused and ready for a fight. My hope is for them to push the dinosaurs out of decision making, and focus more on policy and potential, rather than bank accounts."

"Clearly there are people who are active who weren't active before, young people who are more engaged," said David.

"Absolutely critical," said Vivian. "This vote will not be an election about persuading people to change their minds. People who like Zeldin are not going to turn their back on him. The grassroots who are already engaged start knocking on doors and then you go beyond the Indivisible groups to get out the vote."

But each of them also made it clear that as important as grassroots enthusiasm is to winning, and it would be crucial to a "wave" election, the nuts and bolts that make up a traditional campaign would also be essential to winning, and might, in some cases, even be more important. Funding, advertising, the ability to identify and reach potential supporters beyond the progressive base that were already energized, having a strong message that is not just anti-Trump and anti-Zeldin but states what the Democratic Party stands for, it was clear that they all knew you could not win in this district without these elements.

I asked if they saw a "down" side to the progressive passion in a district that has such a strong Republican base. Did that pose a potential for conflict? Were the grassroots groups more to the left than the established Democratic Committees? How would such activism play with the registered Independents and Republicans in the district? It seemed clear that our nominee could not win with Democratic votes alone.

Their answers depended on how progressive they felt they are perceived. For Kate, who is perceived by many in the grassroots as being the least progressive, she emphasized the support she had garnered from unions and from many established Democrats as a winning formula and thought the real danger came from a candidate being too far to the left.

"This is a very centrist district, not as progressive as people would like to believe," she said, "and we have to work on reaching moderate Republicans, particularly women. Zeldin is moving so far to the right. While Trump is still popular in this district, many people think he is doing a good job, I am not running against Trump, I am running against Zeldin. He has many weaknesses. He is not a pro-labor guy and while he claims that veterans are his biggest base of support, he has disappointed a lot of veterans."

Fairly or unfairly, many in the grassroots perceived her early membership in the Right to Life Party as a sign that she was not a reliable Democrat. She explained that when she first arrived in this country from Ireland, she was not as aware of what these parties stood for and that she had evolved on the subject of a women's right to choose so that she now feels that her personal views have nothing to do with her support for abortion rights. This issue, plus her record in the county legislature, had many in the grassroots opposed to her being the nominee.

One of those people vehemently opposed was Vivian. "If the party supports the least progressive candidate, then there will be a clash," said Vivian. And while she wanted to see the party unified after the primary, she said she personally could vote for all the other candidates, but not for Kate, who she perceived as not really progressive, based on her voting record in the county legislature.

David didn't go so far as saying he would not support Kate but shared his concern that "the grassroots is driven by passion and are unlikely to get so excited by a candidate more on the establishment side," said David. "I actually think the person who has the support of the grassroots has the potential to unify the party, but of course that may be the story I tell myself because it works better for me!" David and Vivian are perceived by many in the grassroots as the most progressive candidates and seem, at this stage, to have very active grassroots support.

Elaine and Perry, with no political record to run on, pointed to their professions and experience as winning strategies to bringing in other voters. For Elaine, she believed that her background as a scientist gave her a unique ability to bring in other voters. "My progressive stance comes from my heartfelt belief that there is money in the wrong places and that we can utilize evidence-based policy and compromise to focus on protecting social security, health care reform, student loans, reversing the Republican tax scam."

Perry said he was "hopeful my business background will appeal to swing voters and help get non-Democratic voters." But he also believed that the Democratic nominee could not win without also rallying the grassroots. "I believe if I am the nominee," he said, "I will have no problem getting people to rally around my campaign, and I think that is true of David, Vivian and Elaine, but I am concerned that if Kate is the nominee, then we won't have progressive turnout and it is my belief that the way we win is with high turnout from progressives."

Brendon saw his strength not in progressive terms but in the fact that "I am the youngest candidate, the only one with a job while campaigning and I bring new ideas to the table. I am the only candidate born, bred and raised in the district and all of my money is from small donations, from district residents who want better government."

2018 AND BEYOND

At this point in the election, it is not clear which strategy - nominating the most progressive candidate to excite the grassroots or nominating the most centrist candidate to bring in crossover voters - will be the winning one. The candidates, based on their backgrounds, their strengths and weaknesses, were positioning themselves in this crowded field and they would have to figure out a way to differentiate themselves from the group. But they also needed to do that without fracturing the party. This would be a tall order.

The importance of beating Zeldin in the fall was voiced strongly by each of the candidates. When I asked what they thought would happen to the Resistance past November 2018 if Zeldin won reelection and the Democrats did not take back the House, this was not a topic they even wanted to discuss.

"Bite your tongue!" said Kate. "It may be hard, but we have to win this fall, because I do believe if Zeldin wins this election, we will never be able to defeat him. Democrats need a coalition, with all the different branches of the party coming together to elect Democrats every year, in local races, state races and congressional races and not just come out in a presidential year."

"The stakes are so high. We must support whoever is the nominee to win this election," said Elaine. "What scares me the most is the destruction of the federal agencies and regulations because they have more dexterity than the legislative process to make rules and address problems. But they need to be funded and that comes from Congress. We have to keep the pressure on Washington to hear the voice of the people."

"I don't want to answer that one," said Perry. "Put this district aside for a moment. If we don't take back the House, it will be really bad for the country, it will be like Trump winning and I don't want to imagine that. If Trump gets that validation, God help us all."

"As far as Trump goes," said Brendon, "he is a dumpster human (using the term human loosely). He is not a person who has ever been concerned with the quality of life of anyone other than himself, and his song and dance has convinced people the opposite. We need to focus on policy that is about the people, not just the mega-wealthy and the corporations if we truly want to win. Relatable candidates are the key to that process. We have to be able to cross the aisle and make it about the country, not the parties. I think there is a good chance of taking back the House if we can break the mold more often."

David agreed that the stakes were too high going forward to even think of the Democrats not winning this year. "I think, in part, things are going to get even crazier, the Trump administration will not settle down, so what we need to do this year is to figure out how to get behind a candidate, bring all the groups together, have the ability to raise money. Being anti-Zeldin and anti-Trump is not enough because that is not a winning strategy. The nominee has to unify people around Democratic principles."

"I perceived the 2016 election as an existential threat to our country," said Vivian. "I thought about Trump campaigning to bring back coal, and my mental image was that he wanted to bring back the technology of a century ago to blacken our lungs. That was my mental image. That is what I mean by existential threat and that has hit home on so many levels. Hurting the most vulnerable, taking them and squeezing them."

Like the other candidates, she did not want to think about Zeldin winning in the fall or Democrats not taking back the House. But when I pressed her, wondering if the grassroots enthusiasm will dwindle if we don't win in 2018, she said she hoped not, because, "we will have to redouble our efforts for 2020, because even more will be at stake."

Chapter 10

January 2018

"We had such a great turnout for the Women's March on NYC Saturday! Thanks to all our members who showed up with loud voices, big signs, and friends and family in tow to support us! Got pictures from the March in NYC, Port Jeff or Sag Harbor? Add them to our Facebook page. We want to see you."

EEAN Newsletter, January 22nd, 2018

Wednesday, January 10th
EEAN Interview with Brendon Henry
This evening, EEAN hosted Brendon Henry at the Westhampton Beach Library meeting room. This was the second candidate interview; the first was last month with Kate Browning.

I got there early to help Sharon at the door signing people up for our newsletter, handing out flyers for our fundraiser in February and handing out Brendon's palm card with his information. Despite being a dreary midweek January evening, we got a pretty good turnout. Rebecca was the moderator, as she was with Kate Browning. She really does her homework, researching the candidate so that her questions are well informed. Afterwards she told me that Brendon was harder to interview than Kate since his answers were short and somewhat superficial. The questions from the audience were sharp and to the point. Some of his answers were specific but too often he answered in platitudes. But he is a likeable, personable person. Still, I am left with the feeling that he is not quite ready for a congressional race since his grasp of the issues is shaky.

EEAN's own Kyle Cranston is Brendon's campaign manager. Kyle is an interesting guy. He is an actor, his brother is Bryan Cranston of Breaking Bad fame, and he is dedicated to his progressive principles, particularly when it comes to issues of economic inequality, war and peace. He was a participant in Occupy Wall Street after the financial collapse. He was a Bernie Sanders supporter in 2016, did not vote for Clinton, because he did not feel she embodied those principles, and voted instead for Jill Stein. This is an issue we try not to discuss because it is hard for me to understand. Along with his acting, he has his own textbook supply business.

I am surprised that Kyle has gotten involved with a candidate in a Democratic primary since I know how negative his feelings are about the Party.

"In 2011, when I was in the city with Occupy Wall Street, I had a question posed to me by one of the participants," said Kyle. " And he said,' Do you really think that there's a difference between the Democratic and Republican parties?' I looked at him like he was crazy. I said, 'Are you kidding me? Absolutely!' He said, 'Really? You think there is?' And I said, 'Absolutely, there's an obvious difference!' Well, I don't feel that way anymore. Any differences are very superficial but at the core, because they're both controlled by the same money interests, then there's really no difference because it doesn't matter, Democrat or Republican, it is more like a duopolistic tyranny. The party of FDR was the party of the people. It was the real reform party that got us through that war and got us out of the Depression and made such social reforms. That's the party I was introduced to that I understood the Democratic Party to be. That's not what we have today. And that started to change in the early 1970s with the Democratic Leadership Conference, the DLC. And Bill Clinton was very much a part of that. Democrats say they're the party of the people, far cry."

We walked out of the library together and he asked me what I thought about Brendon. I chose my words carefully. I like Kyle and I like Brendon so I looked for a way to be honest about what I perceived tonight. I told him that I thought Brendon is the most likeable of the candidates but he needs to learn more about policy because his answers to Rebecca's questions and the questions from the audience were much too broad. I asked Kyle why he was supporting Brendon and he told me that he thinks Brendon is the only one who can beat Zeldin because he is the only one born and raised in the district, spent his adult working years in the district and will appeal to younger voters.

Saturday, January 13th
Candidate Forum

SPC hosted all six candidates in a forum at the Stony Brook Southampton campus, the same location where we hosted the Politics 101 forum last June. The forum was from 3:00 to 4:30 PM and beforehand, in the lobby, we held a grassroots fair, similar to what we had at the Politics 101. Of course, the big difference now is we have a primary and candidates, so the atmosphere is more charged.

We set up tables around the lobby, with tablecloths, and each group had a sign with their name and handouts on the table, along with sign-up sheets. At the EEAN table we taped our large banner to the window behind the table. I said hello to Joy, Robin and Gordon who were at the SHDems table, handing out the flyers we created with all of the candidates' short biographies. I could sit with them but I decided to help out with EEAN. I had prepared handouts with information about the EEAN plan for the Women's March next Saturday in NYC so I handed those out to folks who came up to our table.

What I will remember most about this afternoon was the turnout, the amazing, unprecedented turnout. We thought 60 people, maybe 80 would attend. There must have been close to 200 people, filling the auditorium, overflowing onto folding chairs and standing along the walls. For a candidates' forum in January, before names are on the ballot, when there are still six candidates running, this was astonishing. Maybe this is what a blue wave looks like. No matter which one of these candidates becomes the nominee, it will be up to us to carry them over the finish line.

As to the forum itself, I was surprised at the strength of Perry and David and a little disappointed that Kate was not stronger. I wish we could take the best of each of them and combine that into one great candidate. No one was jumping out as so outstanding that it was a slam dunk to beat Zeldin. Each had a one-line "elevator speech" that summed up their advantage, but digging a little deeper, you came away with a lot of platitudes. David had the most depth. But he was not so personable. Brendon was the most personable but had the least depth.

Most of the audience was older and white, with more men than expected but still predominantly women. Very few minorities and very few younger voters, though there more young people than I have seen at other events. We have yet to figure out how to reach out to other constituencies.

Saturday, January 20th
Women's March NYC

This year we decided to march in NYC, rather than in D.C. It is much closer, a day trip, rather than a whole weekend. I debated marching with EEAN, but decided instead to march again with my sister Nanci, my niece Elyse and this year, her daughter, Mackenzie (age four), who would be joining us in her stroller. Unfortunately, Vicky and Mimi were unable to attend this year but we hoped to meet Joanna and her sister, Elise, in the city.

It was a challenge to wake up early enough on a Saturday morning to get to the city in time for the march. It didn't help that I watched television coverage of the Senate debate that precipitated the government shutdown until after 2:00 AM. On only four hours of sleep, I packed my things and drove to the Long Island Railroad station. As I parked the car, I saw Rebecca, Sharon, Patty and Cindy from EEAN. We were all tired but in good spirits, carrying posters and cups of take-out coffee. As we boarded the train and sat together, we commented that there were no crowds at the station and the train was almost empty. Did that mean the March this year would not attract a big crowd? That would send a terrible signal to the GOP and Trump.

They were taking the two-hour train ride all the way into the city. I got off earlier to meet up with Nanci, Elyse and Mackenzie who are picking me up in Nanci's van. We decided to drive into the city, easier to manage with a four-year-old, a stroller and our big posters. We had our large Michelle Obama signs from last year and were wearing the NYC Women's March 2018 T-shirts I purchased for us. In the van, Elyse created a couple of new signs for Mackenzie to hold in her stroller. Because she still liked the chant from last year, "We will not go away," that was the slogan for one of her signs. She created another one that said "3 Generations."

We were lucky that it was warm and sunny, just as it was last year. We parked in a parking garage further uptown and walked towards the 70s on the West Side. The March was scheduled to be on Central Park West, heading downtown, and then turning at Columbus Circle to continue down to Times Square at 42nd Street. Along the way, I kept texting with Joanna and Elise so we could meet up with them at the March. We had planned on meeting them at 72nd Street where the March was supposed to begin but Joanna sent me a text that the size of the crowd was so large that to enter we needed to go further uptown to 77th Street. The crowd was so massive that all side streets below 77th were now closed since they were already filled with marchers waiting to enter onto Central Park West. We headed to 77th Street and finally found Joanna and Elise.

We stood for almost two hours before merging onto Central Park West. But it was a happy and patient crowd, chanting slogans, dancing, waving posters, taking pictures of each other's posters. Mackenzie in her stroller was a big hit and many people asked if they could take her picture with her two little posters. We even started her favorite chant, "We will not go away!"

When we finally merged onto Central Park West and marched downtown as part of this enormous crowd, we looked up at the people waving to us out of windows from the apartment buildings lining this wide avenue. Together we all yelled "Shame!" and "Shithole!" as we passed by Trump International Hotel. By the time we got to Columbus Circle, we were pretty spent so rather than march all the way down to Times Square, we exited the March. We then took some pictures of all of us with our posters, including Joanna and Elise. Afterwards, we headed to a restaurant for dinner. We went to the same Mexican restaurant we ate at after the Tax Day March last April, our new post-march tradition. Mary and Marge met us at the restaurant. After dinner, we took an Uber back to the parking garage and then drove to Nanci's, where I stayed over that night. Mackenzie stayed awake in the car watching a movie but went right to sleep when she got home. She was quite a trooper at her first protest March.

Even though I wasn't able to meet up with EEAN for the March, they carried our banner proudly.

This is what I posted on Facebook on Monday, January 22nd:

> *Saturday's March was as empowering as last year but different in a significant way. Last year, it was an antidote to the despair and shock we were all feeling that messages of white supremacy, racism, hate and misogyny had elected a president. That a self-proclaimed sexual predator could win the White House. We feared for women's health, for the Affordable Care Act, for immigrants, for DACA, for the environment. At last year's March, discovering we weren't alone filled our hearts with joy and began a healing process, giving us hope that all was not lost in this country we love. And it gave us direction and guidance how to fight back, stay sane and resist. We found huddles to join, rallies to attend, town halls to storm, making our voices heard and learning how to fight back. We won some battles, we lost some battles, but we learned how to engage. We learned that saving democracy is a long haul. We took the empowerment from the 2017 March and brought it into our districts with voter registration drives, knocking on doors and getting out the vote for our local and statewide 2017 elections. It was the beginning of the blue wave. The 2018 March was also an affirmation that we are not alone,*

but this time we are joined as activists, and marching side by side renews our hope that the work ahead is as important to others as it is to ourselves. It was also uplifting to see more men, more children and more young women at the 2018 March. This movement is growing. As we chanted at the March, "This is what democracy looks like." This is also what a blue wave looks like.

Wednesday, January 24th
Sick again

I had two meetings on my schedule tonight, Rebecca's interview with Elaine and a SHDems general meeting. They were at the same time so I opted for the Elaine interview and passed along my EEAN update notes to Andi to give to the SHDems meeting. In particular, we wanted to let people know about a fundraiser we were planning.

Then I got sick with a stomach bug and missed both meetings. There was a vote tonight at the SHDems meeting to make the candidate selection process more open and transparent. David Dubow, the chair for the search committee, asked me to be a co-signer of the motion and after checking with Mike, I agreed. I heard the next day that it passed with unanimous consent. Andi and Sharon emailed me information about both meetings; they went smoothly and both were well-attended.

Wednesday, January 31st
EEAN leadership meeting

I have just gotten home from my first leadership meeting. I had chosen last summer when we first decided to have tiers of volunteering to not be in the leadership because I had a full plate with the SHDems and SPC. That is still true but I felt that I can contribute more to our work if I am part of the leadership. It also gives the reader a closer look at the Resistance from the planning level.

We met at EEAN member Nancy Tuttle's house at 5:30 PM. The drive was a bit outside my comfort zone but at least it was still light outside and I had the GPS on my phone. Also, the drive pretty much stayed on Montauk Highway, which I can handle. Living for 25 years in Manhattan and not driving all that time left me with a driving phobia that I still have not completely shaken. And even though we have been on the East End for almost 17 years, I have yet to be able to drive on Sunrise Highway or the Long Island Expressway. It puts a crimp in my activist work because whenever a meeting or rally is announced, the first thing I have to worry about is, how will I get there? I get rides from my fellow resisters when I can.

Along with Nancy, who is not a leadership member but was happy to host, are Rebecca, Sharon, Syma, Patty, Wendy, Cindy and Kyle. There was wine, some snacks, and we sat around the dining room table. It reminded me of some of the Happy Hours I attended last year. But it was also a working meeting. We talked about the jobs that each of us needed to do to get ready for our upcoming fundraiser, a Charity Bowl. Sharon and Rebecca had already made all of the arrangements but there was work to be done promoting it, reaching out to the grassroots groups, working at the event and trying to get some press attention for it. Everyone signed up for different jobs.

At the end of the meeting, we talked about the candidates. Kyle repeated to the group what he had told me about why he is supporting Brendon. He does not see Brendon's lack of experience in legislating as a disadvantage because he believes that voters are looking for outsiders. But he also said that he had a growing respect for Elaine DiMasi, that she had done really well at the one-on-

one with Rebecca and that she would be his second choice. No one else has really chosen a candidate yet. I know I haven't but am keeping an open mind and still listening.

The chaos in Trump/Zeldin World in January:

- In a meeting with Senators Graham and Durbin who came to the White House with a bipartisan immigration deal, Trump was reported to have called all the countries in Africa as well as Haiti "shithole" countries and asked why we can't have more immigrants from Norway?
- Government shutdown lasted three days as Trump went back and forth on immigration.
- The left was angry that Schumer and the Democrats caved on making sure there would be a vote on DACA in this continuing resolution (CR). Next deadline is Feb. 8th
- We learned that Mueller wanted to talk to Trump and had already spoken with Comey, Sessions, and the heads of all the intelligence services.
- Trump, the GOP in Congress and the right-wing media smeared the FBI in a made-up scandal about text messages between two FBI agents. What they were really doing was trying to discredit Mueller and the FBI to lay the groundwork for the public not believing the results of a report from Mueller.
- Trump levied tariffs on solar panels and large washing machines, likely to start a trade war around the world.
- Trump went to the World Economic Forum. It did not go well. Before he left, he said he can't wait to speak to Mueller and offered to do it under oath. Quickly, his lawyers walked that back.
- Zeldin defended Trump, Steven Miller and hard-line immigration. We kept pushing him for a town hall, which he kept avoiding.

Chapter 11

February 2018

"I'm meeting with Zeldin Monday for a constituent lunch and I wanted to invite you to it."

Ronald Fisher, SHDems

Thursday, February 1st
EEAN Charity Bowl

We began the new month with the EEAN fundraiser. I spent part of the day doing my part to get ready for tonight. Sharon sent me the list of names which I printed, cut up, folded and put into a basket for the door prize drawing. We got to the All Star Bowling Alley in Riverhead early to set up. Sharon drove and picked up Syma then me.

Sharon had already prepared the packets for each team. Since I was not bowling (bad knees that don't bend), I was happy to work at the table at the front door and check everyone in. Most had already paid online through Eventbrite but a few paid at the door. We had door prizes as well as a prize for the top score.

The author, Syma and Sharon at the EEAN fundraiser sign-in table.

Sharon and Rebecca did an incredible job setting this all up. The fee covered everything at the event for the bowlers – shoes, lanes, soda, pizza – and left a portion per person for charity. Many people also gave the fee online but were not bowling and so the whole amount went to charity. This was true of my donation since I not only am not bowling but I can't eat or drink anything due to my allergies. But I was happy to see my whole donation go to the charities chosen. At our last general membership meeting, we voted on which charities to donate to and two charities were chosen to split the donations, one local and one national. Maureen's Haven is a local charity that provides for the homeless on the East End and One America Appeal is the national charity that is providing relief to the hurricane victims in Puerto Rico and the U.S. Virgin Islands.

I described our event in a press release for the local newspapers, though it did not get published.

Press Release from East End Action Network
For immediate release

February 2, 2018: Last night, grassroots activists from the East End of NY's First Congressional District (CD#1) came together for a charity event that raised money for two good causes. Organized by the grassroots group, East End Action Network (EEAN), almost 50 people attended a Charity Bowl at The All Star bowling alley in Riverhead from 6:00 pm to 9:00 pm and enjoyed bowling, pizza and prizes while raising money for two wonderful organizations - Maureen's Haven, a local homeless outreach group and One America Appeal, a nonprofit launched by all former, living U.S. Presidents to help victims of recent hurricanes in Puerto Rico and the U.S. Virgin Islands. Proceeds raised at the Charity Bowl will be donated on behalf of all the grassroots organizations in CD#1. Everyone got into the spirit of the event, arranging teams of six to seven people, with team names like CD1 Strikes, Alley Activists and Blue Patriots. The Democratic candidates vying to run against Rep. Lee Zeldin in the midterm election this fall were invited and three of them were able to attend – Perry Gershon, Brendon Henry and David Pechefsky – each heading a team that they organized. But it wasn't a night of politics or policy but rather spares and strikes and a lot of laughter.

EEAN is comprised of constituents of CD#1 and engages in thoughtful dialogue that serves as a touch-point for those in the district who want to connect with other progressives. As part of this mission, EEAN has been hosting each of the seven Democratic candidates at the Westhampton Beach Library for one-on-one interviews, giving members of the community a chance to ask questions of the candidates and giving the candidates an opportunity to listen to what issues are of paramount importance to constituents. The primary focus for all the progressive grassroots groups this year will be voter outreach, which includes registering, polling and educating voters in preparation for the midterm election this fall.

I was struck throughout the evening at how friendly the three candidates were with each other. Clearly, they respect each other and I hoped this carried over into the primary battle.

It was a successful evening – we raised $1200 to be split between the two charities – and it was great to see everyone have a good time. We should have more social events like this. There is a cohesive bond that is created that helps us all to cope with the work we do.

Once home, I made dinner, then settled down on the couch to watch the news that I recorded. I was very tired which made me a little nervous because I don't want to get sick again. I will take it easy for the next few days.

Wednesday, February 7th
EAN interview with Vivian
Tonight, we had one of our candidate interviews at the Westhampton Beach library. I came close to deciding not to go. It was a cold and rainy night and I was still feeling tired from last week. But the library is only five minutes from my house and I wanted to give Rebecca two letters she asked me to write to go along with our checks to Maureen's Haven and One America Appeal. If not for that, I might have skipped it. I was not feeling as excited to see the interview with Vivian. At the candidate forum in January, she impressed me the least and I was also put off when she went out of her way to attack Kate Browning's record.

There wasn't a great turnout, probably because of the bad weather. And that was a shame because I came away impressed with Vivian, with her passion, commitment, experience and true progressive values. Many people there were moved by her story. Sharon told me that she now knows who her candidate will be. I told her I was equally impressed.

The only note of concern was when Vivian said that if Kate is the nominee, she cannot support her. She feels that Kate is not really a progressive. That would certainly make our desire for everyone to unite around the nominee more difficult. But she said she is impressed with the other candidates, particularly Perry, David and Elaine and would support them.

Some people and some groups were openly endorsing a candidate. Will this lead to hard feelings when the primary is over? We have been working hard to stay on the same page – begin with electing Democrats in the local election last fall, continue the pressure on Congress to save the ACA, protest the travel ban, support DACA, etc., and be vocal and visible against Zeldin through peaceful and organized rallies, protests, town halls, letters to the editor.

But now there are real candidates. None of us want a repeat of the Hillary/Bernie division that split the Democratic Party in 2016. In a year that has the potential to be a Democratic wave and take back the House – essential for a check on Trump and for a potential vote on impeachment – Democrats could blow this chance because there are too many candidates running. Could this also happen in CD#1 and open the door for Zeldin to win reelection?

Friday, February 9th
Are we complicit?
I was recording the Olympics opening ceremony. Good thing because I was on the phone for a long time with Joanna Levinger, who I marched with on Tax Day in 2017 and the second Women's March last month. I have known Joanna since she was born. She is in her late twenties. I could tell from her voice that something was wrong. She said it wasn't serious but that she had a confusing day that left her shaken. She works very long hours at her job in NYC, has a boyfriend that she lives with and an active social life. And in the midst of this busy, 20-something life, she also tries to stay connected to the Resistance movement because she feels strongly that Trump and his policies are attacking the very fabric of our country. She is particularly attuned to the immigration debate.

But everything about where the country is leaves her alternating between outrage, anxiety and guilt. She worries that she is not doing enough and that makes her feel that she is complicit, more part of the problem than the solution. She lives with daily anxiety about the potential for violence and what is her obligation to intercede. As she told me, when she sees a woman wearing a headscarf on the subway, she worries that one of these right-wing-Trumpsters might say or do something and she would want to protect the person, but how would she do that and make sure she is safe? If ICE should come onto a bus, subway or train, should she stand in front of them to protect the undocumented, but would they then harm her or arrest her? She can only take so much time from her job to protest and would like to do more, but also knows that these years when she and her boyfriend can meet with friends are precious because once she starts a family, these moments become few and far between. She envies women who are devoting their lives to activism, but worries that as a white girl, she would be viewed as illegitimate, since she personally is not at risk. And sometimes she falls down this rabbit hole and it is hard to find her way out. Today was one of those days.

I listened and told her that this is now one more reason for me to hate Trump. Everything Trump touches, he infects, including the struggle of millennials who are trying to find their way in the adult world, which is hard enough without being burdened by saving the world from Trump.

I told her that she is the least complicit person I know. She has a good heart and cares deeply and that we cannot all be full time activists. I could not when I was her age. There is a reason so many of us in the Resistance are retirement age.

This is the 9/11 generation. They have grown up in the shadow of terrorism, of fear, of the Afghanistan and Iraq wars. They embraced Obama with hope and then watched the GOP do everything they possibly could to stifle that hope. And now there is Trump. It is so poignantly sad.

I hoped I helped her to feel a little better. Then I turned on the opening ceremony, which was beautiful. I love all the Olympic events, both summer and winter, but I have always had a bit of a soft spot for the Winter Games. They are smaller, Americans are not so dominant so there is less nationalism in the coverage and the athletes compete in sports that defy the boundaries of what the human body should be able to do. Unfortunately, I had to see Vice President Pence there. I fast forward every time they showed him sitting in the viewing box.

Monday, February 12th
Meeting Zeldin
This afternoon, I was privileged to experience life from the other side of the political divide. Ron Fisher, fellow SHDems member, invited me to a meeting where Zeldin was going to be speaking. Ron owns his own business in Southampton, Fisher Signs and Shirts LLC, and is very active in business and civic organizations. Zeldin knows him by name because they have worked on projects for the business community and because Ron is a member of the Riverhead School Board. This is how local politics works. So, when it was announced that Zeldin would speak and take questions at a constituent luncheon in Westhampton Beach, some young ROTC members in Riverhead were invited for a photo-op with the congressman. As a school board member, Ron was invited to accompany them to the meeting and asked to bring along guests. He asked me if I would like to attend. As a constituent I am welcome. I jumped at the chance since Zeldin does not hold town halls and this event was not on his website or Facebook page. Clearly, he only wanted his supporters to be there. I hoped I would have the opportunity to ask Zeldin a question.

I spent the morning researching Zeldin's record on the environment, one of the worst in Congress. I would like to know why he supports the deregulation of environmental regulations because he says they are burdensome to the economy but he never speaks of them in light of public health, welfare, safety and the negative impacts of climate change. Given our district is on an island, this is an important issue for all of his constituents.

Ron picked me up and I did not know until we got there that the event was sponsored by the Veterans of Foreign Wars (VFW) and was held in their hall in Westhampton Beach. Ron parked the car then went to meet the bus where the students were arriving and would then walk in with them. I walked in by myself and was greeted at the door by a man probably just a bit older than me, probably a Vietnam War veteran, who shook my hand, welcomed me and asked me to sign in with my name and email address, which I did. One of Zeldin's aides then also walked up and shook my hand and welcomed me to this event to meet the congressman. I thanked him and let him know that as a constituent I welcomed the opportunity to hear the congressman speak and ask him a question. I also told him that I cannot partake of the meal – pizza, garlic nuts, soda – due to my allergies. It was all very friendly. So different than any other time I have dealt with Zeldin's office. There is clearly a different standard for his supporters.

The hall has a large dining room that was filled with round tables, covered with round plastic tablecloths with a design pattern of leaves, and about eight to ten chairs at each table. The room is surrounded by windows, and after a morning of dark clouds and rain, the sun finally broke through so that by 3:00 PM, the room, despite all the dark wood, was bright with sunlight. Next door to this large room is a smaller room with a long, wooden bar. When we entered and signed in, we were standing in the room with the bar. Most of the guests stayed in this room, congregating at the bar as we waited for the event to begin. Most of them seemed to know each other so the conversations were lively and full of laughter. I did not order a drink but I stood and smiled and said hello to the people there. They were mostly men, mostly middle-aged, and all of them white, with a few women, also middle-aged and also white. Most of the men were wearing pins and hats that connote their veteran status.

I am quite comfortable in the company of veterans; my husband and father are veterans and I wonder to myself, when did the Democratic Party lose the support of veterans? Does it go back to Vietnam, civil rights, Nixon and his Southern strategy? Is it all about race? When did we cede patriotism to the GOP?

After everyone arrived, we moved into the dining room and found seats at the tables. I sat at a table that I thought was in the back of the room. I saw Ron and his students at the other end of the room and figured they were in the front near where the congressman will be since they are the honored guests. They were all in their dress military, ROTC uniforms. I was struck by how many medals were on the front of their uniforms given that they are so young. I was the first to sit at my table. An older man, with grey hair, a grey mustache and glasses and not wearing a VFW hat, asked if he could sit down and I smiled and said of course. We were then joined by another man, taller, younger, with dark hair and with an Irish accent, who also saved a seat for a female friend. When Zeldin arrived and walked to the side of the room where we are sitting, we realized we are all sitting in the front, not the back. I should have realized it since he was standing near a pole with the American flag on it. I thought about moving to the back but there were no available seats. In fact, there were people standing along the walls.

After Zeldin was introduced, we all stood for the pledge of allegiance. As Zeldin began to talk, it was clear to me that he has been there before and many of the VFW members already know him. He was dressed casually in jeans and a button-down shirt and no tie but with a navy blue jacket. He explained that he was there to answer their questions, for about an hour, that this is part of his time speaking and listening to constituents in the district. I cannot help but smile to myself because I know he will not do that with those of us he calls, "liberal obstructionists." He also reminded folks that he had staff members with him in attendance and if anyone had any issues they needed help with, like social security, to just speak to a staff member because they were there to help.

This room is his base and it is clear how much they adore him and Trump. That was palpable. Most of the questions and comments were not a surprise. There was a lot of talk about immigration. Most of it involved talk of dangerous gangs. One woman asked why can't we separate our electoral votes from "those people" in NYC, so that our votes will count more? I couldn't tell if she was referring to Democrats, minorities, immigrants or just anyone different from her as "those people" who live in NYC. From these comments, one would think there are marauding bands of gang members terrorizing CD#1. Trump and Zeldin play on these fears and stoke them to help solidify the support from this group.

It was also expected just how nimble Zeldin is at obscuring facts, at changing the conversation, at steering it in the directions that he clearly believes work well for him. Sometimes he did this by commiserating with the audience, by putting down politics in Washington, by even criticizing the GOP in Congress and complaining about how hard it is to get anything done. And they all had a good chuckle together. The essence of what he was saying was, "Don't blame me for not getting more done, I'm with you guys, but you just don't know how hard it is in Washington." And of course, he leaned heavily into his military service background. He also tried to straddle a line about Trump. On the one hand, he reminded folks about how often he speaks to Trump, letting them know he has the president's ear, but then he criticized the tweeting.

This was all to be expected. What was a surprise were the questions that were not so sycophantic. And these tended to fall into three subject areas: the tax bill and the impact on our district, the potential deportation of the DACA kids and the danger that harsh immigration laws will make it harder to get enough employees for local businesses, particularly for the summer resort season.

Not one person in the room thanked him for the GOP cutting their taxes. Every tax question was a criticism of how this bill is going to hurt this district.

And I quickly realized that if I got a chance to ask a question, it should be on the tax bill. I jettisoned my environment question and formulated a question about the tax bill.

He was having a difficult time, trying to defend his party and what he views as good things in the bill for the economy, but knowing that his constituents are going to get hurt by the bill so also trying to explain why he voted against it. He, of course, left out his vote for the budget resolution that sent it forward. Someone asked him about a lawsuit from New York and he said that will not work and is probably illegal. And he outlined how impossible it would be to get another vote in Congress to reverse this. So, he then landed on what he saw as the only remedy to protect us – blame the Democrats in Albany.

Absurd but clever. If only we could get more Republicans in our state government, then our taxes wouldn't be so high and then the fact that we lost crucial deductions in this draconian tax bill would not hurt us so much. Based on the responses, he appeared to largely succeed in deflecting the ire and attention onto the Democrats in the state government, saying that our best hope for remedy in this situation lies with cutting waste in order to lower our state taxes. He went through a long rambling, almost incoherent answer about doctors scamming the state Medicaid program, and brought the conversation back to those "others" who are receiving benefits and don't deserve it. Folks nodded their heads in agreement.

Few people in the room seemed to grasp the illogic of his argument. As if there is enough waste and fraud to substantially lower our state taxes without having to make cuts to our school districts, police, firemen, and other essential services. Not to mention that Albany is not completely run by Democrats. But he landed on his boogeyman for the harm that the tax bill is going to inflict and the audience bought it especially once he tied it into the dangerous undocumented immigrants.

He finally called on me and I was looking directly at him because he stood right in front of me. As best I can remember, this is how our exchange went.

"Congressman, thank you for coming today to answer questions and I want to follow up on the previous questions about the tax bill. I really don't understand how this happened. With unified Republican government and a major bill to cut taxes and yet my taxes are going to go up and are going to go up dramatically. I have spoken to my accountant about it and I am going to get slammed. And your only answer is to focus on Albany. That's not an answer. I don't understand why you can't join with the representatives from the other states getting hurt by this bill, like New Jersey and California, and offer an amendment that would protect us from getting killed by this."

I heard low voices murmuring in agreement around me. He then gave me an astonishing answer, essentially saying that if he thought he could get the votes in Congress to reverse this, he would, but he can't and he could never get to 218 votes to pass a bill. So, he repeated that our only remedy is in Albany. And he said that many other representatives, even in New York and California, who live in areas, like upstate NY, where their local taxes are low, were fine with a cap of $10,000 for the SALT (state and local tax deduction) so that we wouldn't have the votes even from within our own state. Of course, he did not say that every Democrat, no matter where they were in New York, voted against the bill. It was only the GOP representatives from upstate who voted for it. We would clearly have the votes if we elected more Democrats. Without realizing it, he just endorsed flipping Congress to the Democrats as the only way we will see a remedy.

Before he could move on to the next question, I interrupted him and added, "But Congressman, it is not just the changes to the SALT deduction that are going to kill us. It is also removing the personal exemption so that if we have dependents over 18 and we are not eligible for the expanded child tax credit, we now get nothing for those dependents. And it's making changes like eliminating the interest on a home equity loan that really hurts those of us who made financial decisions based on the existing law and now have the rug pulled out from us. And it is projected that the change in what is allowed in the mortgage interest deduction is going to lower our property values by as much as 10%. My home is my biggest asset. I could conceivably have to move because these changes to the law make living here unaffordable. I really don't understand how this happened and you are not offering us any hope of a real remedy here."

The murmurs at my table got louder and I overheard one man say that he didn't know that his home equity interest would no longer be deductible.

Zeldin didn't disagree or try to deny anything I said. He just tried to deflect blame off himself by saying that he did his best, but didn't have the votes to protect us and that he would be lying if he told me that he could get an amendment passed to change that, that he could tell me what I wanted to hear but he is committed to being honest with us. And he offered no avenue, no remedy for us other than changing the state government in Albany, which he repeated.

It was late and there were only a few more questions. He clearly wanted to pivot away from the tax bill and was grateful when he was asked to explain just how a bill becomes a law. He took up a lot of time with that, eating up the remaining time on a basic civics question. But then he was pinned down again by the man with the Irish accent at my table who asked about the H1B1 visa, the specialty visa that allows American employers to hire foreign workers. These are often used by the tech industry. He explained that he is an immigrant, now a citizen and that he is a large employer in the district and that if the government stops approving these visas, that he will go out of business. He explained that he cannot get enough Americans to fill these jobs and he has tried. "I have put ads in all the newspapers and I am offering salaries above minimum wage and I do not get any response." He never explained what his business is but he was looking to Zeldin for help on how to speed up these visa applications and assurance that retaining these will be part of the immigration overhaul.

Zeldin gave a long, rambling non-answer on this, focusing on the process and time of year for these applications and that the process is slow but people usually get their visas. He did not answer how these visas are going to fare in the immigration overhaul that the GOP is advocating. A woman in the back followed up on the immigration question saying that she works for a major employer in the district and if there is a drop in legal immigration that this business cannot survive. He gave the same rambling, non-answer.

Then the last question was from one of the older veterans in a VFW hat who asked why can't we protect the "Dreamers" who have served in the military and what is Zeldin going to do to help them? Zeldin gave a speech about how anyone who has served this flag, which he turned and pointed to, and has been willing to die for this country we love should automatically be given citizenship. The audience applauded but he never answered about what he personally is going to do to help.

There were a few more questions. The other man at my table said he needed help with social security and he was referred to one of the aides. There was a discussion about the Veterans Affairs (VA) buildings in Northport and how run-down they are. He bemoaned how much money it would take to truly update them and the money is just not there in the budget because there are no longer earmarks. Again, he did not really offer any help or remedy just blamed Washington. Ironically, he never mentioned the infrastructure bill being unveiled the same day. But maybe he didn't because it is reported that this bill will also discriminate against urban areas and blue states.

When it was over, everyone applauded. Ron ushered his kids to the front to have their picture taken with the congressman, while the rest of us moved back into the room with the bar. I left to wait in the parking lot for Ron. Standing in the parking lot, Zeldin walked past me as he left the building. He smiled and said good-bye. I smiled back.

It was enlightening to be in a room with Zeldin and his supporters. He certainly did not speak with us at the one town hall last year like this. And even with these supporters who love him, who love Trump, who are voters he already has on his side, he had to answer some tough questions about the tax bill and about how the immigration debate is going to impact local businesses. Given the visceral negative feelings in the room about the dangerous immigrants, that did not extend to the fear of losing valued workers or of the unfairness of this immigration crackdown on the DACA kids.

That night when I watched the news and learned about the Trump fraudulent infrastructure bill – which further penalizes the blue states – I thought about how important it is that we pin the truth about these economic messages on Zeldin. We need to save our district from the assault from the GOP in Washington. It would be very hard, particularly in a debate with the Democratic nominee, for Zeldin to deflect all of this onto being Albany's fault. But, at the same time, economic policies are complicated and do not lend themselves to a bumper sticker or a message on a hat.

Later that night, after I finished typing up my notes, I turned on my recording of the Olympics. I didn't finish watching until 3:00 AM. But it was worth it.

The next day, Zeldin's office posted a press release on his website about the meeting, which was called a "pizza and policy" town hall.[17]

February 14th-26th
Parkland

I was watching *MSNBC* live when the first reports of a school shooting came in as breaking news. Throughout the course of the day, as I watched more news, more video, more interviews about the shooting, it was heartbreakingly familiar to be witnessing the death of America's children due to gun violence. At the same time, over the week, it became clear that this time a few things are different. For one, the shooter is alive. For another, the surviving students are the ones speaking out about the need for our government to do something about these senseless deaths. I had hoped after the Sandy Hook massacre that the death of young children and teachers in their classrooms would turn the tide and usher in universal background checks and reinstate the assault weapons ban. It did not. Republicans blocked a vote. These were grieving parents advocating for their dead children. But the NRA and the GOP were unmoved. The same was true with the young activists in the Black Lives Matter movement. Their anguished cries about the needless slaughter in their communities were unheeded.

But here was something new – articulate, activist, high school students, predominantly white, shouting down the "thoughts and prayers" contingent. And in a state, Florida, with some of the most lax gun laws - remember Stand Your Ground and Trayvon Martin? - these young people were grabbing the headlines and taking the argument directly to the NRA.

And something else was different this time. Unlike previous school shootings, a national, grassroots, progressive movement is already in place, already energized to oust the GOP from their districts and opposed to Trump and his policies. Indivisible, the Women's March, and the hundreds of grassroots organizations in every district in the country, already pro-gun reform, already against the NRA, leaped into action. Because of this, the students' push against the status quo took off like lightning. They descended on the Florida state capital, in the largest rally in decades to stand for gun legislation. They stood up to Senator Marco Rubio in a CNN televised town hall and confronted him on his NRA donations. And they organized a school walkout planned for March 14th and a national march for gun control on March 24th, called the March for Our Lives. The Women's March organizers joined them, creating the Youth Empowerment program, in addition to their Power to the Polls mission for this year.

And my district was no different. Grassroots groups offered help to the students organizing the MFOL and to connect this students' movement for gun control to the registering of young voters for the 2018 election.

Zeldin's response was typical. Sharon attended one of Zeldin's mobile office hours. She described it on the EEAN Facebook page:

> *FYI: Just a few highlights from my meeting with Rep Zeldin at Mobile Office Hours yesterday:*

1. *He is VERY much in favor of teachers having guns in the classroom, at their choice.*
2. *He TOTALLY denied receiving the amount of $ from the NRA that The Times reported. He is fine with taking $ from the NRA, because the money comes from dues that people who agree with his policies pay.*
3. *He would NOT agree to support a ban on assault weapons.*

He has obviously decided to double down, with full support for the Trump/NRA position, which is a bit strange because this district does not seem like a big gun/NRA district. Activists quickly organized a protest rally in front of his Patchogue office the week after the Parkland shooting and this rally was substantially bigger than any other one we had been able to organize. At the rally, protesters accused Zeldin of taking "blood money" from the NRA.

After a year of trying to get media attention for our protests, after being told over and over again that the local papers would be happy to take a Letter to the Editor but not an op-ed about Zeldin and the grassroots movement here in our district, after a year of asking them to send a reporter to cover a rally, here was press coverage that was finally off the opinion page and onto the front page.

At patch.com, a website for local news, the protest was referred to as, "the largest anti-Zeldin rally held to date, hosted by a coalition of Long Island activist groups."[18]

The difference? The rally came directly after the school shooting, the attendance was substantially larger than usual, the protest organizers were able to get a press release out ahead of time in order to get a reporter to attend and supplied quotes, photos and video footage. It would seem that Zeldin is vulnerable on this issue. He is taking the most right-wing stands in a district that may be majority Republican, but does not seem to be far to the right on guns.

I changed my profile picture on Facebook to the image of Zeldin with blood on his hands created by one of the members of the grassroots.

At the same time, the Democratic primary challengers began to get local press attention. An in-depth article in *The Southampton Press*, titled, "Six Democrats Campaign For Chance To Challenge U.S. Representative Lee Zeldin In November" describes all six challengers and comments on the high level of interest in the district.[19]

Wednesday, February 28th
EEAN meeting with Perry Gershon

Today was not such a good day. I woke up with a sore throat and a runny nose, felt tired and paralyzed to get anything done. But I pushed through because I had the EEAN meeting tonight at the library, where Rebecca will interview Perry Gershon.

I rested during the day. Lying on the couch, I turned on the news. In a rush, it is breaking news after breaking news. The stories came so fast that it can leave you breathless: Hope Hicks is resigning, Mueller is asking if Donald Trump knew about the DNC and Podesta hacks ahead of time, Trump goes after Sessions again, Kushner got loans for his company after meetings at the White House, Dick's Sporting Goods will no longer sell assault rifles, Walmart will raise the age of gun sales to twenty-one, Trump hosts congressional leaders at a meeting at the White House on gun laws and seems to embrace all the Democratic positions on gun control. It is dizzying.

At the library, I helped arrange the chairs for the meeting. One of our members, Bernie Buda, gets there around the same time and we talked a bit about a Riverhead candidate forum from Monday that I didn't attend. All the candidates were there, including Bruce Miller, who I haven't met yet - yes, now there are seven. (Mr. Miller dropped out soon after that). Bernie is also not yet sure who has his vote but is keeping an open mind. He felt the women made the strongest presentations.

Rebecca did her usual outstanding job with her questions. She studies the candidates' positions and her questions are always specific and sharp. Perry's answers were impressive. Free of platitudes and talking points, his responses were nuanced, educated and informed. He has many interesting ideas of how to grow the economy in our district. It was also encouraging that he said he will support whoever is the candidate. He explained that he got into this race to push back against Trump and unseat Zeldin and he will continue on that mission even if he isn't the candidate. He tells a story about how when he was working in real estate finance in New York City he was given a list of builders to never work with and Trump was on the top of the list. He said it was common knowledge that Trump screwed his partners by not paying his bills and also defaulted on his loans.

After the meeting, I approached Perry for an interview for the book project. Asking Perry is my first step outside the world of the three groups I already belong to and the people I know. I spoke to Perry and his campaign manager, Karl. As long as the information is embargoed until after the election, which it is, they said they are happy for Perry to participate with an interview. I need to do the same with all the other candidates.

I came home from the meeting more energized than ever. Watching the news that night I am astonished at how all the stories from earlier in the day are developing. February comes to an end. March is going to be a very busy month.

Chapter 12

March 2018

"Vote them out!!"
March for Our Lives protest chant in Washington, D.C.

Tuesday, March 6th
Petition phase begins
Today the period for candidates to collect signatures begins. Those who collect the requisite amount will be on the ballot for the June 26th primary and those who don't will be done.

Lulu emailed me to see if I want to join her getting signatures for Elaine, her chosen candidate. I explained that I am remaining neutral for the book project but as soon as I am fully recovered from my cold, I will keep her company getting signatures.

The news from the Trump White House was about tariffs and how Mueller is closing in on questions about what Trump knew during the campaign about the stolen Democratic emails and their distribution. A day after his big show on how he will buck the NRA on gun control, he then met with the NRA and there are no more statements from him on gun control. He made a joke over the weekend about the Chinese president declaring himself president for life and how "maybe we need to do that here." Supposedly the people joining him for dinner at Mar-a-Lago laughed and applauded when he said that.

Saturday, March 17th
Requests for interviews
My plans to work on the book the last two weeks were derailed by illness. The cold morphed into a major upper respiratory infection. I couldn't get a doctor's appointment for days and did not want to go to urgent care but luckily, I found some liquid medication for the nebulizer left from the last time I had an asthma attack. That got me through until I saw the doctor but by then, I needed the whole package of medications – asthma medication, steroids, antibiotic. I haven't been that sick in a long time. Struggling to breathe left me feeling shaky about everything.

By Saturday, March 17th I was better and less enervated about taking on the tasks ahead of me. I stepped gingerly back into the arena. It was still too cold out to think of walking and getting petitions signed but there is a hint that spring will soon bring warmer air. Instead of heading out, I spent the weekend emailing folks and trying to set up interview dates and times. I have reached out to the candidates to ask for interviews and have scheduled EEAN to come to my house on Wednesday, March 28th for our leadership meeting, after which I will hold a group interview with them.

I heard back from Vivian right away and we scheduled a phone interview for April 3rd. I am working on dates with David, Elaine and Kate via their campaigns. I will have to follow up with Brendon and Perry again.

And in the news, while I have been recovering: the Stormy Daniels story exploded (she and her lawyer have filed a lawsuit against Trump to free her from the NDA, non-disclosure agreement); Tillerson was fired; McCabe was fired; Trump admitted to lying to the prime minister of Canada; students walked out of class on the 14th for gun control; Mueller issued subpoenas for Trump's business records. The chaos, lying and dysfunction continued.

But the special election results in Pennsylvania shone a light of potential success for what we are doing here in NY01, with Conor Lamb eking out a victory over the GOP-Trump supported candidate, Rick Saccone. In a district that Trump won by 20 points in 2016, this was great news. Even through my haze of illness, I registered the importance of the PA special election on what we are doing. And so did my Dad, Great Grandpa Jack (GGJ), who emailed all of us the day after the special election:

> *Guys, We all know the refrain from this favorite song that goes like this "If you can make it here you can make it anywhere" Well if a D can win an election In PA district 18, they can win an election anywhere. Babs maybe even in NY 1, go baby go GGJ*

Sharon was busy getting signatures for Vivian, while Lulu was petitioning for Elaine and Andi for David. But so far, the fact that folks were volunteering for different candidates has not caused a rift in the group, one of my biggest fears. Still, I will be glad when the primary is done and we have one candidate who we can all rally behind.

Monday, March 19th
SPC meeting

Today was my first SPC meeting in a few months; I was out of town during the last meeting. I was excited to be back connected with Andi, Syma, Sharon and Rebecca as we sat around the conference table in Robin's office in Southampton. There were a few new ladies I had not met before in attendance, along with

Eileen from LVLZ and Kathryn Levy from PEER. The discussion revolved around planning two debates for May, hosted by the caucus. We decided to form a subcommittee to work on the questions. I came home from the meeting encouraged but strangely very tired. I fell into bed early that night. It was clear that I am not completely well yet. The next day I made an appointment with the doctor for blood tests.

Saturday, March 24th
March for Our Lives

I found out the answer to my fatigue when the nurse from my doctor's office called to give me my blood test results and I was shocked to hear that I have Lyme. This is not the first time but I do wonder how I could have gotten bitten in the winter. A new antibiotic is prescribed. I returned to bed, began the meds, and hoped that I will feel better in a few days. I had to cancel everything on my schedule, Rebecca's discussion at the library with David Pechefsky, canvassing with Lulu, and then on the 24th, I missed attending the March for Our Lives.

I was devastated that I wasn't well enough to attend our local March for Our Lives event in Patchogue. I so wanted to be there to support the students. Weeks ago, on our Facebook pages, I joined the discussion of staying in our district rather than traveling to D.C. or NYC for the March so that we can have a massive show of force against Zeldin. The students organized a series of marches across the district: Port Jefferson, Sag Harbor and Patchogue, right in front of Zeldin's office, where we have marched before. Only this time, it will be a very large crowd.

Sitting on the couch watching the television coverage on *MSNBC* in the morning, at first, I was feeling sorry for myself that I am missing joining in this historic event and missing the chance to lend my support to these young people. But as the day went on, I was so touched by the poignancy of the speakers at the rally in D.C., by the power of their stories, that my mood improved and I began to feel a sense of hope that maybe, just maybe, the country is going to be okay.

I was struck by the brilliance of the Parkland students joining with other students from around the country who have also been harmed by gun violence, in their schools and in their communities, students who never make the front pages or nightly news, many of them young people of color. And as each of these teenagers told their stories of losing loved ones, of being threatened themselves, of being shot, students from Chicago, from D.C., I cannot help but feel that something important is taking place here, that this intersectionality and diversity is as important a statement as the March against gun violence itself. And something else stood out all day, that these students are imploring their generation to register and to vote.

Statistically, younger voters vote in lower numbers than older voters. But maybe this is about to change. And if it does, then this high school student movement against gun violence will be another important element in building the blue wave this fall.

The March for Our Lives comes at the end of a tumultuous week, where Trump fired McMaster and is bringing John Bolton, one of the architects of the Iraq War, into his administration as National Security Advisor. At the same time, he fired his lead attorney, John Dowd, and hired Larry Kudlow as Chief Economic Advisor. He also announced more tariffs on China. He is getting ready to start a legal war with Mueller, a trade war with China and possibly a real war with Iran or North Korea. The stock market dropped for two straight days. It was hard to not be afraid. The country is careening out of control with no guardrails by the GOP in charge in Congress. But watching and listening to these impassioned young people at the March gave me hope, because one of the main chants throughout the day was "Vote them out!"

Chapter 13

April 2018

"I'm extremely proud of the movement and what they've been able to accomplish to this point in time, all the different rallies, number of people they've been able to bring out who are articulate and smart and focused. How strong they've been, makes me so proud. But I will be real proud if at the end of the day, it turns into votes. We don't know yet but I don't think this movement is going to die like many of the politicians and people believe it will because as long as we continue to have shootings, these students will continue to be energized."

Paul Guttenberg,
uncle of Jaime Guttenberg who was killed at Parkland.

Monday, April 2nd
SPC meeting

We had our first question subcommittee meeting, which was followed by a general meeting. We were in Robin's office in Southampton. All in all, the question committee went smoothly, mainly because of Rebecca who moderated it well and kept everyone focused on the questions. We asked Rebecca to attend because we have chosen her to be the moderator of both debates. She will have interviewed all of the candidates by then. In the general committee, we decided both debates should have a mix of domestic and foreign policy questions and to keep the locations we have lined up rather than look for new ones.

Tuesday, April 3rd
Vivian interview

I had my first candidate interview with Vivian. It was scheduled for 9:00 AM. I woke up at 7:30 AM to make sure I was ready. I was feeling very nervous and not sure why. I spent years interviewing major figures in less friendly circumstances, but that was a while ago. On the one hand, I am excited to be back doing what I was trained to do as a journalist, on the other hand, almost all my work was in television news, I have been away from this for years and I have never written a book. Just having to use new technology has made me nervous. I tested the phone recording app on my smartphone over and over again, as well as the process of sending it to be transcribed, to make sure it worked. I tested my headphones as well. I was sitting at my desk, ready when Vivian called right on time. It was a wonderful conversation, for about an hour and 15 minutes.

(Vivian's interview along with all of the primary candidates' interviews are in Chapter 9.)

Wednesday, April 4th
David interview
The next day I interviewed David. He was thoughtful and engaged and many of his answers were not what I expected. I am on a high after the interview.

Saturday, April 7th
March for Our Lives Town Hall Project
I got four tickets - for me, Syma, Sharon and my sister Nanci - to attend a forum on guns sponsored by March for Our Lives Long Island (MFOLLI).

All the candidates were invited, including Zeldin. It was held west of us, on the north shore of Long Island at a private boarding school called the Knox School. I drove to Syma's, we then picked up Sharon and we got to the Knox School, way up on the north shore in record time. We were very early. As we drove through the gate, we had to give my name to security because the reservations were under my name; I texted Nanci to let her know to use my name at the gate since she was coming in her own car. We parked the car, talked for a while then headed into the gym. The school is set on a beautiful location, rolling hills, tall trees and stables for horses.

It is a sprawling campus, with a variety of buildings. The gym is a large, open room, with bathrooms and locker rooms downstairs. There were organizers at the front door at tables to check our names a second time and also to go through our bags. We wondered if all this security was because of Zeldin. The room was filled with rows of folding chairs, with tables at the front, microphones, six chairs for the candidates and one on the side for Zeldin, with his name on it. I would bet money he does not show up. He rarely wants to be in any venue that is not his supporters. I would have won that bet. He did not show up.

On the back table, along with handouts, there were voter registration materials. We mingled with the organizers as well as the candidates, as they slowly arrived. It was an interesting dynamic. I have never before gotten to know congressional candidates on this level. Periodically I need to take a step back and take that fact in.

David Pechefsky couldn't make it so his campaign staffer, David Bligh, was in his place. The other five were there. I have interviewed Vivian and David and have scheduled Kate, Perry and Elaine. Brendon is waiting until after the petition deadline closes. We got seats near the front and I saved a seat for Nanci.

It was a large crowd, though all the seats were not taken. The Head of the Knox School welcomed everyone and said that the MFOL student organizers called her and asked if Knox would host. She said her answer was immediately yes, because it is important to teach young people that they can have a voice. “And not just on Snapchat,” she emphasized. “My words in particular are directed to the young people here. This is your enthusiasm. It is important that you vote and that you know the issues.”

The chair of MFOL Long Island introduced the student organizers and explained the structure for the Town Hall. One of the student organizers would ask a question to one of the candidates and if someone else wanted to add a point, they could raise their card. It wasn’t clear if there were limits on the cards. So, every question was not asked to every candidate. And after the candidates answered, the audience asked a question, though the moderator prevented the audience going back and forth in a dialogue.

The candidates all did well, though it was unfortunate that David Pechefsky wasn’t there because Bligh said very little. It was interesting how much they have each grown into this job in the last few months. Each candidate was able to get across the key aspect of their biography while at the same time answering the questions in a substantive way. They all criticized Zeldin’s sponsorship of the concealed carry reciprocity bill, which would give a gun owner with a concealed carry permit from another state the right to conceal that weapon in New York, despite our very strict gun laws. All the candidates agreed on what a dangerous bill it is.

There were two moments that stood out. First, when the uncle of one of the Parkland students who died spoke. He walked up to the microphone and the first thing we noticed was the bright yellow March for Our Lives shirt he was wearing. His name is Paul Guttenberg and he lost his niece in the Parkland shooting. Her name was Jaime Guttenberg, 14 years old. “Zeldin did nothing before Parkland and has done nothing since,” he said. “I have reached out to Zeldin, gotten no response. He is on the wrong side of this issue. A rating from the NRA, 93% of the time supports their policies, Gun Owners of America, 90%, NY Shooters Committee, 100%. Not a record I will vote for.”

He thanked the student organizers and the Knox School for hosting this event. “Our family is spread out, and we are bringing the fight to each state we live in. You’ve all seen my brother on television. He has a big voice and is making sure he is heard. My sister-in-law is too devastated. My niece was the energy in the room. Seventeen kids and teachers killed, twenty injured, that day at Parkland and what has the government done? The President had a listening session, but that's it. Trump, Pence, Ryan and McConnell still have not reached out to us. They think this will go away but the difference is the youth. Your voices count. Make them count, if you have friends that are not registered, bring them to a location to register, and then get all your friends to the polling booths. And use the phrase gun safety and not gun control. I am now a one issue person."

He handed out Zeldin's phone numbers in Patchogue and D.C. printed on a small slip of paper and asked everyone to swamp both offices with phone calls next week, Monday through Wednesday. "We are hoping to get 75-100 phone calls into Zeldin's offices so that he can hear your movement. Let him know that you do not like his NRA rating, he should give back the money they gave him, then leave your name and phone number, and ask that he call you back and tell you what he is going to do to keep you safe."

And secondly, when a young woman spoke about the issue of mental health and guns. "I have been struggling with mental health issues my whole life," she said. "But I'm not violent; I would never pick up a gun and shoot anyone. My brain just doesn't work correctly." She explained that it is hard enough to fight mental illness but now she hears her friends talk about the danger of people with mental illness, the danger of crazy people with guns. She was so honest and so brave that she received a standing ovation.

Watching the growth of the MFOL movement, I had a feeling that this new grassroots organization had the potential to be the X factor in the fall election. Zeldin, who accepted NRA money and support and had benefited from both when he opposed Anna Throne-Holst in 2016, now had a possible vulnerability on this subject. I had no data to evaluate it, but CD#1 did not seem like a big "pro-gun" district. There are a lot of people in law enforcement who live in our district and many were Zeldin supporters, as are veterans, but one had to wonder where they stood on Zeldin's support of the concealed carry reciprocity bill he was sponsoring in Congress.

Before the Parkland shooting and the MFOL, Zeldin may have viewed this as a boost for him with his/Trump's base. But how would this play now against the protests against school shootings that were playing out across the district? Could this issue alone end up being a determining factor in bringing over some moderate Republican voters and independents? Especially once he is confronted on this subject by the Democratic nominee?

After the Town Hall, I reached out to each of our candidates and asked them what they thought about the MFOL movement and what impact it might have on the election.

"A phrase that came up multiple times at the MFOL Town Hall was 'we want our voices to be heard' and I think the ability for these young people to have a voice with this issue can maybe energize other groups to take that example, to take matters into your own hands and make sure your voice is heard," said Elaine DiMasi. "If this brings young people out to vote, helps them to realize that nobody is going to give them a voice, that they have to stand up and demand that their voices be heard, then this is movement building."

"I think they may be incredibly influential in this election, especially because of Zeldin's ties to the NRA and his sponsorship of the concealed carry reciprocity bill," said Perry Gershon. "Zeldin is essentially running against the NY Safe Act and the MFOL movement lets Democrats own this issue and make it clear it is not about the Second Amendment but about preventing what happened in Parkland by banning assault rifles."

Vivian worried that high school and college students have a lot of challenges they are dealing with and often voting isn't the top priority in their lives. "As a high school teacher, I know the energy these kids can have," said Vivian. "But if there is too much going on in their lives, if they are having a tough time, then it is hard for them to stay engaged."

"The question is how will the March for Our Lives intersect with voting?" said David. "A movement that is based on one issue, how does it translate to politics and how does it intersect with voting? Right now, we have all the grassroots movements in our district that are trying to coalesce, but can it translate into electoral wins?" He wasn't sure if it would.

"It is only April," said Kate, "so you never know what is going to happen between now and November. The fact that these kids have come forward now is great, kids are our future, future voters, future leaders. But people don't necessarily vote against someone based on one issue, unless they can tie the issue to the fact that Zeldin is not representing the district, not representing his constituents."

I also spoke with Paul Guttenberg after the Town Hall and we scheduled a phone interview. The following are edited excerpts from that interview.

How are you and your family doing?
I'm doing okay. My brother, his wife and my nephew, are still in a tough place, not a good place. But we are all trying to move forward and work through it.

Do you find participating in a grassroots movement like March for Our Lives a help in coping with such a terrible loss?
Well, it's a good coping tool, helpful because you know there's other people who are working with you and believe in change, in correcting a problem. My biggest issue is not having enough time to do more. I have a job and a family. Also, I'm in the process of training to ride with the Commack Ambulance Corp, to honor my brother who passed away in October of 2017. He was an ER doctor and a 9-11 responder. When 9-11 happened, he was working with the NYC Fire Department. He was on scene when the 2nd tower was hit, he survived but then came down with Pancreatic Cancer. In October, he passed away and for much of the family, that was the last time we saw my 14-year-old niece before the Parkland Mass Shooting.

Were you active before in political issues or grassroots movements?
No, other than talking politics or thinking politics.

Was gun safety an important issue for you before?
Gun safety would have been in my top five regarding political issues, all other issues are now secondary in my opinion to gun violence. There's just no reason in the world anyone should have these guns, and it goes deeper. It's how we just want to ignore the issue and blame it on everything else. The biggest problem is that the NRA lobby is so well financed and so dug in and entrenched. I don't know if it can truly be defeated. It is a complete uphill battle.

Are you encouraged by how engaged young people are by this movement?
Very. If they can increase voter turnout amongst young adults by five to ten percent, I will be ecstatic. It will send a true message, it will change certain races. When I was that age, politics weren't always the first thing you thought about. They need to vote and create change for gun safety issues. So, I guess the proof in the pudding will be in 2018 and I hope they come out and vote because if they don't come out and vote, then everything that they're marching for is going to be watered down.

Do you think this movement is sustainable?
The problem is the media is already gone. They have already moved on to the next thing. Trump and Pence are completely back in line with the NRA. They don't even speak gun safety anymore. It's a completely forgotten event for most of the political leaders already. Because we haven't done enough to prevent the next mass shooting, these shootings will continue, that will make this movement hopefully stay energized and continue to grow, if we don't make the proper changes there will be more shootings and that's the saddest part of it. These kids, especially Parkland kids, have not allowed themselves to be bullied, regardless,

of the smear campaigns that have been placed upon them and the threats that have been made against them. They have managed to stay on message.

Clearly there's not going to be any legislation this year in Congress.
I don't think so. But there are things happening on at the state level in several states. I know my brother is meeting with state legislators in New Jersey and Massachusetts. Problem is with some states, if you try to do it at the local level, the state can overrule it. My brother had something on Facebook recently about Broward County trying to do some things at the local level and Governor Scott came in and said, "Well, if you push that legislation through I have the power to fire you for going against state law." So, at the local level, they could be bullied by the next higher level above them. In this fight, you're going five steps backwards to try to take a small step forward.

If Democrats should take back Congress, would Trump sign a gun safety bill into law?
Maybe. If Trump could sign something that he thinks is a win for him, you may be able to sell it to him. I think he would sign things because he could just put it in the win column. He has no clue what he's doing.

Has your experience changed any minds of people you know?
I find the people who belief in gun safety before this happened, they have become more supportive and the people who were for the second amendment and want guns have dug in and doubled down. I know someone who's an NRA person and I made a couple of comments going back and forth with him on Facebook, he is opposed to any regulations, so I said, what about airplane crashes? We spend billions of dollars to try to find out what happened, then fix it and make sure it doesn't happen again. Or terror attacks? We have a whole government agency that investigates to make sure it doesn't happen again. We have more people killed by guns and we do nothing. It's an issue that people in government and the NRA wants to make sure we never discuss and we don't address and we don't fix so that they can sell guns. The NRA has a strong lobby, they are well financed and they've been doing what they do for a long time. It's a small percentage of the people on the opposite side of the fence from gun safety, ten or fifteen percent of the people I know, and no matter what happens, you're not going to change them. I'm not even going to try.

What impact do you think this issue will have on Zeldin's re-election?
I'm not in his district. I live in Suozzi's district (Tom Suozzi, Democrat CD#3). I used to live in Zeldin's district but he hasn't reached out to me. I left messages for him and said, "I know many people who do live in your district and I will make sure they are aware of this issue." I tell people don't vote for him because

of this one issue on gun safety. Probably a dozen people have told me they will not vote for him and to pass the word around. I don't think Zeldin won because of his stand on guns so I don't know how it will impact the election. After all, Suffolk County voted for Trump.

What is your sense of the potential blue wave for this fall?
You know, one week I feel good about it, then the next week I don't. I think the potential is there, I also think that the potential is there for a lot of gimmicks with voting machines that are not being properly protected within the states, voter suppression, college kids not realizing that they need to register for absentee ballots and then not being able to vote. There are a lot of things that can go wrong and hurt the big blue wave. When you look at what's going on with some of these special elections, all the signs are there that it should happen.

Any fear that the grassroots movements, like MFOL, as well as the Democratic Party will splinter?
Well, I think it's less likely. I think it's more likely in a presidential election year. I'm more afraid of what big money and Republican governors can do to suppress the vote than I am of a Democratic fracture.

Monday, April 9th
SPC question committee meeting
Robin was out of town but she kindly arranged for us to use her office. Rebecca outdid herself in taking on the yeoman job of organizing the questions. It was a productive meeting though by the end, rather than reducing the number of questions, we now had more than ever. There will not be enough time to get each candidate to answer all of them.

I also put on the table the idea that each candidate not answer every question, somewhat like the way the students organized the MFOL Town Hall. I would also love to see more of a real debate. After much discussion, this was voted down and the decision was made to keep the format we had. The last issue discussed was about who will be in charge of the press release and publicity.

That night I talked to Andi on the phone to fill her in on the meeting since she wasn't able to make it. She said she is beginning to feel strongly that we are recreating our forum but that it is not a real debate. She is going to think about a possible new format and run that past the group tomorrow in an email.

Tuesday, April 10th
Elaine interview
A very busy day, felt like more than I can really successfully manage especially while not feeling 100%. I had a conference call with Joy and Ron about the plans for the next meeting of the J. P. Spata Southampton Democratic Club and trying to organize a Youth Forum with a panel of high school students who can speak about issues that concern them in the community. I am not sure if I can manage being on the board of the Democratic Club along with all the other groups I am in but I will see. I am going to be away that weekend so I cannot do much to help but I volunteered to go visit the students at the Southampton Youth Bureau to see if any of them can attend the Club event.

I also had my interview with Elaine and it was fascinating. She is so smart, views issues as problems that can have solutions and tries to find answers.

That evening I visited the Southampton Youth Bureau meeting in Hampton Bays to speak to them about the Youth Forum and to invite them to be part of the panel as guest speakers. I was proud of myself that I drove myself there and back and grateful that it was still light out when I got home. And I was impressed with the focus and interest of this group of high school students from all over Southampton Town. They meet regularly and get community service credit for their work. They have chosen for their spring focus to join with the MFOL mission of gun safety.

The group is diverse and the ages range from 15 to 19 years old. I gave a presentation about the grassroots work we are doing in the district, the importance of voter registration and the chance on Sunday for high school students to speak to an audience of adults and let them know what issues concern them. One young woman raised her hand and asked me to define what grassroots means. A good question and a reminder not to take anything for granted. I explained that it means an organization that started with the public, from the ground up and not top down from leaders. MFOL is a perfect example. We discussed a little bit about historical grassroots groups, those that are successful at sustaining change, and those that aren't. While there weren't any students who are available for Sunday - we really didn't give them enough notice - I found the experience enlightening. For example, when I asked them what is the number one issue for them in the district they said the lack of public transportation, which was a surprise.

I got home that night and was dead tired but was confronted by an email blow up over the two issues that Andi put out to the group during the day, first about organizing the publicity and secondly about discussing a different format for the debate. There was a misunderstanding about just who is doing the publicity which resulted in some hurt feelings. Luckily it was quickly resolved. But the second issue triggered a rather heated online email back and forth argument about the debate format with most people saying they wanted to keep it the way it is. I tried to both support Andi but smooth things over and defer to the majority vote about what to do. It got resolved but I was left feeling puzzled about why it became so needlessly confrontational. Why were people so angry?

Thursday, April 12th
End of petition stage
Sharon texted me that she heard from Patty that Brendon didn't make it past the petitions. I feel bad for Brendon, for Kyle, for Patty. They all worked so hard.

Wednesday, April 18th
SPC Question committee meeting
News is moving quickly: Paul Ryan retires; reports that Mueller has a four-part case for obstruction; the FBI raid on Michael Cohen's home and office; Southern District of New York case against Cohen; the Stormy Daniels lawsuit; the James Comey book release; the bombing of Syria; the looming trade war; the rollback of regulations. Some days it is almost more than anyone can stand. I wonder what happens if there isn't a blue wave in November? What happens if we don't take back the House? What happens if the GOP prevent the release of Mueller's report?

Rebecca and I drove together to a question committee meeting. Sharon is still not feeling well and Syma is away so it was just me and Rebecca. We agreed it seemed strange to have five candidates and not six and that we missed Brendon. We talked in the car about the candidates, the election. There was no more important focus for our group right now than doing all we can to make sure there is a blue wave. All the protests and rallies do not stack up to the Democrats taking back the House. Still, we are both feeling wistful for a time when our activism was less tied to partisan politics and more issue oriented. The antagonism in the email chain over the debate format is only adding to that feeling.

To our relief we had a productive meeting and found a compromise. We would ask all the candidates the same questions and follow ups, but each candidate would get so many cards to add their own follow up and then other candidates would get a chance to offer a rebuttal, which would have them engaging each other. We worked on the timing, figuring out if our plans would run over the two hours and it timed out beautifully. We have two more meetings scheduled, one to practice and an emergency meeting right before the debate just in case breaking news overtakes our planned questions.

Friday, April 20th
Kate interview
I woke up early to get ready for my interview with Kate. She was friendly and personable on the phone, but also a bit more guarded than the other candidates. This is probably a function of being an experienced candidate and elected official, being the perceived front runner and aware of the rumblings out in the progressive parts of the district that she is not progressive enough. But she made some very strong points about how to win in a district that is considered either leaning GOP or likely GOP. "This district is not as progressive as people would like it to be."

Tuesday, April 24th
SPC meeting and special election
At the last minute, I decided to skip today's meeting. There is just too much to do working on the candidate interviews and preparing for the group EEAN interview tomorrow evening. Later that evening, Sharon called me to give me an update on the SPC meeting and I was glad I skipped it. It lasted four hours and was contentious because what appeared at the last meeting to be a resolution about who would handle the publicity became a trip wire in today's meeting because apparently the publicity never got taken care of. Syma emailed us the next day that she found the meeting so difficult that she is thinking of dropping out of SPC and just working with EEAN. I can't quite figure out why these meetings have suddenly become so contentious. We worked so well together all last year.

Also, today were a couple of special elections. In New York, Democrats flipped a State Assembly seat long held by Republicans. "Dems flip New York state seat that Republicans have held for nearly four decades," was the headline in The Hill.[20] Was this a harbinger of what is to come in the election this fall?

Wednesday, April 25th
EEAN leadership interview
I had no ability to write today, probably because I was nervous about our group interview this evening with the EEAN leadership. So, I gave up even trying. I went shopping for wine and snacks for the meeting, rode my exercise bike for 20 minutes and took a long bath to try to relax.

I needn't have worried. The evening was wonderful, though we are all sorry that Patty couldn't make it; she needed to take her 92-year-old mother to the doctor.

The conversation was everything I hoped it would be. I am struck anew by the enormous heart, intelligence and compassion of these women. And maybe that is the only silver lining to the 2016 election. (The transcript from this interview is in Chapter Two).

The month ended with feeling that I have found a handle on the book, that I have realized that I cannot do everything and often have to not participate but one thing has not changed - I am just as outraged over the news as I have been since November 2016. Trump is becoming more and more unhinged as the legal net closes in on him. This is the leader of the free world. While there was some good news to close out the week, like the rapprochement between North and South Korea and a court upholding DACA, it also felt like things are just getting crazier. The destruction of regulations and agencies continues, the economy is slowing, the stock market is down, it appears that the Supreme Court will uphold the travel ban, the EPA will diminish scientific findings in their work, and it goes on and on.

And then we learned the bombshell news that children of refugees who are here seeking asylum are being separated from their parents. Now whenever I start to feel that I can't continue doing this work, I just think about these children. If voters don't produce a big enough wave to take back the House, then more families, more children will be traumatized.

Chapter 14

May 2018

"We have to make sure that we have the highest turnout in the primary, because we have to make it loud and clear to the Republicans that there is not just talk of a blue wave, but the blue wave is crashing over them. And then after the primary, we find Independents who can find a home with us, we find Republicans who are having buyer's remorse to find a home with us, and we make a change in the Congress in November. Because we must make it loud and clear to this president, that we are not going to take the changes that he is trying to do, we are not going to allow him to stack the courts, we are not going to allow him to take away Planned Parenthood, we are not going to allow him to take away our foreign policy."

Robin Long, introduction to the foreign policy debate

Saturday, May 5th
SPC domestic policy debate

Today was the first of the two debates sponsored by SPC. It was held in the conference room at the Southampton Inn. After much deliberation, we decided that this first one would be on domestic policy and the second on foreign policy. Both will be moderated by Rebecca.

I know Rebecca wasn't feeling 100% today but she is a trooper. She, Sharon and I got there very early to set up (Sharon drove me, while Rebecca took her own car). We met Robin there who informed us that the Inn had set up complimentary food and a cash bar for folks coming for the debate, which was very nice. Sharon handed each of us a name tag she had prepared with our names and the words Southampton Progressive Caucus. I was assigned to be the "greeter" at the front door and to direct folks to the room with the food and then to the large banquet room, set up with rows of chairs, for the debate. Before everything started, I reserved three seats for me, Sharon and Nanci, who met us there.

It was a beautiful day, finally a sunny spring day, and one could feel the good mood that pervaded the room. As our friends and colleagues from EEAN and the SHDems arrived, we greeted each other with hugs. The same was true of the five candidates. I greeted each of them with a warm hug. Each of them told me that they enjoyed their interview for the book, which was nice to hear. I also told them that I will be covering one event for each of them which will give me a chance to speak to their supporters.

Several still and video photographers set up around the room, from each of the campaigns, for the Facebook live stream from SPC, and one photographer from Newsday, the Long Island newspaper. I am hoping that means that we have finally broken through to the press.

The five candidates posed for a photo with their hands together. It represented the cordiality that they are maintaining. I have heard from many Democrats who feel that it was the bitter primary fight in 2016 between Anna Throne-Holst and Dave Calone that contributed to the landslide win by Zeldin. No one wants a repeat of that. I have also heard that Robin has spoken to each of their campaigns to insist that such cordiality will be maintained in any SHDems and SPC sponsored event.

Rebecca's introduction and the final questions with the follow up questions for this first debate are below:

> Hello and welcome to the first of two debates presented by the Southampton Progressive Caucus, an alliance of grassroots activists and the Southampton Town Democratic Committee. I'm your moderator, Rebecca Dolber, with me today are the five candidates who will be on the ballot in June's 26th Democratic primary. Please join me in welcoming Kate Browning, David Pechefsky, Vivian Viloria-Fisher, Elaine DiMasi and Perry Gershon. The questions prepared for today's debate were a collaborative effort of Southampton Progressive Caucus members and have not been shown to the candidates. Two minutes will be allotted to answer the initial question and a minute and a half for the follow-up questions. Candidates will receive a warning when they have 30 seconds remaining for each question. Every candidate today has been given three red cards. After every candidate has answered the initial question, they are at liberty to challenge another's answer by using one of those cards. The card will allow a 30 second challenge, and then whomever is challenged, will have 30 seconds to rebut. In an effort to maximize debate time, we've eliminated opening statements and will jump right into our questions.

1. The current administration is dismantling regulations and agencies that protect citizens. Admittedly, some Democrats have even voted for rolling back regulations in banking. What would you as a

congressperson do to put a check on this wholesale destruction and what agencies do you believe have been hurt the most?

a. Similarly, there's been a general attack on the social safety net. How would you protect, support and sustain social programs like social security, Medicare, Medicaid and the ACA?
b. The passing of the Republican tax bill is another means of destabilizing the security of constituents in CD1. Assuming you are our congressperson after the election this fall, what steps would you support to mitigate the negative effects of the tax bill on our district?

2. Income inequality has worsened over the past decade—what are the biggest factors that have contributed to this, and what realistically do you think you can do as a congressperson to address these issues?
    a. Can you give us an example of how income inequality has specifically affected our district?
    b. What ideas do you have that would improve the fiscal wellbeing of our district in a way that doesn't favor constituents based on issues of class, race or gender?

3. The majority of Americans believe that we must come to a consensus around increased gun safety measures. Which proposals do you think we have the best opportunity at passing, and what, in your opinion, are the strongest aspects of New York State law that perhaps could be adopted on a national level?

4. Given the controversy over immigration during the Trump administration, how would you frame the discussion over the fate of immigrants and the impact of immigration policy on our economy.
    a. You are all on the record in favor of creating a path towards citizenship for non-violent, undocumented individuals. How would you work towards that goal, while simultaneously calm fears and anxiety among constituents?
    b. What's your view on ICE working with local authorities using administrative warrants for detaining immigrants.

5. Racial injustice is built into our society; how does that manifest itself in our district and how should government address it?
    a. How do you deal with backlash to any attempts to address remedies to racial injustice?

6. There's been much talk about a blue wave coming for the November election. In your opinion, should Democrats--including the winner of this primary—make it a point to run against Trump, or rather, focus on another set of priorities? In essence, what is the ideal, winning message for Democrats moving forward?
   a. If you were to win the primary in June, how would you counter the issues that Zeldin considers his strengths in the general election? In addition, what do you perceive as Zeldin's Achilles heel?

Later that day, we posted the entire debate on our EEAN YouTube page.[21]

Some of the most interesting takeaways:

- They all adhered to Robin's advice and kept it cordial. In fact, while we gave them the opportunity to use a card and get 30 seconds to directly respond to another candidate, they did not. They all used their cards but always to add additional information. So, where we thought the cards would help us make it more of a debate, it did not because they chose not to. Maybe we over emphasized cordiality!
- The debate was too long mainly because we had too many follow up questions. We will have to make this adjustment with our question list for the second debate.
- All of the candidates have gotten stronger, more confident and more informed as this process has gone along. They are also learning to be more concise in their answers.

I asked Nanci about her impressions of the candidates, now that she has heard from all of them; this was her first time hearing David speak since he wasn't at the March for Our Lives Town Hall. She said she found David impressive but is still leaning towards Kate because she thinks she is the strongest against Zeldin. She feels Kate can really challenge Zeldin on the veteran issue because she has sons in the military and her husband is in law enforcement. And coming from the same part of the district as Zeldin, she believes also gives Kate an advantage. She would also really like to see a woman win.

Monday, May 7th
Ocular migraine

As inspiring and gratifying as Saturday was, Monday was the opposite. I hadn't slept well and was tired but I had a lot of work to do. I had fallen behind typing up my notes and organizing transcripts for the book so after breakfast and coffee I dragged myself to my computer and got to work. While typing and looking at the screen, I suddenly lost vision in one eye while at the same time felt a stabbing headache. I worried I was having a stroke. Looking at the screen, suddenly I could not see the center of the page because the vision in my left eye was distorted as if I was looking through a prism. As it worsened, I ran to the bathroom mirror to see if there were stroke symptoms, such as drooping on one side of my face. I called my optometrist's office and they told me to come right in but the branch office around the corner from me was closed so I would have to drive about 20 minutes into Riverhead. I wasn't sure how I was going to drive with one eye but I had no choice, so I rushed to get ready to go. While changing my clothes, I started to cry.

By the time I was ready to walk out the door, the vision cleared. The headache remained, as a dull ache next to that eye for the rest of the day. When I realized I could see again I sat down on the couch and this time my cries were from relief. With my vision restored, I looked up the symptoms online and when it mentioned an ocular migraine, I remembered that this had happened before, years ago. The primary trigger is fatigue. I wondered if Lyme was a contributing factor. I called the eye doctor back, told them I was better, that I was going to just sleep and take it easy for the rest of the day and if it came back, I would see the doctor on Tuesday at the office near me.

I did not write any more that day. I got into my pajamas, lay on the couch and watched television but stayed away from the news. I didn't read anything since I was afraid of eye strain. I dozed off and on and then went to bed early. But I learned an important lesson. If I am tired, I will not push myself like that again. I am too afraid of another episode like that. This sent me into a bit of a panic about the book because there are so many events, from the candidates, from the grassroots, that I want to cover in person, so many other people's voices that I want to include, that I fear if I cannot stay healthy, then I cannot get this job done. I try to ignore the panic and just get some sleep.

Tuesday, May 8th
More Trump chaos

I was still taking it easy but news crashed through and didn't help my mood. Trump announced abandoning the Iran Deal, the nuclear deal negotiated by Obama and six other countries, approved by the United Nations Security Council, as a way to stop Iran's march towards a nuclear weapon. Despite pleas from France, Great Britain and Germany, Trump blew it all up. Why? Because the Obama administration did it and he is driven to oppose and undermine anything associated with Obama. As one pundit said that night on the news, "Trump couldn't pick out Tehran on a map."

He has no Plan B. He announced he is reinstituting sanctions against Iran. The hardliners in the U.S. and Iran cheered, moving us ever closer to a war with Iran. This is the work of John Bolton. It reminded me of 2002-2003 and the determination of the Bush administration to overthrow Saddam Hussein for regime change in Iraq. No one has any idea what will happen now.

We are all now living in a state of constant agitation because of Trump and the GOP enablers. Every time I think of giving up, of taking back my life away from activism, away from the stress that is Trump, something happens to cement my conviction that our only hope is taking back Congress. That is the only possible check on this madness. There are real, worldwide consequences to this insanity.

Before I go to sleep the news breaks that the lawyer in the Stormy Daniels case, Michael Avenatti, has issued a policy paper that outlines payments to Michael Cohen, Trump's fixer, from a Russian oligarch and several corporations through the same shell LLC in Delaware that he set up in October 2016 to pay Stormy Daniels. Have the Russia probe and the Stormy Daniels/Michael Cohen case now intersected?

Thursday, May 10th
Coffee with Mike
I am now seeing a doctor of Integrative Medicine for my Lyme. This is a practice that combines traditional medicine with alternative medical treatments. I have gone as far as I can go with antibiotics. If it is now chronic Lyme, then just throwing more antibiotics at it is not going to help and could further damage my immune system. This doctor has recommended intravenous (IV) vitamin C. Today, I had my first treatment. I did not experience any ill effects from it, such as a rash, which is a good sign though I can't say I feel any change but maybe it takes a lot more treatments to feel the positive effects.
Afterwards, I met Mike at the Beach Bakery on Main Street for a cup of coffee and to catch up. We have not seen each other or spoken since after the election last fall because he and his wife left for Florida for the winter. I got there first and grabbed a table inside.

After he sat down, the first thing he said was that he had an announcement to tell me. I held my breath, afraid he was going to tell me that he and his wife Ann are moving or he is bailing on politics or something else that will make the work we are doing harder. But instead he smiled and said, "I got my first hole-in-one yesterday." I laughed out loud. I know what a dedicated golfer he is. We have often talked about golf, given how my Dad, even at 94 years old, is an avid golfer.

"Did you get one of those certificates?" I asked, remembering seeing those from my Dad.

"No," he said, explaining that he was playing alone and so no one else saw it. Damn, I said, how frustrating that there was no one else to share it with. But given how scrupulously honest Mike is about his golf score, I know it really happened even without a witness. Mike is one of those golfers that always records his exact score, no matter how many swings he took. He ascribes to that school of golf. I tell him of my Dad's mantra about golf, "No gimmes, no mulligans, just play golf!"

And here, as in almost everything, one can find an example of the corruption that is Trump by how he plays golf. Mike told me about an article he read last year about Trump's golf game and how he freely dismisses shots that didn't work out and puts down a lower score than he deserves. I look online and find the article. It was in Golf Magazine from the summer of 2017, entitled, "First Golfer: Donald Trump's relationship with golf has never been more complicated." It says almost everything you need to know about Trump.[22]

After we talked about golf, we discussed the candidates and it was interesting getting Mike's take on where the race is. We shared many of the same concerns. Will the grassroots end up pushing Democrats to choosing a candidate that is too progressive for this district? He told me he has not chosen a candidate yet. He found the debate on Saturday interesting. He seems to be leaning towards David or Perry, though he has concerns with both, and it is the same concern, that they will get tarred as carpetbaggers.

Monday, May 14th
SPC question committee

Everyone attended our next SPC question committee meeting at Robin's office. First we addressed the issues of the process of the debate, based on what we learned from the first one: we removed the follow-up questions, made each question a standalone and allowed more time for each; Rebecca will give a two-sentence introduction to each candidate so folks who are coming for the first time get a sense of who they are without having to waste time on opening statements; there will be no closing statements but a general closing question. It is a good, solid format. We also hope to reduce the time a bit so that it is less than two hours. Once the process issues were resolved, we finalized the questions.

Here are the final questions for Saturday's debate:

1. *What do you believe are the ramifications of Trump withdrawing from the nuclear deal with Iran?*
2. *What impact has the movement of the U.S. embassy to Jerusalem had, and will have, on our role in the Middle East?*
3. *What would you consider a successful outcome of the June summit with North Korea and what are the shortcomings of the Trump administration's approach to the North Korean challenge?*
4. *What are the effects to Long Islanders regarding the current administration's climate policy, especially with the withdrawal from the Paris Climate Accords?*
5. *We've had covert and overt meddling in our elections. As a congressperson, how would you address these attempts to destabilize our democracy?*
6. *How would you characterize Trump's trade policies, and what impact will they have both nationally and on Long Island?*
7. *In lieu of closing statements, we'd like to know from you, what other issue involving foreign policy that hasn't been discussed, do you think requires action now, and what in your opinion should that action entail?*

When the meeting was over, Robin described what she would like to see the SPC focus on once we are past the primary. She articulated a vision of our steering committee working with and coordinating with the nominee's campaign, and then bringing that coordination out to all of our respective grassroots groups, creating a GOTV army that delivers Southampton Township in record numbers. Not only would this help to unseat Zeldin but would prove to the other townships in CD#1 that the kind of cooperation and coordination that we have created here, between the grassroots and the SHDems, is a template that they should all emulate.

Listening to Robin was riveting. This is, of course, what we all were thinking of when we created this steering committee a year ago and it has been disappointing that other townships did not follow our lead. As she said, the key word in our committee has been cooperation. We have not always agreed and but we have worked hard to arrive at consensus. I left the meeting feeling encouraged.

Saturday, May 19th
SPC foreign policy debate
Sharon picked me up to head to Stony Brook Southampton for our second and last SPC hosted debate. We got there early to set up the tables for the grassroots fair, small though it was with only three groups participating. Still, there was also a table for the SHDems and one for handouts from the candidates.

On our way there, I told her that I made up my mind that I will be voting for Vivian. Once I stopped trying to calculate which candidate has the best shot at beating Zeldin and just went with the person who I think best represents me, the choice was Vivian. Sharon was thrilled. I asked her not to say anything to anyone since I really cannot reveal this until after the primary.

When we arrived, we walked in at the same time as Rebecca and Julie who had brought tablecloths so we helped set them up on all the tables. We set up our EEAN table with our handouts and a signup sheet for our newsletter, and then we taped our banner to the window behind our table. Once finished, we greeted other SPC members from the grassroots who were arriving, Tina Jacobowitz, Nick Michelli and Laura Leever from PEER and David Posnett from Resist and Replace (R&R). Gordon arrived and taped the SHDems banner behind a table. Slowly the candidates and their volunteers arrived. They set up their campaign materials on the front table. I went into the auditorium and taped cards that said RESERVED to four seats, to make sure we got seats and were not left standing. At the January forum, it was standing room only.

I said hello to Mike and Robin, who was in a huddle with the candidates, and then we were all ushered into the auditorium.

I guessed there were about 100 people in the room, a lot less than the attendance at the January forum. I hoped this was because there have been so many forums, interviews and debates and not that people are losing interest. It is likely, too, that a lot of people have now made up their minds.

Still, it was a good turnout. The five candidates were seated at the table on the stage. Rebecca stood at the podium next to them. Before Rebecca began, Robin welcomed everyone, introduced the SPC and explained that this was the second of our two debates. She gave the audience a mission - to grab their friends, neighbors and relatives and make sure they vote in the primary.

Moderator Rebecca Dolber

She then introduced Rebecca. As per our plan, Rebecca introduced each of the candidates with a short biography and then went right into the first question. Based on numbers they picked out of a hat, Kate was asked the first question, which was on Iran.

My takeaways from the debate: removing the follow-up questions improved the flow of the debate and kept it moving, much better than the first one; this time the candidates did choose to use their cards to challenge each other but it was not particularly effective. Elaine, Perry and Vivian were the strongest I have ever seen them. Kate's answers were not substantive enough and David's often sounded muddled, especially his answer on the Russian meddling. Rebecca, as always, was superlative as the moderator.

I walked up to some of the audience members after the debate to get their feedback for the book, but when I told them their answers would be on the record, they politely declined. One group said to me, "No, this is a private conversation." Afterwards, we went out for drinks and several fascinating discussions occurred, involving the candidates as well as politics in our district. When I asked if I could record some of it for the book, I was also told no, that it was off the record.

Sunday, May 20th
Solidarity Sundays

I had been planning for some time to visit one of Solidarity Sunday's meetings. They are a unique grassroots group because their membership is younger women with young children. They meet in Sag Harbor which is about an hour's drive for me and with my driving phobia, it is a challenge. Today I finally made it to their meeting. I planned my route, avoided Sunrise Highway, staying instead on the two-lane Montauk Highway. It was overcast but never rained and there was no traffic which made the drive pleasant. As I drove along the shoreline, I passed farms, wineries and some beautiful homes. I made the turn off of Montauk Highway onto the Sag Harbor-Bridgehampton Road that led me north into Sag Harbor. Once an old whaling village, it has a thriving year-round middle-class community with good schools and a very wealthy, summer home crowd.

The meeting was at the home of Bryony Freij, who along with Emily Weitz and Sarah Cohen, are the founders of Solidarity Sundays. I met Bryony at previous events, such as our Charity Bowl, and I invited their group to send a representative to the SPC, which they have not yet done. The primary reason, I think, is that their group is made up of younger women with young children so it is not easy to attend more meetings.

It is fortuitous that I attended this meeting because along with wanting to see for myself how they organize their group, I plan on visiting with supporters of each of the primary candidates and today they were focused on campaigning for David, who they endorsed last month. Their announced agenda for today's meeting was to fill out postcards about David to be mailed to primary voters in order to spread the word about his candidacy and then go knocking on doors and speaking to voters about him. I let them know ahead of time that I would be covering the meeting for the book and they agreed to be on the record.

After turning off the Sag Harbor Expressway I took several back roads and arrived at a quiet cul de sac. There were many cars in front of the house so I sensed I was at the right place. The house is large, with lots of windows and the kind of shingles that many refer to as a Hampton style. As I walked up the front steps, I heard the voices of women and children inside. This made me smile. In all the groups I belong to, most of the members are older and meetings are rarely filled with the laughter of children.

The front door was open so I walked into the house. To the right was the dining room where about eight women were gathered around the dining room table. Kathryn Levy, who I know from PEER, the SPC and the SHDems, saw me and called out, "You made it!" I had mentioned to her that I was going to try to attend this month's meeting. The group meets the second Sunday of every month.

Bryony, who is tall and blond was holding a child in diapers while describing to the women what the mission was for today's meeting. Wearing a tee shirt that said, "Vote Like A Mother" she greeted me and explained that today was not their typical meeting. Rather than focus on sending out postcards for a particular issue, this month they will be working on addressing postcards to get into the mail for the David Pechefsky campaign. Some grassroots groups, like EEAN, will not be endorsing a primary candidate, but Sol Sun, as they are called, made the decision to endorse David in April.

"We decided to endorse David because we just felt that if we didn't make a statement for the person that we believed had the most progressive agenda, and didn't waver on that, we felt we would end up with the least common denominator, and in the end, no matter what happens, we will fight for whatever Democrat wins the primary. The candidates are very careful, David has been very careful, we are very careful, to not say anything negative about anyone else because we are going to want them to win," said Emily Weitz, one of the founders of this chapter of SolSun.

The postcards they are mailing feature a portrait of David by East End artist Paul Davis. An article in *The Independent* newspaper entitled "Paul Davis Does Pechefsky," explains that the artist, "who has created iconic images of some of the most prominent political and cultural figures of our time, was recently inspired to support the candidacy of Pechefsky, and donated a campaign poster to the cause."[23]

The dining room table had piles of the postcards with stacks of sheets that contained names and addresses, next to a carafe of coffee and bowls of chips and strawberries. Taped to the walls were copies of the poster. It is a beautiful painting though I personally don't think it looks much like David.

I introduced myself to the women around the table and explained why I was there and about the book project. I wanted to know more about how Solidarity Sundays worked. I had read on the website that it is a national organization with chapters around the country. All chapters meet on the second Sunday of each month and work with scripts, called infoscripts that the national organizers provide to them. According to the website, "The infoscripts have background info on the issue/s at hand, along with what to do, how to reach your target, and sample scripts to make the process of calling and letter-writing easy and unintimidating."[24]

"Solidarity Sundays formed around the same time as Indivisible, in response to the 2016 election," explained Emily Weitz. "Three women in California compose the infoscripts, they all have young kids, and they do tons of research for the scripts. They are amazing. We print out the infoscripts and go through them one step at a time and do the initiatives for a particular meeting, like writing postcards or phone calls to our members of Congress. They send us stuff on the national issue and then we research what is happening locally and we take local action as well. There are hundreds of chapters across the country. A lot of what we do involves sending postcards, and most of the time the postcard mailings are coordinated across the country so that thousands of cards are mailed on a single day. We started in January, 2017. Sarah, Bryony and I founded it. Sarah and I went to the Women's March in DC, we took the bus from East Hampton, and I think Bryony went in NYC. We did the second March in 2018 in Sag Harbor."

Speaking to several of the members, they explained that this is the only way they could engage with the Resistance, given they all have jobs and children. Many of them do not have available time to participate in meetings during the week or attend events, but on these Sundays, they can devote two hours to activist work because they bring their children with them.

"Many of us have young children. We provide babysitting so that is a huge part of it. For me, this is my time, my one day a month. I try to do what I can for the rest of the month, but I know every month I have these two hours. Our kids are playing outside with a babysitter. Also, our kids have participated a lot, helping us make signs for the marches. We've taken our kids to the marches, especially for issues that are related to kids. My daughter wrote something about the Muslim ban," said Emily.

Emily told me the story of one time when she and Sarah were with their kids and they ran into Bryony's son, Phoenix, who was with a babysitter and after he got home, he told Bryony, "I saw the girls who vote."

They talked about Liuba Grechen Shirley who is one of the Democratic candidates running in the primary race in CD#2 to unseat Peter King. She has young children and she won a Federal Election Commission (FEC) case to allow her to use campaign funds for childcare. Emily describes what a landmark case that is.

"This is how a Mom can run for Congress. It is amazing!" she said.

Kathryn and Bryony asked for attention from the women around the table. While their leadership made the decision to endorse David, many members are not yet familiar with David, so they filled everyone in and answered questions about why he was chosen.

"You don't have to be doing this without understanding why," said Emily, as she explained how they arrived at this endorsement. "Bryony spoke to David and came back to Sarah and me and said, 'I found the progressive candidate'; she was so fired up and we felt this is so exciting to have found someone like this. The more we read and then met him, the more he resonated with our values, especially understanding a global concept on governing. He has global experience and he cares on a local level and just in terms of passionate immigration reform, which is important to us, and racial equality, which is hugely important to us at SolSun, as well as the environment. But I held on personally for a long time to voting for a woman. I really wanted one of the women to be the one, because I wanted it to be a woman. In reaction to Trump, that began to mean a lot to me. And I said to David, which he heard because he is a good listener that you need to embrace being a feminist. That was very important to me and I believe that he does." She explains that the endorsement came about six weeks ago.

"Feels like two years ago." said Kathryn.

"This is the candidate that we believe can really beat Lee Zeldin. He also inspires us and so we are going all out today, we are sending out postcards urging people to vote in the primary for David," said Bryony. She then explained how the portrait of David on the campaign poster and postcards came about.

"Paul Davis has never done a poster for any local candidate and he is in his 80s," said Kathryn. "He has done all the Shakespeare festivals; he has done Che Guevara, and Martin Luther King and every president."

Bryony, Kathryn and Emily then made a strong pitch to the group for how much help will be needed from volunteers as they go into the home stretch of the primary.

"We need as much time as you can give for canvassing, phoning, texting, recruiting other volunteers, because we will need a size ten times the size of this group on the East End," said Kathryn. "It is very intensive work, since as we all know it is hard to get people out to the polls. We are also trying to do a fundraiser for David, a poster launch, for this amazing poster Paul Davis did. We are looking for a pretty big house that somebody is willing to offer to do a house launch of the poster, but we don't have the house yet. The fundraising is for hiring more paid staff, campaign buttons, lawn signs, mailers, and if we can get enough money, we can then do a television advertisement. David has an incredible video of him walking around Patchogue, talking about after his father died how the community helped him and every time I see it I think it would make an incredible ad, but we don't yet have enough money."

"And all of his staff are pretty much working full time, except for the high school students," said Bryony. "The young people are a big reason why I feel confident in supporting David. His support is not just older, white people. That's who shows up at the campaign events for all the other candidates except for David, who has gotten teenagers in their softball uniforms who just got there from the team practice."

"I went to a town hall that he did on income inequality and it was very different from here, people were not as fancy and it was truly interracial and intergenerational. One volunteer still had her soccer uniform on. One guy was the head of Boys and Girls Clubs. It was inspirational. The East End is not a big percentage of the vote in the general election but it is one third of the voters in the primary," said Kathryn. She explains that after they finish the postcards, they will go out into the neighborhood knocking on doors for Pechefsky.

"If we wait and hold back on the sidelines, and wait to see who wins, then it is probably going to be Kate Browning," adds Bryony. There is then a discussion among the women around the table about Kate. Many expressed dismay over how much of the institutional Democratic support has lined up for Kate. I then hear some very negative comments about Kate: she is "an appalling" candidate, "she cannot win", she won't get "the Latino vote", she has a "shameful record on administrative warrants", she "won't generate turnout", she "won't get people of color" and it would be "suicide" if the Democrats choose her.

I wondered if this group will rally behind the nominee if it is Kate. Just as I was thinking this, Emily interrupted the discussion to reiterate her earlier comment that unity is important. "I think it is important that we don't divide people, we say we support David and why but I don't want to divide the party further." She then added that it is difficult with so many candidates. "The fact that there are five people running is jarring and alarming, I don't want there to be so many options." But she encouraged the focus to be on why they support David, not against the other candidates.

Lorraine Dusky, a friend of Kathryn's, was there not because she is a member of Solidarity Sundays, but because she is volunteering for David's campaign. She has been involved previously in Democratic and political campaigns on the East End. She hosted a large benefit for Tim Bishop and is considering doing one for David. She sees the energy in the district this year as bigger than in previous midterm elections.

"More people signed petitions than voted in the last midterm election," said Lorraine. "Thirteen thousand voted in the last midterm."

She didn't bash Kate but did express concern that all of the institutional support, like from the County Democratic Party, lined up behind Kate. I told her that at the Southampton Town Democratic Committee we are not endorsing anyone. She was surprised to hear that. But then Kathryn told me that the Riverhead Democratic Committee had endorsed Kate. I said I hadn't heard that but it seemed unwise to me for any of the Democratic Committees to endorse any of the candidates.

I walked into the backyard where about six children were playing. Some were in the playground, others ran on the grass and two small children sat and ate watermelon, cut into pieces for them by a young woman who was watching them. She told me that she is the sitter the members hire for every Sol Sun meeting and that the kids have all gotten to know each other and view the meeting as a playdate.

But as with all young children, there are also moments when there are tears and they only want Mommy or in one case, Grandma, who was at the meeting with her young granddaughter. While I sat at the table taking notes, the granddaughter, holding onto a stuffed Winnie the Pooh, came up beside me so that she could tell her Grandma that she really needed her dolly, which was in the car. Grandma was busy writing a message on a postcard, copying it from a large sheet of paper taped to the dining room wall. The message was, "Vote For Bold Progressive Vision, Vote for David." She put down her pen, picked up her granddaughter and they went out to the car to retrieve the missing baby doll.

A group of boys dashed in from outside and began to play the piano which is in the dining room, but were quickly ushered out of the room and back outside to play with the other children.

One woman, who was also wearing a "Vote Like A Mother" T-shirt, was filling out postcards while her young daughter sat on her lap, drawing a picture with markers. I asked about the message on the T-shirts. The message and the T-shirts are from the website votelikeamother.org where the watchword is "parenthood as a lens for politics" and all the profits from the sale of their merchandise go to "mom-centered non-profits."[25]

The pile of postcards with handwritten message grew ever taller. Another woman with young children, Deborah Oppenheimer, said, regarding the election postcards, "I know this is important but I kind of miss when we were focused on the issues instead of the election." We then all had a wistful discussion about 2017 and how we all miss when the focus was on issues, rallies and resisting, instead of the election. This is much harder work. And there is a real fear that if there is a not a blue wave, that there will be no check going forward on Trump's agenda.

Bryony walked around with a clipboard and wrote down their names on a schedule for making phone calls, sending out text messages and knocking on doors for David. I asked if the group will stay focused on the election up until the midterm election and there is general agreement that this will be the mission this year.

As I drove home, I had a couple of nagging thoughts. Watching them participate in the Resistance while juggling jobs and young children is inspiring. And they are clearly passionate about David. He is lucky to have such devoted supporters. But will they be just as passionate if someone else is the nominee? That was my concern, especially if the nominee is Kate.

Monday, May 21st
Take Action Suffolk County (TASC)
I was tired from the weekend and busy typing up my notes from the weekend events so I was not planning on going out canvassing or covering anything today. But then I got an email from Syma that she has been canvassing for a group called Take Action Suffolk County (TASC) and asked if I would I like to go out with her today. Canvassing is the backbone of election work. Going door to door, speaking directly to voters is still, despite the age of technology and social media, the most effective method to get your message out to potential voters.

TASC is a district-wide nonprofit that focuses on promoting progressive values and supporting progressive Democrats without being affiliated with any campaign or candidate. It started in 2017.[26]

This is the email Syma sent about her experience canvassing for TASC:

> *At Rebecca's suggestion, I've started working for TASC, since I could not decide on a candidate I wanted to support. They gave me a walk book for a small area in Center Moriches--approximately 20 houses--and I went out Sunday afternoon. Everyone on the list was a registered Democrat, some with an irregular voting history. It was a great experience--every person (woman) I spoke to was delighted to talk with me--it also happened to be a sunny day, but for me it was fun and lifted my spirits. It's easy because we ask nothing of people except that they remember to vote--and then we ask about what issues--from a list we have--are troubling them most. To paraphrase something Sharon said to me--many of these women are hungry to talk to people about politics. Most of the ones I met have conservative husbands and feel isolated in Brookhaven. Two of them are interested in volunteering and I put them on our mailing list.*
>
> *Perhaps that's something you might want to consider . . . walking outdoors is therapeutic anyway and the warmth of the women was reassuring.*

We made plans to go out together around 4:30 PM. But then she got back late from a meeting in Riverhead with a client and so we postponed our canvassing walk until another day. I am glad, though, that the experience left her uplifted. When we talked on the phone she described the number of women she spoke to at their doorways who felt compelled to whisper about their support of the Democrats running so that their husbands would not hear this. It is eye opening to realize that even in the 21st Century this is still the case with so many women.

Thursday, May 24th
League of Women Voters primary debate
This evening, the League of Women Voters hosted a primary debate in Hampton Bays. As far as I know, it was the first time the Southampton League had hosted a primary debate.

In the afternoon, while taking a break from writing, I came across an article in *Politico Magazine*, entitled "Why Long Island Still Loves Trump: In Suffolk County, N.Y., where the Hamptons collide with MS-13, the president feels like a local." The article, by David Freedlander, zeroes in on the rise of Zeldin and Trump having been fueled by anti-immigrant feelings. It also casts doubt on whether or not any Democrat can unseat Zeldin this year.[27]

The article shook me to my core. I did not want to believe that this is so prominent in our district. But if this is true, then our candidates need to have answers on how to address these fears and prejudices. It explains why Trump and Zeldin won so big in 2016.

That night Sharon picked me up and with her in the car were two other EEAN members, Pat Falk and Diane Bavosa who are also Vivian supporters. They all wanted to know when I am going to go public with my support for Vivian and I said not yet. They brought handouts and a sign for Vivian but when we got there, we were informed that the League does not allow giving out candidate materials.

Some of the candidates had not arrived yet and we heard that the traffic was terrible. I ran into David Dubow and his wife in the lobby. I know that David is supporting Pechefsky. He asked me who I was supporting and I explained that I am neutral because of the book project. I asked him if he heard about the Riverhead Democratic Committee endorsing Kate. He said yes, it is true, though he says he heard that there was limited attendance the day they voted and that this is mainly coming from their chair. He said he has not heard of any other Democratic Committee in the district endorsing. He said his sense of the campaign as it stands now is that the grassroots are supporting Elaine, David and Vivian but that the institutional support is going with Kate and that Perry is the only one with the funds to run a major advertising campaign. He told me that he thinks David is the best candidate and is the best to go up against Zeldin.

All the candidates finally arrived so we all moved into the auditorium. We were given index cards to write a question on that were then collected. Mike was there as was Gordon. I debated sitting with them but I am here with Sharon and EEAN so I sat with them. I realized afterwards that this probably signaled that I am a

Vivian supporter. I hope this does not inhibit any further interviews with the candidates and their supporters.

It was my first time in the Hampton Bays high school auditorium and it is a lovely setting. The candidates were seated at a table on the stage, each with their own microphone. It was more formal than our debate setting was. There was a good-sized crowd though the auditorium was not filled to capacity. The moderator from the League, Kathy Peacock, stood at a podium to one side and on the other side were two individuals who had the questions from the audience and asked them of the candidates.

The candidates were introduced and then gave opening statements, something they didn't do with us. The format, otherwise, was not that different from ours. The questions, since they were from the audience, were more general than the ones we asked, and I heard the standard answers from them that I have heard them say many times. They were asked: what motivated them to run; what strategy did they think will be the most effective in the district - motivating the left or appealing to moderate Democrats and GOP voters; did they support Pelosi as speaker; if you are not the nominee, what will you do to support the nominee; would you amend, improve or replace the ACA; the opioid crisis?

The one surprise was that someone posed a question based on the Politico article. It was the same question that I wrote on my card, which was how to counter the anti-immigrant feelings in our district that propelled Zeldin and Trump to victory? They all agreed that it is important to emphasize the value of immigration, to not allow the GOP to control the narrative, to acknowledge the fears of criminals, to remind voters that most immigrants do not commit crimes and that we need a path to citizenship.

Perry came closest to answering it and even referenced the Politico article. But all their answers left me worried. They were reasonable and filled with facts. But we saw in 2016 that facts seemed no match for hate-fueled rhetoric,

The month ended with the race heating up as we got closer to the June 26th primary. In the news, Trump's on-again, off-again summit with North Korea is back on, though he is no longer talking about denuclearization. It seemed clear to me that he is being played by the North Koreans and the real fear is that he will give away the store at their June 12th summit. We seem to be inching closer to a constitutional showdown over whether or not Trump will speak to Mueller as Trump starts throwing pardons around.

Meanwhile, Zeldin continued moving to the right. He sponsored a resolution, H.J. Res. 132, that was signed into law by Trump that the GOP claimed will make it easier for dealerships to provide auto loans. The reality is the resolution overturned a previous Consumer Financial Protection Board (CFPB) guideline that protected consumers. The Consumer Federation of America (CFA), a coalition of consumer groups, issued a press release with a subtitle that stated: "Consumer Finance Expert says Congressional Invalidation of the CFPB's Auto Lending Guidance Would Grant Car Dealers Free Reign to Discriminate Against Minority Borrowers and Set a Dangerous Precedent for Future Guidance." [28]

Chapter 15

June 2018

"Whoever wins, I vote for him or her. Any one of them is better than Lee Zeldin. Doesn't matter who wins. The turnout will probably be low. It is very confusing with so many candidates. My biggest concern is if the Democratic Party becomes split. We are supposed to work together and support each other. This primary is not the end, it is the beginning. People shouldn't withdraw, since this is the start of the campaign, not the end."

Lulu Bouvier, SHDems

Saturday, June 2nd
Newsday article
An article in Newsday, entitled, "Progressive groups looking toward LI congressional primaries," mentioned how progressive grassroots groups are keeping it together to avoid the divisiveness that doomed the Throne-Holst vs. Calone primary in 2016. It features the photo from our first debate of all the candidates with their hands together and several of our grassroots leaders are quoted, like Laura Leever from PEER and Eileen Duffy from LVLZ.[29]

Wednesday, June 6th
Andy Kim
Andy Kim, the founder of Rise Stronger, won the Democratic primary in New Jersey. I am thrilled for him. Analyzing other primary results, Democrats avoided a shutout in the bizarre California primary system, but it still does not look likely that they will flip these GOP districts. I feel a growing anxiety about a blue wave. Today, I received a mailer from Zeldin and it is all about MS13. He is running again on hyping fear of immigrants.

Thursday, June 7th
Indivisible North Fork
I attended an event at a restaurant in Riverhead called The Dark Horse. It was organized by Laura Venugopalan of Indivisible North Fork and co-sponsored by EEAN, to make phone calls or write postcards to protest the separation of families. This is what Rebecca posted on our Facebook page:

> *Join Indivisible North Fork and the East End Action Network this Thursday afternoon as we flood our representatives' offices with phone*

calls regarding the Trump administration's horrific policy of separating families at the border. We'll be there to help with call scripts, post cards, moral support and light refreshments!

Do you have a friend who's interested in getting involved? Bring them. This is a great introduction into the work of the grassroots and the important role we play in keeping a check on power and policy. If you work and cannot make it, please try to call from home.

When I got there, only a few people were in the room. Rebecca had already left. Wendy arrived after I had been there for about an hour and Sharon arrived after that. Along with filling out my postcards, I got a chance to speak with Steven Kramer, a member of Indivisible Northfork leadership. It was interesting to get a male point of view. I asked him what impact he thought the grassroots might have on the election.

Steven Kramer

"The sense I get is that I don't think people in the media are doing a very good job of measuring. I don't think that there's a lot of engagement with the media to the grassroots, and I think there's an underestimation of the passion that's out there. And I think that they're content to denigrate the movement in a lot of ways. If you look at the way that a lot of the major outlets covered Hillary Clinton, the takeaway is pretty much that there's an ingrained sense of misogyny. And that so many of the major reporters were then implicated in their own #metoo moments. It was amazing to me that the people that were charged with covering this race were so blatantly anti-woman. No wonder the coverage is so skewed. It definitely brought a lot of things to a head in my mind that was already there. I did have sort of a moment at some point listening to one of my coworkers complaining about something where I said in my mind, what are you doing about it? He was looking for a reason why tech schools aren't funded with scholarships. And it is a very sound question, and one that should be explored. But what are you doing about it? You're just sitting here complaining about it. And then I sort of had a man in the mirror moment where I was kind of like, well, what are you doing about it? And I said, oh. That's not good.

I think that men in this society have a very privileged position where they don't need, as a man, to be politically active. Because your needs are already taken care of. The only people that have to fight are the people that aren't fully represented. People of color, LGBTQ people, the disabled, those people who know that their rights are going to get run over. And personally, I think that if we're going to change the way that politics function in this country, it has to come from a different place. It can't come from a white male perspective; it has to be a different perspective. Because if you keep electing white men, I'm telling you right now, nothing will change. They don't need it to change. And that's why you see so little activism from men. What's the percentage of white males that voted for Trump? Almost 70%."

Friday, June 8th
Perry meet-and-greet

I drove to Jamesport, on the North Fork of the East End, to attend a meet-and-greet for Perry. I have heard him speak before so my goal here was to speak to some of his supporters.

It was a beautiful evening, not very hot but sunny. I forget how lovely the North Fork is, rural with farms and farm houses, and the drive heading east was easy for me.

The event, called Pints for Perry, was at a micro-brewery called the Jamesport Farm Brewery, from 6:00 to 8:00 PM. Perry arranged to pick up the tab for the beers being served. About 25 people were there. Before Perry spoke, I walked around and asked people why they came, who are they leaning towards and what are they hoping to hear tonight from Perry?

The first person I spoke with was Alan Fishbein who lives in the city but has a vacation home in the area. He changed his registration to be able to vote in this district. He has not made up his mind yet who to vote for in the primary but whoever wins has his vote against Zeldin.

"I voted in the general election in 2016," he said. "I can't stand Zeldin. I thought Anna was going to do better in 2016. Whoever is the candidate is going to need a ton of money to beat Zeldin. Expect a lot of dirty money behind Zeldin this year, Koch money, Mercer money. That's Long Island."

I also spoke with a young man, Robert Steven, who is a student at the State University of Stony Brook here on Long Island and majoring in political science. It is over an hour drive from the campus to the brewery here in Jamesport.

"I found the last debate very interesting. Perry was very confident and I liked that. David and Kate seemed uncertain. I am leaning towards Vivian, Elaine and Perry. I drove all the way from Setauket to Jamesport, because I wanted to hear Perry," he said.

Another young man, Mike Hilt, told me it is about Trump for him. "I am upset with Trump's rhetoric," he said. "But will it motivate Democrats to show up and vote? We need a candidate who is both progressive and pragmatic. We need to express support for hard working Latinos but also show that Democrats can be tough on MS13."

Perry spoke briefly. I didn't hear anything that I hadn't heard before from Perry - progressive causes and plans for Long Island economic revitalization, that he is a strong progressive but also strong for jobs, that the tax plan is Zeldin's Achilles heel, and to win we must bring non-progressive voters to the voting place. Even though I have heard these ideas before, many in the audience hadn't and he made a strong presentation.

Then he took questions. The first one was about immigration. He gave a strong answer: "Farmers in the district need migrant labor, Trump and Zeldin use MS13 as a deflection. While what the gang does is sufficiently awful, if it went away, Trump and Zeldin would find something else. Saying immigrants taking your jobs is not true."

The next question was on the value of running negative ads in the primary. Perry's answer was on the danger of going negative: "I'm on television now but I am not going at the other candidates, I have the resources to go negative on them and am not going to do that. But if anyone else went negative, I have the megaphone to answer that."

He answered more questions on economic development on Long Island, social security and Medicare, the tax bill and how Democrats plan to undo the tax bill. He ended by saying, "My campaign is one of high integrity and you know where I stand because I wear my heart on my sleeve. The way we win is turnout."

I got a chance to speak to two people after Perry's presentation. Kathy Haft told me that after meeting Perry, she has made up her mind. "I was looking at all the candidates then got to meet Perry and thought, too good to be true!"

Desiree Martyn, a young woman who it turns out went to high school with my son, came after work because, "one of my best friends is the bartender here, and I had stopped by to visit, not even knowing about the Perry event. But after speaking with his wife, Lisa, and then hearing him speak, I am convinced. Perry has my vote."

Sunday, June 10th
Meet-and-greet for Elaine
The event for Elaine was at a house party in Baiting Hollow, also on the North Fork, on a Sunday afternoon from 2:00 PM - 4:00 PM. It was at the home of Gail Donoghue, an active volunteer for Elaine. The house was filled with a very large crowd, a mixture of men and women, mostly my age, all white, with a smattering of some younger voters. Many of them are apparently neighbors.

When I got there, Elaine was already speaking. Like with Perry's event, most of what I heard, I have heard before - the importance of trade schools and community colleges, a need for jobs, and that as a scientist, her message for the general election is the same as for the primary.

For the first time, I heard Elaine address her opponents, though not by name. "My opponents talk about what they are against, but I am telling audiences that are two-thirds Democrats and one-third Independents what we need. Congress invests huge amounts of money in maintaining the status quo, the extremely wealthy, to keep people uneducated, and we need to put progressives in office to change that. We are preparing ourselves already for the dark money that will enter this race."

I asked Tim Freeman, Elaine's campaign manager, what their strategy is in the primary. He also referenced the other candidates. "In the past ten years, the GOP has been proactive, while the Democrats have been reactive, and we are now eight years too late, in terms of GOP super PACs. Are we being proactive this year? Some of these online grassroots groups are just keyboard heroes and that doesn't turn out the vote and voter turnout is the key. We are not blanketing houses, we are being very strategic. Look at our opponents - real estate businessman with his own money, two former legislators, all these years voting in Suffolk County legislature and we are left with a huge deficit. Pechefsky has a lot of support but ran in the city several times and lost. But Elaine as a scientist is the problem solver. We are getting good crowds at house parties. I believe if we can win the primary, we can win the district because we are in a race in a district that can be flipped."

I also spoke to Elaine's supporters. Bernadette Nendza told me, "I'm supporting Elaine because she cares about the environment. This is a very scary time, killing off animals and trees. The polluters are paying people off to get around regulations. I believe Elaine will really stand up for the environment."

"I worked with Elaine at the lab, I know Elaine," said Pat Johnson. "I am disgusted with the Democrats and the GOP, no one wants to compromise, so polarized, we need to see the Democratic Party move away from Hillary and show a positive message. Elaine represents the scientific approach, not the radical left."

Ed Goldstein, a former Republican, told me that he had concerns that Elaine didn't have enough name recognition to win district wide but despite this being considered a Republican district, he thought there was Democratic enthusiasm in the district. "I had lunch today with a good friend whose wife is a crazy hater of Trump. He said from what he knows and speaking to all the people out here, they still love Trump. I said, 'Well, they should go to Setauket, Stony Brook and the more progressive areas because I don't think that's the case throughout the whole district.'"

He then told me a story about his son, who worked for Trump in Atlantic City. "For the Taj Mahal, and he's told me about all the bills Trump never paid, the gym that was never finished. He had enough of Trump and he moved into the Hyatt. My other son works for Coke and he was saying that they would never deliver Coke unless they got paid cash because Trump never paid his bills."

Jon Marko, who works in IT for a public school district, told me he first met Elaine last fall at a small meet-and-greet. "After communicating with her for a couple of days, I decided that I had to help out because she's exactly the kind of person I would want representing me in Congress. I've been volunteering for her campaign since then. At that point, I simply started to see about helping to get her name out there. I would post things on Facebook or things like that. I started an email group for her as a way of communicating with the other volunteers. So that kind of put me in the position of being a bit of a volunteer organizer because I was the one managing the email group that all of the volunteers belonged to."

He hoped that once the primary is over, Democrats will come together to support whoever is the nominee but is worried that some people won't. "There is an undercurrent of divisiveness on a couple of the campaigns so there might be some people who won't come together from that. This is a concern for me that there are some people who got involved with certain candidates because those candidates inspired them and then, if their candidate does not become the nominee, they will fall out for lack of inspiration. I'll be honest. Elaine inspired me but I will still, of course, support and vote for whoever the nominee is."

Tuesday, June 12th
Fundraiser for Vivian

I went to the home of Peggy Ann Jayne in Westhampton Beach for a fundraiser for Vivian. Sharon invited me and she was one of the organizers. She is working her heart out for Vivian. There was a large crowd, mingling in the backyard and in the house, a total of about 33 people. There was an amazing array of food and wine. Peggy explained how she chose Vivian to support. "When we heard her entire background and where she stands on several issues, we said, this is the person that we want. And we definitely don't want to see Zeldin carry the torch. We do not want him any longer. So, I think she's the one that's going to do it."

I walked around speaking to the guests. Most of them were already supporting Vivian and they told me their reasons. For Becky Wiseman, it was Vivian's outreach to the agriculture industry in the district. "This is an important industry in our district and is very Republican but Vivian reached out to them and has built bridges with them." For Carol Passarello, she said it was important for her to vote for a woman. Several people were excited that Vivian is a Latina woman and hope this can bring in more Hispanic voters.

Diane Bavosa, from EEAN, who is also volunteering for Vivian, told me a story from her canvassing. "I knocked on the door and this woman came to the door. She had a Spanish accent. And I was telling her a little bit about Vivian Viloria-Fisher who's also a Latina woman. And she was so excited. She goes, 'Does she speak Spanish?' I said, 'Yes she does.' She goes, 'Oh, she has my vote.' And the woman was so nice. She invited me in the house. Not many people invited me in the house because they're a little wary. And then I told her a little bit more about Vivian. And she was really excited. She was going to vote in the primaries."

Diane Bavosa and Sharon Adams canvassing for Vivian

Maria Tursi said she is not yet sure who she is going to vote for, but the environment is an important issue for her, as well as stricter gun laws and equal rights so she is interested in hearing Vivian's stands on these issues.

Interestingly, I spoke to one woman who is a Republican. "I am a registered Republican," said Melina Hale, "So I can't vote in the primary." But she told me she will definitely be voting Democratic in the fall and would like it to be for a woman. "I feel very disenfranchised in the Republican party, which is now a white, male patriarchy."

Sharon introduced Vivian and thanked everyone for coming. Vivian spoke, and she repeated her key message that she also emphasized at the debate. "Long Island is my home. You know what I will do, because you know what I've done."

I have one more meet-and-greet for Kate, but I am struck so far that the candidates who have inspired their supporters are David, Elaine and Vivian. They are passionate about them. Perry's supporters have made the calculus that he is the person to beat Zeldin, and that is the most important thing to them. They sound practical and dutiful but not passionate. I don't know if that will make any difference in the final vote count for the primary. More likely Perry being the only candidate with enough funds to have television advertisements will be a more decisive factor.

Monday, June 18th
Meet-and-greet for Kate

My last event was a house party at Susan Blake's house in East Setauket. This is too far for me to drive but since Nanci is interested in Kate, she suggested I take the train and she will pick me up at Patchogue and we will drive together. She has liked Kate from the beginning and was eager to meet her in a smaller setting. Elyse and Mackenzie also joined us, as did Nanci's good friend Laura Mirabella, and Laura's mother Alice Coccorese. We met at the diner first for dinner before heading over to Susan Blake's house. Alice reminds me of my Dad – so sharp and active that you would never guess she is in her 90s.

We had trouble finding the house and even more trouble finding parking, so when we got there Kate had already started speaking, but folks moved around to make room for us, got us chairs and we sat and listened. There were about 40 people there, so it was crowded and not everyone had seats. Kate welcomed us and then continued speaking about her experience.

She talked about her experience in the county legislature, endorsements by Bridget Fleming, talked about Parkland, the AR 15, Zeldin and concealed carry and then opened it up to questions. There were some questions about how much funding she has and she admitted not as much as Perry. But she said that if she wins the primary, she feels she is the strongest candidate to beat Zeldin because she will pull support from Zeldin's base and unlike Vivian or Perry, her support is in Brookhaven, where 60% of the population of the district resides and that she is more well known in Brookhaven than the other candidates because the legislative district that she represented is there. She also said that her district, the 3rd legislative district, has connections to the farming community, blue-collar voters and the bread and butter issues that will be needed to defeat Zeldin. She also emphasized how people are being screwed by the tax bill. She talked about her husband being in law enforcement and 9-11, and her three grandchildren.

She was asked a question about the controversy with Vivian about abortion and that she used to be a member of the Right to Life Party. She said that she is for a woman's right to choose and supports Planned Parenthood and that she was a member of the Right to Life Party when she first moved here from Ireland but that was a long time ago. She also addressed MS13, said it is a real problem but it is a crime how Zeldin is using it to bash immigrants. Her key question she posed was, "Who do you think he least wants to face? Me."

Given how crowded the house was and that we got there late, I didn't get a chance to speak to her supporters, but from the comments and questions I heard, many of them strongly believe that she has the best chance to beat Zeldin. I did not sense the kind of inspiration that I heard from David, Elaine and Vivian's supporters. The calculus is more aligned with Perry's supporters.

Tuesday, June 19th
Petitions with Lulu in ED 19

Lulu picked me up in the afternoon and we went to our ED to get petitions signed for us as ED leaders. Our ED has a large African American population. We knocked on a lot of doors and most people were happy to speak with us and happy to sign our petitions. They told us they will be voting Democratic in the fall since they are deeply unhappy with Trump, but many of them were unaware of the primary coming up in a week. I was surprised given the number of flyers the candidates are mailing and the amount of television ads that Perry is running. But it goes to show how little attention even dedicated Democrats are paying to the primary race.

Thursday, June 21st
CD#1 Leadership meeting at Eileen's house
I attended the CD#1 leadership meeting with EEAN members Rebecca, Patty, Sharon and Syma. Normally Rebecca attends as the EEAN rep to this group. This is a steering committee with representatives from grassroots groups across all of CD#1. It is the same idea as the SPC in Southampton, with hopes of coordinating initiatives across the district.

The following people and their groups were represented there that day:

1. Julie Sheehan, Progressive East End Reformers
2. Sharon Adams, East End Action Network
3. David Posnett, Resist and Replace
4. Patty Callan, East End Action Network
5. Barbara Weber-Floyd, East End Action Network
6. Amy Turner, PEER
7. Rebecca Dolber, East End Action Network
8. Steve Kramer, Indivisible North Fork
9. Laura Venugopalan, Indivisible North Fork
10. Eileen Duffy, Let's Visit Lee Zeldin
11. Syma Gerard, East End Action Network
12. Shoshana Hershkowitz, Suffolk Progressives, TASC
13. Jackie Gavron, East Hampton Democrats, Background Check, Zeldin Watch
14. Phyllis Hartman, Bend the Arc
15. Judy Meserve, SWR Persists
16. Darcy Stevens, South Country Unites
17. Barbara Fontana, Indivisible Patriots of Long Island
18. Dan Fingas, Long Island Progressive Coalition
19. Chris Cangelari, Organize Plan Act
20. James Bertsch, Sayville Citizens for Political Activation, Bayport-Blue Point Indivisible
21. Cindy Morris, TASC

It was interesting meeting people from the grassroots from across the district. The meeting was very lively though it was hard for Rebecca, who was chairing it, to keep everybody focused because conversations kept veering off topic. The group came up with an extensive list of collaborative activities; we then organized into sub-committees for things like canvassing, social events and messaging.

But it was very chaotic and, in the end, I wasn't sure how many of these initiatives would ever become reality. The level of confusion was a little too much for me. I think each individual group is active and organized and involved. The idea of a joint steering committee to coordinate across groups was a good one, but other than helping to alert people across the district about rallies and upcoming events, I was not sure how effective this group was.

Tuesday, June 26th
Primary

Finally, it is primary day. Six months of active campaigning, beginning with six Democrats, then five, it feels endless and I will be happy when it is over and we have one candidate.

The New York primary comes on the same day that the Supreme Court rules in favor of Trump's travel ban. The vote is 5-4. I am shocked that the Supreme Court has ruled in favor of bigotry. The Supreme Court also ruled that the state of California could not require pregnancy centers to give patients information about abortion. That vote was also 5-4. The villainy of what McConnell did in stealing this Supreme Court seat from Merrick Garland is blatantly obvious in both of these decisions.

This is all happening at the same time that thousands of migrant children are still separated from their families. This is Trump's America. The news of the day just emphasizes how crucial this midterm election is. There must be a blue wave. We must take back the House.

I voted this morning at the firehouse around 10:00 AM. Matt and Eugene both voted by absentee ballot since they are out of the district today. I walked up the steps to the polling place and was flooded with memories from voting in the general elections of 2016 and 2017. In 2016, I had great hopes but nervous fears about Hillary's chances. In 2017, I had PTSD from the 2016 election and anxiety that the results would reveal that the Resistance was not having any impact. My fears were justified in 2016 and proven wrong in 2017. With all that in mind, I really didn't know what to think this time around. Granted, this is for a primary and not the general election so the concerns are different. I can't even remember if I voted in the primary in 2016. I knew almost nothing about either Anna Throne-Holst or Dave Calone and didn't really care which one won the primary since I would vote for any Democrat against Lee Zeldin.

In speaking with Mike last week, he mentioned that he thought the voter turnout would be low today. Not because Democrats aren't focused on unseating Zeldin in the fall, but because most people are not paying close attention and with five

Democrats running, they can't choose between them so why vote? They are probably saying to themselves that they will vote for whichever Democrat wins. This was my thinking in 2016.

I walked up to the desk and signed in. I was handed my ballot - which I am familiar with from seeing the absentee ballots that Eugene and Matt filled out - and I walked over to one of the desks and filled in the bubble for Vivian. Eugene and Matt both voted for Perry because they believed he was the strongest candidate and had the best chance to beat Zeldin. After vacillating for months, going back and forth, and keeping my own counsel of who I was supporting because I was covering all of them for the book project, I was finally able to cast my vote. When my ballot slid into the optical scanner, it gave me a read out that said I was the fifth voter in my ED as of 10:00 AM. That seemed incredibly low even for a low turnout primary election.

That afternoon, Lulu and I traveled to our ED to finish getting the signatures for our positions on the Democratic Committee. We decided to go to the polling place for ED 19 rather than the street addresses in our walk book, thinking we could get a lot of Democrats after they voted. It was about 5:15 PM. We knew we had to stand 100 feet away from the polling location but we decided to walk into the building first to see if there were any voters inside. There were none. So, we went back to the neighborhoods. We only needed a few more signatures. We walked on several streets, getting four signatures. Two of the Democrats who signed told us they had voted in the primary earlier in the day. One of these Democrats asked how she could get more involved to help take back the House in the fall and we took her contact information. That was encouraging.

Then it was time to wait for the results. While waiting, I reached out to family, friends, grassroots activists and Democratic Party members across CD#1 to get impressions from them about primary day.

Below are the email responses I received, in alphabetical order by last name:

Sharon Adams, EEAN

"I was on the road at 5:30 am. Shifting yard signs to be near the polling places from WHB to East Moriches. I was #2 voting at 6:30 in Eastport. Then a successful afternoon of canvassing in East Quogue again. I want to share a special canvassing story from yesterday. I came upon a woman who was mowing the lawn. She stopped for me, but said she had a lot going on and really couldn't deal with politics. She was overwhelmed by the mess Trump has made. Somehow during her venting, she asked about clean water. After I told her about Vivian's work with the farmers to reduce pesticides and fertilizers, she reached for the door hanger, folded it and put it in her pocket. She said "I'll be there tomorrow. I'll vote for her." Prayers for this voter please. She is having surgery for breast cancer on Thursday but wanted to mow the lawn and vote for our Vivian for Congress. We persist!! Proud to be walking and sharing the message of this important campaign. GO TEAM VIVIAN!!"

Mike Anthony, SHDems

"Ann (Elaine) and I (Perry) split our votes. Ann and I were 52nd and 53rd voters in ED23. At that pace - 11:20AM- it looks like turnout might approach 2016 Hillary/Sanders level, if 23 is representative. I would say that favors someone other than Kate Browning if that vote goes to one or two other people primarily (rather than split evenly). I hope the turnout is larger than expected so that pundits and prognosticators talk about an energized Democratic Party. My main concern is Party unity: this is not a time to squabble over who has the best single-payer plan or who wants to raise the minimum wage the highest, this is a time for moral clarity and for Democrats to take a stand for compassion and decency. As Thomas Friedman recently said, the worst Democrat is better than the best Republican because Republicans refuse to address the dumpster fire in the White House. Dumpster fire is my word."

Victoria Aspinwall, fellow marcher at the Women's March 2017

"I'm hoping for a strong Democratic turnout and result. Democrats have to turn things around and the word has to go out to all Independents and Democrats to vote in the mid-terms and change Congress. Positive results for Democrats in the primary could be just the impetus people need."

James Bertsch, Sayville Citizens for Political Activation, People Power Patchogue (civil liberties but non-partisan ACLU grassroots group)

"My impression is that voter turnout is low, which is not unusual for a primary. In light of today's context, I think that means we'll see the further polarization of politics as the most impassioned people turn out to get their candidate the party endorsement. Regarding both CD 1 and 2, I predict the party favorites (who are generally more moderate which is not my preference) will both lose. Browning (1) will lose as will Gregory (2). To me, that means a vocal minority controls the party which is something to think about. We've seen the pendulum swing back and forth between a Democrat (Obama) and a Republican (Trump). With Obama we had the Tea Party; with Trump, we have the

Indivisibles. With a zealot like Trump, we'll see a more radical swing of the pendulum, with Democrats taking back Congress and eventually the Presidency. Yet to a large extent, low voter turnout and a high intensity group controlling the party speaks to the same force: people don't trust politics. The apathetic majority are shutting down further while more vigorous people (on both sides of the aisle) are crawling out of the trenches expecting to fight a pitched battle."

Patty Callan, EEAN

"I am anxious about the primary today. I really want Vivian to be our Democratic Candidate to stand up to Zeldin. I am going to cast my vote after work and will be praying for a win for Vivian."

Rebecca Dolber, EEAN

"I voted for Kate and I have to say, I went right in and did it with no hesitation. I was the 14th ballot cast and my poll worker friends (Anne, John and Barbara) were encouraged and said that was above-average for that time of day during a primary."

Shannon Dupuis, SPC

"I was very disheartened to see the low turnout in my polling place today. I had hoped more people were paying attention and getting involved at the local level. People clearly don't perceive the severity of our situation and where the movement needs to happen, which is within our local communities. But I am optimistic about rallying for whichever candidate wins the primary to turn CD1 blue again!"

Matthew Floyd, my son

"I'm not expecting a very large voter turnout. Choosing between the five candidates was very difficult because of all of them had distinct viewpoints, and, in my opinion, different ways of winning. My only hope is that people don't get divided by whatever today's decision is. Losing Bernie supporters in 2016 was one of our biggest mistakes. Whoever wins today, we must jump in the proverbial pool of support, with both feet, for the next four months."

Syma Gerard, EEAN

"In ED 29, in Remsenburg, turnout was almost 100 by 1:00 PM. They were delighted and so was I. Diane Novak, however, told me that when she voted, around 11:30 AM she was only # 5 in Brookhaven. I'm personally down—not sure we will get the turnout where we really need it—Brookhaven Town. Throughout the day I have been feeling a kind of overarching anxiety—worried about low turnout—not sure what it would mean—not even certain what I was anxious about. Finally decided to vote for Perry because I believed he would be our strongest candidate to defeat Zeldin—but wavered all the way to the voting booth. So much anxiety around Trump's recent activities, and particularly the ongoing damage from the Supreme Court."

Susan Habermann, SPC

"I voted early and was #7 on the sign in sheet (my son was #1 in Sag Harbor). It's a spectacular day and I hope that doesn't negatively affect the turnout. My support right now is for Perry Gershon, but I am committed to supporting the winner as I am fully behind ousting Lee Zeldin and getting this country back on the right track."

Phyllis Hartmann, Bend the Arc

"I am concerned that there are 5 candidates in the CD1 primary. The winner will have only a small percentage of the vote, and this will weaken the candidate in the November election. Also, having so many candidates makes it seem like real work to educate yourself about the candidates, especially for voters who have limited time to read or those who have limited interest in or understanding of the primary process. I have canvassed a lot of Hispanic voters, and they really don't understand it at all and why it is important. I will be interested to see the percentage of Hispanic voters who vote."

Elyse Hennes Sheehan, my niece

"I had a pretty hectic day, a perfect ingredient for someone to say 'it doesn't matter if I vote in the primary or not. All that really matters is the midterm election.' But, I refused to think like that and I dragged Mackenzie, in the midst of everything, to exercise my right to vote. We met Nana at the polling place and cast our ballots together. The reason why I didn't just say "oh, F--- it" is because it mattered to me that the voter turnout for this election was big. I didn't expect it to be huge, but I still hoped that it was an increase from years past. After we voted Mackenzie said "That's it?" and I turned to her and I said "That's it! It takes 2 seconds, I can't for the life of me figure out why people don't do it." It is so important to vote; it is a right that is taken for granted. My biggest concern is that my generation is going to lose their interest in politics. It is a growing trend among my friends (myself included) to distance ourselves from this crazy sideshow we call American Politics nowadays."

Gordon Herr, SHDems

"My concerns are always about voter turnout! I expected a much higher turnout so far than I've anecdotally heard is the case. Hopefully there will be more people voting this evening."

Sarah Hunnewell, SPC

"My impression going into today was that, given the hard work, activism and involvement of so many people I know, there would be a great turnout. Quite the opposite seems true, which is very disheartening. At my Water Mill polling place, as of 1 pm, 39 people had shown up to vote (out of an eligible 400+). Rebecca Dolber had warned of a projected turnout of only 10% and I have urged everyone I can think of to vote and encourage others to do so. I know the polls are open to 9 pm so perhaps the numbers will pick up. I am supporting Perry Gershon and hope he can win. I am perhaps most worried about a potential win by Kate Browning. I am very sick of hearing from LI politicians like Tim Bishop that she is the only one who can beat Lee Zeldin. I don't believe that and think they are backing the wrong horse and that she can't beat him."

Andrea Klausner, SHDems

"I just went to vote in the primary, and the polling place was pretty empty. I don't know what that bodes, but my sense has been that it has been hard to garner enthusiasm around the primaries. With so many running, and no clear frontrunner, the process has felt fractured to me. My hope is once we finally know who our candidate is, that we can get all progressives to mobilize around that candidate. I'm committed to working hard to defeat Lee Zeldin, no matter who our candidate is. We MUST flip the House! Also, it will be interesting to see whether more moderate or more progressive Democrats will win in our district, as well as around the country. I hope the DCCC pays attention to this in articulating its platform. The primaries will also show us around the country whether the GOP remains a legitimate and independent party or just Trump's cult."

Laura Leever, PEER

"The only thing I can say is that I'm concerned about individual citizens not taking ownership of the personal responsibility they have in regard to the success (or failure) of the electoral process and our democracy in general. Everyone is so quick to blame parties or candidates or whoever, but they don't look to see the part that they are playing. They want democracy and fair play handed to them; they don't want to have to do the work that is required."

Robin Long, SHDems

"This is not just a primary day. This is the first battle to defend our democracy. That which is being perpetrated by the Trump administration is fascism in its infancy and the franchise is the only ammunition we have to defeat them. We need a larger than usual turnout on Tuesday and an immediate unification on Wednesday. If either is lacking, it will not be our Party in jeopardy...it will be our country. This is not a push back to a "Bush" or "Reagan" Republican...this is a push back against fascism."

Steven Lupo, Let's Visit Lee Zeldin

"What "protest voting" brought us: A Supreme Court voting 5-4 to uphold the Muslim travel ban, gutting the Voting Rights Act, discrimination against gays based on supposed religious freedom; withdrawal from the Paris Climate Agreement, trade wars, white supremacist rallies, the most unethical and corrupt administration — ever, etc. To those folks on Facebook sowing the seeds of the division, on the left, do you want more of the above? Because … sometimes … it appears THAT'S exactly what you are looking for. Just sayin'."

Cindy Salwen, EEAN

"I voted at about 9 in Center Moriches and I didn't catch the number but it looked like 20 or so before me on their list. Remember this is a primary. If someone feels like all the candidates are reasonable they might not bother voting. I think the turn out will be considered an indicator of enthusiasm, but I'm not sure how clear its meaning is when there are five candidates and their positions aren't that different. Basically, I don't think it's time to worry."

Julie Sheehan, SHDems

"I got a call from another voter in my Electoral District. She was only the 7th person to vote today. So, my fear is that we will have extremely low turnout. That favors Kate Browning, the establishment candidate, and bodes ill for progressive energy in the fall. SCOTUS just ruled 5-4 in favor of the Muslim ban, thanks to the seat stolen by Mitch McConnell and handed to Gorsuch, against the will of the people. Things look grim for our democracy."

Amy Turner, PEER

"It is an incredible relief to know that the primary will be decided by the end of today. The primary period has been divisive and very uncomfortable for me. During the primary, we lost that sense of unity and common purpose that had made our efforts (despite being exhausting at times) so inspiring and actually fun. Without a collective focus, the anti-LZ activities felt, to me, like they lost a little steam. I desperately hope that we'll rally around the candidate, no matter who it is. I tried not to get too attached to any of them because I wanted to be able to "switch gears" easily if my candidate (I made my decision only two weeks ago: Perry Gershon) doesn't win. I'm hoping for a turnout that is significantly larger than 2014. We need a large turnout to demonstrate that we have the necessary momentum to defeat Zeldin and that will energize Democrats and attract large donors."

That night, Lulu sent me a link to watch the results coming in live. At 10:15 PM, with 20 districts not yet in, Perry won with more than 35% of the vote.

The final vote count, with all 100% of ballots counted, was similar to the results on election night.

Congressional District 1 – Democratic Primary 2018
Election Districts: 473
Votes Cast: 22,240 out of 143,700 (15.48%)

CANDIDATE	PARTY	VOTES	SHARE
Gershon, Perry	Democratic	7,902	35.53%
Browning, Kate M.	Democratic	6,813	30.63%
Viloria-Fisher, Vivian M.	Democratic	3,616	16.26%
Pechefsky, David	Democratic	2,565	11.53%
DiMasi, Elaine	Democratic	1,344	6.04%

Source: Suffolk County Board of Elections[30]

Perry had hinted that his polling indicated it would come down between him and Kate. Clearly spending so much on advertising was a key factor in getting his name recognition out to the district, which was the strategy Perry outlined to me back in April. Perry had a plan, he stuck with it and executed it well and he got stronger as the process went on, though I am sure many activists are going to be angry that his money gave him an advantage. And for those who wanted a woman nominee, in this year of the woman, with the vast majority of the grassroots made up of women, Perry being the nominee will be a bitter pill to swallow.

On a personal note, my heart is aching for Sharon who has invested so much into Vivian's campaign. And for Nanci, who so wanted Kate to be the nominee. At least both of their candidates had a respectable showing, Kate with over 30% and Vivian with over 16%. If David and Elaine had dropped out, I wonder where much of their support would have gone?

As to voter turnout, at about 22,000 votes, this is higher than in the 2016 primary, when it was about 12,000, but with more than 140,000 registered Democrats, that percentage seems pretty low to me.

This long primary is over. We now have a nominee.

Wednesday, June 27th
Post-primary thoughts and EEAN leadership meeting
So far, the chatter on Facebook among the different grassroots groups has been supportive of Perry. This was in contrast to just how divisive it got right before the primary. I think the overall sentiment today was whether Perry captured your heart or not, we cannot afford to be divided if we have any hope of defeating Zeldin. Kate posted a statement thanking her supporters and congratulating Perry and I saw postings from supporters of Vivian and David, but nothing yet from the other candidates themselves. A Unity Rally is planned for tomorrow in Smithtown, with all the candidates from the primary there to support Perry. It is not a coincidence that Zeldin will be hosting a fundraiser close by.

Meanwhile two progressive women in other New York districts won their Democratic primaries. Luiba Shirley beat the establishment man, Dewayne Gregory, in CD#2 and Alexandria Ocasio-Cortez beat a ten-term Democratic Congressman, Joe Crowley, in a Queens/Bronx Congressional district. She is young, progressive, and passionate.

And my analysis of who was inspiring and who wasn't and whether or not that would affect the outcome, based on visiting with supporters at the meet-and-greets, ended up being meaningless. The two candidates who seemed to be the least inspiring to their supporters, Perry and Kate, whose supporters approached choosing them in a matter of fact, dutiful calculation, were the two top vote getters. And the three who had the most inspired supporters, Vivian, David and

Elaine, lagged far behind. Clearly inspiration was not that important, nor was nominating a woman in this year of the woman.

And then, as we are trying to absorb what happened in the primary, news broke that Justice Kennedy is retiring. Now conservatives will have a solid five member majority on the Supreme Court, with no swing votes. We can say goodbye to Roe vs. Wade, to any protections for civil rights, voting rights, unions; the list is almost endless. It was almost more than I could bear.

Rebecca commented to me, before the primary, that maybe what has driven us in the Resistance to get involved is instinctual, that it was instinct that caused us to join right after Trump won and it is an instinct that keeps us involved. "We knew we had to act, such a gut-pull, such immediacy to it and zero hesitancy. I think maybe many of us can't put our fingers on it because it was partly primal."

I think there is a lot of truth to that. I never hesitated after the 2016 election to jump in and get involved. But as the blows keep coming, one after another, how long can we keep going, how far can our instinct carry us? As the country lurches further and further hard right, as the policies - like family separation for migrants at the border - become ever crueler, as the Trump agenda evolves into being worse than I could ever have imagined in November 2016, the question of just how much we in the Resistance can bear is now always on my mind.

Tonight, the EEAN leadership met at Syma's house but the Kennedy announcement permeated the mood of the group with a sense of despair and we were collectively unable to make decisions about what, as a group, we want our mission to be from now until the general election. In the primary phase, our focus was on voter education. Now, we assume we will all work for the candidate but in what way, we cannot decide. The burden felt too heavy tonight to make plans.

Instead we talked about the primary. Sharon and Patty were active volunteers for Vivian. Rebecca voted for Kate, as did Cindy and Wendy. Syma went with Perry. We all agree that we will come together and rally behind Perry - most of us have nothing against him personally - but as Sharon said, she is not yet ready to talk about Perry. It is going to take some time to process the loss. She told us about the speech that Vivian gave at her headquarters last night once the results were in and how classy it was. She thanked her supporters and pledged her help to Perry.

I cannot shake off how despondent I am about the direction of the country. And that leaves me unsure if I have it in me to go forward with the book project, the grassroots and the Democratic Committee. I am not sure, as of this moment, that

I see the point in it. Trump and all the ugliness that he stands for are succeeding. Maybe I do not have what it takes to stick with this.

In the meantime, Zeldin's campaign issued their first statement about Perry and the focus is on their "Park Avenue Perry" moniker they have given him. The primary is over. The cordiality between our candidates ends and the nastiness of the Zeldin/Trump treatment begins.

Thursday, June 28th
Unity Rally
"Flip the House!"

That was the chant that rang out from the crowd at the Unity Rally. In front of Smithtown Town Hall, with all of the candidates in attendance, a very large crowd of excited Democrats, with posters and flags, chanted over and over again, that our goal is to "flip the house." Rich Schaeffer, Democratic County Chairman, introduced Vivian, Kate, Elaine and David, congratulated them on their races, and then introduced the winner of the CD#1 primary, Perry. There were smiles and hugs all around, though I am sure it was not easy, so soon after their losses, for the four who are not the nominee to project so much cheer. But they did. There is one goal on everyone's minds, to project unity now that the primary is over.

Perry stood next to Liuba Gretchen Shirley, who won her primary in CD#2, our neighboring congressional district, beating the establishment candidate who had been endorsed by Rich. I am sure that felt awkward for both of them but they didn't show it. She will now oppose the long-serving GOP Congressman Peter King. She and Perry stood side by side, with raised arms together, to the cheers of the crowd. This location was chosen for the Unity Rally because down the street, Zeldin was having a kick-off event for his campaign, with Sean Spicer and Sebastian Gorka as the guest speakers. Later that night, I saw the video online of his speech. Just like his mailings on MS13, he is going with a hard-right fear campaign.

I drove to the event with Syma, Wendy and her husband Art, who did the driving. We got there early and we waited in the car as a sudden violent thunderstorm swept through. But as it got closer to 6:00 PM, the rain stopped, the sky lightened, and the sun came out. We looked at each other and wondered if this was a sign.

We saw so many people we know at the event, including Julie and Eileen. Gordon stood by the candidates, as did Dave Calone, who lost the 2016 primary.

Vivian, Kate, Elaine and David smiled, joined hands and chanted "flip the house" along with the crowd. The message was clear - that this had not been a divisive primary like in 2016 and that Democrats were going to be united going forward. There was too much at stake to retreat into our corners, especially coming this week, on the heels of the terrible Supreme Court decisions on the Muslim Ban, pregnancy clinics, union dues as well as the announcement of Justice Kennedy's retirement.

Several Zeldin hecklers stood on the sidewalk - it was hard for me to see just how many - and at first, they were yelling while Rich was speaking. But then three policemen appeared and put themselves between the protesters and our crowd. This essentially stopped them from yelling at us. It also made sure there would not be any contact between our rally and them. I was very grateful to the police for doing this. I wanted to thank them after the rally, but when it ended I looked for them but they were gone.

I was able to speak to each of the candidates, give each a hug, congratulate them on their races and ask if they are doing okay. They all smiled and said they were fine. A couple of months ago, I thought I would be feeling very sad about the primary ending, knowing that four people I had come to know and admire would be feeling disappointed. But instead I am so relieved that the primary is behind us and we now have a nominee. I didn't vote for Perry but he has my total support. And I was hearing these sentiments from everyone. Even on the Facebook pages that just a few days ago were becoming more and more divisive as different people defended their chosen candidates. I think if the race had gone on much longer, it would have been very hard to pull the party back together.

But this sense of unity is a testament to the candidates who all ran clean races as well as their abilities to put aside their own, individual disappointments and stand there in the sunshine together and support Perry. I am sure there are supporters from their campaigns that are finding it hard. Sharon didn't come with us; she said she wasn't yet ready to talk about Perry, though she also said it was without question that she will vote for him. And I am sure that for many of the supporters I spoke to, particularly from David's campaign, who resented that Perry had the advantage due to money, are not yet ready to publicly back Perry. But with the candidates working hard to show unity, it will be harder for supporters to splinter off, like what happened in the Anna/Dave split in our district and the Bernie/Hillary split nationwide.

Instantly, with the primary over, all the press attention that we could not get for the candidates before the primary was evident now that we have a nominee. News 12 Long Island posted a great video about the Unity Rally. At 58 seconds into the tape, it was great to see Wendy, Cindy and Syma. EEAN was well represented! If you look closely, I am tucked behind Syma.[31]

After the speeches, I spoke with Perry. We hugged, I congratulated him on the win, jokingly told him that now I really needed a follow-up interview for the book, which he agreed to. And we repeated what we had said to each other at the Jamesport Brewery. That he has to win, so much depends on it.

Some excerpts from his speech at the rally:

> *"Lee Zeldin, we are going to beat you in November! The five of us ran a great race, plus Brendon Henry, who is not here. We had candidate forums and we got to know each other and respect each other. And I am so grateful that they and their supporters are here and we are all united together. This is a day for all Democrats to send the message to Lee Zeldin that we are going to defeat you. We are done with you being our congressman. We don't want Steve Bannon in our district. We don't want Sebastian Gorka in this district. And we surely don't want the president and his vile rhetoric in this district. We are going to flip the house."*

> *"This campaign is going to be about issues, like healthcare, protecting the environment, gun safety and bringing back good paying manufacturing union jobs to Suffolk County. We don't want the Trump tax cuts, we don't want the caps on our property tax. We are going to send a message to Zeldin and Trump that we, the Democrats, are going to take back the House and put a check on the Trump presidency."*

I came home from the event tired but heartened. Certainly, in less despair than the day before. Standing there together, chanting, cheering, with the sunshine warming us, it lifted my spirits in a way I handed felt for days. At that moment, my biggest fears - that the fractures in the party might prevent coming together after the primary, that the grassroots and the Democratic Party would not work together, that we might end up with a nominee far to the left of the district - seemed behind us. And after a week that felt like the Trump agenda is winning, at least standing there, shoulder to shoulder with all the candidates, all their supporters, with people from both the party and grassroots, with a nominee with progressive beliefs but a solid business background, I got to end the primary phase with some hope going forward. It was now onto Zeldin and the general election.

Saturday, June 30th
Families Belong Together

A rally at an East Quogue park to protest the Trump family separation policy marked the end of the month. It was organized by a number of grassroots groups and we were asked to all wear white in solidarity. It was a brutally hot day, so I was grateful to be wearing white. I got to the rally with Mike and his daughter, who was visiting. There we met up with Sharon, Syma, Cindy and Wendy. Sharon is not quite ready to talk about the primary but she brings her usual smile and optimism to the event as well as her poster that looks like a picture frame. Many protesters at the rally asked to have their pictures taken with her poster. We took pictures of fellow EEAN member Kim O'Reilly and her son, Miles, first with their hand-written posters and then with Sharon's picture frame poster.

It was a large crowd. Perry spoke to the crowd about the Trump agenda, which Zeldin supports. He got a very enthusiastic reception. There were several speakers, including a woman who was undocumented, who came to the U.S. because her husband tried to kill her. Several immigrant organizations were involved, such as Sepa Mujer.

Julie and Eileen helped to organize the rally and both of them spoke. Julie waved a giant American flag and led us all in singing America the Beautiful. I was surprised when the singing of this song brought me to tears. Then we marched and while near the road, people honked and waved and cheered us on. At a time when our country is espousing bigotry and harming children, solidarity at moments like this makes it bearable.

Keep
Families
Together
Families
Belong
Together
#Remember
the
Children

Chapter 16

July 2018

"There's a huge difference between the Republican and the Democratic philosophy. The Republican philosophy says, 'if we want to do this, this and this, we have to have some income. And if we don't have the income we can't do it,' and that's exactly what Trump is aiming for. He's one of the few people who really recognize that. Now the Democrats on the other hand, pay no attention whatsoever to the income, except to say we want to spend X number of dollars, and we want to tax the rich to get it. The Democrats are acting like a bunch of petulant children. He won't give me this. So, I'm going to holler at you. Now I don't blame Zeldin for not speaking with you, because all you want to do is holler at him. You don't want to listen."

Lloyd Gerard, Trump supporter

Monday, July 1st
SPC meeting
The two rallies last week – the Unity Rally last Thursday in Smithtown and the Families Belong Together Rally on Saturday in Quogue - gave me a sense of optimism that we would go forward united against Zeldin. I carried this feeling into our first SPC meeting since the primary. We met in Robin's conference room in Southampton, squeezed around the table because we had the largest turnout we have had in months. But from the beginning, discord and division dominated the meeting.

The meeting opened with a suggestion from some supporters of candidates who didn't win the primary that we discuss "what went wrong on Tuesday" and "why the progressive candidate didn't win." Some even questioned if we were really a "progressive" organization and if we had the right to keep the word progressive in our name. I was taken aback by their anger and confused given that all five of the candidates had the same platforms. If their frustration had emanated from the impact that Perry's money had on the primary race, I would have understood that. But their argument was that Perry was not progressive enough to represent us. Those members who had actively campaigned for Perry did not look happy.

During this conversation, there were verbal shots thrown at Robin because she was pushing back on a suggestion that we should work to oust certain leaders of the Democratic Party, to root them out for not being progressive enough.

Robin and Andi worked at calming things down. We then discussed what our next mission should be. It was suggested that we could host a series of community forums to educate the public on specific issues such as healthcare. But I left the meeting distressed, so much so that I thought about dropping off of this committee, even though I was one of the founders. When I got home, I reached out to Rebecca, Sharon and Syma to vent my frustration. Syma called me that night and I got emails from Rebecca and Sharon. We shared similar feelings.

A few days later, Robin sent out an email to the group.

> *I have spent many hours thinking about my following decision and I hope you all will receive it with the same level of consideration.*
>
> *I am reversing my own participation in the health care forum for the following reasons and with the following suggestions:*
>
> 1. *I believe that the defeat of Trump through his proxy Zeldin is the priority. Nothing should take energy away from that endeavor and the election of other Democrats. Educating and energizing the electorate can be accomplished through the campaigns.*
>
> 2. *I would suggest cooperating with the campaigns that match our personal convictions...be it Perry or Luiba or any other local or state race.*
>
> 3. *I would further suggest that we set up a series of educational symposiums including topics such as health care and taxation for after the elections. The work we need to do will not end with a single win. Trump has already undermined so many of our nation's structures and the fight for the soul of our nation will be longer than one election. But unfortunately, I need to fight one election at a time.*
>
> *I speak only for myself and of course, will continue to assist.*
>
> *Robin*

When I interviewed Robin shortly after this, she told me what had motivated her to send that email.

"I don't have the time to go back and fix what the Democratic Party did before because we're on the verge right now with the whole crux of our country, our checks and balances, about to be gone. We're losing the freedom of the press. The veracity and trustworthiness of the press is being lost. Not because the press is not truthful. It's because people are buying the bullshit that's coming from Trump."

Her email gave many of us cover to withdraw from the forum idea and go connect with Perry's campaign. That night I registered with Perry's campaign online and received a phone call from one of his volunteers. I am scheduled to knock on doors on Sunday, July 22nd in Southampton.

Wednesday, July 4th
Independence Day Fundraiser for Perry
Eileen, from LVLZ, organized a one-day online fundraiser for Perry. I thought it was a brilliant idea. We shared it with all the grassroots groups in the district so they could also post it on their Facebook pages.

The online message from LVLZ is included here.

> *We the People for Perry*
>
> *This July Fourth, be a part of the largest online fundraiser EVER!*
>
> *On Independence Day grassroots groups, Democratic committee members and engaged citizens pledge to raise a cool half million dollars IN ONE DAY to support Perry Gershon, OUR Democratic candidate for New York's 1st Congressional District.*
>
> *Give what you can to be a part of the world's largest online political fundraising event. If 5,000 people give an average of $100 each WE WILL DO THIS.*

By the end of the day, Perry posted this statement on his Facebook page.

> *Thank you to the more than 400 people who took action and contributed today. This campaign is going to be won with grassroots energy, and everyone at LVLZ and others contributing online are showing how wide and deep our support is. We are just under $50,000*

> *raised for the day, and with another five hours, let's keep it up to show that NY-01 is united for a change in Washington! Your support is what will power this campaign and it is what will take us to victory. Thank You!*

Not quite the half million dollars Eileen had hoped for, but still an amazing return on the investment, which was just posting it on Facebook across the different groups. Here is where the thousands of Facebook activists can come into play. It was exciting.

As our general election campaign heats up, women, just like us, are beginning to get more notice from the press. I love the headline on an opinion piece by Jill Filipovic on the CNN website on July 3rd: "Trump's worst enemy: Middle-aged moms."[32]

Monday, July 9th
The Supreme Court

Over the weekend I was off the Resistance grid while I took a trip to visit Matt in Pittsburgh where he is attending graduate school. On the Amtrak train ride back to New York City, I was seated next to a woman my age. We got to talking and she told me about her efforts to create a Democratic Club after Trump's election. Her name is Ilse Buzzanca. I took her card and after I got home, I emailed her to get more information on what these Democrats were doing in red-state Florida.

"In Polk County, our Democratic Executive Committee has been in disarray for years. The leadership was incompetent and ineffective (and sometimes, crooked). The first meeting that I attended (shortly after the election) had only about 6 attendees. During our attempt to get a handle on the Democrats in Polk County in 2017, many changes occurred. First and foremost, an incredible couple surfaced, Richard Sutherland and his wife Dr. Katherine Sutherland. Before retirement, Rich was an attorney and Kathie an OBGYN, both from California. Among other university degrees, both are graduates of Harvard. Rich decided to start a Democrat Club in their development at Lake Ashton, sent out a notice, and 100 people showed up! Lake Ashton is decidedly RepubliCON and they were amazed at the turnout. Kathie became President of the DEC and has turned that group around. Not only has she recruited Precinct chairs (125 for 167 precincts), rented a 2,000 square foot office space manned by volunteers, organized precinct training sessions, walkathons. postcard writing sessions, phone call groups, socials, rallies, visits to elected officials, Democratic gala events etc. and more importantly, she is raising money for a previously bankrupt DEC . Both Kathie and Rich have contributed their time (60+ hours per week), talent and treasure! In this respect, Democrats have not only prospered, but leaders have emerged and the attendance at the DEC has surged to 75-100 people per meeting....mostly precinct chairs and hard-core volunteers. . Smart and FOCUSED LEADERSHIP IS THE KEY!"

How inspiring to hear that even deep into Trump country, there are activists working hard against the Trump agenda.

I got home late on Monday evening and discovered that Trump announced his nominee for the Supreme Court, Brett Kavanaugh, a former author of the Starr Report in the Clinton impeachment. He also worked in the Bush White House. Appointed to the federal appeals court, he is solidly right-wing and in fact had just ruled on a case against a young migrant woman requesting an abortion. I had no doubt that he will work to overturn Roe and probably a whole litany of rights. He also wrote a Law Review article in 2009 about how presidents should not be burdened by court cases while in office. Very likely this is the main reason Trump chose him.

The fight is now enjoined. It is so disheartening because we don't have the votes to stop it. The court will then have a permanent right-wing tilt for at least 20 years, probably more given the ages of Ginsberg and Breyer. And now the election becomes about abortion, something I had hoped to avoid. When we fight in the culture wars, despite every poll showing the majority of Americans support a woman's right to choose, we lose. Right now the country is under the tyranny of minority rule. I went to bed saddened, tired and angry at every Democrat who sat out the 2016 election or who voted for a third party because they didn't like Hillary Clinton.

Tuesday, July 10th
Outreach meeting and SHDems meeting

Julie Sheehan hosted an outreach meeting at her house for me, Laura Leever and Mike. She served a lovely gluten and dairy free lunch that perfectly accommodated my allergies and we came up with a plan to host "potluck" ED events, social events where Democrats could meet fellow Democrats in their ED. We finalized the parameters for the plan so that Julie can present it at the SHDems meeting tonight.

At the meeting I sat at a table with Andi. It was good to catch up. We hadn't seen each other since her move further east to Sag Harbor. One grandchild is due in a few weeks and a second at the end of the year.

During the dinner portion, Perry spoke and received hearty applause. He was there with his wife and one of his sons as well as his finance chairman. That was a high point of the evening. It devolved after that.

What should have been a pro forma discussion about the updated platform document became a contentious argument about why this policy document did not contain stronger language about what Democrats stand for. I was surprised by the angry tone and it was reminiscent of the last SPC meeting. I felt bad for the chair of the platform committee, who was presenting the update on the document – which had been on the website for months for people to comment on or add changes – and instead had to field a confrontation from a small handful of members.

People tried to explain that this was a policy document that was a help for the elected board members on legislation going forward, which is why it contained specific and concrete statements. This same small group argued that it needed to be a mission statement espousing what the Democratic Party stands for. I raised my hand and said that a strong mission statement and a policy-oriented platform are not mutually exclusive and that we could have both by adding a mission statement to the document we have. Robin agreed that a strong mission statement was a good idea, that it would reflect the change in the country now since the original policy document was written in 2014. There was no reason to not have both. Anyone who wanted to help in writing this mission statement was asked to join the platform committee.

That seemed to be the end of it. But I was still confused. I did not understand what this small group was so angry about. After the meeting, Robin, Andi and I spoke briefly before I had to leave with Mike and Katey. I told Andi I was surprised at the level of vitriol and asked what that was about. Andi explained that it is all about a problem with transparency and recounted to me the difficulties she had experienced two years ago with the committee, in particular how hard it was to find out information about the subcommittees we well as her feeling that she wasn't heard. But, I answered, what does that have to do with now? Hadn't we conducted the Politics 101, formed the SPC, wasn't the committee filled with new and active people? I told her I still did not understand. Andi agreed that much had changed. Given that, I said, this level of vitriol was mystifying.

In the car ride home, I had a lot of questions for Mike and Katey about the angry tenor of the meeting. What was that about? They filled me in on a movement behind the scenes by David Dubow to challenge Gordon for the chairmanship. That there is a faction on the committee that believes Gordon is not effective as chairman and has not run the committee with enough transparency and in a democratic fashion. Mike explained that David wanted to challenge Gordon two years ago and didn't but that he feels this is the year. I asked Mike if he agreed with those criticisms. He told me that Gordon would be the first to admit that there had been a learning curve for him as chair, and that he had overseen the period of a lot of growing pains for the committee, but he adamantly disagreed with the contentions from this faction. He said he works with David on the executive committee and usually supports reforms he is recommending but does not agree with this movement to oust Gordon.

After I got home, I thought a great deal about all this divisiveness, about what I witnessed at the SPC meeting and now at the SHDems. It reminded me of the Democratic divisions in 2016 that paved the way for Trump. I didn't like it and didn't want to be around it.

But by the time I went to bed, I realized that these divisions are an important part of the story of our mission in 2018 and that if I am going to write an honest book about this year, I could not ignore it.

The next day, I emailed both Gordon and David requesting interviews with them so that I could better understand the issues. With Gordon, it required little in the way of introduction. But I really don't know David and he doesn't know me. This is the email I sent to him:

> *Hi David,*
>
> *As you may know, along with being a member of the grassroots and the Southampton Democratic Committee, I am a journalist. After my experience last year working on the local election, I got the idea of writing a memoir of the twelve months in between that election and the midterm election this fall to chronicle, in real time, all of the efforts by both the grassroots and the Democratic Committee to unseat Zeldin. In many ways everything we are doing is a microcosm of what is happening around the country. I have been honored to interview all of our candidates, their supporters, our nominee, many members of both the grassroots and the Democratic Committee. I continue, each day, to report on our efforts to unseat Zeldin and to try to flip the House and place a check on Trump.*
>
> *It is not easy to wear three different hats - EEAN member, SHDems member and reporter - particularly when I have my own opinions on an issue. It is clear to anyone with eyes that there is a rift in the Committee.*

That was clear at the last Southampton Progressive Caucus (SPC) meeting as well as last night. While I am not unbiased on this issue - I came to the Committee at the invitation of Gordon, helped to form the SPC thanks to Robin and have been lucky to have Mike Anthony as my mentor - as a reporter, I would be remiss if I did not listen to all opinions. Given that, I would like to know if we could sit down for an interview. It could be in person or over the phone, whichever is most convenient for you. Let me know when might be a good day and time for you. I am free this Friday afternoon, at about 4:00, if that might work for you.

I have attached my resume and if you have any questions about my background or the book project, please don't hesitate to ask. I should also add that everything in the book is embargoed until after the election.

Many thanks,
Barbara

This is the email I got in response.

Hi Barbara

I would be happy to talk with you – either in person or over the phone. I am in the city today and tomorrow – on the Jitney at the moment, in fact – but will be back on the East End from Thursday night. I would be delighted to have you come to our home in Hampton Bays to talk over coffee, or do it by phone if that is easier. I always prefer face to face if times and schedules allow.

Both interviews are scheduled, Gordon's will be over the phone, and David's in person.

Wednesday, July 11th
EEAN Summer Party

Instead of our usual huddle this month, we have an EEAN summer party, hosted by Wendy and Art at their house, with Perry as the honored guest. We got a great turnout, with more people than we have seen for months. Perry spoke and answered questions and I was struck by his sincerity when he told the crowd that during the primary, while he hoped he would be the winner, he could take solace from the fact that if he lost, then one of the other good Democrats would step up and oppose Zeldin. But it is all on his shoulders because if he loses, then that means Zeldin is still our Congressman. He pledged to work as hard as he could to make sure we Flip the First and help Democrats take back the House. He said the road to taking back the House runs right through CD#1. We got a picture of Perry with the whole group and also one with Sophie McHeffey and Kim O'Reilly's babies, Rex and Paige, in their EEAN outfits.

Thursday, July 12th
Interview with Lloyd Gerard

The next day, I woke up early and prepared my questions for my interview with Lloyd, Syma's husband. Knowing that Lloyd is a Trump supporter, I asked Syma to reach out to him to see if he would sit for an interview with me. I thought it would be interesting for the reader to hear his point of view. He said he would be happy to speak with me and we scheduled it for today.

Yesterday, as we drove together to the summer party, I mentioned to her my concern if Lloyd should say something that might embarrass her. She said there is nothing he could say that she and their friends don't already know. She described her ongoing conflict, that Lloyd is very good to her and cares about her welfare, but his support of Trump and his policies are painful to her. Mostly they try to not talk about it. He watches *Fox News* in one room, while she stays in another.

I drove to Lloyd's store which is on Main Street in Eastport and is called Lloyd's, an antique furniture store. The store takes up the whole building, which is large. I parked in the parking lot to the side of the building. I walked in the front door, which is on Main Street, and met someone working for Lloyd in the front of the store. When I told him that I was there for the interview, he asked if Lloyd is interviewing me for a job and I say, no, I am interviewing him for a book. He then directed me to the back of the store, to a warehouse section. I walked into this very large, cavernous space that was filled with furniture and other antique items. I found Lloyd sitting by his desk. We greeted each other and then moved to two chairs across from each other and I placed my phone on a large vase next to his chair to record our interview. Luckily, the opening of the vase was small enough that the phone did not fall through.

Unlike other transcripts I have included in the book, this one required more of the back and forth between us to be able to understand Lloyd's answers. To make that easier, the interview is organized into eight sections.

Below is the lightly edited and condensed transcript from our conversation.

TRUMP

Lloyd: He is doing things that I've championed forever.

Barbara: Like what kinds of things?

Lloyd: Like the Chinese, what's going on with the Chinese and how they've been beating us up for years. It's about time somebody said, "Hey, you can't do that." NATO is something else. We pay for almost the entire bit of NATO. And the people who we're supposed to defend don't do it themselves, and they hate us for it. Now, why should we defend and support them at all? Cause we give them money, and they hate you.

Barbara: The leaders of NATO?

Lloyd: I don't see any country in the world that is on our side, except for possibly Israel. I don't think they have any choice because without us they're dead.... Look at the national debt. Look at what happens. You want to know one difference? Mr. Obama doubled the national debt the first year he was in office, from seven to 14 trillion dollars.

Barbara: But that was because of the economic collapse.

Lloyd: What collapse? They're just cycles... It just went up a trillion dollars so Trump had no choice.

Barbara: I don't understand ...You're talking about the tax cut? But isn't that what is now exploding the debt?

Lloyd: No, I'm not talking about the tax cut, I'm talking about the amount of money that he had to borrow from the treasury, borrow from the country just to keep the country going, because it has to finance our national debt. We have no choice at this point.

TRUMP FAMILY SEPARATION POLICY

Barbara: I think people are upset about the family separation policy.

Lloyd: Who started that? Who initiated that law?

Barbara: That came from Trump.

Lloyd: No, it didn't, it was the law, and he's only been president for a year. He did not enact that law, Obama did. Wait a minute now, wait a minute. You don't know what you're talking about. And I do okay? Trump reversed it.

Barbara: That's not true.

Lloyd: It is true. It is true. Well, first of all, if you don't like the way you're being treated in this country don't come here. Okay, that's a very simple process; if you don't like my apples don't shake my tree. And that's exactly what these people are doing. Now I'm not in favor of separating children from their parents, and neither was Trump because he reversed that by presidential order. You don't know that. And the original one came from Obama's law.

Barbara: They didn't separate the children from their parents.

Lloyd: The law said that if you come to this country illegally, and that's all they are. I mean do you want to open the border and let everyone in? I say fine, but they got to come in legally and who believes that? The Democrats don't believe that. They say just open the border and let them in.

Barbara: Well I am a Democrat and I don't say that... I'm not aware that the Democratic philosophy is just opening the borders. Obama was very tough on border security but he did not have a family separation policy. Children were kept with the parents.

Lloyd: When the parents came to this country illegally they were put in jail. You don't put the kids in jail.

Barbara: They weren't put in jail... They weren't criminalized. It was a misdemeanor. So, when they came to the country, the parents and children were kept together.

Lloyd: Boy, are you brainwashed.

Barbara: I can show you the data on that. That is actually a fact.

Lloyd: Did Trump recently reverse that?

Barbara: Yes, the zero-tolerance policy was new. That was his policy last fall, which reversed what George W. Bush and Obama had done.

Lloyd: His policy last fall was to follow the law and he did not enact that law.

Barbara: I can send you the information for it.

Lloyd: Let me say this to you as far as the liberals are concerned. And I assume you're a liberal. Liberals are liberal until they find somebody who doesn't agree with them, then in that case, if they don't agree, then liberals say they can't think the way they want, and they can't talk the way they want.

Barbara: Well, can I ask you this?

Lloyd: You can ask me anything you like.

Barbara: The immigration policy that Obama had was the same as George W Bush. George W Bush has come out and said the family separation policy was not their policy. That it was new under Trump. So, I'm just telling you the facts.

Lloyd: Well Trump did not say separate the kids from the parents. It was the law of the land, which he did not enact. What he did was he said, "We don't separate children from their parents."

A WOMAN'S RIGHT TO CHOOSE

Lloyd: I am all about freedom, freedom of choice. I don't necessarily believe in abortion, but I'm in favor of freedom of choice.

Barbara: That's interesting to me. There are not many pro-choice Republicans.

Lloyd: I'm not pro-choice, but I believe in a woman's right to choose. It's about freedom of choice.

Barbara: You believe in freedom of choice?

Lloyd: I do.

Barbara: Okay.

Lloyd: I believe in freedom period.

Barbara: What about Planned Parenthood?

Lloyd: Planned Parenthood. Okay, what do you want to believe? Which side of Planned Parenthood are you willing to listen to? The part that says we do women a lot of good, or the part that says we take these unborn children, and sell off their parts? Which of those do you want to listen to? It shouldn't be supported by the taxpayers.

Barbara: Planned Parenthood isn't supported by the tax payer.

Lloyd: Sure it is.

Barbara: How is it supported by the tax payers?

Lloyd: If I'm a taxpayer and I donate to them, it's being supported by them.

TRUMP'S VERACITY

Barbara: Many Republicans have taken issue with the tweeting.

Lloyd: That's nonsense. Why shouldn't he tweet? Any American is free to tweet. He's an American, he can tweet if he wants to. He's not supposed to tweet? He's supposed to do something that is "more presidential than tweeting"?

Barbara: The tweeting doesn't bother you?

Lloyd: No, not one little bit.

Barbara: Even though sometimes the tone of it is very disparaging?

Lloyd: It's freedom of choice.

Barbara: Okay.

Lloyd: And he can disparage anybody he likes, but he doesn't do it first. He doesn't pick on them first, they pick on him and he's supposed to sit there and take it? I don't think so. He's like Harry Truman when somebody picked on his daughter, said she had a lousy voice ... he called him a son of a bitch, in public and he wrote him a letter and his main claim to fame was the letter that he wrote. He actually bought the postage stamp.

Barbara: What about the times when he is not truthful? Does that bother you at all?

Lloyd: Not one little bit. Because you're telling me that he's not truthful. Now, you tell me what he has ever said that is not truthful. It's a matter of, he's a great negotiator. The law will allow a salesman for instance to say almost anything you want when you're selling something to someone, did you know that?

Barbara: I didn't know that.

Lloyd: There's a special part of the law that gives salesman a right to do that.

Barbara: There are people who have compiled lists of the number of untruths. Some of them are basic facts that are wrong. None of that bothers you?

Lloyd: None at all. Nobody's perfect including Trump. And Hillary, you want to compare Trump to Hillary. Is that what you want to do?

Barbara: That's irrelevant right now, the questions are about Trump. He is president.

Lloyd: Of course, it's irrelevant. Because you're a liberal and liberals are very upset she didn't get elected.

Barbara: I was upset she didn't get elected.

Lloyd: Of course you are.

Barbara: But I will tell you honestly, if she had been beaten by a McCain or Romney, a traditional Republican. I would not have become an activist. It was not that she lost, it is that Trump won.

Lloyd: Reporters claim to be independent, but you know, you pick up any newspaper. They're always beating up Trump, beating him up for one thing or another. We were in Austin a couple of winters ago, when we went to the Lyndon Johnson museum, and I really had to laugh when I walked through the door and saw one of his quotes on the wall, which said, "If I walked across the Potomac River, the press would say Johnson can't swim."

Barbara: Good line.

Lloyd: I mean, okay, that's the same thing here. The press, to sell newspapers or whatever you want to say, they make a big thing of whatever Trump does. He's a perennial sales person, and you have to understand that, you have to understand where he's coming from. He's always selling something. It's not the usual "presidential approach".

Barbara: No, but a lot of it just isn't true.

Lloyd: For instance.

Barbara: He had a number of bankruptcies because he made very bad business decisions.

Lloyd: Nobody's perfect. I don't blame him for that. I don't fault him at all.

Barbara: But then be truthful about it.

Lloyd: Because not everything worked. Everything in our lives work?

Barbara: No, but then be truthful about it. Donald Trump was never a great businessman. Donald Trump ran companies into bankruptcy, ended up so deep in debt that no one would loan him money except the Russians.

Lloyd: You know that for a fact?

Barbara: Those actually are facts Lloyd… You can see the documents of the bankruptcies.

Lloyd: I know that there have been bankruptcies, but Harry Truman went bankrupt.

Barbara: These are multiple bankruptcies where people got stiffed for money he owed them.

Lloyd: If you go bankrupt your creditors lose.

Barbara: Well, he used bankruptcy often as a way to get out of debts.

Lloyd: Is that good business, bad business or being a crook? You tell me.

Barbara: All I know is that people stopped doing business with him in New York.

Lloyd: How did he make his billions of dollars then?

Barbara: Well I don't think he has billions, but he started out pretty wealthy to begin with.

Lloyd: I think his father gave him seven million dollars.

Barbara: A lot of people in New York would no longer do business with him, they wouldn't lend him money. They wouldn't do alliances with him. They wouldn't go into partnerships with him because he ran businesses into the ground and that happened over and over again. So much of what people know about him is from The Apprentice, which was not his business.

Lloyd: It was a success.

Barbara: It was NBC's business.

Lloyd: He ran it though.

Barbara: No, he didn't run it.

Lloyd: What part did he play in it?

Barbara: He played a part in it, but he didn't run that show, the producer did. So, here's my question. It's questionable whether he is as successful as he says he is, and that is borne out by documents, does it bother you then if he portrays himself ...

Lloyd: I know what I see.

Barbara: In terms of his business?

Lloyd: I know what I see, what he's doing with this country now, and I like it. And so should you because you would not have the things that you will continue to have if somebody else was running the country, he's making the money to fund what you want to do.

Barbara: So, you don't think they have any legitimate right to be upset?

Lloyd: They have a legitimate right to do anything they want. It's a free country. However, the way they're acting is not doing them any good. Don't you understand that? The more they beat up Trump, the more Trump supporters will support him. If you want to get somebody elected, for instance Perry Gershon, he's got a good chance against Lee Zeldin because he's got a Republican silhouette. He looks like a Republican to me.

MUELLER INVESTIGATION

Barbara: Let me ask you a little bit about the Russia investigation. What's your feeling about it? What's your feeling about Mueller?

Lloyd: I think Mueller has overstayed his welcome. I think if he hasn't discovered anything by now, he should just write his final report and say just that. And what he's doing now with Trump's lawyer and with ...

Barbara: With Michael Cohen? Well that's actually in the southern district of New York that case.

Lloyd: Whatever. Which is ran probably by Democrats. It's obvious with this ... They indicted an aide of Trump, they said they put him in solitary confinement.

Barbara: Manafort.

Lloyd: Why did they do that?

Barbara: That I can't tell you.

Lloyd: Well the theory is, that they're trying to break his spirit, so he will agree with the powers that want to give Trump a hard time. What I really believe is, suppose there was some connection between Trump and Russia, so what? The Russians are part of the world, an important part of the world.

Barbara: I actually would consider it treason. You would not?

Lloyd: No, I wouldn't.

Barbara: If we discover that a foreign power colluded with a candidate to win an election to be able to then make money by having sanctions lifted ...

Lloyd: That's a huge effort ...

Barbara: I'm just asking you, if ...

Lloyd: You can't even answer that question because it's not a possibility.

Barbara: Why is it not a possibility? If it turns out that that Mueller can prove …

Lloyd: He can't, it's been two years.

Barbara: I'm just saying, if it turns out that he can prove, through documentary evidence through a trail of ...

Lloyd: I won't even answer the question because it's not a possibility.

Barbara: Why in your mind is it not a possibility?

Lloyd: Because if it was a possibility it would have come out by now.

Barbara: Let me ask you another question, because back in the 80s and 90s, Trump was accused and there was some evidence that he was involved in money laundering. There was a quid pro quo. No one else would lend him money, his entire empire was ...

Lloyd: That not a question that I'm willing to answer because it's a big if, and it'll never happen.

WHITE NATIONALISM AND CHARLOTTESVILLE

Barbara: Any concerns about the rise in hate crimes and anti-Semitism, like what happened in Charlottesville, that has come along with Trump?

Lloyd: You're now accusing him of bigotry, are you?

Barbara: Well, I lived in Manhattan 25 years and Trump was there, and there were a lot of statements.

Lloyd: There is no more anti-Semitism or bigotry here than when I was growing up.

Barbara: Okay.

Lloyd: It hasn't disappeared.

Barbara: No.

Lloyd: It has just become a little bit more difficult to find, a little bit more cloak-and-dagger if you will. I know, I've been through many situations where I was the only Jew around, like I was on the bank board for 30 years, and it was hard to find another Jew anywhere. And I really didn't care, as long as you don't start calling me names and its meaningless because I am what I am, and if you don't like it, that's tough. And certainly, Eastport was a seed of anti-everything. The Klan ...

Barbara: Really? The Klan?

Lloyd: Yes, the Klan had parades right down the street into the church, and they all claimed they didn't do it, but I have the Klan records for Eastport and I can tell you, both chapter and verse, who was and who wasn't.

Barbara: People that you knew were in the Klan?

Lloyd: Of course.

Barbara: And did they know you were Jewish.

Lloyd: Of course.

Barbara: So how did they reconcile those two things?

Lloyd: I'll tell you what my grandfather used to say. They never bothered him because he was the only one, the only Merchant who would sell them their sheets on credit.

Barbara: Oh my God.

Lloyd: My father used to tell me about the big Klan rallies up behind the school, the big cross burnings and all that stuff. The Klan became merchants, mechanics, Masons and they became a lot of other organizations, and people will deny it, but I have the records which I got from an old house right up here in Eastport. From a guy who was in charge and I got photographs of the Klan parades, right down the main street here.

Barbara: Wow.

Lloyd: With wagons, and the guys with their hoods and the kids dressed in Klan costumes.

Barbara: What year would that have been?

Lloyd: Probably in the 1930s, late 20s, early 30s. And letters that they wrote to school districts telling them to fire all the Jews and Catholics, and if they happened to have a colored teacher, they were liable to lynch them.

Barbara: That was right here at Eastport?

Lloyd: The Klan was big and also in Hampton Bays.

Barbara: So, from your point of view, whatever is going on now is nothing compared to the Klan having a parade right down Main Street?

Lloyd: I don't believe Trump has anything to do with any increase, decrease or leveling off, of racial bias, anti-Semitism or anything like that. I think that's the farthest thing from his mind because it wouldn't help him.

THE ECONOMY

Barbara: What would you say for you are the biggest issues, that are the most important to you, that he take care of in his first term?

Lloyd: He has got to keep the economy healthy.

Barbara: Okay.

Lloyd: If you keep the economy healthy, everything else will take care of itself. That's the big difference between the Democrats and Republicans. The Democrats want to give everything away and they want somebody else to pay for it. If you look at what's really happening … they want all the grants to continue, and that's fine. I have nothing against those grants to the arts, medicine, grants to everybody, but it's got to come from somewhere, and you have to make it before you can spend it, although in this country that's not so. I mean if you are deeply in debt, and you have credit cards, as this country is deeply in debt, what do you think they would do to you? They would take away your credit cards for one thing. And I think Trump is that person who will turn the country around, either have a balanced budget or a surplus, so we can either pay off some of our debt which I think would be a great idea, or continue giving it away. And also, I think that what Trump is going to do, is these countries to which we are giving billions of dollars, he's going to say, "Sorry fellas. I mean we give you money and you hate us." There's got to be something wrong with that.

Barbara: I agree the economy is always a paramount issue. I think when we go into severe downturns and severe recessions that the damage is great. Where we disagree is I am not seeing policies from Trump that will make the economy healthier.

Lloyd: They're long term. You have to cut the spending. That's simple. That's what he's going to do.

Barbara: I don't see any spending being cut. And I think that tariffs are going to hurt consumers terribly.

Lloyd: You don't think he's already told our European "allies" that they need to support themselves? My opinion we have to get what the French owe us from World War I. We ought to repossess the Eiffel Tower. They still owe us money. And so does most of Europe. How about lend lease? We lent but we never got anything back.

Barbara: What do you think about tariffs?

Lloyd: It's about time, because I think in the long run, it will benefit us. It will bring the Chinese to the table. All the tariffs will disappear from their end and from ours, but you've got to twist their noses first.

Barbara: But then why institute tariffs on the Canadians? Why put tariffs on our allies?

Lloyd: Because they're doing business with the Chinese.

Barbara: So somehow this is to squeeze the Chinese?

Lloyd: Yes.

Barbara: What if they don't come to the table?

Lloyd: They will. They have no choice because we're one of their biggest customers. We can live with what they're doing to us. We've lived with it for 50 years.

Barbara: But by putting tariffs, I mean, they're essentially a tax on consumers. We're going to all pay more for every item that uses aluminum and steel so whatever little benefit we all got from the tax cut, we're going to lose.

Lloyd: You don't understand the long term. What will happen is the Chinese, as they've already started to say "Well, we'd like to talk with you."

Barbara: I think they have a greater ability to wait it out than we do. They don't have a capitalist system like we do. Ours is far more complex, than theirs. They can make an edict, and it goes across. It's a planned economy.

Lloyd: Won't happen because the Chinese will come to the table with us. Trump will decide with whoever their leader is, and you get rid of yours, and I'll get rid of mine. We're now on a fair footing. Long term planning and he's very good at that that. True not everything he will do is right, not everything he will do is successful, but in the long run, we'll be a stronger country for it. You don't understand that.

Barbara: See my concern is I think it's the opposite. I think in the long run we're going to be a weaker country, because I think we're doing systemic damage to the economy, and to some of the agencies of government.

Lloyd: That's because that's your Democratic philosophy. I'm an optimist. I know what will happen, because I've seen it and I've done it myself, and I know what succeeds, and what doesn't. And if it doesn't, you just push it aside, and you keep on going with what you know is right. That's what will happen. Because this guy is different from any President we ever had.

Barbara: Well, that's the truth.

Lloyd: The results and his approach will be different, and the results will be different, but in the final analysis, it will be on the plus side.

THE DEMOCRATIC PARTY

Barbara: What do you think about the midterm elections this fall? Do you think there's going to be this blue wave?

Lloyd: I think the Democrats are deep trouble.

Barbara: You do?

Lloyd: I do because they're a bunch of complainers. That's all they do, and the more they complain the more the Republicans feel, "To hell with you, stop your complaining get to work." Like Maxine Waters and a bunch of others, like Rachel Maddow. They're actually funny. I mean I listen to Rachel once in a while. I mean, she's a hoot. And Maxine Waters could be on Broadway. She's one of the greatest actresses in the world.

Barbara: So, you don't see the Democrats taking back Congress this fall?

Lloyd: I think the Democrats are in deep trouble. I think they're going to lose. They won't gain anything. First of all, there are 10 states that they have to keep and they are Trump States. That's number one. I'm not that familiar with all our Republican candidates. But if they have Trump's support, I think it's a dead issue… I don't think Gershon can get elected, but I think he's going to give Zeldin a run for his money.

After the interview, we stood up and shook hands and I said goodbye. My overall takeaway from our conversation was a feeling of sadness. I am not sure what I expected, but based on how gracious Lloyd was to me last year during the Jewish holidays when I was at their home and each time I have met him when I meet up with Syma, I expected more insight and humor in his answers and in his reasoning. I know, from what Syma has told me, and from things we discussed in the interview, that he is a person of substance. And for a person of substance, to answer questions with nothing but *Fox News* talking points was profoundly sad.

What do I mean by substance? For one, Lloyd is a veteran. Syma told me that he is a Korean War Veteran, who saw active duty during the war. For another, he has deep family ties to the community, going back several generations. He purchased the building his business is in from his father who was in retail but not antiques. "He was in the new junk business and now I am in the old junk business," he told me during the interview. His father sold everything. "You name it, he sold it and if he didn't have it, he could get it for you." He told me his father wondered if Lloyd could make a living selling "this old junk."

Lloyd is college educated, appreciates the intrinsic value of things like antiques, was friends with Harry Truman, who he admired - he did not want to talk about how he had been friends with Truman, who he said was his presidential hero - had cared for his first wife when she was ill with cancer, and clearly cared deeply about Syma. He told me that the first Republican he voted for was Eisenhower. And that he believed in the traditional GOP mandate of smaller government and freedom.

Yet in our conversation, when it came to Donald Trump, he blithely repudiated everything he supposedly stood for as a Republican to completely stand behind Trump. His love of Trump is unbounded. He was unable to look deeply at any issue involving Trump and became angry when any facts related to Trump were challenged.

The only moment that gave him pause was our discussion of the Russia probe. He just shut down, did not want to talk about and would not even consider the possibility that the accusations could be true.

Later that evening, I rode with Syma to Riverhead where we were meeting up with Rebecca, who had a booth selling her jewelry at a summer event called Alive at Five every Thursday, and we planned on giving out flyers we had printed outlining Zeldin's positions on the issues. Patty and Wendy also met up with us. In the car on the way there, Syma and I talked about my interview with

Lloyd. I told her how he shut down when it came to the Russia probe. She said that his complete denial about this concerned her that when it does all finally come out, how will he handle that? And his denial about it is the issue that poses the most conflict for her. How can he not see that colluding with Russia is treason?

In handing out flyers, I realized very quickly that I had much better luck when I approached women than men. Almost all women took the flyer and many stopped to then discuss the issues with us. A couple of people thought we were handing out pro-Zeldin flyers, to which Patty said, "They will get a real surprise tonight when they settle into bed and read the flyer!"

We handed out our whole stack of flyers. It felt good to think that maybe some of these women might turn out to vote because of our efforts. We also ran into Perry, his wife Lisa and one of their sons who were making the rounds talking to people there on Main Street. This was good because one of Zeldin's campaign offices is right there on Main Street.

Sunday, July 22nd
SHDems Summer Party
I met up with Syma at 3:00 PM to drive together to the SHDems Summer Party. It was in a lovely outdoor setting at the Southampton Social Club, with an open bar and appetizers, none of which I could eat due to my allergies. I sipped slowly on a white wine spritzer. Syma and I sat by the front door signing people in, and taking checks from those who hadn't paid already online. It was interesting seeing so many people who I did not know since they are Democrats in Southampton but not committee members. They all seemed very energized and excited when Perry spoke to the crowd. And it was wonderful to see Lulu, Joy, Gordon, Mike, Eileen, Julie, Robin and several others. I realized that I draw energy from their enthusiasm even when my own is flagging, as it often is right now.

I was relieved the next day when our SPC meeting, which had been scheduled for 5:00 PM, was cancelled. I had already decided I was not going anyway. Until we decide what our mission is going forward in 2018, it feels like a waste of time and to be honest, I am having trouble handling how heated the meetings have become. Last year I thought this would be the singular accomplishment that I worked on as an activist. Now, it may have ceased to be effective. Just as earlier this year I thought the young people involved in the March for Our Lives movement would be a key component of winning this fall. It is now July and I hear very little from them, at least in our district.

Later on in the day I learned that Donald Trump Jr. called Perry a "leftwing nutjob" and urged his supporters to rally behind Zeldin. Interesting that the Trump family has jumped into CD#1; could this be a sign that Zeldin is worried?

Tuesday, July 24th
Wine and Signs for Perry

A wonderful EEAN event, organized by Sharon and Rebecca, hosted by Rebecca's Mom, Debra Dolber, had 20 of us gathered together to write postcards to Democrats for Perry. The cards will be mailed in October so we have time to put the addresses and stamps on them. This evening we focused on writing and decorating the cards. I have never received a handwritten political card and the hope is this will help motivate Democrats to come out and vote. Several people joined us who have not been to recent meetings and there were also some new faces. I sat next to a woman I met at the meet-and-greet for Elaine who was very instrumental in her campaign but is now all in for Perry. She was next to another woman who hosted a fundraiser for Vivian and is also all in for Perry. And I got to catch up with Joy who I had seen at the SHDems summer party but we didn't really get a chance to speak. It was a lovely evening, sitting outside at large tables, chatting with other people who feel invested in fighting back by helping Perry win.

The author and Joy Flynn writing postcards to voters.

After most everyone left, Rebecca, Kim, Wendy and Cindy painted a white sheet with the word "TREASON" in big red letters and planned to hang it from a bridge in the Moriches area. They waited until it was dark. We had a lot of jokes about bailing them out and who would drive the getaway car, but there was also a sense that this came out of our frustration that we are not doing enough, directly to counter the damage of Zeldin and Trump.

Debra Dolber, Florence Wiles, Kim O'Reilly and Rebecca Dolber

It gave us all a great feeling. I asked Rebecca the next day to write a few words for me about the experience. She emailed me her thoughts about the experience and it is reprinted with her permission.

> *EEAN turned an exhilarating corner last night. I'd been thinking about doing this for weeks now, and everyone I mentioned it too brushed over it--except Kim, who, on Sunday texted me that she was at Michaels buying red spray paint. On Tuesday, she said she got the sheets and asked if there was anything else she could bring to the Wine and Sign to*

make this happen. This Thelma had finally met her Louise. We'd asked Wendy the week before to do some due diligence on the matter to see what the implications were of hanging a banner over a bridge. Could we get arrested? Ticketed? I didn't think so, but with protesters getting arrested all over the country for lesser actions, I just wanted to know where we stood legally. Wendy didn't turn up answers, so instead, she volunteered to be the getaway car. Fair deal! Cindy jumped in too, and on the way over, Kim and I called Sarah to assist. This was the plan--Kim and Sarah (the tallest) would get the top two corners, and Cindy and I would secure the bottom. We played Bobby McGee en route and as we approached the overpass, Kim and I squealed. We scanned the gas station parking lot for cops. Wendy pulled over onto the shoulder and we jumped out. Kim and Sarah weren't tall enough, so I had to climb the railing to secure the corners. We acted fast and quickly secured the first banner under an almost-full moon. Meanwhile, Wendy "flipped a bitch" and positioned the car on the other side of the bridge. We ran across and she tossed the second banner out to us. Second verse, same as the first. We quickly tied it up and ran back to the car, zooming away seemingly unnoticed. IT WAS INCREDIBLE!! I think of everything we've done as a group, this was the proudest I've been. Between all the interviews, debates, action items, nothing felt more satisfying than calling this President out in this way. We drove all the way to the next exit and turned around so we could see it from the highway. SUCCESS! We decided this wouldn't be the last--next banner goes up in William Floyd, Zeldin's hometown. I'm so proud I want to claim this action in the name of EEAN--but at the same time, I want to see how and if it spreads on its own. Will someone take a picture and start a thread on Facebook? Will the news cover it? I don't intend to stop until someone makes us.

The next day, Rebecca let me know that around noon the banners were still up, based on Wendy's reporting. Rebecca texted me around 4:30 PM that the banners were gone. Did the highway department remove them or a Trump supporter? No matter, this is the beginning.

Wednesday, July 25th
David and Gordon

After a few postponements on my part, I met with David today for our in-person interview. A few days later, I conducted a phone interview with Gordon. I also reached out to several committee members to get their insights on the division in the committee. To make it easier for the reader to follow, I have put all this information here in this one section.

David Dubow

I spent the morning preparing. I did not know exactly what to expect. I had only met David a few times. He knew going into the interview that I was brought to the committee by Gordon and I have no issues with his work as chairman of the committee. And he also knew that I was aware that he was considering challenging Gordon this fall. Would it be cordial or would it be as confrontational as the last SHDems meeting?

When I arrived, he welcomed me into his home, showing me around and then asking if I would like something to drink, coffee or water. He even had gluten free cookies for us, which was very thoughtful. We sat out on his screened in porch, overlooking his lovely backyard and pool. He told me a little about the house, which had been his parents' vacation home years ago. The slate tile on the floor of the screened in porch reminded me of tile in our front hallway in the house I grew up in, in Dix Hills, in the Western part of Suffolk County. The house and tile dated from the early 1960s. Extensive renovations had been done to create a wide-open kitchen and great room with a cathedral ceiling.

Below is a lightly edited and condensed transcript of our conversation:

I am seeing some of the same rift here in our committee that we saw nationally in 2016.
Well, if there is, it's not coming from me or anybody else who is working with me, because we're very clear ... and in fact, again, I said to the gathering here last night, should we proceed, and should we be successful, that this is not about getting rid of the old. It's about building for the future. And if I challenge Gordon and I win, as far as I'm concerned, there's an honored position for Gordon within the party. I hope that if he were to win, he'd still want me to be part of the party.

What I don't want this to be, and it certainly won't come from me, I don't want this to be personal, I don't want to be acrimonious. Despite what some people have said, I am not looking to radicalize the party. I'm looking to democratize the party.

What concretely would that mean? Tell me in concrete terms, what would be different ... and I'm not talking about going back to two years ago, three years ago. I'm just talking about the last year, which is my only experience in our committee. What would be different?
What we should do is set out rules and conditions under which candidates are put forward, and candidates are selected by the various stages of the process. And to create, and this is a word that makes a bit of sense for all of them, but to create "transparency" and involvement. As you know what we did with those rules, is we involved the whole committee, so we have got to test them. It's going to happen this coming year where candidates are made known to the full committee, that the proceedings of the search committee and the executive committee are made known to the full committee, that those candidates who are not recommended by the various bodies within the committee, still have the opportunity, and we provide the facility to make their interest in running and their candidacy known to the full committee, and then the full committee votes and selects the candidate. It's never happened that way before.

What I will propose whether we win or not is the opaque way in which committee members are effectively selected has to change. Gordon's notion, after we worked together very closely for a while, that his decision that the names of the candidates for committee are confidential, that's ridiculous. They're not confidential. And that we stop sharing committee names. And in fact, well, Gordon eventually relented. He made a commitment, and then he reneged. I insisted on a certain number of people from a list that I had provided be added and, in other words, we were going to jointly endorse a committee for this year. And he wouldn't do that, because he was really looking to block as many of the people from our list as possible, maybe in anticipation of a leadership contest.

Were you stacking the committee with supporters?
No, it was never, and you can ask, by the way, any of the people over the years who I've added who have come from our list, people like Julie Sheehan and Laura Leever, I never ever asked the question if I were to run for the leadership, "Would you support me?" People who I've added this year, like Kathryn Levy, it never came up. In fact, Jessie Herschell's husband, Greg, who was a former Republican, may wind up being the most conservative member of the committee, I didn't say, "Are you going to vote for radical things?" What I wanted to do was add people who were open-minded, who were prepared to be active and

involved, and to make this town a better place. I would hope that they would see what I was trying to do as being in that direction and because of my actions, would want to support me if I ran, but I never asked them to.

But don't you think the people that Gordon added in the last year were of the same ilk?
Some. If you look at the list of 84 names, you will see that there are some names on there that you have no idea who they are. You haven't seen them. And some of them are not new. You wouldn't have seen them last year or the year before or the year before that or the year before that. And what I want to see is a committee of people who are there because they want to be there, because they're interested in the principles of what we should be doing there, which is not just selecting candidates. It's about serving the community. And it would have ideas and thoughts, and be prepared to be involved in, if need be, in vigorous debate, and then they will support the things that's right, whether it's on the agenda of the whoever is the chair. Add that if we are forward thinking and positive and Democratic in the way we approach things, we will all come together to support whatever the majority decides. Obviously, there are things that many of us cannot support. But I don't think that the group I'm talking about putting together would ever put us into that territory.

I think you won the war. The composition of the committee now, since 2016, with people like me, and Julie, and Laura, and so many people who have come over from the grassroots, is pretty much what you're talking about. We're all working so hard, and there's this animosity toward other Democrats that to me seems so counterproductive. People have told me that historically this is a committee that didn't have transparency. What is not transparent right now?
Well, what were we just talking about? The selection of the committee. And that's fundamental, I would think. People should not be piggy backed so that they become votes when the votes are needed. So, if they don't carry petitions, they don't get involved in the community, they don't get involved in campaigns, they don't come to committee meetings, except when they're asked to come and cast a vote, then that's wrong.

So how many people are we talking about, of the 84?
Probably about 30. But that's a big number out of 84.

So, you're going to go to these 30 people and tell them to leave?
No, you can't. The issue is the way in which people get onto the committee, and this is ... it's not a job for life. It's a two-year term. And it's as the result of carrying petitions. So instead of pairing people, a carrier with a non-carrier, to effectively

carry that inactive person onto the committee, I wouldn't do that. I would say to those people, "If you want to be on the committee, tell me why. What contribution do you feel that you can make that you will make? And if you're not prepared to carry petitions, tell me why and I will see if there is someone who is prepared to carry petitions for you as well."

I guess I'm just trying to understand, what is going to be so dramatically different with this overhaul of the committee than it is now?
I don't know that it is going to be dramatic on day one, or even on day 100, but as you have conceded, though it's not a concession, because you weren't there before, but based upon what you know, you are aware of the substantial changes from the way the committee operates now from the way it did two and three years ago. And it's my feeling that if we're going to continue that progress, that changes are now necessary. That we spent the last two years working in parallel with the old guard so as to embed in our systems, some of these changes. But I think there are more things that have to happen. And the backroom deals have to stop. That the way in which we select candidates, the way in which we select committee people, the way in which we appoint people to the appointed boards and the advisory boards, have to be more democratic and more open, to not just the committee certainly, but to the community and the committee being the representatives of the community. Reflecting the views, the attitudes, the dreams, the desires, of the community they represent. Amongst other things, one of the things I've been trying to do, and we've had some success in this, is rather than simply assigning people to an ED that they might not know, to move more and more people into the EDs where they live. Or at least that they have a connection to.

My biggest concern with the leadership battle is you're going to have people that feel very loyal to Gordon. There are going to be people that feel loyal to you. And there are going to be hard feelings, and some people may walk away.
I know.

And to me, I can't think of a worse time to split the committee, than right before this election.
It will come up every two years. Two years ago, I decided not to challenge Gordon, as I said. Four years ago, Bridget Fleming was challenging Gordon, but withdrew for the sake of unity. And you can trace it back. There will always be a congressional election. There will always be a state of affairs in the country or in the town, or in the state, or on a national level or international, there will always be a reason. There is never a good reason to set democracy aside. And there is good reason for there not to be acrimony. There is good reason for there

not to be the kind of infighting that overflows into the other important things that the committee should be doing.

One of the things that's fundamental, and the difference in perspective that I have, and the people that I'm talking to have from the, let's call them the powers that be, is that they see, and the County will tell you the same thing, they see the function of the committee to identify, select candidates for office, work for their election, and to continue to fill as many elected posts with their friends. I agree that that is a fundamental part of what the committee should be doing, but it's only half. And that's where we disagree. We should be involved in the community.

We should not just find out what the national issues are, or the local issues that motivate people. We should understand about people who are upset because the streetlight on their street is out. We should care about people who are unhappy about noise pollution in their area.
That's a fundamental difference between what I want to do, and what the party, as it now is constituted, wants to do.

The problem is, I'm not seeing that, so I'm on committees with Gordon. I'm on committees with Mike…
There is no one I have greater respect for than Mike. He's a friend and although sometimes we have disagreed about particular issues or candidates for office, there is nobody with greater integrity, greater commitment to the principles of the party, and to doing the right thing than Mike. And it was in fact, in part, because of Mike that I drafted that resolution, because I said we have to stop grumbling about, after the fact, about the way we select candidates.

And I'm on committees with Robin. If they are the old guard, I have not found in any committee that I'm on, this lack of interest in the community affairs that you are describing. So, you haven't answered my question which is what are people so angry about? We're talking about this anger towards fellow Democrats.
It becomes contentious because there are people that go there too quickly. I have not made, and to my knowledge, nobody on my behalf, has made one phone call or made one effort to tell people that Gordon is a bad guy, and that he shouldn't be reelected. I've tried to keep dialogue open with Gordon, and it has been, at least to this point.

When I announce, which will happen in the next few days, the first phone call I'm going to make is to Gordon. And it's going to be about letting him know what my intentions are, although he probably already knows, and looking for a way that we can approach this in a fair and democratic and honorable way.

The amount of animosity that was over something like a platform document, as if the people who had worked on it are not good Democrats, don't care about diversity, don't care about minorities, don't care about the Democratic philosophy. And this is my concern about a leadership battle coming up this year. I think you're going to have people that are going to retreat to corners, who are going to say I'm a "David person" or a "Gordon person," and that really concerns me because I just want to see Perry get elected.

I'm saying I sent a very clear message, and I have a lot of support in the room. Just saying that that's not what we want to do. I am reminded because I still think it's right, what Michelle Obama said. "When they go low, we go high." I'm not suggesting that they will go low, but whether or not they do, we make it about the issues and strategy and plan and philosophy, not about personalities. And I think even to try not to make it about past bad behavior, because whatever happened, happened. The question is, "What do we need to do to be a better party tomorrow, next month, next year, and so on?" And people are entitled to evaluate their choices and to do that.

It doesn't have to be uncivilized. Go back to people who sat in Congress, far longer than they should've done, they were always better off with the incumbent because if we challenge Joe Crowley, there's going to be upheaval, and it's going to be bad for the party, and it's going to be hard for us to maintain the leadership in the House. I think simply maintaining the status quo is not in and of itself a good thing.

I think it's been, and I'm saying this not in a disparaging way, it's to Gordon's credit that he is a pragmatist. He's the ultimate pragmatist. Gordon will kick and scream if he thinks that you're banging at the door and want to get in. But if Gordon recognizes the door is off the hinges and you're coming in, Gordon's going to say, "Welcome to the table. Have a cup of coffee and join us." That doesn't make him a bad guy, but it also doesn't make him a progressive or a Democrat at heart.

You don't think Gordon is a Democrat at heart?

A Democrat with a large D, that is for the Democratic Party, most certainly he is. I think that Gordon along with many others probably believes that sometimes the party leadership has to do what's good for the party, even though the members of the party may not recognize it. It's almost like a parent saying, "You are children. You don't really understand." And I think that probably we're in a world where we need to all be treated, that is all Democrats, all party members, as grownups. And these grownups will sometimes make mistakes, and sometimes exercise bad judgment. Hind sight is always easy.

I'm a strong believer that democracy must be allowed to play out, even when we get it wrong. Because we learn from our mistakes, and we become stronger and we become better. But what's important all along the way is that we're reflecting the will of the people and the population. I know you can argue that that's how we wound up with Donald Trump as President. I think as Democrats, we screwed up. I don't give Trump credit for a victory. If you saw that, which I'm sure you did, the looks on the faces of Donald Trump and Mike Pence looking at the results, they were as stunned as the rest of us.

Nobody thought it was going to happen. And it's because, I'll talk about the Hillary campaign, but there are lots of other examples, it's because there was a total misjudgment. There was arrogance. There was a sense that we got this locked up. That's not a fault of democracy. It's a fault of understanding the needs of people, about understanding that Wisconsin could go the other way. That Pennsylvania could go the other way.

I think whether we're talking about for the Town of Southampton, or CD#1, or the country, and in many respects, I can give you arguments about the world, democracy must always prevail. And if we screw up, then we should use the tools of democracy to fix our mistakes.

I absolutely believe, and whether it was me or somebody else, that there's not only a right, but a responsibility to challenge leadership if we think that something better can happen. And it's the right of all of you to say, "You know what. I understand what you're saying, but I think we're doing just fine. And I wish you weren't running, and if you're running, I'm going to vote against you." But it's still my right to run, and your right to vote against me.

We had talked for a long time. I had liked him more than I had expected. He was eloquent in speaking about the importance of democracy, openness and transparency and that his challenge was to create more of these things. Much of his challenge had to do with the way he viewed the selection of members to join the committee and a belief that too many people were not pulling their weight regarding canvassing and getting petitions signed. He viewed a chairmanship challenge as taking a stand for democracy and fighting an entrenched power structure that wasn't caring enough about residents' local concerns. He clearly felt Gordon was lacking as chairman in all these areas.

I thanked him for the interview. As he walked me to the door, he asked me what I thought about his arguments. I told him that, in theory, I took no issue with his arguments about the importance of democracy and the need for transparency and that from what I had heard, the ideas that he had brought to the committee – like holding more frequent meetings - were valuable. But I still disagreed with his challenge. I did not feel that Gordon was doing a bad job as chairman. In his ten years, he had overseen the greatest growth in the Democratic Party in Southampton Township and helped to put a supermajority on the Town Board that now enabled the Board to pass more progressive policies. And that my experience with Gordon was that anything I asked for, he was open to, such as working more with the grassroots. I told him I wished that he and Gordon could work out these differences so there would not be a chairmanship challenge out of my concern it would split the party. I feared that the result would be divisive at a time when we needed unity.

A few days after my meeting with David, Gordon and I spoke on the phone. Below is a lightly edited and condensed transcript of our conversation:

Gordon Herr

I keep hearing this complaint from people on David's side of this lack of transparency, that it's an old boys' network and it's closed and yet that hasn't been my experience.

Well, it's a question of history. I first came out here in 2007 actually in October 2006. I'd been at an event when Tim Bishop was speaking and I said to Tim, "Look, I want to get involved with the party. How do I do that?" And he said, "I think there's a new chair" and he gave me Mike's contact info and I told Mike I wanted to get involved and he said, "Please do!" So we started working together and I met people who had been in the party a long time like Grania Brolin and Hank Beck, and I got involved in the various things which we organized, including fundraisers. We had our first Annual party in 2007 and that was a great event and I got more and more involved and Mike and I worked together and then he wanted to retire and I became the chair in 2009. So it's been a slow process.

And I think that yes, I was new to this as well. And I didn't realize how much time it was going to take, it was a tremendous amount of energy and time and effort and, honestly, I did what I thought we had to do. We didn't have meetings every month or every two months, then just the required minimum meetings, which was four times a year. I just didn't have the time and I was working full time. And so, we did quite well and we got more and more people elected and we started registering second homeowners and we got more people registered and elected more Democrats and then what happened was that we were able to get more people on the committee who wanted to get involved. Yes, there are some who never do any work. Like with Obama's second election in 2012 and there was OFA and they never did anything to help us on a local level. People would always say they worked for the national presidential campaigns, but they were never involved with local town elections.

I was actually one of those people. I was affiliated with OFA and I never did anything on a local level. I was one of the typical Democrats who focused on the presidential and never did anything else, though I was not a committee member.

Then John Bouvier wanted to run for trustee and Anne and David got involved because they like John and had worked with him. So that was the first time I heard of them and seeing them. David came in and obviously, there were various people that he spoke to, some of them were on the committee who weren't happy with the way things were being run and there were other people who he wanted to bring onto the committee which he did, which I agreed. This is what I did with a lot of people. And then there were these continued complaints about transparency, which quite honestly, I'm still not 100% sure what they're referring to.

I believe that there are two main reasons why this is happening. Number one, there are certain people who want to move the party much further to the left and that's absolutely fine. The problem is if the party is so far to the left we will never win elections in Southampton Town. These are a lot of Bernie people who worked in the Bernie campaign and if you look at all the David supporters, there are probably 16 diehard supporters out of 82 people on the committee right now.

So that's number one. Number two, which I think is probably more important in terms of how they feel, is we've always had a disagreement about running non-Democrats. Some of these people want to only run people who are registered Democrats and my feeling is I'm prepared to run people who are not registered Democrats, but have the principles and values of the Democratic Party, like Jay or Anna. And they absolutely oppose any arrangements that we might have with the minor parties, like to get a spot on the Conservative Party, or Working Family Party line and their feeling is that we need to be pure, you need to enter only Democrats on the Democratic Party line without any endorsements on the minor parties. Well, the reason that we've been so successful is that we have managed to gain the lines of the minor parties, certainly the Working Family Party.

If I had my way I would rather not accept endorsements of the minor parties but the reality is that this is what's allowed and if we don't take these endorsements the Republican Party is going to take them. So we're going to be left with just one line. And if it was just the Republican or Democratic Party we would probably win 80% of all the elections but that's not the way it is. So we need the party lines but this group wants to move away from that.

The other thing they feel is that we haven't included minorities as much as we can. Although we've been doing outreach for 10 or 11 years, including the efforts of the search committee, and we have added some minorities, we haven't been as successful as we would like to be. It is something that we've tried to do; it's not just that we've ignored it.

Same with reaching out to younger voters. As you know, I brought Jake in. Even though he's Brookhaven he's allowed to be on the committee because he's part of the assembly district and I brought in a few more new names and new people and we continue to try and bring people in, who are going to do the work.
You know I credit David that we have more meetings and changing the nomination proceedings and things like that. And that's all great, but I'm more focused, as Mike describes me, focused on candidates and elections and Dave is more focused on process.

David says that you reneged on a list of names that he gave you and that is what triggered his challenge.
David did promise me that if I agreed to put on the people he really wanted, 12 people, on the committee, which would have meant removing some people, then he wouldn't challenge me. I didn't want to remove some so eventually I accepted

nine out of 12. He wanted two of his cousins on but I didn't think his cousin was qualified. And he said, "I'm sure lots of people don't want to see you as chair, but nobody else would challenge you except me." So he basically went back on his word.

Do you think this challenge from David and his supporters mirror the rift nationally in the Democratic Party, you know, the Hillary/ Bernie people or do you think this is more sort of sui generis to our district?
I think it does. There's some other national stuff that's going on and look I'm not denying that there are people who don't like me and you know I think I've been told by Rich Shaeffer that if I don't have enemies, then I'm not doing my job. Now you know I can't please everybody and if I'm doing something right, well then, some people aren't going to like it. And I think there are a handful of people who just do not like me and they want to see me go. Some arguments or differences of opinion, I don't take it personally. I've had a responsibility to make sure that people get elected and to raise money and so they say I am not democratic enough, with a small "d" in terms of my politics.

Do you think you will win the vote?
Absolutely. But the problem is getting people to the meeting because we don't have proxies in the Democratic Party. People have to attend in order to have their vote cast. If the person who opposes me is at the meeting and the other person is not, that costs.

If you win the vote, how will you then keep the David supporters who are going to have very hard feelings within the tent?
That will be David's responsibility as well since he's the one who's kind of created this situation, it is his responsibility to make sure that people are retained and obviously I will make my best efforts to reach out and make sure everyone feels respected. But you know unfortunately some of these people are going out there, telling very untrue stories. Someone apparently said to one of my supporters who professed loyalty to me, said to her, "Well, why would you vote for a racist?" I complained to David about this person calling me a racist and he said, "Well, you know, I told everyone if that's how they're going to talk, then they should not make phone calls for me" but he said you can't control everybody.

Even after speaking to both David and Gordon, and trying to get a better understanding of what the issues were in contention, I still did not understand the depth of the animosity that I had witnessed at the SPC and the SHDems meetings from this small handful of members. Even if everything David said was true, that didn't explain the anger and the condescension. In my discussions with other committee members, I asked many of them for their take on this chairmanship challenge and the vitriol that was underneath it.

A few comments stood out and summed up the different points of view.

"I had not been happy initially with the job Gordon was doing, but things have improved, and I see things getting more transparent and inclusive," said Andi Klausner. "At first, I felt that change would be good, but as I see the anger and contentiousness starting, I think this is the wrong time for in-fighting. We need to pull together and not fracture ourselves. Everyone needs to put ego aside and work on getting Perry elected."

"Gordon will win and I take David at his word that he wants more transparency," said Joy Flynn. She told me she was supporting Gordon because she believed he had done a good job as chairman and deserved another term. She did not think this would split the committee. She had seen this before in a previous chairmanship challenge.

I asked her about the anger emanating from the David crowd. "It's Bernie/Hillary. They fancy themselves these big progressives and that everybody else is sold out somehow and they are holier than thou and just pissed off. Some people are just angry people, it doesn't matter what the issue is, they will create it," she said. "I've told David that he's done really good work. He got more people on the committee, more regular meetings, a bigger executive committee, all good stuff. But he just doesn't have the talent that Gordon has."

I knew Julie Sheehan was supporting David. She too believed it would not split the committee.

"Oh, I don't think it will. It doesn't have to be divisive. Don't be afraid, because fear is what got the Democratic Party into the pickle it is in. Fear did that. The fear, the sort of Clinton fear of, 'you can't say anything, let's split all the hairs' and just navigate some tortured path because of this imaginary swing voter that we don't even know the first thing about who is probably far more willing to vote for someone who has passion and conviction," she said. "It is time to open up the ranks, make the system more transparent so that it's easier to get involved. How decisions are made, that information is tightly held. Let it go. It's scary but you have to have faith, and you are rewarded by democracy. And I disagree with this argument that this isn't a good time. There is never a good time, but it does feel like it is time for change, time for transparency."

I was surprised when Julie expressed the opinion that Gordon had brought me on the committee "because he realized that the seats were going to be filled by David supporters if he wasn't careful." This was news to me. But it explained some of the animosity I had felt from some members of the SPC who seemed to view me as not progressive enough. I guess I was viewed as a non-reformer by supporting Gordon, as someone who didn't care enough about the issues. I told Julie that I found this whole approach from fellow Democrats insulting and hurtful.

She did not disagree that I was viewed that way but she did seem concerned that I was feeling insulted by it. "I don't think anyone is saying that you don't care. I just don't believe anyone could have met you and not get the glaring fact that you care. It's very hard if you feel like, 'Are you saying I'm not a good Democrat or I'm not a good person or I lack passion?' It's very hard to do anything but suffer. I'm sorry you had that experience and I hope you never have it again."

I appreciated her empathy, but she completely missed the point.

As always, Mike put it all in perspective.

"I don't think David realizes exactly what he is taking on. He wants an improved Committee - one that is more inclusive, democratic, and transparent - all good things. However, our main purpose is to find good candidates, get them on the ballot and get them elected. He will find out that that is a lot. Internal process is only a part of what his responsibilities will entail. He needs to be the face of the party, the person the press goes to, the person most responsible for keeping our coffers full, or, at least, adequate, the one to soothe wounds, the one to negotiate with minor parties. And not all decisions need to be made in a democratic fashion, sometimes deferring to a wise leader is paramount. I hope he has the time and support to get these things done. He won't have my help."

Sunday, July 29th
Opening of the Southampton for Perry Office

I woke up early and drove out to Southampton so I could attend the opening of Perry's campaign office. The event was from 10:00 AM -12:00 PM. Luckily, I was able to drive to this location. There was a pretty big crowd and I saw a lot of familiar faces- Eileen, Andi, Ron, Robin, Gordon, David as well as Perry and his staff.

A lot of local elected officials were also there. Gordon introduced them and Perry, who then gave a wonderful speech. Afterwards, Perry and I talked about when we can schedule a sit- down interview. To speak to me, he moved us off to the side of the crowd because he said he is now being followed by Zeldin trolls. He explained that he now must be careful with every word he says. At a campaign event, he mentioned that what is going on in our country right now is analogous to Germany in the 1930s. He was recorded by a Zeldin troll and the video has been turned into ads criticizing Perry for attacking Trump.

It was a lovely summer morning but underneath was a not-so-lovely subtext, which had to do with David's decision to challenge Gordon in the fall. Many of us were worried about how this might impact our getting out the vote for Perry. I heard that Gordon had spoken to Perry, who was also concerned about how this might impact the congressional election. Andi had an idea, which was to postpone the SHDems convention and the chairman challenge until after the midterm election but when we approached Robin she explained that this is not possible because of the county rules. But she told us not to worry. She was sure that Gordon will be reelected by a very large margin and that will be the end of this. I told her that I hoped she was right.

The author with Andi and Ron Klausner

A great turnout for the opening of Perry's Southampton office.

Chapter 17
August 2018

"This split in the Democratic Party in our district mimics a little bit about what happened in the last election with this whole Bernie/Hillary thing. I feel like that's happening on a smaller level here. I am getting that same vibe and it's infuriating, but also not surprising… People just kind of lose sight of the big picture and maybe it's because we're too in it right now.... I'm always motivated by the fact that we have an illegitimate president… That's my motivation, to flip Congress so we at least have a chance of getting him out. That's why I keep doing it."

Rebecca Dolber, EEAN

Wednesday, August 1st
Chairmanship challenge

David Dubow confirmed his decision to challenge Gordon when he emailed a letter and a manifesto regarding his run for the chairmanship to 50 people on the Democratic Committee. I asked him if I could include his email and manifesto in the book and he agreed.

Wed., August 1

Dear Barbara,

As you know, I have decided to run for Chair of the Southampton Democratic Committee. This was not a decision taken lightly. I have tried to articulate in the attached 'manifesto' why I am running and what I think we can all accomplish together.

Many people encouraged me to run for Chair two years ago. Committee people old and new have asked me to once again consider running. Two years ago, I believed that more could be accomplished by working in partnership with Gordon to improve democracy, transparency and inclusiveness in our Party. Through my efforts, and those of many other dedicated, committed people, we have brought about real change in these two years. I believe that there are many challenges ahead and a great deal that still needs to be done. I believe that a change in leadership is necessary to make that a reality.

Some will argue that now is not a good time: we have an important Congressional election ahead. I know that is your view. The reality is that the schedules for these two contests are beyond our control – there will always be a Congressional election within a month of a Party leadership election. They will always compete for attention and will always run in parallel.

I am committed to a fair and open leadership contest, without acrimony or ill will. I applaud the contributions Gordon has made over many years and I value the contributions he has made to building our Party. If I am successful in winning the leadership, I would hope to have Gordon be an important part of the transition and the future.

I am committed to working hard for Perry Gershon's election, as is everyone else on my team. The shared commitment of all Democrats to do whatever we can to ensure Perry's victory in November– whoever they support for leader – should unite not divide us.

I hope to have your support in building a better Democratic Party.

Best regards
David

Attached to his email was David's manifesto titled Working For a Better Democratic Party.

Working For a Better Democratic Party

Being a Democrat means more than being a member of the Blue Team fighting the Red Team. For me – for most of us – it is about a set of core values, principles, goals, dreams. It is about making our community, our town, our country and our world better. It is about ensuring access, opportunity and quality of life for everyone. It is about integrity, decency, humanity.

In my view, the Southampton Town Democratic Committee must fulfill two critical roles:

- Identifying, nominating, supporting and helping elect good Democrats to public office
- Engaging with the diverse communities that make up our Town, understanding their needs and concerns, addressing the quality of life

issues that matter most to our constituents, and making their issues our issues

As a local Party we have, in recent years, had substantial success in the former and have fallen woefully short in the latter. Now, more than ever, it is critical that we address and embrace our community role.

It is not just that we have a Committee that is older and whiter than many of the communities it should represent, but that our Committee disproportionately reflects the values and experiences of that age and complexion. We can and must do better.

There should be three governing principles in all that we do:

- Democracy
- Transparency
- Inclusiveness

These must be reflected in how we conduct ourselves, in both what we do and what we are seen to do. If we hope to engage with the broader community, we must demonstrate that these values represent who we are.

Nearly three years ago, I came to Gordon with a series of proposals to take us from a small, entrenched, closed group to a more open, more democratic, more welcoming and more representative Committee.

Those proposals included

- Filling long vacant Committee seats
- Expanding the Executive Committee to better reflect the views of the membership
- Holding regular Committee meetings (we had gone nearly a year without a meeting at that stage). We now have 6 a year
- Producing an agenda circulated in advance and minutes of the meetings circulated after (at that time we had neither)

Gordon and I worked together to make those things happen and did so with the support of many others – both longstanding Committee members and newcomers. To Gordon's credit, he recognized the groundswell of support for change and made significant efforts to accommodate our goals. This was all before the shock of the 2016 Presidential election that unsettled and energized the grassroots.

Last year we moved further towards increasing democracy, transparency and inclusiveness. I drafted a resolution to identify and codify the process for selecting, endorsing and nominating candidates for elected office in the Town of Southampton. I was joined by 14 of you as co-sponsors of this resolution. I presented it to the full Committee who voted unanimously to adopt these new rules. They will be employed for the first time next year.

There is still a great deal to be done and I want to work with all of you to build on our accomplishments and create an even stronger, more inclusive Southampton Democratic Party.

Today I am announcing my intention to run for Chair in October's leadership elections. If I am elected I pledge to:

- Work with communities throughout Southampton to engage on the issues that matter most in their daily lives. We will build a broader Outreach team and involve ourselves in community activities, not just invite them to be involved in what we think the agenda and structure should be
- Make diversity a priority – and work towards a Committee that represents the African American, Latino, Native American and LGBTQ communities – as well as our Town's resident labor force
- Continue to democratize the ways in which we select candidates for public office, and Committee membership
- Create a clearer Committee structure and a more democratic, inclusive and transparent decision making process
- Act proactively to defend the rights of those residents of our Town least able to do so, both documented and undocumented
- Work toward creating a platform that reflects our values and articulates them clearly
- Support a program of interactive communication with Democrats and other voters – through our website, print materials, social media and ED-based and Town wide events
- Bring an end to unilateral and opaque decision making. We have 84 Committee seats. Each Committee person must have the right to play a part in how we define ourselves and the actions we take.

I believe it is time for leadership with a new perspective. It is my objective to democratize not to radicalize. I want to begin the process of building an open, welcoming and durable Democratic Party for the future.

I ask for your support, and to join me in building that future.

David Dubow
July 30, 2018

Thursday, August 9th
Gordon Responds
A week later, Gordon emailed his own letter and his own attachment to the Committee members. I can see why he needed a week to get everything in order because it included endorsements from Democratic elected officials in our district.

Below is Gordon's email and the attached endorsement letter.

Dear Fellow Committee Members,

In these critical times, I am certain that all Democratic Committee members will continue to support the issues for which we have always fought on the local level. This year, in particular, we need a united and strong Southampton Town Democratic Committee to help Democratic Congressional Candidate Perry Gershon beat Republican Congressman Lee Zeldin in November. So many issues have become divisive under the Trump administration - his immigration policy is a key example. We have to respond to this congressional race as a cohesive force, to ensure that Perry helps Democrats take back the House of Representatives.

Now, more than ever, we need experienced and effective leadership in the roles of Chair, Outreach and Campaign Committees, not only for this national midterm election, but for our local elections in 2019. Over the years, we have developed an outstanding leadership group that has brought us incredible success in registering Democrats, raising money and winning elections.

Our Outreach Committee, under the chairmanship of Mike Anthony, has worked hard in identifying Democrats of all backgrounds. In 2017, his team engaged hundreds of new voters face-to-face, used social media aggressively, advertised on Spanish-language radio, and reached dozens of Latino voters on their doorsteps. We recently sent a mailing to 500 new Democrats, inviting them to our 2018 Summer Party, resulting in a 50% increase in new attendees. This year, Jake Grier is coordinating a Facebook effort, to attract and activate newly registered Democrats, between the ages of 18 and 35.

Robin Long, who heads our Campaign Committee, has achieved unparalleled levels of electoral success in Southampton. She is also a vice chair of the Suffolk Country Democratic Committee and a powerful and articulate voice for our Party and ideas. Robin and I have worked successfully over the years and we will continue to do so in order to elect more Democrats in Southampton.

Since 2009, when I became Chair, there has been a 14% increase in the number of registered Democrats in Southampton, while the number of registered Republicans decreased by 7%. As of July 31st, we have 12,890 Democrats compared to 12,306 Republicans, which indicates a significant change from the old "one party rule". We have enrolled more new Democrats than at any other time in our history, resulting in more registered Democrats than Republicans. Many of us share the credit for this.

We now have a super-majority on the Town Board, Democrats are the dominant party in our Town and we are able to advance a progressive agenda. We have a lot to be proud of, notably the changes made in the composition of the Town's major land use boards, which now include many individuals who have much more sensitivity to environmental issues than their predecessors. The whole tone of Town Hall has changed.

Another key to our successes has been our ability to fundraise. Over the past ten years, I have been the primary fundraiser for the Committee, raising more money than any previous chair. I do not say this to boast but because, unfortunately, money continues to play an increasingly pivotal role in our ability to win political campaigns at all levels of government.

With regard to our elected officials, I am honored to have the full and complete support of County Legislator Bridget Fleming, Town Supervisor Jay Schneiderman, Town Councilman John Bouvier, Town Councilwoman Julie Lofstad, Town Councilman Tommy John Schiavoni and New York State Assemblyman Fred Thiele. Please see the attached letter.

> *Beginning with Mike Anthony's chairmanship in 2007 and under my leadership since 2009, we have dramatically changed the political landscape in the Town of Southampton and created a "big tent" party for all members of our diverse and growing Democratic Party, from left to right to center, with respect, inclusiveness and opportunity for all perspectives. With your support and the continued great work of our elected officials, I promise to continue to move our Party forward and I anticipate an even stronger, more effective and more unified Southampton Town Democratic Committee.*
>
> *Sincerely,*
> *Gordon*

Attached to Gordon's email was an endorsement letter from the Democratic elected officials.

> August 7, 2018
>
> We the Democratic Elected Officials of Southampton, fully and wholeheartedly endorse GORDON HERR to continue as Chairman of the Southampton Town Democratic Committee.
>
> The two principal tasks of the Committee are to elect Democrats to public office and to grow the Party. When Gordon became Chair in January 2009, there was only one Democrat out of five members on the Town Council; now there are four Democrats out of five, plus our County Legislator, plus two Town Justices.
>
> Since 2009 there has been a 14% increase in the number of registered Democrats in Southampton, while the number of registered Republicans decreased by 7%. As of July 31st, we have 12,890 Democrats, leading all other parties, including the Republicans.
>
> Fundraising is a vital support function of the Democratic Committee. In the four years, 2014 through 2017, Gordon Herr was personally and solely responsible for securing 80% of the monies received by the Committee, an extraordinarily high proportion for a single individual.
>
> Gordon Herr's record of striking success speaks for itself and we are proud to support him in the expectation that he will only add further accomplishments for the Democratic Party going forward.

Suffolk County Legislator BRIDGET FLEMING
Southampton Town Supervisor JAY SCHNEIDERMAN
Southampton Town Councilman JOHN BOUVIER
Southampton Town Councilwoman JULIE LOFSTAD
Southampton Town Councilman TOMMY JOHN SCHIAVONI

Tuesday, August 14th
The work goes on
There is much going on across the district that is worth mentioning, even though I can't attend everything. Perry's campaign is opening up offices across the district and people can go online to schedule time to canvas and to phone bank. Yesterday Perry spoke at an event to prevent gun violence. Here is how Perry described it on the campaign's Facebook page.

> *Last night, I had the honor of standing side by side with Fred and Paul Guttenberg in Patchogue for a discussion on gun violence prevention. Nearly 200 people joined us to honor Fred's daughter, Paul's niece, Jamie to talk about how we can and must go about finding solutions to the epidemic of gun violence in our country. Change is long overdue, starting with banning the sale of assault weapons. Enough is enough.*

It was my hope after the horror of Parkland that gun safety and the March for Our Lives movement would be the sleeper issue that would hurt Zeldin in this election, given his support for concealed carry reciprocity. So, it was good to see how many people showed up for this event.

Friday, August 17th
Trump comes to the East End
As the news spread yesterday that Trump would be arriving at Gabreski Airport aboard Air Force One, meeting up with Zeldin and driving together to a fundraiser at a wealthy mogul's home in Southampton, the grassroots quickly organized two protests, one at Gabreski in Westhampton and one in Southampton, and spread the word across all the Facebook groups. For all the privacy and misinformation problems of Facebook, activists could not have organized these two events so quickly without it. Gordon also sent an email blast to all Southampton Democrats with alerts about the protests.

I had a doctor's appointment that day so I could not attend. But I was well represented by both the SHDems and EEAN.

I saw some coverage of the event in our local press which included quotes from several grassroots activists.[33]

Sharon texted me about the protest: *Protest was good. Attendance was a disappointment though. Wish it wasn't on a work day. Trump supporters definitely outnumbered us.*

EEAN members Sharon Adams and Wendy Turkington

SHDems member Mike Anthony

Sunday, August 19th
Democratic Potluck Party

An influential week of the Trump presidency began for me focused locally on the potluck events we on the outreach committee arranged. Postcard invitations to registered Democrats in specific Election Districts were mailed inviting them to a meet-and-greet with other Democrats in their neighborhoods.

Julie, Mike and Gordon shepherded the events to completion. I was part of the Westhampton event hosted by Mike and Ann at their home. Julie hosted an East Quogue event in the park and Laura Leever hosted an event in Sag Harbor. The response rate was pretty low, not even 10%, but given it is the summer, the busiest time of the year here on the East End, we were thrilled with the response.

Our biggest worry the morning of the event was rain. It had poured the day before and while Mike and Ann had enough room if the event had to be moved indoors, it was going to be crowded. That morning it was raining and when I arrived at their house an hour before the event to help set up, we were still waiting to see if the rain would stop or continue. As it looked like the skies were going to stay clear, we quickly set everything up outside, on the deck next to their pool. They had done such an amazing job of organizing everything and once all the tables, chairs, decorations, food, drinks - wine, water and beer - were all arranged, I was impressed at how warm and inviting they had made the event.

Sharon was also there to help set up. Ann was busy cooking sliders and other appetizers. The ice-breaker fun event that Ann planned was a board where folks could pin up captions to pictures of Trump, his son and Sarah Huckabee Sanders. There were also red, white and blue hats, noisemakers and scarves so people could take selfies, as well as mardi gras beads for everyone to wear.

My job was to sit at the sign-in table which we positioned on the driveway and when I signed people in, I also checked them off the RSVP list, gave out the beads, had them choose one of the pictures for the caption game and then directed them to the side door to Mike and Ann's backyard. SHDems member Jorge Balan was sitting with me at the table. I had printed out two copies of our RSPV list so there could be two lines to check people in and we would collate the list afterwards. We also wanted to make sure we got everyone's email addresses so we could continue to stay in touch with them.

Almost everyone on the list who had RSVP'd arrived, along with about ten additional people who had heard about it and wanted to come. At one point we had so many people at our table that it was hard for just the two of us to welcome everyone. What a wonderful dilemma to have! We had worried what it would mean if no one showed up. In total, with those of us hosting and helping out, we had almost 60 people in their backyard. Thank goodness it hadn't rained.

Mike spoke as did Sharon, Perry's son Logan and Town Board member John Bouvier. People were energized and ready to sign up with the campaign to canvas, make phone calls and spread the word. It was heartening to speak to so many people who were eager to meet other Democrats and to get involved.

Later Mike corresponded with Julie and Laura and they also had higher turnout than expected. I wondered if there might be a way to host more of these across the district between now and election day. When polls and pundits say that there is enthusiasm and energy on the Democratic side, here was an illustration of just what that looks like.

Tuesday, August 21st

"This isn't the end; it isn't even the beginning of the end. But it is the end of the beginning."

My brother, David, texted me the above quote today by Winston Churchill. It is an apt description of how the investigations of the Trump presidency entered a new phase and went in a new direction, starting with this day. When the history of the Trump era is written, will August 21st mark the inevitable drive toward impeachment or resignation?

During the afternoon, in a split screen, the news media attempted to keep up with the fast-moving legal events: the Manafort jury convicted him on eight counts of tax and bank fraud and Cohen pleaded guilty in the SDNY case. In his oral plea deal in court, Cohen uttered the most consequential words yet in the Trump investigations when he stated that everything he did, was at the direction of Trump.

Trump is now an unindicted co-conspirator, the first time a President is in that position since Nixon and Watergate.

Republicans are silent. While few are publicly supporting him, few are also condemning him. It is shameful. This election is crucial because the Democrats must take back the House so they can investigate the President. The country hangs in the balance.

Saturday, August 25th
John McCain

In the afternoon, I learned that John McCain, who had stopped treatment the day before for terminal brain cancer, had died. Given that this is the same diagnosis that my brother-in-law died of two and a half years ago, it felt very personal to me, even though I had never voted for Senator McCain and was not one of his supporters. But I did always respect his service to this country and he was one of the very few GOP luminaries who called Trump out. I will never forget my relief when his thumbs down gesture defeated the repeal of the ACA. Now there may be no one on the other side of the aisle who will speak truth to counter the Trump lies.

Monday, August 27th
The Interfaith Forum

McCain's passing still dominated the news, as it should. The weak tweet from Trump that didn't mention McCain's name just emphasized how petty and small he is. Nothing should ever shock us about the depths of Trump's crassness. It is bottomless. News articles emphasized again that Trump is not invited to attend McCain's funeral in D.C. later this week, after his body lies in state first in Arizona and then in the capital. How ironic the people McCain requested to give his eulogy are the two men who denied him winning the presidency, George W. Bush and Barack Obama.

In the morning, I got a call from Gordon. He wanted to make sure that I will be there on October 9th for the vote at the convention and I assured him I will. He asked me if I would enter his name in nomination. I was surprised. I told him that I would be honored but did not feel that I am the right person, given that I am so new to the committee. But he felt that this made me the perfect person and I told him I would be happy to. I was very touched at being asked. He suggested I speak to Mike about his background as chairman.

That evening, I got a ride with Mike to Southampton for an Interfaith Forum hosted by a coalition of religious leaders on the East End. Both candidates were invited and Zeldin will not be attending. I was a bit shocked to read on The East Hampton Star website that Zeldin declined to attend because he felt the religious leaders who organized the event were biased against him.[34]

The Forum is in the evening in a church in Southampton. There was a pretty good crowd, though I am guessing that without Zeldin it is primarily Democrats so, once again, we are preaching to the converted.

We sat down in the audience as the panel of interfaith leaders and Perry arrived and took their seats in the front. There was an empty seat for Zeldin. Without him, it was not a debate since only Perry was answering questions but I thought he did well and his answers were thoughtful and authentic.

One of his key comments for the evening was in answer to the question, "What values and moral commitments were prominent in your household growing up and which ones have you strived to instill in your children?"

> "I grew up in a household here in New York. My parents were both doctors and academics. We did not have religion in our household for my first ten years of life. I grew up knowing I was Jewish, and hanging out with the Jewish kids in my classroom. And in third grade I started to attend synagogue on my own with some of my Jewish friends. And through that, the Rabbi at the synagogue, who I got to know very, very well and am still in contact with, reached out to my parents and said "Your son is attending Hebrew school here, don't you think you should join the synagogue?" They thought about it and said, "That's probably right." So my parents joined the synagogue and they became members.
>
> Now that was how I got involved and how my values came together. But in terms of the values that I'd like to see with my children, I have really basic human values, for caring, developing and being. Not to lie, not to cheat, not to steal, to be charitable and compassionate and have a strong work ethic. Those are the values that define me and what I'd like to instill upon my children. It is really unfortunate to see a president who does not know the meaning of the word lie. To me, that is not what America is supposed to be, and that's what's motivating me ... a large part of what's motivating me to run. And it's most unfortunate that Mr. Zeldin can't see to it to criticize a president who lies routinely. That just goes against everything that I believe in."

After the event, Mike and I stopped and spoke to Perry for a few minutes. He pointed out that the other camera there recording him was from a Zeldin tracker who follows him around. He won't show up but sends these camera people to follow Perry around and try to catch him in a gaffe. Mike asked Perry if the other candidates have been helping the campaign and he told us about a Latino event that Vivian hosted for him and canvassing that Kate and Elaine have done for him. He said that he has reached out to Brendon but not heard back and has not heard back from David Pechefsky. He and Mike also discussed the David Dubow challenge to Gordon which Perry said he really doesn't understand and is concerned will interrupt the committee's commitment to the election. Mike tried to assure him that this will not weaken the SHDems commitment to his election.

Before we left, Mike introduced me to Elena Adelita Rivera-Williams, who is a SHDems member, a zone leader and a member of the executive committee. She is also an active member in several other organizations, such as the Eastern Long Island chapter of the NAACP where she is the 3rd Vice President. I had heard of her from Robin Long but we had never met. Mike said she is someone I should speak to because she is a voter-registration powerhouse, in particular on the Shinnecock Reservation in Southampton. Shortly after the Forum, we sat down together. Hers is such an interesting story.

Born in Brooklyn but raised in Cypress Hills, N.Y. (on the Brooklyn/Queens border), her mother was a Shinnecock Native American, of the Shinnecock Indian Nation in Southampton. Her father is Taino, the Indigenous people of the Caribbean and Puerto Rico. He was born in San Juan, Puerto Rico. Elena learned her incredible work ethic from her parents who both worked at full-time jobs, her father with the Transit Authority and her mother as a supervisor for a computer information firm, but in the evenings and on weekends they ran their own business, a hot dog stand that offered a fusion of Hispanic and Native American recipes. On the weekends, she worked with her parents at the hot dog stand. She would visit the Shinnecock Reservation with her mother and grandmother.

After a series of careers, including modeling, and a first marriage that ended in divorce though gave her the son she adores, she met her present husband, Donald Williams Jr., a Shinnecock Native American who is a retired Marine, at a family funeral at the Reservation. They married in July, 2012 and both live on the Reservation, even though her work for American Airlines at LaGuardia Airport in the control tower necessitates a very long commute. But she feels that she has now found her voice and she and Donald, who is a tribal elder, are instrumental in the annual Powwow event on the Reservation that features Native American music, dances and food and is a major tourist event in the Hamptons. In 2018, Donald was elected Sachem or Chief, on the seven-person Trustee Board. The Sachem is a position of leadership that is reserved for elders.

Elena's involvement with voter registration goes back many years to an early job in the garment industry when she was a union member with the International Ladies Garment Workers Union and they sponsored voter registration drives. Thanks primarily to her efforts, there are now more registered Democrats than Republicans on the Reservation. Elena joined the SHDems in 2013 and on the strength of her voter registration efforts she was invited to join the executive committee, which she did in 2015. She encouraged her husband to join in 2018 and they are now the ED representatives for ED26. Elena explained to me that when the district was predominantly Republican, people had to join the Republican Party to be able to get a job.

"A lot of the elders were listed as Republican, because in the past, they couldn't get the government jobs without being in the Republican Party. They are now changing to Democrat," she said.

She told me that when she is working to register members of the Shinnecock Nation to vote, in particular younger voters, she tells them that by not voting, it is too easy for elected officials to ignore their needs.

"Voter registration is very important. Some of the youth today don't see the importance of being a registered voter. I try to bring that importance to the forefront. There are things that the youth feel are not being addressed. I said, 'Well, the way to get heard is to be a registered voter. If you want some of these things addressed, you need to see who is going to take on those issues.'"

SHDems members Jake Grier, Elena and the author at the Interfaith Forum

Tuesday, August 28th
Wine and Sign

A frustrating day. I have developed a pain in my right wrist which is making typing a struggle. Then I had to take my car to the mechanic and get a rental car. Still, I was determined to make it to another wine and sign event for Perry tonight. It was in Patchogue. I drove with Sharon and met my sister Nanci and her dear friend Laura there.

Sharon had organized all the colored markers, postcards and stickers and we set up two stations, one inside and one outside. She is amazing! About 13 people attended and we used all the postcards the campaign gave Sharon. A lot of good conversation, wine, snacks and we created personal postcards that we hope Democrats will post up on their refrigerators to remind them to vote for Perry on Nov. 6th. In talking to some of the women I learned that they don't feel comfortable going door to door so the postcards give them a way to be involved.

That night Mike emailed me the information about Gordon's chairmanship that I need.

Gordon's tenure can be bullet-pointed thusly:

1. *Financially sound.*
2. *Since taking office, by a wide margin in each election, local Democrats have won 5 straight Town Supervisor races.*
3. *Although not as successful as in the Town Supervisor races (not all council races have been won) we currently have a 4-1 majority on Town Board.*
4. *Successful Town Board winners: Bridget Fleming, Brad Bender, John Bouvier, Julie Lofstad, Tommy John Schiavoni. Sally Pope and Anna Throne-Holst won Council seats before Gordon became chair.*
5. *Created a campaign structure that recognizes the independence of each individual campaign while simultaneously providing oversight for all campaigns. (Robin's role)*
6. *Created various subcommittees to promote candidates, support and assist electeds*
7. *Created a brochure to introduce voters to the party and a party platform*
8. *Has fostered good press relations and has secured third party endorsements (a bone of contention in this Dubow/Herr race).*

Regarding the third-party endorsement disagreement: some of the Southampton Dems think that we should not accept third party endorsements, however, NY is a fusion state, meaning third parties do not have to run their own candidates, they can cross-endorse major parties. And they do. In fact, they cross endorse more frequently than they run candidates. See # 2 above: in each of those 5 winning Town Supervisor races, the Democratic candidate was cross-endorsed by the Independence Party.

Of note, too, many Democrats have been critical of Gordon and the party leaders for running Anna Throne-Holst for office; likewise, Jay Schneiderman -- both were registered Independents when they accepted the Democratic Party line. Their values, though, are our values. Both eventually changed their party affiliation to Democrat (to help advance their careers, admittedly).

Our view has been, all along, that we'd love to only run Democrats and we'd love not to have to deal with the slimy Independence Party (endorsed Zeldin this year) but, as we were in the minority (enrollment wise) for many years, we thought that was a necessary concession to reality. We are now at the stage where we can decide to run only Democrats.

According to Mike and George Lynch, the SHDems treasurer, based on the phone calls they have been having with committee members, Gordon has the votes and it probably will not be close. It is a strange voting system, mandated by the state, that each ED is weighted based on the vote in the last gubernatorial election. When I spoke to George, his sense is David is running this time to make a showing and then when Gordon is looking to retire in two years, he will be the assumed front runner. I told him that was not the impression I had. I think he is running because he believes he can win.

Wednesday, August 29th
Zeldin flyer

A flyer from Zeldin arrived in the mail. The headline is about Park Avenue Perry with a picture of Perry in a tuxedo. I was surprised that Zeldin is going so negative this early and equally surprised that he wasted his money mailing it to me. But it is also the one thing he can throw at Perry that we have all been worried about, that he is new to the district. I only pray that it doesn't take. The irony is it is a nice picture of Perry.

Thursday, August 30th
A tragic loss

We met today at my house not for a meeting but just to socialize. We also felt the need to gather together to support Syma. It was her first time back with us after being away for several weeks. That is because she has suffered a terrible tragedy. Her daughter, a civil rights attorney in Denver, died of a sudden heart attack. She was only 58 years old. I can't even imagine how Syma is coping with losing a child. Rebecca set up a charity fund for us to donate in her daughter's name, Danyel Joffe, with an organization called the Human Rights Campaign.

Danyel, like her mother, was a tireless champion for people in need. "The 58-year-old Denver attorney devoted her life and her legal career to those who otherwise might not have had a voice in the courtroom," was how she was described in a lengthy obituary in The Colorado Sun.[35]

Syma has just gotten back from Denver, from Danyel's funeral which was held at her daughter's synagogue. She and her other two daughters as well as other family were all there. Lloyd was not able to go because of his health which cannot handle the high altitude in Colorado but Syma told us that Lloyd has been very supportive. I was grateful to hear that.

We all listened as Syma talked about her daughter, her work, the funeral. She looked very tired. She left early because she said since she got the news of Danyel's passing, she gets very tired. We each gave her a long hug. There are no adequate words. I am heartbroken for her.

Chapter 18

September 2018

"Perry is a good man. We spent many events seated next to each other and talked frequently. I respect his decision to run a clean campaign from start to finish. I will be voting for him. I truly believe he is in the race for the right reasons. His chance of winning is going to depend on the turnout and the climate of those wanting change."

Brendon Henry, CD#1 Democratic primary candidate

Thursday, September 6th
Two months until Election Day

While I spent the Labor Day holiday weekend with family and was somewhat disconnected from the news, it was there in the background, especially the McCain funeral and burial. Seeing all of Washington, D.C., though notably not Trump, there to commemorate McCain, one couldn't help wondering if the McCain message of honor and duty to country would break through and we might begin to see some profiles in courage against this renegade administration from the GOP.

Then this week, breaking news came at us in a rush. Just like the day when the court decision convicting Manafort and the guilty plea for Cohen hit the news at the same time, there is a sense that something big is happening and we are hurtling forward at top speed toward some kind of reckoning.

First came excerpts from Bob Woodward's new book, Fear, and while the revelations that officials like Defense Secretary James Mattis were disregarding Trump's unhinged orders was not new, it now came with credibility because it came from Woodward.[36]

Then an op-ed article published in *The New York Times* titled, "I Am Part of the Resistance Inside the Trump Administration," by an anonymous senior administration official, validated everything Woodward wrote.[37]

Trump was tweeting and ranting about "treason" and asking *The New York Times* to hand over the individual to the government.

And on the heels of that, Democratic Senators on the Judiciary committee, in particular Corey Booker (D-NJ) put their jobs in jeopardy to make sure the GOP cover-up of Brett Kavanaugh's record would not stand. Chairman Grassley and the GOP were systematically excluding thousands of documents from Kavanaugh's past on the grounds of national security, documents that would expose just how right-wing his record is, and at risk of expulsion from the Senate, first Booker and then other Democrats, like Senator Hirano (D-Hawaii) brought to light emails written by Kavanaugh about Roe vs. Wade, affirmative action, warrantless wiretaps and more. *The New York Times* then published the same documents after they were emailed to the newspaper.

From the article, "Leaked Kavanaugh Documents Discuss Abortion and Affirmative Action," we learned that Kavanaugh questioned whether or not Roe vs. Wade was settled law.[38]

Exactly two months from today is Election Day. There must be a reckoning, there must be a blue wave.

On a personal note, I saw the doctor yesterday for my sore wrist, which feels worse. He does not believe it is carpal tunnel but did recommend bracing it, Advil and rest. He told me to expect it to take two weeks to heal. As long as the brace is on, he said I could type but it has certainly slowed down my writing, which is frustrating given how much work needs to be done. But then today, after very little typing, the wrist started to throb and my hand began to spasm, despite the brace and Advil. So, what I focused on instead was reaching out to arrange events to cover for the book, such as spending a day with Perry on the campaign trail, a day with Wendy at the campaign office that she just took over organizing and scheduling a day and time to canvas with Lulu in our ED. I also registered online for several upcoming Perry events.

Friday, September 7th
Canvassing in ED 19
I stopped working today to listen to President Obama's speech at the University of Illinois where he was receiving the Paul H. Douglas Award for Ethics in Government. He spoke about the greatest threat to our democracy being indifference.

Thank you, President Obama. You are speaking about us. How very much I miss you. You always inspire me to keep going, one day at a time, one door knocked-on at a time, and to not give up despite how often I feel that I cannot keep going. Today was one of those days. I was tired, my wrist was sore, I was feeling anxious about how far behind I am on the book. Given all that, it would have been easy to skip going out today with Lulu to canvas. But I got dressed and was waiting by the front door for Lulu to pick me up at 5:00 PM.

As I have written before, Lulu is my co- ED representative. She is also the wife of John Bouvier, member of the Town Board. She has her own business knitting extraordinary items for babies and children, which she sells at craft fairs and farmers markets across the East End.

At the website for her company, LuluKnits, she explained how she came to be in the business of creating one-of-a-kind hand-knit items for children.[39]

> They say "when life gives you lemons, make lemonade". This proverb makes it sound so simple, but in real life some lemons aren't always so easy to squeeze.
>
> 20 years ago, life gave me a lemon: a 5 hour daily commute between my home in Westhampton and my job in New York City. The journey was a necessary evil I would have to put up with if I wanted to keep my life as it was. I didn't want to choose between my home and my job, just because of the commute. I loved my job in the city! It provided a stable source of income as well as meaningful work. But I also loved my small-town home. Living outside of New York provided plenty of indoor and outdoor space for my children to enjoy their childhood. It enabled me and my husband to take care of my aging in-laws.
>
> However, sitting still for 2 hours on the train without getting bored is not easy. Each morning when I boarded the inbound train to Penn Station, I felt like a child being relegated to the time out chair. But when I realized that these were some of the few -moments in my day that I had control over-- I was not reporting to my boss, nor to my family, I should use the time to do something I love. My grandma taught me how to knit when I was a little girl. So, whenever I knit, it triggers the sweet memories of my childhood. But who has time for that in the 21st century?
>
> This "lemon" of a commute gave me time to brush the cobwebs off of my beloved childhood pastime. Popping in my earphones and listening to a good audiobook, I started to knit on the train. I would knit for family, for friends, for the baby showers of co-workers.... Any excuse was a good one! People started to ask me to knit one-of-a-kind pieces with custom patterns, such as baby names or a favorite animal. Every new request was an opportunity to take on a challenge, expand my collection and hone my design skills.
>
> As the requests started to pour in and my skills developed, I found what I enjoy the most about knitting -- the design. I love that every custom

piece I knit brings the ideas of my customers to life. Each new Lulu Knits commission is an opportunity for me to touch a new family. All of my pieces are knit from cotton yarn, so they're perfect for a baby's sensitive skin, also they are machine washable and easy care for Mom. Whether it's a little sweater, a knit cap, or a cute dress, Lulu Knits become woven into the life of your family as everyday art work. Today, your Lulu Knits are keeping your little babies warm, and tomorrow will become a memento of their childhood.

Now here I am, some 20 years later, finally rid of that 5 hour commute. While I can breathe a HUGE sigh of relief that the Long Island Rail Road is no longer a part of my everyday life, I don't take for granted what it gave me. I'm still addicted to knitting, and I have so many touching stories of clients in my own life's record. I know that when life tells you to make lemonade and gives you nothing but lemons, you just need a bit of creativity. Please enjoy the following pictures of some of my commissions, and if they inspire you, let's work together to bring your ideas to life.

Lulu

Lulu is a fascinating person. Born in Beijing, China, she experienced Mao's Cultural Revolution during her teens and worked in a local factory for years until the Cultural Revolution was over. She came to the United States as a graduate student at SUNY Stony Brook in the Linguistic Department. When she finished her master's degree, she enrolled in the Political Science Department at the same school. After she received her Ph.D. in Political Science, she worked for the headquarters of the Girl Scouts of the USA for 20 years. So, her interest and affinity for politics is in her DNA. She and John have two children, now grown, and since she has her own independent business, it affords her the time to volunteer with the SHDems. She and I are a good team when we go canvassing, because I don't like to drive and she prefers not to be the one speaking to voters because she fears her accent hinders them understanding her.

Lulu, as always, got here on time. This is Lulu's first year with this ED and my second. Reading the materials Gordon sent out about the points assigned to each ED based on voter turnout in the previous gubernatorial election, ours is the lowest. Lulu told me that the ED has more unaffiliated voters than either registered Democrats or Republicans - these are voters who have not registered with either party. This ED tends to be low and moderate income. Our goal, as ED leaders, is to reach out to the voters in our ED and see if by doing so, we can try to raise the voter turnout.

New York does not make it easy for people to vote. One thinks of New York as such a progressive state but when it comes to voting, it is not. We do not have early voting, we do not have vote by mail, we have one day to vote and that day is not a holiday. Yes, one can vote absentee ballot if you are going to be out of the district on Election Day, but just getting the absentee ballot requires several steps - download the form, print it out, fill it out and sign it, mail it then wait for the ballots to arrive for the primaries and general election, fill them out, sign them and get them in the mail on time. Both Eugene and Matt have requested absentee ballots for this year. But how many people take the time and effort to do this? And if you are working on Election Day, especially if you do shift work, and you have a family to take care of, it is not easy to go out and cast your vote. It is not an accident that the United States has such low voter participation. We don't make it easy.

Today was my first time knocking on doors for Perry as our Democratic nominee. We have been out here twice this year for signatures, but now we are speaking to people about the importance of voting for Perry on November 6th. We have palm cards about Perry and a flyer with the truth about Zeldin's record. This is the same flyer that we handed out over the summer.

There are some streets in our ED that are hard to canvas since the houses are on busy roads. We look for a street to start on that makes it easy to park the car and then walk to reach the houses. We usually park, knock on several houses that are on our list and then go back, get the car and drive it forward and then repeat.

We used a walk list the campaign gave us. Lulu entered the walk list number into the app MiniVAN which was loaded onto her smartphone. For more information on how MiniVAN works, you can go to their website at **https://act.ngpvan.com/minivan**. Years ago, before this technology, one went canvassing with paper and pencil, filling in the information – was the person home or not home, what was their reaction, etc. – and then would have to scan and email the lists to the campaign office. A walk list shows us the person's name, age, gender and how they are registered. The lists we were using did not show registered Republicans because we were not knocking on those doors. We were focused on Democrats, as well as those voters not registered with any party, called Blanks or Unaffiliated (U), and voters registered with the Independence Party (I).

No one was home at half the houses. So, we left the palm card on their front door. We are not allowed to put them in mailboxes. Of those who were home, probably half were Democrats and the other half were split between the U and I.

Mostly they were women. And they were all receptive to taking the materials, which was encouraging. A few women were very enthusiastic. One woman, who is U, told us not to worry, that while she is not a registered Democrat, she knows all about the race and will make sure she votes for Perry.

Some of the streets had small homes, with small yards that were not well tended, and overall looked in a state of disrepair. Being a homeowner myself and knowing how high the cost is for upkeep, one can assume these are homes that if they have to decide between food, medicine, and other basic necessities versus having the house painted or a broken wooden door replaced, that repairs have to wait. Financial insecurity is a terrible state of anxiety to live in. No wonder voting is at the bottom of the list, though these are families who need a government that provides services and if their voices are not heard, they tend to suffer the most. The greatest con that con man Trump has pulled off is promising low income Americans that he would be there to help them.

We turned a corner and entered a street where the homes are equally small but in far better shape. Many of the houses are made from red brick, with neat slate walkways, lawns that are mowed and small gardens in front of the house. The distance in the lives of the residents from one street to the other is the difference between hanging onto a rung in the middle class and falling further behind.

Yet, when we found people home, no matter which street we were on, they were receptive to taking the materials and receptive to speaking to us about the election and voting for Perry. That gave me hope. The other commonality between all the homes is how many of them have a dog, with a sign in the window that says, Beware of Dog.

One of the last houses we went to, an older couple were sitting on their front porch, smoking cigarettes. We walked up to the front steps and greeted them. Only the husband was on our list, and he is a registered Democrat. We know the wife is either not registered or a Republican. When we told them who we are and why we were there, the husband smiled at us, took the materials and said he will be voting for Perry. The wife, half joking, said don't hand them to her because she is a Republican and wouldn't vote for a Democrat if her life depended on it. I smiled and said that maybe her husband could convince her and she answered, "Not a chance."

When we meet a mixed political couple like this, usually the woman is the Democrat and the husband is the Republican. We thanked the husband, smiled and walked away. We do not try to convince her. And I wondered what kind of discussion they will have after we leave.

All in all, our canvassing was encouraging. Many voters already knew about the election, knew that Perry is the Democrat and were interested in information about the race. Many of them mentioned anger at Trump. One senses, from speaking to these voters, that some of the Democratic votes this fall will be anti-Trump votes.

The other takeaway is a reminder that most people appreciate the effort that the canvasser is making to come to their door and speak with them in person, about the election. I am struck by how many people thanked us.

Lulu dropped me off at home around 7:00 PM. We made a vow to go out to our ED at least once a week from now through the election. I laid down on the couch. I was very tired and my wrist was throbbing but I would rather be out walking and knocking on doors than making phone calls. I think it is the most effective way to reach out to people and I hope that the personal touch will motivate them to make the effort to get to the polls on November 6th and vote.

Wednesday, September 12th
Postcards!
Perry's campaign posted this today on their Facebook page.

> *We've hit a milestone that we're extremely touched by and couldn't wait to announce. YOU have written 20,000 postcards that will be mailed across the district, spreading the news of our campaign, what we stand for and why we believe our solutions will be better for this district and this country.*
>
> *Think about that. Twenty. Thousand. Hand written. Postcards. All written with love, with passion and with conviction, by people who want change and who believe in our message. Some were even embellished with drawings and other designs. This is so heartwarming and energizing for our campaign and I can't thank you enough.*
>
> *There are more postcards to write, though. Many more. A hundred thousand more. We need your help. A hand written postcard coming from a neighbor is one of the most effective ways for us to cut through the noise and reach our voters, and we need to keep them coming.*
>
> *To get involved, keep an eye out on this FB page for postcard party events, hold your own party, or simply request some blank postcards for you to complete at your leisure.*

Quick shout out that our friends at the East End Action Network are hosting a postcard writing event today (Sept. 12th) to benefit our campaign.

Postcards are a vital and incredibly effective way to get the word out about Perry and our campaign and we are so thankful for our entire postcard writing army.

See below for EEAN's blurb about the event. Can you attend? If so, please please please let us know below.

PLEASE SHARE!

"This Wednesday, September 12th, the East End Action Network will host its 4th postcard writing event! To date, we've created over 2,000 postcards that will be sent to democratic voters, encouraging them to get to the polls in November. Your neighbors need to hear from you! Join us this week at the Westhampton Beach Public Library from 6:30 to 7:30PM. Everything will be provided for you."

Our event that night at the library was terrific. We were expecting about 15 people. We ended up with closer to 35. Along with being posted on Perry's Facebook page it was also on EEAN's site and in our newsletter. And we had a lot of new faces, people who have never come to one of our meetings before, who wanted to be involved in helping to flip this district.

We had five tables. Sharon did her usual amazing job preparing it. She had printed out a packet of materials for every person who sent an RSVP – 14 of Perry's postcards, address labels, suggestions of what to write – along with two baskets of art materials for each table that contained permanent markers, scissors, ribbons, stickers, all kinds of things to decorate and personalize the cards. Then we had a lot of people come she wasn't expecting but Sharon is always prepared, having brought extras of everything. Retired teachers make the best activists.

It was tremendous to see so many new faces, so many people who want to be involved. Of course, a lot of camaraderie and talking while we're doing it, but everybody made sure they got their postcards done.

Today, as well, Indivisible Northfork hosted their Action Wednesdays with their weekly postcard writing event, coordinated with Perry's campaign. Next Wednesday we will join with them in Riverhead rather than host our own postcard event. Other grassroots groups around the district, such as Solidarity Sundays and Resist and Replace, are also hosting postcard writing parties.

And Perry has opened up more campaign offices that are coordinating with the Democratic committees and grassroots groups for canvassing, providing postcards and lawn signs, and voter registration drives. This Saturday, Mike is helping to spearhead a Latino voter registration drive in Hampton Bays, in coordination with the campaign and several grassroots groups in the district, in particular, Neighbors in Support of Immigrants (NISI).

This is the way Mike explained the project in an email.

> *I've done an analysis using the last three years registration data to determine that 40% + of newly registered Latino voters in Southampton Township have registered from Hampton Bays, with, potentially, more eligible voters waiting for us to show up to register them. (I hope.) Our plan is to fan out into HB with a focus on registering more Latino voters.*
>
> *We are using a method developed by Brookhaven's EJ Lopez. EJ found that registering voters at set locations yielded meager results, so he decided to "go where the voters are." So, door-to-door registering became the preferred method.*
>
> *The beauty of EJ's method is that it combines registering new voters with canvassing. We will hit every door (except Republicans) and address each door as presented. I've been out twice doing this and found the method very beneficial.*
>
> *By using MiniVAN app that provides house by house registered voter info:*
>
> 1) *Registered Democrats - urge them to support Perry, provide palm card, ask if any other eligible voter needing to be registered*
> 2) *Registered Unaffiliated/Indy - Urge them to support Perry, provide Palm Card, if positive response ask about voter registration*
> 3) *No apparent voter at this house -- ask occupant if they are interested in registering*
> 4) *Registered Republican - Don't bother*
> 5) *Mixed house - Republican and Dem; or Indy and Dem; or 2 Rep and one Dem -- Use discretion*

> *We will report results through MiniVAN -- that is responses from registered voters.*

An update on the debate situation between Perry and Zeldin: up until now, Zeldin has been refusing to debate. Now he has agreed to three, but only right before the election. Perry posted about dual interviews he and Zeldin gave to the local newspaper, *The Independent*.

> *Since Lee won't debate live, The Independent was able to simulate a debate through interviews by reporter T.E. McMorrow. The attached article provides an account of my views and Lee's on a variety of issues. I tried to provide in-depth and concrete answers to the questions. You can come to your own conclusions on Lee's responses to the same questions.*
>
> *I'll leave rebuttal of his positions for another time. We touch on healthcare, woman's choice, immigration, energy policy, transportation and the Mueller inquiry.*

Right now, this article, "Zeldin and Gershon Square Off: The Candidates Discuss the Issues in Separate Interviews," is the closest we can get to a debate between them.[40]

Perry's answers are clearer and more forceful than Zeldin. I am feeling encouraged. I am not the only one.

"I'm naturally optimistic. I mean, that's my nature and I think Perry's got a really good shot," said Gordon. "He's got a really good organization. I think that obviously depending on what happens over the next couple of months with Trump and how it plays out with the Mueller investigation and whatever else is going on that might play a role in it. You know, a year or two ago when Perry first came to me, I said to him, 'this is such a long shot, you really sure you want to do this?' But now, he's really come a long way. I think he's got a really good message, I think he presents himself well and he has a lot of volunteers out there working for him. I think he can make it."

Thursday, September 13th
New York State Primary

The tendonitis in my right wrist is worse so I am stuck having to record my thoughts rather than composing them in writing. I use the same app on my phone that I use for recording sources in interviews that provides me with a written transcript. It is not perfect but better than nothing.

Today was the NY Primary. New York has this ridiculous primary system where for federal offices, the primary is in June and for state offices, the primary is in September. And this year is even more confusing because it was moved from Tuesday to Thursday so it wouldn't be on the Jewish holiday. Given that we never vote on Thursday, how many people are going to remember to go vote? I am sure that turnout will be low.

But it appeared to be the opposite. From the reports I got today from Gordon, voter turnout all across Suffolk County was high. Across the state, it's kind of a mixed bag for progressives. Many of the progressive candidates that we were supporting did not win, but they did make it close.

I did not vote for Cynthia Nixon. While I'm not crazy about Governor Cuomo, I just did not feel that Nixon was qualified. It's not enough to be a celebrity. She has been very involved in the New York City education reform movement but has no background managing a large business or legislative experience or legal experience. And while I agreed with her platform, and I thought she did fairly well in the debate with Cuomo, I just did not feel she was ready to be the governor of such a large and diverse state.

I did vote for the other slate of progressive candidates, and it is disappointing that none of them won their primary. But we did get an African American woman as attorney general, Letitia James. She will be the first African American woman to hold statewide office in New York. And it is very exciting that of the eight incumbent Democrats in districts around New York who were running for the State Senate, who were part of the IDC movement, the Independent Democratic Committee that voted with Republicans and stood in the way of progressive legislation in the State Senate, six of those eight Democrats lost in their primaries.

The hope is these six Democrats will win against the Republicans in the fall, which they should. These are districts that normally vote Democrat. But by electing true progressive Democrats and getting rid of Democrats that voted with the Republicans, maybe, just maybe we can start putting into law some of the legislation that comes out of our Assembly, things like the New York Health Act, a single payer system for New Yorkers, more gun control and election reform.

One of the things I have learned in the last year, as I got involved in this journey, is to pay much closer attention to local, county and statewide elections.

Also, today the DCCC announced that they see our district as competitive. This is a huge step forward. Zeldin won by such a large margin in 2016 that we were not considered a swing district. They have added our district to their Red to Blue initiative, which hopefully means more help and more money coming in. This is a very exciting step forward for us. When we were knocking on doors last year for the local election, the hope was if we could show how energized Democrats are, that we would start to be seen more as a swing district instead of a solidly Republican district.

Everybody says this will be a turnout election. I believe that to be true. It is up to us. Perry's doing his job. We have to do ours.

Monday, September 17th
Immigration
Back at the doctor yesterday and this time they took blood for tests. Since the soreness has moved to acute pain in both wrists as well as spasms in both hands, the fear is it is something more systemic rather than tendonitis in one wrist. I will find out in about a week. Is it arthritis? Is it rheumatoid arthritis? Is it stress from typing?

The doctor's appointment forced me to miss an important Zeldin event yesterday. He held what his office called an immigration forum at the Suffolk County Community College in Riverhead. But, like all Zeldin events, it wasn't a forum, it was just a photo-op because he did not invite any of the organizations who are advocates for immigrants in this district. People found out at the eleventh hour and organized a fairly large protest in front of the campus.

I gather that professors and students on the campus joined with the protesters. They were very upset that this kind of hate event was on their campus, and it was encouraging that in the articles that I have seen in the press about the event reporters covered the protest as much as they did Zeldin's forum, and that is really important.

Perry issued the following statement:

Statement from Perry Gershon on "Immigration Roundtable" at Suffolk County Community College, Eastern Campus, Riverhead

> *Immigration is a serious topic for serious reform and debate. The Trump administration's policy of detaining immigrant children in cages is abhorrent to humanity and the rule of law. Snatching babies from their parents is simply un-American.*
>
> *Lee Zeldin's taxpayer-funded, closed-door "immigration roundtable" is no more than a charade. It was designed by his campaign for Lee to look tough on immigration—without the inconvenience of including advocates for immigrant communities.*
>
> *This is textbook Lee: espouse extremist xenophobic views in front of TV cameras, while not allowing his own constituents in the room. Because Lee did not announce the event would be closed until just before it was scheduled to begin, dozens of people showed up to attend and were prevented by police from entering.*
>
> *If I had been given a seat at the table, I would be advocating for bipartisan commonsense immigration reform: more sophisticated border security including investments in technology, keeping families together, and creating a fair legal path to citizenship. In Congress, I will make all of those a priority.*
>
> *We must remember immigrants are a vibrant part of our Suffolk County communities. I'm rooted in lasting, practical and comprehensive policies that respect the rule of law. Enough of this unproductive showmanship. It is time for Lee to face his constituents, the great people of NY-1.*

Wendy, who was there, posted this message on the EEAN Facebook page:

> *Great turnout today at Rep. Zeldin's unrepresentative immigration forum. Only "invited" guests were allowed in so we stood quietly outside to not disrupt classes. Many varied groups were there who are fighting for fairness and justice and many of their spokespeople spoke eloquently about their work, and opposition to Rep. Zeldin. During class changing times, Perry Gershon staff and volunteers fanned out with voter registration forms and Perry literature to speak to students! Quite a few returned completed returns to us, and both they, and students already registered, expressed strong support for Perry Gershon. WE CAN DO THIS!! YES, WE CAN!!*

In reading Perry's message and Wendy's, I was struck by how rational, reasonable and compassionate they are. But we still have not come up with an argument that addresses the irrational fear stoked by Zeldin and Trump. Is reason enough?

We also got some good news yesterday. According to a poll commissioned by Take Action Suffolk County (TASC), Zeldin is only up by three percentage points, which is within the margin of error. With six weeks to go for Perry to get his name and his message out there to the voters, that seems like a margin we can make up.

In the national news an accuser has come forward against Judge Kavanagh claiming that he attempted to rape her when they were in high school. She did not want to come forward and be quoted on the record, but her information was leaked. They have opened the hearing back up for her to speak next Monday.

I am reminded of the Anita Hill hearing in 1991. I was working as a producer at PBS, but I happened to be home the day she spoke. It was infuriating. It just heightened my sense of the importance of women achieving more power in our political system, in the media, and really, in all forms of life, because the way Anita Hill was treated in front of that committee was a scandal. And Clarence Thomas was confirmed anyway.

Friday, September 21st
The Montauk Lighthouse
Zeldin starts running a new ad that is very slick, with beautiful aerial shots of historic locations around the district. I was worried because I thought the ad was effective. But then I saw on Facebook that the video in the Zeldin ad of the famous Montauk lighthouse was actually stock footage of a lighthouse in Estonia. This gave Perry an opportunity to say that while he only recently moved to the district to live here full time, he certainly knows the Montauk lighthouse when he sees it.

In addition, the campaign put out a new ad on healthcare. I do think Zeldin is vulnerable for his vote to repeal the ACA. I think people are genuinely worried about the loss of protection for pre-existing conditions. I know I am worried about it.

Sunday, September 23rd
Swing state family focus group
As we got to the end of September, we saw the winding down of our EEAN postcard-writing events. Soon, instead of writing new postcards we would be

busy addressing the thousands of hand-written postcards and getting them in the mail so that voters received them in October before Election Day.

EEAN postcard event

I was off the political grid this weekend because we had company. It was a lovely visit with Eugene's cousins. Claude and Janie traveled from Ohio and Marilyn, Claude's sister, came from Pennsylvania. We went sightseeing around the East End, including a trip out to Montauk to see the lighthouse.

They are all Democrats and were intrigued with what we are doing in our district and with my book project. They are African American and live in swing states that went for Trump, so I asked if I could get their thoughts and insights about Trump on the record. They agreed but given the recent increase in hate crimes, they requested only using their first names.

What was it like in 2016 in your district during the campaign? Did it feel different than previous years? The polls were showing Hillary up, I think in Pennsylvania.

Marilyn: Well, I think like most people, I thought that Hillary was going to win, according to the polls on television. However, I did notice early on that there were no signs in front yards, for Trump or Hillary, so we didn't know where the community was going. But based on the polls, we assumed that Hillary would win the election. When I went to the polls on Election Day, I did sense a little bit of quietness and distance but didn't pay any attention to that until afterwards, then it registered with me. And while my district did not vote for Trump there were a lot of Trump supporters. That's why there were no signs on the lawns. I thought they were probably not willing to let on that they were in favor of Trump.

Claude: I also noticed there were fewer signs than usual. I thought Hillary was going to win. I was totally surprised by the results. Even though my county voted for Hillary it appeared that the blue-collar areas had predominantly supported Donald Trump.

While both of your areas voted for Hillary, were the margins of her victory say, lower than you saw for Obama?

Claude: Yes, the margins were lower. Surprisingly, in contrast with the 2008 election and 2012, you had a feel for where your neighbors and your community were, by just the showing of signs which way they were going to vote, but in the 2016 election, nobody was willing to commit or show a commitment of which way they were leading to vote. That was a scary feeling because even though in your heart and going into the polls, you felt that Hillary was going to walk away with a marginal victory, you didn't see it displayed by the voters. Even talking with co-workers or friends, nobody really revealed themselves but after the election you can tell by one's actions who voted for him and who did not vote for Trump. Unfortunately, this particular election, like I said before, there seems to be a sense of fear, not wanting another person to know where you stood on each candidate.

Trump has given license to the racism and white nationalism in the country. Does it make you feel differently about the country that we live in?

Claude: I have not personally experienced any increase in racism since Trump but I have noticed that Trump's reaction to race, his negative reaction to African Americans and people of color has entitled racists to feel comfortable in saying and doing things that they had not been doing but had wanted to do.

Janie: Yes. I've always known that it was there, even though people didn't talk about it, but the problem now is that people are showing their bias more. I mean, especially, when you hear it from the top, in the president and the people that he has surrounded himself with and the things that they're doing. You knew people had those feelings but it wasn't sanctioned, I would say almost like it is right now and encouraging people. What is even more disturbing is at the Trump rallies, I see young kids and they are being indoctrinated into that negative, racist, divisive rhetoric that he espouses. So, that to me is very worrisome and bothersome. I have grandchildren and I worry how will this impact them. Some of them are too young to feel it now, they are four years old, five years old and seven months, but my oldest granddaughter, who is 15, I think she's beginning to experience some racism, particularly in school. I do encourage her to think black and to be black.

Now, tell me what that means. Describe what that means, to think black and to be black.

Janie: That to me means recognizing first of all, who you are, being okay with who you are as a black person and being a part of the black race. Recognizing that there is racism amongst some people but not all people and feeling that you have just as much right and you're just as smart as someone else and not to let someone tell you differently or treat you differently. I see her responding to that. In particular, she'll wear her hair natural. I know some of her friends say, "I like your hair better when you have it straightened out." She says, "But, I like it the other way." Like, "You can't tell me what to do with my hair." That kind of stuff. She has a pretty good sense of self.

Would you say that's the same message that your sons were raised with? This idea of be black, be proud of being black, be who you are. Did they, in their education, in their careers, did they ever experience any sort of overt racism or are they seeing more now than they did before Trump was elected?

Janie: Our youngest son recently had to deal with a boss that was saying things, calling him, boy. This was about three weeks ago. So, he handled it. He went and spoke with this person's superiors.

Claude: We all live in the suburbs. And, they still do have white friends, which they get along very well with. I don't know how their friends are reacting to them in terms of Trump or anything like that. But, I want to say this, I want to say as a veteran, a Vietnam veteran who has gone to war for this country, I am embarrassed how Trump has made the country look to the rest of the world. To anybody that served in the military, it's a disgrace. Would you go put your life forward to protect this country, then you have someone come in office that has never been in the military, found ways to stay out of the military and then tear down the military and then tear down the image of the country on a global scene? And I think it would be a difference between African American veterans and white veterans, in terms of supporting Trump. A lot of those white veterans they're also the people that live in the coal mining regions, Trump's base, so it is less about being veterans and more because of their economic status now and the communities they live in.

Do you find you have more awareness or hyper-vigilance to what messages might be coming at you from people than you did before?

Marilyn: Trump encourages racism. I have to say that I'm a little bit more open to seeing if anyone is feeling freer to express racism when dealing with me. I'm looking out for that in other words. I'm changing the way I deal with people and how I see people. I'm trying to be more aware of it. If you're black in America now, you're always on your toes just a little bit more. Are there any changes around me? Is it injuring my small world, my arena, where I operate from? A little bit … because of Trump other people feel free to share their racism. Sharing their racism instead of, you know, keeping their personal feelings to themselves.

Claude: It is a survival mechanism. Assume when meeting a white person that they are racist until they prove otherwise.

Wednesday, September 26th
EEAN leadership meeting and Candidate Forum

I drove with Sharon to Rebecca's house for our EEAN leadership meeting. I got to finally meet her fiancé, Sarah, who is a nurse. Rebecca had gluten free pizzas for dinner and we discussed what we want the group to be doing going forward, between now and Election Day. We discussed what events to focus on in support of Perry and to also work on registering voters. We decide on two more postcard parties and a pop-up canvassing weekend in Center Moriches.

After the meeting, we all drove together to the Mastic Fire House for a candidate forum. It ended up being a wild experience. Below is a description on Facebook from Steven Lupo of Let's Flip CD-1 of what happened there.

> *I attended the Mastic Park Civic Association tonight. The event was hosted by the Civic Association but Nancy Marr, the president of the LWV, acted as the moderator for the question and answer portion. Unbeknownst to many of the candidates, if only one of the two candidates, for a particular office was in attendance, the attending candidate would only be allowed two questions. Since Zeldin did not attend, Perry was limited to answering two questions.*

After he received his two questions, he proceeded to leave the building. He was followed by a throng of Zeldin loyalists. Luckily, we had promoted this event amongst our team, so there were plenty of his supporters following too.

Zeldin's team tried to say Perry was lying, by saying Zeldin was too afraid to face him. They said Perry should've known that Zeldin was going to be in Washington tonight. The president of the Civic Association, Ray, was right next to Perry. Perry informed the crowd that he was told in the initial email that Zeldin would be in attendance. Ray backed Perry up, he said he would provide the email to the crowd, to prove Perry correct.

Zeldin's team came well prepared. They were hitting Perry about some ridiculous story of spending a lot of money on a bottle of wine and loaning money for offshore drilling. To be perfectly frank, I couldn't help but giggle to myself. Zeldin's team was taking Perry to task for such ridiculous things, while Zeldin has been hiding from us for the last two years.

Zeldin's Director of Constituent Services, Bill Doyle, was stoking the flames with his team.

Perry handled it like a Mench. He did something that Zeldin would never do, he faced an adversarial crowd—on camera.

They were some heated side arguments. But I had a very, very pleasant conversation with a young man, who was a Zeldin supporter. He actually said to me that he respected the fact that Perry was standing there answering questions.

The crowd in the parking lot was probably 50-50. Thank God, Perry had supporters there to speak in his defense.

Many of our Let's Flip CD-1 members were there. It was a pleasure to meet some of you in person. Please, by all means, post your thoughts here. There was no way any one person could've observed everything going on tonight.

I admired the way Perry handled it but it really shook us up. The threat of violence was in the air. Below is my comment on the Facebook chain:

> *Yesterday was outrageous. I hope the campaign has given this information to the press. Those Trump/Zeldin supporters who ambushed Perry Gershon_are thugs. As I stood there, watching Perry calmly and graciously answer their ambush questions, behind me were a group of white males yelling at Perry and at us. I felt a real fear they would become violent. I am grateful to Perry and his staff for keeping it from escalating.*

Thursday, September 27th
Christine Blasey Ford
After a whole day of watching these hearings, what is the bottom line? Christine Blasey Ford was credible and Kavanaugh was not. He came across as a privileged, white, male jerk. It sickened me. Senators Jeff Flake and Chris Coons are asking for an expanded FBI investigation. We will see. I don't trust Flake. He talks about standing up to Trump but then always votes with Trump and the GOP.

Saturday, September 29th
Perry Facebook video
Perry has a great new video on Facebook. Here's the script to it.

> *I'm in this race to bring the voice of everyone in this District to the halls of Congress. It's not about politics, it's about doing what's best for the people of Suffolk County and this country. I've now driven over 35,000 miles from hamlet to hamlet and back again, listening to people's concerns and sharing my vision.*
>
> *I am energized in this last month to bring home a win for everyone who thinks we can do better, who thinks that government can and should do more for every American, who knows that that the direction we're currently headed in is wrong and wants to make change. I hope you'll view this look into just one day on the campaign. Please share if you're on #TeamPerry*

PART III
RACE TO THE FINISH: OCTOBER – NOVEMBER 2018

Chapter 19

October 2018

"Kavanaugh was one of the lowest points for me since the Trump election. After the Women's March and after the #MeToo movement, I was hopeful that we would have been able to affect a different outcome. And, the fact that we weren't really shows what we are up against. It is the last gasp of the white male patriarchy. And they are going down in a really ugly way. That concerns me and is why I think it may get worse before it gets better. However, if America survives the next 30 years, people of color will be the majority; and that's coming whether they want it or not. They can't stop it, though they are trying their damnedest."

Kathryn Szoka, PEER

Monday, October 1st - Monday, October 8th
A hard week

The first week in October was difficult. I was often torn between what I should be covering for the book and what I should be doing to help elect Perry. The book required staying on top of interviews and covering events while activism pulled me from one postcard-writing event to another, with long days canvassing in between. It was also a week of emotional whiplash, lurching from inspiration to despair.

One of the inspiring moments was EEAN's last postcard writing event on October 3rd. Another great crowd, another great event organized by Sharon. Soon these personalized cards would be mailed to Democratic voters throughout the district.

At the end of the week, the Senate voted to confirm Kavanaugh, and plunged us into one of the lowest political points of 2018. I posted this comment on Facebook in response to Kavanaugh's confirmation:

> *The federal courts are now packed with right wing conservatives, up to and including the Supreme Court. We have lost the judiciary for a generation. What this means is the loss of voting rights, civil rights, immigrant rights, gay rights, consumer rights, women's right to choose, protection for pre-existing conditions, union rights, privacy rights, environmental rights. The list goes on. The courts are now set up to protect the profits of wealthy privileged white men. But the truth is that for most of our history, this has been the case and after a brief period of the Supreme Court standing for equality, it has been moving in the direction away from that for a long time (Citizens United, Hobby Lobby, etc.). It will not stop the march of history, of a more diverse, more tolerant country. To continue that progress we MUST take back the levers of legislative and executive power, both federal and state. Then we pass laws that reinstate those protections. And each time the courts knock them down, we vote them right back. The judiciary is lost but this war for the soul of our nation is not over. It all depends on our ability to rally the majority of the country to vote, to rise above all the voting obstacles that have been placed in front of us, to shake the majority out of their apathy, and vote these people out of office. Election Day is one month from today. Vote, make sure your friends and family vote, and never stop voting. Our rights depend on it. And come help us in CD#1*

to vote our Trump clone Tea Party Congressman out of office and elect Perry Gershon_our next Congressman.

Immediately we saw a Kavanaugh backlash hit our district. *The New York Times* had been conducting real time polling of our district. The first day, Perry and Zeldin were nearly tied. Then the Senate voted to confirm Kavanaugh and that weekend Zeldin increased in the poll, in the end widening the gap to 9 points. As Trump and Zeldin hammered away at how the rabid left slandered the poor privileged white man, one could see reflected in this poll how this roused the Trump/Zeldin support, awakening their base. I feared this was a turning point in the race and we would not have enough time to recover.

The news outside my door was dispiriting this week and then within my immediate world, it became even sadder. Marge Copeland, my dear friend Mary's mother, died suddenly from leukemia. We had all marched together at the Tax Day March last year in New York City and met for dinner after this year's Women's March. Even in her 90s, Marge was a warrior for the Resistance. Below is a photo of Marge with her family. Instead of traveling to D.C., they stayed in New York City. Marge walked the whole distance.

Elise Levinger, Marge Copeland, Mary Copeland, Bob Spatafora and Joanna Levinger at the 2017 NYC Women's March.

Mary described Marge's decline to me in an email. While her passing was sudden, her decline was not:

The course of Mom's decline was a slow process. Her main issues were the osteoarthritis, severe macular degeneration (she could see very little) and atrial tachycardia for which she was on daily heart meds. She had been getting progressively tired/exhausted for about two months, had stopped cleaning her house (which was shocking since she was a compulsive cleaner), asked me to look into assisted living residences and was finding it harder and harder to get to the senior program at the 92nd Y where she was an active member. For several weeks Bob and I repeatedly took her to the doctor at Mt. Sinai Geriatric clinic thinking it was her heart condition, atrial tachycardia, but that looked fine and it wasn't until her visit on Sept. 18th that the doctors did further blood work. I was called by her doctor Thursday, Sept. 20th at 6:00PM to tell me that she had acute leukemia and told me to take her to the ER immediately to get a bone marrow biopsy. When I told her about her diagnosis, her immediate response -- "Well, if you're going to get leukemia, 93's a good age to get it." Always the trooper.

In the ER, when a third- year medical student conducted the cognitive exam and asked her if she knew who the president is, she said Trump was the reason she was sick, that as soon as Trump announced his candidacy, she's been going downhill ever since. Later that day, the oncologist came to discuss her leukemia. She said that the only reason a bone marrow biopsy was necessary was to do targeted chemotherapy, but since she didn't want treatment there was no need to put her through that. The only available bed in the hospital was on the palliative care floor and her decline was rapid. Her care there was extraordinary -- compassion, kindness and support, but that floor was designed for patients who required extreme symptom and pain management and she just required a little morphine to keep her comfortable. She spent her last 36 hours there and passed on Oct. 4th.

She was a great lady. I will miss her and I am heartbroken for Mary and her family.

Tuesday, October 9th
SHDems convention

Because of my sore wrists, I am not yet typing so I am reduced to recording my thoughts every evening. The blood work came back negative and the doctor referred me to a hand specialist. After X-rays, he said it is not arthritis and not a systemic disease. Evidently, there is a ligament that is in this wrist joint that just wears out over time, it is called a TFCC tear. He gave me one cortisone shot in the right wrist, which does feel a little bit better. I will go back in two weeks for a shot in the left wrist. That is really all I can do. It is a chronic condition, brought on by age and wear and tear. There is a surgery if it should get much worse but it is a big deal with no guarantees. Not something I would even consider right now.

Today was our convention for the SHDems leadership positions. I spent last week working on my nominating speech for Gordon, based on the information Mike sent me and my own experience. I tried to be thorough and hit all the pertinent facts about why I believed Gordon deserved another term. The top of the speech was similar to the information Gordon emailed, Mike sent me and the endorsement letter from the elected officials. The last part of the speech was based on my personal experiences with Gordon. I showed it to Mike and he approved. I practiced the speech and the total time came to six minutes. I was concerned it might be too long but Mike thought it was fine.

It was a very long night. Each candidate, for each executive position, had two people speaking to put their name in nomination. Along with David's challenge, he had also put forward a slate of candidates to challenge the other executive positions. This made for a lot of speeches. In addition, David had requested a debate before the vote, then a question and answer period as well as allowing anyone who wanted to speak on behalf of the candidates to come up to the podium and talk. David clearly needed the speeches. Gordon had a ten-year record to run on. David just had the head of the search committee for the last couple of years.

Gordon's supporters who spoke, including many elected officials, praised how he had guided the committee through that ten-year tenure and helped shepherd Democrats to the majority party in Southampton Township. They pointed out his skills as a spokesman for the SHDems, as a fundraiser, as a partner to the campaigns and how his knowledge and experience had helped create the supermajority on the Town Board and would help the candidates and campaigns of the future.

Most of David's supporters who spoke in support of his challenge praised his efforts to open up the committee with needed reforms. They had nothing bad to say about Gordon and his tenure but wanted to move the committee into a new direction and felt a new chair would help make that possible.

But there were several who made outrageous attacks on Gordon. There was that same vitriol that I had witnessed months before over the platform. One member gave an angry and divisive speech claiming that Gordon had kept her off the committee because he is a racist and thanked David for her now being a member.

She accused Gordon of not caring about minority populations in the Township and that this was the reason there were so few minorities on the committee. It was hurtful and offensive. In contrast, not one of Gordon's supporters said anything derogatory about David or his slate of candidates.

One questioner stood up and asked, "What is each of you going to do as candidates to reach out to the grassroots? I know several people in the grassroots who don't feel welcome here."

I looked around at all the new members, like myself, from the grassroots, ushered in by David and by Gordon.

Since the election of the chair was the last event, these nominating speeches came at the end of a long evening. Gordon had me and Mike as his nominators. Mike went first and his speech was similar to the email he had sent me but with more humor. As always, he hit all the right notes, getting straight to the heart of the matter.

Then it was my turn. It was very late, we still had to vote and I could tell people were getting restless. So, I made a quick decision to jettison most of my speech. Much of what I had been going to say had already been said many times by others. In retrospect, I wish I had given the whole speech but at the time it seemed like the most prudent thing to do, to just go with the end of my speech which was the personal part. I realized after listening to all of the speeches supporting David, that it was this part of my speech that directly countered their arguments against Gordon. I understood then why Gordon had asked me to do this.

I stood at the podium and explained why I was shortening the speech – so much had already been said, it was late and we were short of time. But I did want to give them my personal reasons for supporting Gordon. Then I read the last paragraphs, slowly and emphatically. I looked down at my paper then looked up and stared intently at the crowd. I worked hard to not raise my voice. I wanted to convey authority but not seem strident.

> *Let me tell you a little bit about my own experiences with Gordon, experiences that I believe are equally informative about why Gordon deserves another term as Chairman. I reached out to Gordon in March, 2017. I was a member of a national grassroots policy group called Rise Stronger and a local grassroots group, East End Action Network. Like so many women across the country, I had been motivated to get involved first by the election of Trump and secondly, by the Women's March. My*

focus then was solely on trying to stop the repeal of the Affordable Care Act and I contacted Gordon to see if there would be a way to form a coalition of the Democratic Party and the grassroots to organize protests together.

In these conversations, Gordon asked me if I would be interested in joining the Committee. At first, I said no. I already had a lot on my plate. But more and more I realized that the only clear check on the destruction of our democracy by Trump and the GOP was going to come at the ballot box and I did not believe that the energy of the grassroots alone would be enough to win elections. So, I said I would join the Committee but only if I could continue to work on finding ways to combine the electoral expertise of the Committee with the passion and energy of the grassroots.

He never hesitated for a minute, immediately connecting me to a number of Committee members who were interested in the same thing and he has continued to support this effort ever since. The result – the Politics 101 Forum which led to the creation of the Southampton Progressive Caucus, a steering committee that coordinates groups like EEAN, PEER, LVLZ, R&R and others with the Southampton Democratic Committee. Together we organized voter registration drives, sponsored forums and debates during the primary and have joined with Perry's campaign to canvas, phone bank and help to flip our district.

To me, what could be more democratic with a small "d" than inviting me, an outsider, into the process and then helping that outsider work to open the Committee up to more people from the grassroots?

In addition, when I told Gordon almost a year ago that, as a journalist, I was interested in writing a book about this journey leading up to the midterm election, to chronicle all of our efforts to flip our district, he encouraged me to go forward with the project and in our ongoing conversations for the book project, he has never once asked me to put any discussion we had off the record or on background.

What could be more transparent than allowing a reporter to be part of this process? Trust me on this. I have been a reporter for over 30 years. I have interviewed leaders of Congress, diplomats, corporate CEOs, union heads, hospital directors, and chairmen and women. People who are more interested in closed door, backroom deals than an open, transparent process do not allow a reporter to witness their leadership of that organization.

For all these reasons, I am honored to place Gordon Herr's name in nomination and strongly endorse his election to another term as our Chairman. Thank you.

Then we voted under the strange system I described earlier, where each ED is assigned points based on the voter turnout in that ED in the last gubernatorial election. These are called GUBI numbers. I was surprised to discover this was a voice vote, not a private ballot. None of the candidates on David's slate won. The votes weren't even close. And Gordon won by a substantial margin, two to one, whether it was by a head count of EDs or by the GUBI numbers. The GUBI numbers were something like 4000 votes to 2000 votes.

I was relieved. I was not surprised because it had been clear all year that Gordon had the support of the majority of the committee. But the surprise came listening as many of the people I had worked so closely with all year voted against Gordon. Robin, Elena and I were the only SHDems members on the SPC to vote for Gordon.

I knew that I should reach out to each of them and hear their thoughts, on the record for the book, about why they voted against Gordon, even after everything Gordon and Robin had done for us on the SPC all year. But I didn't. It was just too hard.

Mike was determined to see it in the most positive light and in an email he listed the reasons why. "Democrats are stronger than ever; Gordon has been highly successful; Gordon won the chairmanship in a rout; Democratic registration is now more than Republicans; Democrats control the town board 4-1; and all elected Democrats supported Gordon. After 10 years it is to be expected that Gordon would find some opposition, and although we have differences we welcome input and they have a chair at the table, make that several chairs at the table. We welcome diverse opinions, and hope that all members can contribute to the well-being of the party."

Wednesday, October 10th
On the campaign trail with Perry
The next day I woke up to an email from Gordon to all the SHDems members.

Dear Committee Members,

A great thank you to everyone who attended our Organizational Meeting last night at the Southampton Inn. Of the currently 82 members of the Committee, 72 members were in attendance - an outstanding turnout!

Thanks to ***Sally Pope*** *for moderating the supporting statements and the Q & A. Sally was very professional and did an amazing job. Also, thank you to* ***Joy Flynn*** *for being the timekeeper and then the temporary secretary during the official voting - a really great job. I would like to recognize Joy's previous role as the second vice chair of the Committee, where she was always involved and active. Thank you Joy! Our fantastic* ***Robin Long****, as temporary chair, was once again superb and kept everything running smoothly and efficiently - thank you very much Robin!*

A very special thank you to ***David Dubow****, his slate and supporters. I include my slate in expressing our appreciation: First Vice Chair, Robin Long, Second Vice Chair, Andi Klausner, Treasurer, George Lynch and Secretary, Alexis Mayer.*

One more thank you to ***Hank Beck****, our previous secretary for many years, who has done so much for the Southampton Town Democratic Committee, in every possible area and has worked so hard to contribute to our success. Hank received a standing ovation from the members.*

David and I will be getting together soon, to talk about some of his ideas for growing and strengthening the Party. I know that we are committed to doing what's best for the Committee and the overall community and I welcome everyone's involvement. Our revised platform will be voted on at the next full Committee meeting, scheduled to take place December 19th.

So, now on to making sure that Perry wins in November! Perry hasn't yet decided where his election night get together will be, but perhaps we should also have an election night event in Southampton. If anyone has any suggestions, please let me know.

Thank you again for allowing me to serve another term as Chair of the Committee!

Being a gracious winner was Gordon's first step to help the committee move forward.

But I needed to turn my focus away from the SHDems and toward the campaign today because I was going to be spending several hours with Perry on the campaign trail. I had requested time to follow Perry to several events and to get a chance to speak with him about the campaign. Today was the day. To start, I needed to meet the campaign in Setauket. Since that is too far for me to comfortably drive, I took an Uber there. It was expensive. Geographically we are a very large district so this was over an hour away from me.

This first event in Setauket was a veteran's forum. There were about 30 people there and it was held at the Setauket Neighborhood House, a beautiful historic building with a large room that can be rented for events. The oldest part of the building dates from the 1700s.[41]

This forum was being hosted by several groups. The goal was to give Perry an opportunity to hear directly from veterans about their issues and concerns.

I was deeply moved by the stories I heard many of these people telling. One was from a woman Navy veteran who has been trying for years to get the Northport VA hospital and clinic to have a female gynecologist/obstetrician which they do not have. Another was the story of a man who needed a stent for his heart and was told he had to go all the way into New York City since they did not have anyone here to do the procedure. Over and over again we heard stories from people who had given their time and often risked their lives for this country but did not feel that they were being heard by Zeldin or Trump or the Republican Party. It was extremely moving.

Several of the veterans advised Perry not to be shy about veterans' issues just because Zeldin is a veteran and Perry is not. They even advised him to apply to be on the Veteran Affairs committee once he got to Congress.

When the forum ended, people drifted outside and onto the front porch of the building. Many of them lingered and asked Perry questions. He answered their questions until he had to leave for the next event. He assured them that he would always listen and be honest with them. A student reporter from the Stony Brook University college paper asked Perry for a quote about the forum. I also recorded his answer.

"Veterans want and need to be heard, we owe it to them. And as I said, not every problem can be solved, but people appreciate the effort and it sounds like they're not getting that right now. And the other thing that I took away, the one story that resonated with me the most, is not having female gynecologists available to veterans. That makes no sense. It's so easy to correct. You'll hear about it on the campaign tomorrow because it's atrocious. My father-in-law is an OBGYN and I get the need why women like to talk to women. If we don't provide that service to our veterans, we're letting them down."

Perry said good-bye and we left together to travel to the next event. Perry and I were riding together in his car to the Setauket campaign office so I would have a few minutes alone with him. After the campaign office stop, I would be riding with his communication associate, Ali, who had helped arrange the day for me, to the next forum, this one at Stony Brook University with students. Ironically, there was also a reporter from *The New York Times* spending time with Perry today and this time at the campaign office gave her a chance to speak to Perry privately. Ali told me that a reporter from Newsday had spent time with Perry earlier in the day.

As Perry and I walked to his car, I told him how moved I was by listening to the veterans and their stories. He was clearly moved as well and he looked me in the eye and said, "I really have to win this thing" and I knew exactly what he meant, that he had to win it for the people who are being forgotten. In the end, this is what this race is about, the people in his district who need help.

We then talked briefly in the car since it was a short ride. I asked him how he thought the race was going.

"It's so hard to know. If you asked me last week, I was super optimistic, and I haven't lost any of that, but I just don't know where we are, because this Kavanaugh thing turned everything upside down a little bit. The thing that concerns me most is that Trump has somehow finally got himself out of the headlines. And I am counting on Trump to get back in the headlines. Hopefully he will do it. I don't want to root against the country, but the stock market could be the thing."

The market had taken a hit that day. I asked him if he thought the emerging horrific story about the killing of *The Washington Post* journalist, Jamal Kashoggi, by the Saudis might resonate with voters.

"I'm trying to decide what to do about that. On one hand, people in this district don't care that much about international stuff, but this is so atrocious, it's what scares me about what this country could be coming to."

I asked him about the live polling *The New York Times* was doing on our district. I mentioned that Zeldin's unfavorable numbers were high and his favorability numbers were under 50 percent and there were still a large number of undecided voters. Did that give us an opening?

Perry said it did if he could end the race strongly. "I need my last two ads to be very powerful." And he thought his closing issue should be healthcare. "That is the one thing that, when I'm talking, I always come back to it. Not only did he vote to repeal healthcare, but his reaction to that vote was to go into hiding and to stop facing people."

He believed the race would be close, possibly coming down to the absentee ballots. I asked him what more we in the grassroots should be doing to close that gap?

"Keep knocking on doors. It's all a matter of door knocking now. This election is going to be about turnout. As long as we get our voters out to vote, we will win. I've been saying that for so long and I still one hundred percent believe it, with no equivocation."

After waiting at the campaign office, Ali and I drove to the University for a town hall organized and hosted by the Stony Brook College Democratic Club. She parked in the parking garage and we walked together into a very large conference room that was packed with students. At a table right outside the room, there were voter registration forms and applications for absentee ballots. I was impressed at how large the turnout was. Perry was there with several other Democratic elected officials and candidates. At one point Perry asked the students how many of them were registered. From where I was sitting, it looked like the majority of them raised their hands. He was told that they have been doing voter registration drives on campus all year.

I struck up a conversation with a young woman sitting next to me, Ifunanya Ojukwu. She told me she is a freshman and she is from Albany, in upstate NY, but that she registered to vote in this district, so she could vote on campus.

Perry did a terrific job answering questions. Many of them, not surprisingly, were about student debt. When the town hall ended, students gathered around Perry to continue to ask questions. Some of them seemed to be Zeldin trolls based on their questions, but there were others who were genuinely interested in his answers. Perry looked tired. It had been a long day. It was late and I had to catch an Uber home so I said goodbye.

This is what the campaign posted on their Facebook page about the town hall.

> *More than 250 Stony Brook University students gathered with us last night to talk about the issues impacting campus, our state, and our country. From student debt, to Title IX, voter suppression and the environment, these young people are well aware of what is going on in the world around them, and have real concerns and thoughts about how to make change. The highlight of this event for me was when I asked everyone who is registered to vote to raise their hand- over 75% of the room had hands up. Between my campus visits, my presentation to a political science class, and through participating in this forum, it is clear to me that students are more energized to vote than ever before.*
>
> *Thank you to the Stony Brook College Democrats for organizing and hosting this forum with Congresswoman Grace Meng, Assemblyman Steve Englebright, and State Senate Candidate Kathleen Cleary.*
>
> *Our future is looking bright!*

By the time I got home, it was very late and I was exhausted. It had been an important day for the book project though I felt a little guilty that I had not done anything to advance the vote today. That push/pull again. My predominant feeling from the day is how important this election is. I thought of the veterans and their healthcare, the students and their student debt, the houses in need of repair in my ED, the hurricane bearing down on Florida, of climate change and what is at stake with the environment.

As tired as I was I jotted down a note to myself. "We have to work harder. We only have three weeks, we have to knock on more doors and make more phone calls. We have to win this election."

Friday, October 12th
Last Day to Register

It was the last day to register to vote and so we were making a full court press to get this information out on social media. We posted registration information across all of our grassroots Facebook pages as well. I was pleased to hear back from friends and family members who had not been registered that they were now. Several registered through the DMV website. If you already have a New York State driver's license and you are not changing any of your information, such as your address, you can register to vote with them online.

Saturday, October 13th
Fundraiser

After a day canvassing, Mike and I drove together to a Perry fundraiser that we both signed up for at the Southampton Inn that evening. As committee members, we received a discounted fee.

The event was a cocktail party and then the showing of a documentary about Trump and his history with Russia, Putin and money laundering. I had read about it in *The New York Times* and in *Vanity Fair*. The film is called Active Measures.[42]

The filmmaker, Jack Bryan was scheduled to present the documentary at the fundraiser along with Congressman Eric Swalwell, (D-CA) a member of the House Intelligence Committee, who is interviewed in the film. They would also be introducing Perry who would speak after the showing of the film.

Unfortunately, the Congressman couldn't make it because his wife was in labor but he did speak with us via Skype to talk about Zeldin – how right-wing he is – and the importance of Democrats taking back the House and how Perry winning would be part of that. He also talked about the film and his part in it. Then Jack Bryan spoke and introduced his documentary. It was fascinating and incredibly depressing. Looking at the evidence it was clear how corrupt Trump is and how much Putin's goal was to destabilize the West.

After the film, Bryan answered questions and then Perry spoke about the race and how it was going. He said we have to try and raise more money since he's going to need funding for the next three weeks of the campaign to do more television advertising. He said the *The New York Times* poll showed a wider split in support for Zeldin because it came right after the Kavanaugh hearing and that they've done their own polling since then that showed a closer race.

It was an interesting event. I wish there had been a larger crowd so that Perry raised more money for the television ads. Most of the attendees were SHDems committee members. Things were still a bit awkward after the convention, with the two sides sitting on opposite ends of the room.

When the event ended, I spoke with Andi, her husband Ron, Robin and Irene Donoghue, another SHDems member. We all talked about Perry's chances. The discussion focused on the challenges of winning in Brookhaven. Robin mentioned that maybe we on the East End, which seems to be on board with supporting Perry, should be focusing our canvassing efforts more in Brookhaven. I mentioned that EEAN was planning a Brookhaven weekend of canvassing and asked if maybe the SHDems would like to join. A plan evolved to arrange a caravan of SHDems to travel west together and join with EEAN to canvas in Brookhaven. Andi and Robin offered to make the arrangements.

Monday, October 15th
Zeldin tactics

A drizzly day but it wasn't enough rain that it would stop us from going back to ED19. Lulu picked me up at 3:00 PM and we drove to a neighborhood that borders a small lake. A lot of people weren't home but we left Perry's card on their front doors.

The author canvassing for Perry in ED19

We then drove to another part of ED19 that I remembered going to several times last year with Mike when he was showing me how to canvas. My memory was a lot of the names on the list did not match who lived in the houses; that people were either renting or there had been a lot of turnover. That was true today as well. It was a neighborhood of small houses, some in need of repair.

Most of the people we spoke to were committed to voting for Perry, particularly the Democrats and many of the Unaffiliated, especially Unaffiliated women.

Lulu and I gave out three lawn signs. We spoke to one African American man, probably in his early 70s, who said he would definitely be voting for Perry. He was very upset about what's going on with Trump and was happy to take a lawn sign. That was one of the highlights of the day.

One of the lowest points of the day came right after that. We walked up to a house that, according to our walk book, had a couple in their thirties living there who were both registered Democrats. The outside of the house was decorated with a lot of Halloween decorations, including a sign on the door that said "Beware of Witch" and these decorations were fitting for the house of a young couple with young children. But the door was answered by an older woman, probably a senior citizen. I stood there with a smile on my face about to give her my spiel about Perry. Before I could say a word, she looked hard at me and then in a voice filled with venom, yelled, "Get off my lawn and get off my property" and slammed the door in my face.

Lulu and I walked away feeling quite shook up. I wondered what made a person so angry to express such animosity to a complete stranger? It seemed fitting for a Trump/Zeldin supporter. Lulu pointed out that the sign on the door was certainly accurate.

We finished canvassing around 4:30 PM then went to a little café in Riverhead to get a cup of coffee before going to an environmental forum, hosted by the League of Conservation Voters, at a location within walking distance from the café. Perry and Zeldin were scheduled to speak. It was not a debate since they would each be speaking separately, Perry for an hour with the League moderator asking questions and then a Q&A with the audience and then the same for Zeldin in the next hour. But it was the first time they would be speaking at the same event since Zeldin avoided showing up if Perry was in attendance. We had registered for the event through Perry's website online and had encouraged people to sign up because we wanted a large contingent of Perry supporters there to both have Perry's back and to show the press how strong the support for Perry is in the district.

We walked over around 5:00 PM and there was a large crowd outside including a loud and obnoxious Zeldin guy with his pickup truck blasting music. We joined Lulu's husband, John Bouvier who was already on line. We saw many other people we knew. We were all outside since they were not yet opening the doors and it had become very chaotic with no one knowing what exactly was happening. Finally, the outdoor glass doors were opened and we made our way into the lobby at which point it was announced that only people who were members of the League would be seated or people who had registered with the

League on their website. They said it was a small room and everyone else, such as people who registered on Perry's website, would have to wait to see if there would be room. They asked the very large group of Perry supporters to stand off to the side.

We were surprised but we did as they asked, all moving to one side of the lobby. During this time period, they continued to seat other people. Then the same woman from the League who had informed us we had to wait, came out and told us the room was full and we couldn't get in. By this point, we were not so friendly any more. We had seen them seating Zeldin supporters before the announcement that League members were being seated first, which would explain why there wasn't one single Zeldin supporter in the holding area of the lobby with us. Maybe they had all registered through the League website but I doubted it.

In the midst of this chaos, Perry arrived and I felt bad for him because he had gotten caught in traffic, was running late, and the first thing he encountered was a mass of his supporters now being told they had to leave the building and could no longer stand in the lobby because of fire regulations.

Perry apologized for whatever the screw-up had been, whether it was the League or his website, or a lack of coordination between them or if this was some shenanigans by the Zeldin campaign. Perry offered for people to watch the live stream from his campaign office which was just down the street and most of the crowd headed that way. Lulu and I looked at each other and at the same time both said let's just pack it in. We were both tired from canvassing so we just decided to go.

After I got home, I saw that Steven Kramer of Invisible North Fork posted some pictures on Facebook showing that the police had been called in out of some fear that we weren't going to clear the lobby. His pictures showed all these police cars in front of the building. The whole thing was really strange.

Before going to bed, I read *The New York Times* article on their website about the CD#1 race. It is a pretty good article for Perry because it exposes how right-wing Zeldin's voting record is. I liked the title, "Will Too Much Love From Trump Be a Bad Thing for a Long Island Congressman?"[43]

Tuesday and Wednesday, October 16th and 17th
How we are doing…
I took today off from canvassing in order to rest and so instead emailed folks to ask them what they have been doing for the campaign and their assessment about the race, the chances of a blue wave and the state of the nation.

Below are a few of the responses, including from two of Perry's opponents in the primary, Vivian and Elaine.

Vivian Viloria-Fisher

"I see Perry well positioned to win this race due to the phenomenal grassroots movement that has emerged after the Trump 'win'. I have been involved in small ways: postcard writing, rallies, delivering lawn signs, sharing big sign material left from my campaign and canvassing. Perry is projecting a more powerful presence as he grows more comfortable with public speaking. This reassures his supporters. I also wrote a neighbor to neighbor letter in support of Kathleen Cleary (NYS Senate 2). The tide lifts all boats, so it's important to support the slate."

Elaine DiMasi

"Regarding Perry's race, I'm glad I've been able to budget some time to help. Canvassing is key for the Democrats in our district this year. I'm proud that we've shown ourselves to be willing and able to train each other and keep up morale. The race will be close. The 2016 Democrats' Congressional GOTV has to be out-performed by more than 30%. And we might just be doing it! But we will not know the answer until the eleventh hour."

Cindy Salwen

"I am somewhat encouraged by how things are going. My sense is that there are more Perry signs than I saw in the past for Democratic candidates in Brookhaven town. The canvassing I've been doing is somewhat mixed, but good enough to be encouraging. On the other hand, I am on Zeldin's email list and he lies and I'm sure all his supporters believe him. I suppose I've never had a really strong expectation that we'll win, but who knows."

Ilse Buzzanca

"We have had meetings devoted to making phone calls to Democrats in our districts. I didn't think that it went well. The phone numbers were almost always disconnected or with weird recordings. I waded through at least 100 phone numbers and left a few messages and spoke to only five people (already voting). Until we get decent information from the Board of Elections, it seems like a waste of time. We also have been canvassing for local and state candidates. The extreme heat (often 100+ with the humidity) has kept many of us off the streets. Most of our membership is 'old' and unable to stand the heat. We have a handful of die-hard volunteers who canvass. I have had several postcard parties at my house with at least 20 men and women who have filled out 1500+ cards within two big districts in Florida. These cards were sent to 'Democrats only' urging them to vote. I have had three big fundraisers for candidates that raised $10,000; a lot of expense and work on our part to give parties for a 100+ people at our houses. All in all, lots of work and, still, unable to predict an outcome."

Mike Anthony

"*The Southampton Press* has an article in the most recent edition that Zeldin has an eight-point lead, same as in 2016 at the same point in race. I would be shocked if the results are similar. Democrats have closed the registration gap in CD#1; more volunteer energy compared to other years and the issues are on our side. I help the campaign in several ways: I canvass frequently, I coordinate the letter writing team, and I produce various segmented new voter lists from a database. Reports such as: 2nd homeowners, new Latino voters, young voters. I'll add that Perry is at a disadvantage because he is so new to the voters."

Andi Klausner

"Mainly what Ron and I have been doing for the campaign is knocking on doors to get people to vote, and donating money to the campaign. We will be pounding the pavement again and making phone calls as we get closer to the election. The good news is that the DCCC now considers us a swing "Red to Blue" district and not a lost cause, so at least we are in play. But it's just so hard to feel optimistic about anything political these days because it seems like one assault after another by this administration on a daily basis. The confirmation of Brett Kavanaugh to the Supreme Court left me reeling and depressed. It is now crystal clear what the GOP thinks of women, minorities, Jews, Muslims, dark-skinned immigrants, LGBTQ, the disabled and anyone else who is not a White Christian male."

Robin Long

"Unfortunately, I do not feel as optimistic as many. A wave is neither a lasting phenomenon nor a real change in the nature of the body of water. The wind can whip it up but it doesn't go deep. Similarly, the winds of

> discontent in this country with the President do not go deep. Moral outrage is like the wind, it can whip up a big wave but it doesn't change the tide. While financial issues resonant, moral outrage is fleeting. Until Trump takes an action on the level of removing pre-existing conditions or touching Social Security, he will be allowed to continue destroying the moral fiber of this Country."

Thursday, October 18th
Meeting the Perry campaign staff at a Brookhaven office
Today I woke up early and drove to Wendy's house. Together we drove to the Farmingville campaign office so I could spend the day there with her and the campaign staff. She had recently started working at this office, at Perry's request. It is located in the crucial Brookhaven Township where CD1 races are won or lost.

Below is an excerpt from our discussion in the car on the way to the office.

How did it come about Perry asking you to help out in this office?
I was at an event for Perry, against Betsy DeVos's proposal to take money away from educational funding for inner-city kids and use it to buy guns, or to arm teachers. It was held in Patchogue, we were all talking, and Perry came over, and said that he was very frustrated, that the 'Farmingville office is driving me crazy. I really need somebody to take charge.' So, I told him that I was looking for a place to fit in and help out the best I could, 'so if you'd like me to go to Farmingville, I'd be glad to'. He said, 'would you really?' And I said, 'yes I will do it' and he put me in touch with Joanne Young, who's up at the Setauket office. I went up there for training, and I asked Joanne, 'are you sure I'm not stepping on anybody's toes here?' So, I went to Farmingville and of course, I was stepping on peoples' toes. They are paid staff there... But they're young, mid-twenties. I have come to know all of them, and I call them the guys. They are just a group of characters.

Perry picked the right person for this job. They needed a mother figure to come in, and kind of get them into shape. Though it sounds like at the beginning they were a little miffed.
There was some back and forth phone calls and texts about 'who is she?' And then, I stepped back because I realized, no I'm really not in charge. Perry didn't say that to anybody, he didn't clear the path for that. It was ambiguous. I realized that and sat back a little bit, and looked at where I could be helpful. So, I buy all the snacks, I talk to a lot of people, I do data entry. We have good political discussions because they're there from 10 in the morning until 8 at night. It's a long day. Then they start getting on each other's nerves a little bit. And so we

have good discussions. I am there on Tuesdays, usually a full day, from around 11:00 AM until 8:00 PM. Thursday, Friday, Saturday are also pretty full days.

Are you getting volunteers walking into the office?
We are getting more and more. Farmingville has been the quietest office for volunteers… The middle group of Long Island is probably the most conservative area… We really, really need walk-ins, but we are getting there. And the paid canvassers are all young students primarily from Stony Brook University.

What about the grassroots groups like EEAN, Let's Visit Lee Zeldin, etc. are you seeing any volunteers specifically that have come from the grassroots?
None. They may be going to the Stony Brook office, but I have no idea. Debra Dolber came in one day to help me make signs, which keep getting taken down. It could be there aren't as many grassroots volunteers here because Brookhaven Town is thoroughly Republican, from top to bottom. That is also why people can get away with taking down our signs… Their town employees know, or businesses know that they are safe to put out a big Zeldin sign whereas, if they put up a big Perry sign then the building, zoning, and all the compliance boards can have a heavy hammer and even if they don't use it, the fear of them using it, is profound when the town is completely and totally owned.

On our way into the office, we stopped at a supermarket. I waited in the car while Wendy bought snacks and drinks for the staff at the office. I asked her if the campaign reimbursed her but she said she didn't mind paying for it. She considered it a campaign contribution.

We arrived at the office which was tucked away in a small shopping mall, in the back. We parked the car and I helped Wendy carry groceries into the office. I wondered if this out of the way location had something to do with the lack of walk-in traffic for volunteers.

On the walls of the office were maps of all the EDs in Brookhaven. It is substantially larger than Southampton. Southampton Township has 42 EDs. Brookhaven Township has 296 EDs. Brookhaven Township is the largest of all the townships in CD1 and leans Republican. To win a district-wide race, a Democrat must turn out every non-Republican vote they can find.

The following table compares the population of the two townships as well as voter enrollment. Population data is from the U.S. Census Bureau 2018 estimated population statistics; voter enrollment is the most recent (November 2019) data from the N.Y. Board of Elections. The percentages listed under each township represent the share of that party's registered voters residing in that township. For example, in the first line under Brookhaven, 66.2% of registered Democrats in CD1 reside in Brookhaven. The percentages listed under CD1 represent the share of the district's registered voters that are in that party. For example, in the first line 31.8% of all registered voters in CD1 are Democrats.

Congressional District 1 Voter Enrollment (November 1, 2019)

Party	Brookhaven		Southampton		CD 1	
	Number	Percent	Number	Percent		
Democratic	110,596	*66.2%*	15,017	*9.0%*	167,149	*31.8%*
Republican	110,951	*64.2%*	13,123	*7.6%*	172,766	*32.8%*
Conservative	8,202	*65.7%*	726	*5.8%*	12,485	*2.4%*
Green	808	*68.8%*	118	*10.1%*	1,174	*0.2%*
Independence	16,146	*64.3%*	2,330	*9.3%*	25,125	*4.8%*
Libertarian	426	*69.8%*	26	*4.3%*	610	*0.1%*
SAM	1	*20.0%*	1	*20.0%*	5	*0.0%*
Working Families	1,667	*75.8%*	164	*7.5%*	2,198	*0.4%*
Other	223	*74.1%*	21	*7.0%*	301	*0.1%*
No Party	95,919	*66.4%*	11,990	*8.3%*	144,560	*27.5%*
Total	344,939	*65.5%*	43,516	*8.3%*	526,373	
Population (7/1/18)	486,040	*67.6%*	58,314	*8.1%*	718,726	

Sources: Census Bureau and New York State Board of Elections[44]

Registered Conservatives and Independence Party members are what give the GOP an advantage in Brookhaven since they tend to vote for the Republican candidate. But the largest bloc of voters after the two parties is the No Party affiliation. We have to turn out those voters to win.

It was the middle of the day but there were several volunteers working the phones.

There were five paid staffers in the office. I asked if I could speak with them on the record for the book. They asked if I knew if it would be okay with Perry and I told them that I had interviewed Perry and that the book would not be published until after the election but certainly if they wanted to check with Tim, his communications director, first that would be fine. In the end, they all spoke on the record.

As Wendy had told me, they were all young, in their early and mid-twenties. While I was there a few others drifted in and out of the office. They had different assignments, from coordinating the volunteers to managing the database of voters. They were all interested in politics, many majoring in political science, many at Stony Brook University and many had just graduated. It was interesting getting the point of view of millennial voters, an age group that will be crucial to our voter turnout efforts and rarely encountered in the grassroots groups, Democratic Committees or when canvassing and speaking to voters. Some had been with Perry since the primary, others had signed up just a few weeks ago after responding to an advertisement that the campaign was looking to hire paid workers.

"I just graduated and I was looking for something to start my career with and I think the midterm election coming up is the perfect time," said Conor Stevens who had joined the campaign two weeks ago. "I wanted to get involved with the campaign and try to contribute as best as I could." Conor went to college in upstate New York at the State University of Geneseo, one of the top colleges in the New York State University system. He was a political science major and had interned in Senator Schumer's upstate office.

Conor said he was pleased at the large number of younger volunteers. "I never expected so many young people to be involved at this stage, so joining the campaign and seeing how many people are working or volunteering from Stony Brook and Suffolk County Community College is a surprise."

"I have some friends who say, 'what election?' But those are my friends that I don't discuss politics with," said Bradley Schlotz, another paid staffer who started a few weeks ago. "But I also have friends who are interested in politics and this election is everything to them… I think young people know that this is their chance to have their voice heard and they haven't really had that chance because we haven't really shown up to vote. I think we saw that with Bernie, we lost that opportunity, because a lot of young people who supported him had the opportunity to vote and didn't come out for him and I think that we'll correct that mistake."

Both Conor and Bradley were assigned to canvassing. Paid canvassers are crucial to any campaign, to not just be dependent on volunteers. They said most of the paid canvassers were out in the field almost all day.

Bradley said his time was split about half and half between being in the field and in the office. I asked him who the canvassers were focusing on, what kind of feedback they were getting from voters and what issues were voters most interested in talking about?

"We mainly target Democrats who might be on the fence, so when we talk to them it is about getting out and voting rather than persuading, whereas with Independents and Unaffiliated voters, we try to persuade them to vote for Perry," he said. "I think enthusiasm has been picking up. Our numbers have been looking great, with more and more people recognizing Perry's name. And I think healthcare is the biggest issue. People are concerned about the rising cost of healthcare and whether it is going to be expanded or not. The Republicans are looking to just repeal Obamacare. I would put healthcare first with taxes second."

Conor and Bradley then left to go out into the field. I sat down to speak with another staffer, also in his mid-twenties. I only got his first name, Owen, and he told me he started with the campaign in September and was grateful there was an opening so he could get involved. Also a political science major at Stony Brook but he graduated in 2017. He agreed that more millennial voters like himself were involved – he was about to turn 25 years old – but he said he also had a lot of friends his age who were not engaged. He told me one example.

"I was at the gym with a long-time friend and we were watching the news and it was about the Russian investigation and I was going into intricate details about where Mueller was and it became clear to me that this individual had no idea what I was talking about. Nor did he seem to be interested in finding out." He said that the involvement from 16 to 17-year-olds due to the Parkland tragedy was encouraging to him, "because my generation, just looking at turnout, especially among those who didn't go to college, is not where it needs to be. And that's another reason why I felt like I had to get involved. I felt like somebody from my demographic – young, white, straight and privileged – had to do something."

Most of his work of late was focused on recruiting volunteers for the get-out-the-vote (GOTV) effort the last weeks of the campaign. Like everyone else I spoke to with the campaign, he thought the race would be close and would come down to turnout. He described the different kinds of volunteers that they needed to line up for GOTV.

"There are certain levels of supporters," he said. "You have the person who is going to vote but not do anything else. You have the person who will phone bank for a few hours. And then you have the diehards who are willing to climb over glass to canvas if you ask them and that's who we want to find because they are the ones who are going to go door to door. We have volunteers who are like employees at this point because they donate so much of their time here."

He told me about one woman who has, "reliably been here every day and working hard. We are seeing, this time for this election, people who just can't stay silent. Especially a lot of retirees who are using their free time to be unpaid employees, who come in for hours at a time, entering data, making phone calls, canvassing and they are really the backbone of this. They are coming in, frankly, out of just disgust and goodness of soul. We have some people who have disabilities who volunteer at the Setauket office on a nightly basis. It's an honor to see them. They come on a bus and make calls for us."

Owen agreed that healthcare and taxes were the predominant issues, both with the voters and the volunteers.

"I would say it is healthcare and all the associated tentacles to healthcare, like protection for pre-existing conditions, a woman's right to choose, accessible birth control, etc. That is number one. Number two is taxes and the economics that play into it because at the end of the day, I think it all intersects."

I asked him what his plans were after the campaign and he said he was looking to work for a nonprofit, particularly in the arena of human rights and then another campaign, "maybe Perry's reelection campaign here in 2020 or a presidential campaign."

Before Wendy and I left, I got a chance to speak with Dan Sweeney who throughout my entire time in the office, had been glued to his laptop. Dan was a field organizer, in charge of working with volunteers, recruiting them, staffing Perry's public events and trying to recruit more volunteers at the public events. Dan was a student at Stony Brook when he reached out to the political science department last year and applied to be an intern during the primary. He has since graduated. He told me, "I've been with Perry since late October or November of last year."

I asked him what made him pick Perry and why he thought Perry had won the primary.

"The reason I picked Perry was because they asked, they were looking for interns. I got involved, I liked Perry and came to respect him a lot and so I stuck around with him," he said. "All in all, I think he won the primary because he had a district wide game. We saw a lot of the other candidates really strong in certain areas, they had one location where they did well. But only Kate and Perry did well across the district. She just didn't do as well as Perry."

I asked him what he had been working on all day on his laptop and he told me he was inputting information into the voter database.

"The way the voter database works, you can target people based on voting history, demographic information. Then once you build up your system, you have your own list of frequent volunteers, contacts, people that are supportive, unsupportive and what issues they like and don't like."

He said he thought the race was close, closer than *The New York Times* poll indicated. He agreed that healthcare was the top issue but that in places like Smithtown the GOP tax bill that capped state and local taxes (SALT) was important. The only problem was it took time and effort to get people to understand it.

"In specific parts of the district, such as Smithtown, if you can sit down and explain it to people, to get them to care, they really respond to the issue."
On the ride back to Wendy's, she talked about these young staffers with affection, like their mother hen. She said they discovered that they were all fans of the television show The Office. "You get so tired doing this work, the days are so long, that I mentioned that some days I just wanted to go home and watch some light television and I mentioned that I am an Office binge gal. So, it turns out that Dan and another staffer, Brian, are huge Office fans. Brian does a killer impression of the character Kevin from the show."

Wendy told me her experience in the campaign office was more tiring than she thought it would be but also more fulfilling than she expected. Her disappointment was more with the grassroots groups than the campaign. One day she had busloads of volunteers coming in from New York City and needed drivers with cars to take them door to door. She put the word out on all the different grassroots Facebook pages. No one responded. She said she was the only driver that day and so she spent the day chauffeuring different groups of volunteers around the district.

I got home late from Wendy's. I was very tired and despite how upbeat I felt about the young people I met there, I could not shake a vague feeling of sadness. Over the last few days, people I have spoken with, such as Rebecca and Wendy, have a sense of unease, that the blue wave will not be coming, that Trump is winning, from Kavanaugh to the Kashoggi murder to his lies at his rallies, to the GOP calling us a mob. Or maybe this is a function of fatigue. Trump, and the constant state of chaos he engenders, is exhausting.

Zeldin has cancelled the Smithtown debate. Will he get away with not facing the voters and Perry? Is the Resistance still viable or are people just worn out? Wendy sounded exhausted. The split in the Southampton Town Democratic Committee is still there. When I spoke with Robin the other night she still sounded hurt. No one wants to give up, but it is getting harder to keep going.

All I can hope is that this work we are all doing will result in the blue wave in November that we desperately need.

Saturday, October 20th- Sunday, October 21st
Brookhaven canvassing weekend

This was a big weekend for EEAN. It was our Brookhaven canvassing event – in Center Moriches, East Moriches, Mastic and Manorville - in a joint effort with the SHDems. Our goal was to speak to as many voters as we could and to minimize the GOP advantage in Brookhaven. We met at Wendy's house for two shifts of canvassing, 10:00 AM -1:00 PM and 1:00 PM - 4:00 PM on Saturday. Wendy had all the materials from the Farmingville office. Dan organized the walk books using the MiniVAN app. We were set up to train new people how to use the app and the fine points of canvassing. And then Sunday we did the same thing but working out of Rebecca's house.

I spent Friday putting the last touches on all the arrangements. The event had been listed for weeks on our Facebook page and was linked to the other grassroots' Facebook pages. It was featured in our newsletter. Gordon had sent an email blast out to the SHDems about it. So, when I noticed on Friday that fewer than 20 people had signed up, I was disappointed. EEAN has hundreds of members. The SHDems have over 80. LVLZ has thousands. Where were they all? The fact that we were not getting more involvement had me very nervous.

I had to be at Wendy's at 10:00 AM. I woke up at 8:00 AM feeling groggy and tired. It was drizzling and dark out and I did not feel like getting out of bed. I hadn't slept well. I debated not going but I didn't want to leave Wendy with all the work, though I knew Patty would be there. It was slow going but I finally got myself moving and drove to Wendy's. Both wrists hurt a lot these days – any benefit from cortisone shots had not lasted- and driving really aggravated them even with the braces on. By the time I got there the rain had stopped and it turned into a crisp, sunny fall day.

When I got there a few other people had already arrived. Wendy had coffee and pastries. She and I shared our concern that not as many people signed up as we had hoped. But the people who did come were excited to be there. Nancy Rose from EEAN was there. Carolyn, an older woman, who had recently moved here a year ago from Missouri, told me she hadn't knocked on doors since the Vietnam War but she was eager to get started. Patty was there with her friend and neighbor, Roland. There was also a young man who grew up in the area but lived in the city now and can't even vote out here but he wanted to help. Another woman arrived, with her two young daughters. She wanted them to see what democracy in action looks like. I tried to focus not on the people who weren't there but on those who were. Wendy gave everyone training on how to download and use the MiniVAN app on their phones. Then she gave them their walk list numbers to input into the app so they could get started. There was a lot of laughter and jokes as we all headed out into the field to canvas.

Carolyn and I were paired together. She drove and I handled the app on my phone. Our territory wasn't that far away, in East Moriches. It felt good to be outside. It was a large list, and we finished about half of it; three streets, two very long ones and one small cross street. Many people were not home, but we left Perry's palm card on the door. Of the people who were home that we spoke to, most told us they were voting for Perry. At one house, it turned out that the Unaffiliated resident on our list had passed away. When the daughter told us this, we gave our condolences and asked her if she would like information about Perry. She declined saying that she was a registered Republican. But she was friendly, thanked us anyway and at least we didn't get the door slammed in our faces.

At one house, an Unaffiliated woman told us she had never voted Democratic before but she would vote for whoever the Democrat is because she can't stand Trump. We spoke with her at some length. She talked about following Trump over the years and how we in New York always knew he was a con man and she could not believe that people fell for it. She assured us she would be voting on November 6th and took the palm card about Perry, though she said it didn't matter who he was, she was voting for whoever had that D after his name.

We finished our list and headed back to Wendy's. We got there around 1:00 pm, just when the afternoon shift was arriving. There were more people scheduled for this shift, including Syma, and several other EEAN members. There were also eight SHDems who came as part of the caravan from Southampton. They talked about the training that Andi and Robin had given them at Perry's Southampton office. I had planned on going out again in the afternoon, but I was too tired. I visited with the afternoon shift for a bit before they headed out to canvas.

Talking to Wendy later we both agreed that the day had been inspiring and, in the end, there were more people than we originally thought. Not quite the army I had envisioned last year but still a lot more than a candidate normally has for a midterm election.

The next day, on Sunday, I drove to Rebecca's with Mike. He picked me up at 9:00 AM. Today there was only one shift, in the morning.

On the way to Rebecca's, Mike told me how his Latino voter registration initiative was going. He and Jorge had gone out yesterday in Hampton Bays. Mike said that Latino interest in voting seemed higher than in previous years.

"I don't know if that's a result of having an active outreach and building the foundation or maybe the rhetoric about MS13 is turning off the Latino voter here with Trump and Zeldin painting the entire Latino community with a brush of terrorism and gangsters. So that could be what's driving some of the enthusiasm, but each time we've gone out we've had comments about people saying, 'Yeah, I'll talk to my brothers and my sisters and my nephews.' Overall, I would say that I find more enthusiasm for Perry, much more enthusiasm for him than for Anna Throne-Holst in 2016, not just in the Latino population. And also a lot of people just don't like Zeldin. Then there are others who say, 'Who's Zeldin? I don't know who he is; I don't know who Perry is. But I don't like Trump, so I'm voting for whoever the Democrat is.' I think it's anti-Trump fervor."

I asked Mike if I could go along on the next Latino outreach so I could chronicle it for the book and he said sure, he would set it up for me.

Rebecca had coffee and bagels and even had a gluten free bagel for me. While we sat around eating breakfast and drinking coffee, I spoke to a woman named Kathleen who was new to canvassing so I partnered with her. The campaign suggested we finish up the list I started yesterday that was already on my phone. Unlike yesterday, today was cold and windy, not the most comfortable day to be out canvassing.

Yesterday was a brighter day not just because of the weather. Yesterday, most of the Democratic houses we went to were enthusiastic and most of the Unaffiliated women were as well. Today was more of a mixed bag so it ended up feeling more frustrating. I felt bad for Kathleen because it was her first time canvassing and some people were not friendly. Like most canvassing days, there was no one home at the majority of homes, so we left Perry's palm card.

There were also a few Democratic households who said yes, they're voting for Perry, but they weren't as enthusiastic as we would have liked to have seen and the concern you then have with these voters is will they make the effort to come out on Election Day, especially if it is raining? We tried to impress upon them just how important this election is. Another disappointment was a couple of Democrats who said they were still thinking about it and hadn't made up their minds yet. I said to Kathleen, what the heck are they waiting for? But she said that maybe these were Democrats who voted for Trump and Zeldin but didn't want to tell us. That made more sense.

We spoke to one enthusiastic Democrat who said he's voting for Perry and he wanted to know how his wife could register. It broke my heart to have to tell him that the deadline for voter registration was last week. And I thought, if someone had knocked on his door last week, we could have registered his wife and she could vote.

One of the last houses we went to was a registered Democrat, a woman who was not home but we spoke to her husband who is a registered Independent and he said, "Don't worry. She's voting for Perry and I am as well." Nice.

Mike and I had left but we heard that Perry came later in the day to canvas alongside our volunteers. Imagine the surprise of the voter who opened the door and the candidate himself was standing there!

That night, I was tired but proud of what we achieved with our Brookhaven event. We are now just a little more than two weeks to the election. I think we did a pretty good job this weekend, though I had thought more EEAN and SHDems members would have joined in.

I tried to focus on the positive aspects of the weekend, the people I canvassed with, the voters we met, the group that traveled from Southampton to help out. Maybe ten people came from Southampton, including Andi and Irene Donaghue, and without them, that's ten less people we would have had.

While outside walking and knocking on doors, we talked about how we are all going to cope if we wake up November 7th and there isn't a blue wave, if the Democrats don't take back the house, if Zeldin is still representing us.

My son said to me the other night, "No matter what happens, Mom, it can't be as bad as election night, two years ago when Hillary lost." I've thought about that a lot. I don't know, on some level if there isn't a blue wave, this election night might be worse for me than two years ago. Yes, it is true that two years ago I was crushed. But very quickly that despair turned to anger and I was determined to do everything I could before the next election to right the wrong of a racist, misogynistic con man becoming president.

Now, after two years of activism, of channeling that anger into action, if the Democrats don't take back the House and the GOP retain all the levers of federal power, I don't know if I have it in me to keep fighting. Today, when we were canvassing, Kathleen said to me that if it's a bad election night she is going to turn off the news, stop watching *MSNBC* and put her head in the sand for the next six years because the country will have made a statement, a statement that this is the country they want.

Walking outside this weekend, I was struck by the beauty of this district. It looked like an Impressionist painting - leaves of vibrant fall colors, against a background of a deep blue sky, with sunshine shimmering on the ocean waves along our shoreline. This is a place worth fighting for.

I tried to go to sleep but I just couldn't shake off my concern that more people hadn't come out to canvas this weekend. Unable to sleep, I signed up online with the campaign for more canvassing days. I stayed up and composed a comment for the EEAN newsletter, which Rebecca and Sharon put together on Sunday and email every Monday morning. I finished writing and emailed my comment to Rebecca in the early hours of the morning. She got it in time and included it in the newsletter.

Here's what I wrote:

> *This past weekend, East End Action Network, in conjunction with the Perry Gershon campaign, sponsored two canvassing events in Brookhaven, hosted on Saturday by Wendy Turkington and on Sunday by Rebecca Dolber. We are grateful to them for welcoming us into their homes. On Saturday, members of the Southampton Democratic Committee came to help and on Sunday, Perry, the candidate himself, joined the canvassing team for a truly special experience.*
>
> *Together, in teams of two, we knocked on hundreds of doors, and either left information for voters about Perry if no one was home, or spoke in person to registered Democrats, Independents and those who are not registered with any party, the Unaffiliated, about what is at stake in this election and how important it is for them to cast their vote for Perry. For everyone who knocked on the doors, it was inspiring. But it was much more than that. Because those conversations and those flyers left on their doors could end up being the reason those voters make the effort to come out and vote on November 6th.*
>
> *For that reason, we can call our weekend a success. But think how many more doors, how many more voters could have been reached if we had marshaled an army of door knockers? What if instead of 20 people, it had been 40 people, or 50 people, or 100? Instead of hundreds of voters, we might have reached thousands. And in a race that is statistically tied and will be decided by turnout, each house, each voter, could be the*

deciding factor in whether or not the result is a new Congress or if the status quo of total Republican control is left intact, which will embolden Zeldin to continue to ignore us and Trump to be even more aggressive on his assaults on our democracy.

In these last two weeks before the election, it is incumbent on all of us to do all we can to bring Perry over the finish line, and that means canvassing, phone banking, even contributing financially if we can afford it, so that Perry can keep his ads on television to counter the smears and lies from Zeldin. Listening to the news, posting on Facebook, even reading this newsletter will not win this election. But reaching out to voters will.

On January, 21st, 2017, the day after Trump's inauguration, we stood up and by the millions we marched, all over the world, to make a statement about his election. That inspired us to keep the movement going by joining EEAN and other grassroots organizations in our district and together we have spent nearly two years protesting, calling Zeldin's office, registering voters and writing letters to the editor. But now, in two weeks, comes the only statement that really matters, when we get to make our voices heard through our votes. We have a chance to flip our district, to unseat Lee Zeldin, to help the Democrats take back the House and place a check on Trump.

Between now and November 6th, go to https://www.perrygershon.com find the closest campaign office near you and sign up to reach out to voters, through canvassing or phone banking. If you have never done either before, do not be afraid because they will help you and teach you what to do. These last two weeks are crucial. We mobilized a movement when we marched. It is now up to us to mobilize people to vote.

Monday, October 22nd
The Zeldin/Gershon race in the national news

The New York Times endorsed Perry in a group endorsement. "New York Times Endorses Antonio Delgado, Liuba Grechen Shirley, Perry Gershon, Anthony Brindisi, Tom Malinowski and Mikie Sherrill: Democrats in six races in New York and New Jersey can see their party restore good sense in Congress."[45] It was not unexpected but a nice confirmation nonetheless.
Then a story linking Zeldin to voter suppression added to the national news coverage of the race.

The story was about a mailer that Zeldin sent out that listed the date to return absentee ballots as Election Day, November 6th, which would be too late. Absentee ballots in New York have to be postmarked by the day **before** Election Day. I heard something about this mailer over the weekend and saw some text messages going back and forth about it, particularly from some parents who said their college student got this mailer which had the wrong date on it.

But what made it a story is that Zeldin did the exact same thing two years ago in 2016, leading many people, including Perry, to say it was a deliberate attempt to suppress Democratic votes. Zeldin's office issued a statement that it was an error at the printer.

The story was not only on our local news but also featured on multiple national news sites, such as *The Hill*[46] and *Axios*[47]. It was even part of a larger story on the many forms of GOP voter suppression on *The Rachel Maddow Show* on *MSNBC*. Rachel Maddow cautioned voters who live in Zeldin's district to "hold onto your wallet."[48]

The story blew up all over my Facebook feed, across all the grassroots groups. Which was it Zeldin, purposeful voter suppression or incompetence? Either way, I hoped exposing it helped Perry.

Also, in the national news today was a story about pipe bombs being sent to George Soros. I was grateful nothing exploded and no one was hurt but I went to bed wondering, what was that about?

Tuesday, October 23rd
Healthcare
Lulu and I went back to ED 19 today and spent time in a predominantly African American area of our ED. While more than half of the people were not home and we left Perry's flyers on their doors, those who were home came to the door, often with young children by their sides, and we probably had the most engaging conversations about this election with anyone we have encountered in our canvassing. Many of these people we had met when we were getting signatures in the spring, for ourselves to be ED leaders and for the petitions for the primary. Some remembered us. Most thanked us. But what I found so touching was how genuinely interested they were in knowing more. And this even though they were clear from the beginning that they were Democrats and would vote for whoever was the Democrat. But they wanted to know more about Perry. Some of them listened while studying the palm card. Issues like taxes, jobs, the environment mattered, as did placing a check on Trump, but their number one concern was healthcare. And it was personal.

They didn't know that Zeldin had voted to repeal the ACA, or if they had known, they didn't necessarily remember. These were not voters who had joined us in the protests in front of Zeldin's office. They were voters with busy lives – juggling jobs and young children. But they had a lot of questions and concerns about healthcare.

We were told about children on Medicaid, family members with pre-existing conditions, senior citizens on Medicare. One house had a walker outside the front door. I will never forget one mother, who stood in the doorway asking us questions while her two young children stood behind her. She asked us if the GOP would really take away her children's healthcare. We said yes, that is their plan, along with cuts to social security and other forms of the social safety net. She asked us for extra flyers to give to her mother and sister. And she asked to confirm where her polling place is. We asked her if she needed an absentee ballot and she said no, she would make sure she went to the polls on November 6th.

She was not the only voter who wanted to speak to us about healthcare. We told them to not be fooled by the GOP now saying they will protect pre-existing conditions. The truth is that Zeldin and the GOP voted to remove it, over and over again. We didn't have a lot of time at each house, so I am sure there are other issues that these voters care about. But our experience canvassing matches the polling that indicates healthcare is an important issue.

Even a *Fox News* poll revealed the popularity of the ACA (Obamacare) at an all-time high.

In response to these numbers, the GOP was now lying about their history with healthcare legislation. New ads were running all over the country claiming that they are the party that will protect coverage for pre-existing conditions. I hoped people were not that gullible.

But in the age of Trump, all bets were off. Trump has been particularly unhinged out on the stump at his rallies, and the lies have been coming at an unprecedented rate. And yet his poll numbers were climbing up. Even worse, his rhetoric was becoming more dangerous: the migrant caravan is coming for us, there are Middle Easterners in it, George Soros is paying for it, Democrats support open borders, etc. That coupled with his weak statements on the killing of Kashoggi and praising a GOP congressman who assaulted a reporter last year, and we now have a toxic stew to rile up his base. I was afraid it was also the kind of language that incited violence.

Wednesday, October 24th
Pipe bombs

I had finished some phone interviews, scheduled several others and was busy reading the transcripts from last week's interviews when a Facebook notification went off on my phone. I reached over, picked it up and saw that it was a post from Andi. She said that pipe bombs had targeted the Clintons, just like George Soros on Monday. I felt a deep chill run through me.

I stopped working and went downstairs and turned on the television. Slowly the news emerged that the people targeted were the Obamas, the Clintons, *CNN*, Eric Holder, Rep. Deborah Wasserman Schultz, all perceived as Trump critics by the right-wing media. I watched the press conference with Mayor DiBlasio, Governor Cuomo and the New York City police commissioner. I watched the statement from Hillary. I admired how they all tried to tamp down any rhetoric to calm things down while not denying that the Trump playbook had contributed to this inevitable march to violence. Right-wing extremists, conspiracy nuts with guns and weapons, something I have been worrying about for a long time.

Shoshana Hershkowitz, of Suffolk Progressives and Bend the Arc, posted these insightful comments on Facebook.

> *Today's lesson: words matter.*
>
> *Exhibit A: Barack Obama, Hillary Clinton, George Soros, and CNN headquarters have all had suspicious packages containing bombs mailed to them. The common thread? Donald Trump has continually railed against and vilified them. Public office is a powerful medium, and the words our leaders use matter and have influence.*
>
> *Exhibit B: the murder of Jamal Khashoggi. When the president of the United States continually refers to the media as "the enemy of the people", it sends a signal to bad actors that we don't respect freedom of the press, nor will we look out for them. The Trump administration's refusal to face what the crown prince of Saudi Arabia has done is yet another green light for terrorism and violence from our so-called allies.*
>
> *I could go on and on, as there are endless examples of ways that the Trump administration, and the Republican Party, in its silence, is complicit in spreading falsehoods and hurting innocent people, including immigrants and transgender people. But my message to you is bigger than this. WE NEED BETTER LEADERS. We need moral leaders. We need change, and we get the chance to make change on*

November 6th, 2018. It's time to send a message that we expect better from the people we elect. #NovemberIsComing #VoteThemOut

Trump was speaking, reading from a script. Listening to him say that we have to unify is such a joke. No one has inflamed the country more with hate than him. Everyone on this list has been the subject of attacks by Trump or critical of Trump. He is such a hypocrite. His recent rallies have ramped up his incitement to violence. He has a rally tonight. Let's see what he says.

In the meantime, polls showed races so tight that there was no indication of a blue wave. One pundit said it might be a trickle. There was a question of whether or not Democrats will take back the House. Trump and the GOP could be rewarded for everything they have done, tearing this country apart.

And here in CD#1, along with the voter suppression of the Zeldin mailer with the wrong date, we learned that the Suffolk County Board of Elections will not be accepting walk-in absentee ballots, as they have in the past. The announcement came from the Republican commissioner.

This was Perry's response.

More Attempts at Suppressing Votes
Updated 10:30 AM:

After further research, it seems that the Board is not giving in person absentee ballots to people who have already been sent such ballots by mail. But you may go to the Board and request an absentee ballot on the spot, if you have not already done so by mail. Further, you may no longer fill in the ballot on premises (as that would be deemed "early voting"), but you may leave the building, fill out the ballot, and then return with the ballot in a sealed envelope to submit it. It is unfortunate that the Republican commissioner of the Suffolk County Board of Elections has decided to change the procedures from the historical norm, but that is the case.

One more update - a different problem seems to be occurring - many voters in Smithtown CD-1 have reported receiving CD-3 absentee ballots (with CD-3 congressional candidates listed). We are looking into this problem and believe it is equally serious with the other issues, though there is no reason to believe it is more than a clerical error by the Board at this point, and not partisan motivated (we have been told of complaints from Democratic and Republican leaning voters).

Perry also asked for an investigation from the Attorney General about the Zeldin mailer with the wrong postmark date.

Luckily the Suffolk County Board of Elections reversed course and will allow walk-in voters, as they always have in the past.

In the evening, I learned that both Perry and Zeldin attended a debate that was conducted and filmed by *News12* and it will be on their website. This was how Perry described it on the campaign Facebook page.

> *Perry Gershon for Congress FB*
> *Debate Season Has Started*
>
> *I enjoyed spending 30 minutes with News12 today actually debating with Lee Zeldin. He showed up. Unfortunately, Zeldin was more interested in attacking me for phantom positions than talking about the actual issues. Sometimes it's easier to create a fantasy about what your opponent stands for and attack it, than to actually discuss meaningful issues to NY-1 constituents.*
>
> *Tonight, we get another crack to address each other, this time with a live, but unfortunately limited, audience. Once again, I will focus on healthcare, and our urgent need to preserve coverage for people with pre-existing conditions (Lee voted to take it away). And I will focus on the environment, and our need to stand up to Trump's assault on the air we breathe and the water we drink (and that surrounds us). And my plans to grow wages through infrastructure investment and repeal of the hurtful Republican tax plan.*
>
> *Please ignore Lee's misdirection. I am focused on issues, and I hope Lee properly and fairly represents his votes this time as well.*
>
> *The News12 debate should be publicly available for viewing within the next day or two and we will post a link to it as soon as possible.*

That night I got a phone call from a polling organization asking me if I would be willing to answer some questions about the midterm election in my district. Assuming it was a legitimate poll, I said yes. But after a few preliminary standard questions, I was asked, "if you knew that Perry Gershon was so liberal that it would give parents nightmares, would you still vote for him?" I knew then it was a Zeldin push-poll designed to try to change my mind about voting for Perry. I told the caller that the statement was a smear and a lie and I enthusiastically will be voting for Perry. The caller hung up.

Before I went to sleep, I learned about more pipe bombs that were also sent to Rep. Maxine Waters and former Vice President Joe Biden. This was horrifying. We have to be grateful that the bomb maker wasn't very good at his work and none exploded and no one was hurt. I tried to imagine what I would be feeling this night if these had been successful and the entire Democratic upper echelon had been wiped out in one day but I can't hold onto that thought. It was too exhausting. If there isn't a blue wave in two weeks, it this country does not repudiate Trumpism, then God help us all.

Thursday, October 25th
***News12* Debate**
I watched the video on the *News12* debate on their website. I thought Perry did a pretty good job of not taking the bait as Zeldin continued to try to smear him and lie about his positions. I loved when he said, "There you go again," an echo of Reagan that might resonate with some of the anti-Trump GOP in our district. Perry appeared uncomfortable at first and was unsure what camera to look at or when to smile. But overall, he did a good job countering Zeldin's smears and lies. And the moderator worked hard to keep Zeldin from eating up all the time with his usual word salad of nonsense. A particularly good answer was after Zeldin tried to tout all the money he has brought to the district for environmental causes. Perry said that was good but not enough if you stand with Trump and the GOP to gut the EPA and remove regulations for clean air and clean water and do not recognize climate change given this district is an island.

But their biggest exchanges were on healthcare, with Zeldin saying that Perry is lying about Zeldin voting to take away coverage for pre-existing conditions and Perry countering that Zeldin can't hide from his vote.

We have to remind people on just what Zeldin voted for in the GOP replacement bill. To try to claim anything else is an outright lie.

Friday, October 26th
Mail bomber suspect arrested
Today law enforcement arrested a suspect in Florida. The news reports show a MAGA supporter with a history of arrests and stickers on the outside of his van with crosshairs over a picture of Hillary and the words CNN Sucks. It knocks down the right's "false flag" theory that the bombs were sent by an anti-Trump critic to smear him. The arrest comes right after an announcement that two more

bombs were found, addressed to Senator Cory Booker and former Director of National Intelligence (DNI) James Clapper. He seemed to have a list of every prominent Trump critic.

Lulu picked me up at 3:00 PM but instead of going to our ED, the campaign asked us to go to Westhampton to canvas there. It was not our most inspiring afternoon of door knocking. Most people were not home, some had moved and many of the Unaffiliated or Independents were leaning toward Zeldin, particularly older, white men.

It was a mixed area of small houses on some streets, then very large homes closer to the water, many which appeared to be summer homes so we wondered why the campaign was sending us here since most homes seemed closed for the off season. Yet, people were registered to vote in our district so maybe they were planning on voting by absentee ballot. There were only a few on our list.

At one of the last homes on our list, which had an Independent male and a Democrat female, we got lucky that they were home, since it appeared to be a summer home. The husband answered the door and after I gave him my spiel on Perry, he took the palm card and told me that he would look at it because he was still undecided. At which point his wife walked in the vestibule and stood next to him. They were both in their 60s. He told her who I was and she smiled and said, "Honey, you are not undecided. Perry is the Democrat and we are voting for him. Remember, this is why we switched our registration to vote here so we could vote against Zeldin."

I thanked them both and walked away with a smile, remembering all the door knocking that Lulu and I did in the summer of 2017 on our Second Home Voter Registration initiative. Here were two votes for Perry that probably came from that project.

Later that day, the news announced that another bomb was sent to Senator Kamala Harris. This really was a right-wing hit list of Trump critics.

Saturday, October 27th
Pittsburgh Tree of Life Synagogue shooting
I took the day off from canvassing to attend my great-niece Mackenzie's fifth birthday party. While I was running around getting ready to go in the morning, the phone rang and Eugene answered it. It was Claude and Janie asking if Matt was okay, if he had been near the shooting in Pittsburgh. He was in graduate school at Carnegie Mellon University in Pittsburgh. We didn't know what they were talking about. I checked the news on my phone and learned more about

the shooting. I read that it was a hate crime, an anti-Semitic attack on the Tree of Life Synagogue. We knew that building. We had passed by it many times when visiting Matt in Pittsburgh. It was a few blocks from his house. We frantically reached out to Matt and learned that he was okay. Before I left for the party, we stood and hugged each other for a long time. Eugene said he would call Claude back to let them know Matt was safe.

Eleven people were dead, killed at a Saturday morning prayer service. According to *The New York Times*, the gunman told the police officers when he surrendered that "he wanted all Jews to die."[49]

That night, after getting home from the party, I called Matt and we finally had a chance to talk. He told me he had never been in danger. The school had sent out a text message alerting students of an active shooter and telling them to stay inside. But having such a horrible act take place in his neighborhood left him feeling numb. And filled with guilt that he was okay and had not done anything to help. We talked about how there really wasn't anything he could have done but such a feeling is normal, it is called survivor's guilt. He wondered what the answer to mass shootings was. There would always be people unhappy with their own lives and blaming others, there would always be people with mental illness. But I said that for me the answer was twofold - people like Trump had to stop stoking the fires of hate and that we had to find a way to get assault weapons off the streets.

I had needed to hear his voice. When we said good night, it was almost 5:00 AM. He went to sleep but I was wide awake. I stayed up for another hour reading the news online. The election was in a little more than a week. It felt like the country was coming apart.

Sunday, October 28th
Latino Voter Outreach and the *Newsday* endorsement

I finally had fallen asleep around 6:30 AM and woke up at 10:00 AM. I had but a few hours before Mike was picking me up to go out canvassing in Latino neighborhoods in Hampton Bays. Being tired, I almost cancelled. I could feel a sore throat coming on. But there won't be too many more opportunities to participate in this initiative so I got ready to go.

The news was filled with more information on the Pittsburgh shooting. The more I read, the more sickened I felt. Many of our activists were posting moving comments on our Facebook pages about their feelings of being Jewish and going to synagogue in the wake of the shooting.

This Facebook posting from Shoshana really hit home.

> *I drove the kids to Hebrew school this morning. They don't know what happened yesterday, and it took everything I had not to just keep driving, because I am sad and angry and scared. We pulled up to a police car in the parking lot.*
>
> *Normally, I drop the kids off and leave. But today I went into the sanctuary for services. I don't consider myself to be particularly religious, but I felt the need to pray and not be alone today. The Rabbi told all of us who felt moved to that we could stand and recite the Mourners Kaddish. We did, and I cried as I said these words that end with the phrase "He will create peace for us and all Israel, and let us say Amen."*
>
> *The attack on the Jewish community of Pittsburgh is no different than the attack on the black church in Charleston, the gay nightclub in Orlando, the Sikh temple in Milwaukee. We are a diverse nation, and some folks can't handle that. But we're not going anywhere, and when we stand together, we outnumber the bigots, the racists, the xenophobia, the homophobes. Love is stronger than hate.*
>
> *In January 2017, at my kitchen table during a winter storm, I started Suffolk Progressives to create a community group with my like-minded friends, to figure out how to make change where we live. The group grew well beyond people I knew, and I gained lots of knowledge, and lots of new friends. Together, we've marched, called our elected officials, written petitions, letters to the editors, and postcards, knocked on doors, volunteered in primaries and elections, and become an important part of civic life where we live.*
> *Today we hit 2,000 members. In these dark times, these folks are a silver lining, a reminder that there is so much good surrounding us, and so many people ready to be the change they wish to see in the world. Amidst the sadness, I am deeply grateful to these beautiful people for making my world better.*
>
> *#SuffolkProgressives #MakingChangeSince2017 #JustGettingStarted*

Mike and Katey picked me up and we headed for Hampton Bays to meet up with the rest of the canvassers, including Jorge. There were three teams of two people with each team having a Spanish speaker. I was there to observe.

It was a perfect fall day. Such a contrast to yesterday's rain and wind. Today was the kind of fall day that is made for being outside raking leaves, then sitting down inside to watch football. Instead we were canvassing. Giving up a Sunday to knock on doors was just one sign of how important this election is to each of us.

Mike explained that we would be working from lists of new voters, Latino and others, and because they were new, they weren't in MiniVAN yet so we couldn't use the app as we had been doing but had to go back to the paper and pencil version. This list was specifically new registrations. He said there were about nine EDs and the campaign needed us to cover three of them.

Jorge explained that the way he approached the Spanish-speaking residents was to just have a conversation. Not so much to tell them but to listen to them. And if they speak English, it is okay to speak in English but if it seems that they would be more comfortable in Spanish, then this is when he switches to Spanish. He said the key message for the Latino community is that it is important to show up and vote.

While we were getting ready to go out canvassing, we all got messages at the same time on our phones that *Newsday* had endorsed Perry. This was stunning, given that the newspaper had endorsed Zeldin in the past. Checking out the endorsement, it was even bigger than I could have imagined. Not only did they endorse Perry but they methodically laid out the argument why Zeldin had disappointed the district, why he didn't deserve another term and why Perry deserved a chance.[50]

Perry Gershon to represent 1st Congressional District

The Newsday editorial board's 2018 endorsement for Congress.
By The Editorial Board

Updated October 28, 2018 4:18 PM

When Newsday endorsed Shirley Republican Lee M. Zeldin in his 2014 run to unseat Democratic Rep. Tim Bishop, the fact that Zeldin could have the power to help Eastern Long Island as a member of the dominant Republican majority was a prime reason.

The GOP wanted the seat badly. It had repeatedly and unsuccessfully targeted Bishop. Once the party won the district, Zeldin should have had power. He should have been willing and able to make the case that he'd have to take care of the voters' needs and perch on the party's moderate wing if he wanted to keep the job and fairly represent his diverse district.

Zeldin didn't do either. Instead, he embraced an extreme brand of conservatism, and failed to secure some crucial Long Island needs.

Then he got worse.

President Donald Trump came on the scene and Zeldin quickly became a reliable cheerleader for Trump's divisive, dismissive politics and disastrous policies. Most troubling are Zeldin's feverish efforts to discredit the federal investigation into Russia's involvement in the 2016 election. Zeldin joined with the most right-wing elements of his party, even speaking on the House floor in a #releasethememo campaign. More recently, he sponsored a bill to create a second special counsel to investigate the FBI's probe of Hillary Clinton's emails.

Zeldin, 38, says a top priority is the preservation of Plum Island, which hosts a federal animal disease research center just off Long Island. The lab's functions are moving to Kansas, and federal law requires that it be sold to the highest bidder, which would likely lead to commercial development. That's an unacceptable outcome. The prospect led the Town of Southold to pass zoning laws making the island essentially impossible to develop. But zoning can change. Federal protection is needed.

This is exactly the kind of local need a majority-party legislator with power in his caucus and the ear of the president ought to be able to satisfy. But Zeldin has gotten nowhere. His bill to stop the sale and have the government draw up a plan to preserve and protect Plum Island has passed in the House more than once but gone nowhere in the Senate. Plum Island has no more federal protection today than the day Zeldin was elected.

The same is true of 1st District residents who bought their homes counting on federal deductions for state and local income and property taxes. Those long-standing deductions were limited to $10,000 annually in a tax bill Republicans passed last year. That added $1.5 trillion to the deficit and used the loss of Long Island homeowners' deductions to help pay for a huge corporate tax cut. To his credit, Zeldin fought limiting that deduction. To his detriment, no one listened.

In perhaps his worst vote in four years, Zeldin joined his party's efforts to repeal the Affordable Care Act. Except for the courage of the late Sen. John McCain, who defeated the effort in the Senate, as many as 1 million New Yorkers could have lost Medicaid benefits over time and more than 60,000 1st District residents could have lost their insurance.

Zeldin is often vocal. Up until the time he had to protect his seat in a swing district, he had been a regular on cable channels, lambasting the investigation into Russian interference in the 2016 election. He made his voice heard fighting for billions of dollars in cuts to Environmental Protection Agency funding.

And he's a leader in the crusade to gift the National Rifle Association with a 50-state reciprocal concealed-carry weapon law. Such a change would give anyone legally allowed to carry a concealed semi-automatic handgun — and in at least 13 states there are essentially no requirements to get such permission — the right to conceal and carry such weapons in New York and in his district. That would mean a gun right that is extraordinarily difficult for Zeldin's own constituents to obtain, thanks to reasonable state and local legal restrictions here, would be freely granted to millions of unscreened out-of-staters.

Perry Gershon, 56, of East Hampton, is a successful financier spurred to get into the race by the election of Trump, and by Zeldin's support for Trump's policies. This has prompted Zeldin to repeatedly criticize Gershon for only recently moving his voting registration to Suffolk County from Manhattan, although he's owned a home in the district since 1999 and has spent considerable time there, and before that with his wife's family. It is a legitimate criticism.

But not being a native and wanting to stand up for residents of the 1st District is better than being from the 1st District and repeatedly letting them down. Gershon is smart, motivated, tireless and a listener, and his is the kind of private-sector success story many conservatives want to see more of in government. He says he has driven his blue Chevy Volt more than 38,000 miles across the district to meet with voters since the campaign started.

Gershon has made fighting climate change central to his campaign. Zeldin stands against policy changes that would keep rising waters and increasing storms from swallowing the district.

Gershon wants to strengthen the Affordable Care Act and push for a public insurance option all Americans can buy into, and thinks the nation could get to single-payer health care over time. Zeldin and his allies weakened the law in a way that over time will drive up rates for New Yorkers who need coverage most.

Gershon wants to give people brought illegally to the United States as children a path to citizenship. Zeldin staunchly opposes such a path.

Gershon wants a huge increase in infrastructure spending. Zeldin and his party pay that priority lip service, and do nothing to bring it about.

Gershon wants to act as a brake on Trump. Zeldin's support enables the president's worst behaviors.

Gershon promises to be a strong voice trumpeting the right policies for the district and the nation. Zeldin has been a voice for neither.

Newsday endorses Gershon.

By The Editorial Board

Wow! The *Newsday* editorial board had outlined, clearly and succinctly, everything we had been saying for two years about Zeldin and Trump. Now it was up to us to keep knocking on doors and getting the word out. We had about a week left to do that. We all agreed that going forward we will print out the endorsement and give out copies, along with the palm card. We hoped this endorsement could be a game changer.

I joined the team of Jorge and Katey. Jorge drove while Katey sat in the front seat and managed the list. It was harder than dealing with the lists in MiniVAN since there were only a few houses on each street. And these streets were more spread out. It took us about two hours to cover a list of only 15 houses.

It was beginning to look like I would not get an opportunity to see the Latino outreach at work since most people were not home but towards the end of our canvassing, at two houses, I got to see just how crucial having a Spanish-speaking person was to this effort. At the first house, we were looking for a 19-year-old first-time voter. His parents and what seemed to be his younger brother were in the driveway, working on a car. The father told us the son was not home. He spoke English but his wife did not so Jorge switched to Spanish. I could not understand what they were saying but the change in the body language and tone from the mother and father was so striking. They began to smile and seemed less stiff and tense. There was a lot of laughter back and forth. They shook Jorge's hand as we said good-bye.

As we walked back to the car, he explained to us what they had talked about. Their son is a citizen and was registered to vote in his first election. He knew where his polling place is, he was voting Democratic. The parents said they have green cards but are not citizens yet and so they cannot vote. They smiled with pride that their son, who was born here and is a citizen, will be voting.

At the last house on our list, a Latino woman was the registered voter. A man answered the door, opening it only a crack, and told us she wasn't home. Katey was at the door speaking to him in English. He seemed very wary. Katy called Jorge over to the door and he struck up a conversation in Spanish. As they spoke, the man opened the door wider and they shook hands. By the time Jorge said good-bye, the man was smiling and laughing and waving goodbye to us.

We got back in the car and Jorge explained that this man was the husband of the woman we were looking for. She was newly registered but that he had been registered for awhile and voted regularly. He said that they would both be voting Democratic.

It was clear just how powerful it was for this voter to speak to Jorge. Jorge was able to turn it into a conversation. Maybe it will be these conversations that inspire these voters to make sure they get to the polls and cast their votes. Someone had not only cared enough to come to their door but had gone the extra mile to speak to them in the language that they felt most comfortable with. To me, these exchanges were the most moving of all of my canvassing experiences.

I learned later from Mike that canvassing with Jorge is always illuminating because he speaks five languages in total. Mike told me that once, when he was out with Jorge, the voter had been more comfortable in Portuguese than Spanish so Jorge was able to switch to Portuguese.

Monday, October 29th
League of Women Voters debate in Hampton Bays
Getting ready to attend the debate tonight, I saw on Facebook that a series of Perry's lawn signs had been defaced with hate speech along major roads west of the district. We had been getting reports of signs disappearing and then suddenly the missing signs reappeared, dozens of them, with anti-abortion and anti-gay language stenciled on them. Perry's supporters who saw them along the

highway, stopped and took pictures and posted the photos on the grassroots' Facebook pages.

News12 covered the story of the stolen and defaced signs and included interviews with both Perry and Zeldin about them.[51] While Zeldin denounced the hate speech, he did not take responsibility for how his and Trump's inflammatory rhetoric contributed to such a climate.

I was sickened, especially coming on the heels of the shooting in Pittsburgh. In response, I posted this on Facebook with the picture of the signs:

> *Beautiful, vibrant, welcoming Pittsburgh. I am heartbroken. Never having been to Pittsburgh before Matt started at CMU last year, we have so thoroughly enjoyed each of our visits there. It is a youthful, diverse, affordable, energetic, tolerant small city. Last year, after the hate rally in Charlottesville, I wrote to my Congressman, Lee Zeldin, and begged him, as an American Jew like myself, to separate himself from Trump and the hate speech. Instead, he moved even closer to Trump, and attended a fundraiser this year hosted by white nationalists Steve Bannon and Sebastian Gorka. He spouts the anti-immigrant Trump party line, stoking fear to maintain power. Yesterday, when our local newspaper, Newsday, endorsed Perry Gershon, his Democratic*

> *opponent, the Editorial Board took Zeldin to task for being "a reliable cheerleader for Trump's divisive, dismissive politics and disastrous policies." Today, we discovered Perry lawn signs, along major roads, defaced with hate speech. Enough is enough. This has to stop. Hate begets more hate which leads to violence and death. Vote Democratic on Nov. 6th.*

I traveled to the debate with Mike, Katey and John Bouvier, with John driving his car. On the way there, we talked about the race, Zeldin and Perry's chances. John said that one of the key things that he doesn't like about Zeldin is how little he helps on local issues. He explained that to get funding for local projects, you need cooperation from the federal government, and unlike previous representatives, he said Zeldin is always AWOL.

When we got to the Hampton Bays High School, around 5:30 PM, there was already a long line outside with people waiting to get in. We ended up outside on line for quite a long time. It was cold out and John wished he had dressed in warmer clothes. I was glad I wore a heavier coat and equally glad that I found gloves in my pocket.

Ahead of us on the line were a group of Zeldin supporters. We knew that because they were wearing shirts and sweatshirts with the word Zeldin in large letters. Mike joked that all we got from Perry were buttons.

They were a group of white men and women, probably in our age group. They were hugging and greeting each other and were as friendly with each other as we were with our group. Given we are usually only in our own silos, it felt strange to be in such close proximity to people who support the Trump and Zeldin agenda. I cannot help but wonder what it is about that agenda that they liked? Were they bigots? Were they anti-immigrant? Did they excuse the hateful rhetoric that led to the pipe bombs and the Pittsburgh shooting? They did not look like wealthy people. Why weren't they worried about the burden of the GOP tax bill on our district? Why weren't they worried about losing their healthcare?

I grappled with the urge to tap them on the shoulder and ask these questions. It would be interesting to hear their answers and include them in the book. But I did not. I was wearing my Perry buttons. I am clearly not unbiased. I did not think they would welcome my incursion over to their "side". And, to be honest, I was fairly certain of what they would say. I did not believe it would be that different from the answers I got from Lloyd in the summer. After the last two years, to hold tight to supporting Trump and Zeldin has to mean either willful ignorance or embracing bigotry. Especially after Saturday's shooting.

Also, to be honest, asking questions in this setting did not feel particularly safe to me. So, I behaved less like a reporter and more like a supporter, staying on my side of the divide.

Mike, Katey, John and I were soon joined by fellow activists Eileen Duffy and Lisa Votino and by Lisa Gershon, Perry's wife. I gave her a hug and asked her how she and Perry were doing. She said she was fine and that Perry was tired but energized. And she was amazed at the energy and organizational ability of Logan, their son who was helping to manage the campaign. Talking to her now seemed like a million years away from when I first met her at the Westhampton Beach library when Rebecca was interviewing Perry. It has been a long journey.

Amanda, one of the campaign workers, came up to our group and said hello. She had a clipboard and was signing people up for GOTV. No need with our group, we were all already signed up. We saw other Democrats we knew and waved hello. Robin walked over and joined us. This is the first time we have been together since the fundraiser in Southampton. When I emailed Robin and asked her for her sense of where the race is and where the country is, she was not feeling optimistic. Now after the shooting on Saturday, she was feeling even less optimistic.

Finally, the line started to move. Thank goodness because I began to shiver from the cold. My biggest fear is getting sick now in the last week before the election. Once we got in the front doors, in the lobby we were given programs while people working there tried to count how many people were walking in. There was a bit of confusion at first that they were directing campaign supporters to two different sides of the auditorium but that was not the case. I was surprised there were no metal detectors, and no one looked in our bags, really no security at all. Given the events of last week, that was not only a surprise but forced me for a minute to think about now being in a room with Zeldin/Trump supporters who might have guns. I had to quickly put that out of my mind, otherwise I would not be able to sit in the room.

We got a row of seats. I looked behind me and saw Syma several rows behind. We smiled and waved hello. I had not spoken to her since the shooting. I could only imagine how upset she must be. Jorge arrived and we found a seat for him. Gordon waved as he headed for a seat towards the front.

The room was packed. I asked Mike if it was bigger than the usual crowd for a congressional debate and he said yes, though Robin said that could be a consequence of only two debates, one on the East End and one further west tomorrow. Everyone who was interested had to pack into just these two debates. High school students were walking around handing out index cards and pencils if people wanted to hand in questions. All of us focused on writing questions. I took two cards and posed two questions, one on the tax bill and one on Trump's rhetoric and the violence in Pittsburgh. The format had four people asking questions: members of the League of Women Voters and journalists so it seemed unlikely to me that there would be time for a lot of questions from the audience. Still, a lot of people were asking for cards and pencils to write questions.

On one side of the stage was a podium. In the center was a table with two microphones and two chairs for the candidates. And on the other side of the stage was a large table with four microphones and four chairs for the questioners. When Perry walked into the auditorium, there was a large cheer and a chant of "Perry" from our side. The host walked to the podium and said into the microphone there would be no more outbursts like that during the debate so "get it out of your system now." We did. And she said that when Zeldin walked out, his side would also get a minute to holler.

When Zeldin walked out, his supporters stood up and cheered, getting their one minute to holler. Interesting, when they stood up, it was clear that three quarters of the room were Perry supporters. I asked Mike if that was unusual and he said he did not remember in Zeldin's other two campaigns that the other side dominated the room. If that was the case, that had to rattle Zeldin a bit since he had not spoken in front of a gathering of all of his constituents since that one town hall in May, 2017.

Soon the stage was filled with seven people, one standing at the podium and the other six in their assigned seats. The superintendent of the Hampton Bays Union Free School District was at the podium. He explained that high school students were helping at the debate and he asked that all the adults in the room model good behavior for the students. He left and the moderator, who I remember from the primary debate which was held in this same auditorium, walked to the podium and explained the LWV rules for the debate. A question will be asked, both sides answer it, and if they want a rebuttal, they raise a red card.

Then the debate began. I was not able to record it since that was forbidden so I did my best to take notes despite my sore wrists. Luckily, I was able to check the live stream which was on YouTube by the next day.[52]

They each made an opening statement. Based on a coin toss, Zeldin went first. They each gave their usual speech about themselves. For Zeldin, he talked about being born and raised here, his military service, being a state senator and now a congressman, how much he has done for the district and why he thinks he deserves your vote on November 6th. Perry gave his story of being a businessman, an innovator but then asked the question: since Zeldin is such a vocal spokesman for Trump, is he still working for you? He mentioned Zeldin's votes on healthcare, the environment, taxes, wages and said we need a change, that he is running on these issues, that he is all about solutions and that we need to come back together. It was a very effective opening for Perry. Just like in the primary debates, right from the beginning, he did a very good job of tying three things together - Trump, Zeldin's record and the issues. He was off to a good start.

The first question was on healthcare and Perry answered first. He talked about the value of Obamacare and the GOP efforts to kill it which are ongoing, Zeldin's vote to take away protections for pre-existing conditions and then explained what can be done to better reduce healthcare costs, that the ultimate goal is single payer but that is far in the future and will need to be a bipartisan initiative.

Zeldin then defended his vote on the GOP American Health Care Act (AHCA) of 2017 and said it was a better step forward and that he disagreed with the ACA but that his vote was not to take away the protection for pre-existing conditions. He talked about tort reform, the need to negotiate drug prices, the comprehensive recovery act for opioid addiction and the need to invest more in the NIH (this is laughable given the administration's budget) and said he doesn't agree with the cost of Medicare for All, which is government takeover of healthcare and a one size fits all solution.

Perry held up a red card for a rebuttal. "Medicare for All is not a one size fits all, it just means a single source of payment and it is far from the government takeover." He then said how much the ACA stabilized the New York healthcare market and the AHCA would have allowed insurers to charge extra and gave states the ability to let protection for pre-existing conditions go away. It was not a way to maintain what we have today. I was pleased that Perry got that in there because it is the counter to Zeldin trying to argue that he didn't vote against preserving that protection.

Unfortunately, Zeldin got the last word on that question with his red card and Perry could not come back and rebut his argument that the ACA did not stabilize markets. Then he read the section from the AHCA that states it protects coverage for pre-existing conditions. Perry did not get a chance to come back and read further into the law where states and insurance companies are given the ability to remove coverage for essential health benefits which makes protection for pre-existing conditions meaningless. This is the GOP shell game that Zeldin is hiding behind. But if you don't know the details of the law, he can get away with it.

There were questions on the Pittsburgh shooting, the environment, transgender rights, social security, the opioid epidemic, gun violence, Trump's border wall, water quality and term limits. There were no surprises in any of their answers. Perry was straightforward and Zeldin used his word salad technique to run out the clock and hide how far to the right he is.

In their final statements, Perry talked about the differences between the two of them on healthcare, taxes and how getting rid of the full SALT deduction discriminated against New Yorkers. He mentioned the *Newsday* endorsement and how it emphasized that Perry is more concerned about the issues and the district than Zeldin who stands with Trump. When it was Zeldin's turn, he rambled on about Nancy Pelosi and Maxine Waters as some kind of scare tactic, and said that he was born and raised on Long Island and Perry wasn't. The moderator had to interrupt him to let him know he ran out of time.

The questions were thoughtful, mostly from the panel with a couple from the audience. They included national issues and purely local issues, particular to our district. I was impressed with the breadth of Perry's knowledge. It was his best debate and he kept his cool while Zeldin tried to rattle him with attacks and lies. He really did his homework.

I am shocked that Zeldin attacked Maxine Waters who was just targeted with pipe bombs. It made his repeated entreaties to "bipartisanship" throughout the debate sound pretty hollow.

Kathryn Szoka posted her assessment about the debate on Facebook.

> *Perry Gershon for Congress_done good. He was passionate in his support for environmental and social justice issues. He declared, "discrimination is wrong," "we need to work towards a Medicare for All health care system," "we need to support immigrants living in the shadows." Perry accurately countered Zeldin's attempts to finesse his extreme record on votes for national issues, he challenged LZ for supporting the US leaving the Paris Accord. He was knowledgeable, passionate, and commanding. Let's get this vote WON.*

We filed out of the auditorium and while we were lingering and talking in the lobby, Perry walked out and we gave him a loud round of applause. My feeling about a political debate is it can't win you an election but if you make a major gaffe, it can lose you the election. The Zeldin folks seemed unusually quiet as we all walked outside.

That night, in looking through my mail that had been delivered that day, I laughed out loud to discover a postcard addressed to Matt. Someone at one of the many postcard parties around the district had written this card to him. I took a picture of the card and texted it to Matt, who had already voted by absentee ballot.

Tuesday, October 30th
Final Debate
The newspaper *Riverhead Local* said over 600 people attended the debate and that, "the candidates' positions were a study in stark contrasts on most issues."[53]

I had planned on making my way to the western part of the district to see the second and final debate but had to change my plans. Because I don't drive that far, I was going to take the train to Patchogue and meet up with Nanci, Laura and her mother, Alice. But track work on the Long Island Railroad caused the cancellation of several trains and so I would not get there on time. The campaign was telling supporters to get there early because the room is small, holding only 90 people. It was in the Sachem Library. We didn't want a repeat of what happened at the League of Conservation Voters forum where we could not get in. So, I decided not to go, instead I watched the live stream, but Nanci and her group did go and were able to get in.

At this LWV event, the two candidates were standing at podiums, with one table in the middle that held one moderator. It was hard to tell how many people were in the room or how large the room was from the camera angle on the live stream.

They had their opening statements and they were both similar to last night. Then the single moderator asked questions, though I wasn't sure if they came from the audience or not. The questions covered many of the same topics from last night - social security, Medicare, Medicaid, immigration, the Pittsburgh shooting and gun safety, climate change, deficit and debt, polarization, education, healthcare and covering pre-existing conditions. They were also asked about rising income inequality. Their answers to this question were very different. Perry emphasized the GOP tax cut and how it increased income inequality and the war on unions and organized labor by the GOP while Zeldin danced around the issue, focusing on the importance of education and apprenticeships.

There was more applause for the answers from the audience, especially earlier in the debate, unlike last night when it was made clear that no responses from the audience would be tolerated. But then the applause stopped, though I wasn't sure why.

Then they came to their closing statements. Perry went first. Based on my notes, this is what he said: "I have talked about what I stand for. Grateful there have been less personal insults than last night. One issue we did not cover is a woman's right to choose. The country is going in the wrong direction. My campaign signs were stolen, over 50 signs, then they reappeared and they were spray painted with the words baby killer on them. This is not acceptable. I hope Lee condemns this. We have to protect women's rights, for healthcare, for equal pay. In a week you will decide who to vote for. I hope you make an informed decision. I have enjoyed this evening."

There was lots of applause when he was done. He never raised his voice, was calm, but definitive about how heinous these defaced signs were. I was glad he brought it up since it hadn't been mentioned last night and it had gotten a lot of press attention, and not just from local press, but from the national press as well.

Then Zeldin spoke: "I do condemn that, I have no idea who did it. But it is unfortunate that my opponent embraced his supporters when they said Zeldin is a Nazi." Zeldin was yelling and pointing his finger. And then he started ranting about a pro-choice flyer that was being mailed out by Perry tomorrow that showed a coat hanger and referred to it as Zeldin's healthcare plan for women. I had no idea what he was talking about. He was yelling and came across as quite unhinged.

At this point half the room was booing and it seemed like the other half was chanting USA. Zeldin then began to read comments from online against him and his family, a comment like "I hope you choke on your dinner." Perry said that of course he condemned a comment like that at which point Zeldin yelled, "I had to shame you into doing the right thing!"

Now the mixture of boos and USA chants grew louder. At which point the moderator quieted down the room and then interrupted Zeldin and said, "This is not an appropriate closing statement."

The room erupted in a mixture of applause and people yelling, while Zeldin tried to interrupt to say, "Was it appropriate when he did it?" But of course, Perry hadn't been yelling and accusatory.

The moderator quieted the room and said that Zeldin would get time to finish his closing statement. People were filing out of the room while he was speaking. And then the live stream shut off.

My phone rang and it was Nanci. She had just left the room. She filled me in on what had been happening. She said the library had opened up another room which is why it held more than 90 people. They were there very early but were able to wait inside and the library offered them refreshments. She said they let them in the room around 6:30 PM. It seemed to her that there were more Perry supporters in the room than Zeldin but that the Zeldin people were very loud. She was sitting in the 10th row, right behind a large group of Zeldin folks. She said it felt very tense in the room.

Soon after they sat down, Perry arrived and there was a lot of applause when he came into the room and that he walked around shaking hands. She said Zeldin didn't arrive until the debate started and went right to the podium. One member of his staff made a big deal out of moving Zeldin's podium forward so he wasn't in shadow.

She said the crowd was boisterous, with applause on both sides, until the moderator asked them to all stop. She said the Zeldin supporters sitting in front of her would mutter comments about Perry under their breath while he was speaking. At one point, Zeldin made a snide comment about hoping Perry's supporters will listen. That didn't go over well with the audience.

Most of this I hadn't heard since it wasn't picked up by the live stream. She felt Perry was very strong, focused on policies and was clear and articulate. Much of the time when Zeldin was speaking she said she had no idea what he was talking about.

But she said when Zeldin went after Perry in his closing statement they booed and then walked out. She wasn't going to stick around and listen to his smears. In fact, by the time he began to redo his closing statement and talked about thanking the LWV, most people had already left.

Wednesday, October 31st
Final Canvassing
I had planned on staying in today and trying to catch up with the book project but when Mike called to say he wanted to try to finish the walk book that we had started, I said sure. He had Andrea Spilka with him so there would be three of us, which helps it go faster. I had never met Andrea but I knew she had gone out canvassing with Mike before.

They picked me up around 3:30 PM. There weren't that many houses to finish this territory. They were spread out, one or two houses on each street, so it took longer even though we weren't covering as many houses. Most people weren't home but we left Perry's flyer and a copy of the *Newsday* endorsement at each house.

Mike told me that Andrea is a powerhouse in Southampton working on different issues through a variety of civic associations. Andrea explained to me that in the past she has tried to be more non-partisan but today's politics pushed her to be out here knocking on doors.

"As a community advocate who feels strongly about working with all levels of government, I'm often reluctant to get involved in party politics. However, I've come to understand that in standing up for the East End community there are times when the issues on the ballot are so important that I need to take a political stand. I can't complain about government inaction if I don't try to elect people who will make a difference. In prior years I've worked to elect/re-elect both Democrats and Republicans. Whoever wins, I'll keep pressuring them to take action on issues important to my community but my heart is hoping that my choice is elected."

Chapter 20

November 1st – 5th

"Hopefully Let's Visit Lee Zeldin is obsolete in November. God willing."

Eileen Duffy, founder of LVLZ

Thursday, November 1st
Sweeping the table on endorsements

Election Day is less than a week away. To add to the endorsements in *The New York Times* and *Newsday*, every newspaper on the East End endorsed Perry. The campaign gave us a new flyer to give to voters with a graphic that included the logo of every news source that has now endorsed him. Not one had endorsed Zeldin. Impressive for a challenger. The campaign posted this message on the Facebook page:

> Perry Gershon for Congress
> *My campaign has been about focusing on the needs of the District- how we can improve peoples' lives, how we can ensure that the District has a voice in Congress, how we can boost the middle class, how we can steward the environment and our beautiful surroundings, how we can finally stop senseless gun violence. Across the district, from Newsday to The Smithtown News to The East Hampton Star, local media voices have expressed their trust that when elected, I will do everything I can to fight for what's best for Long Islanders in Congress. I won't let them, or the District down!*

Friday, November 2nd
GOTV in Riverhead

I woke up very slowly today. It was a rainy, dark, windy fall day; a day to stay inside. But today was the first day of GOTV, those crucial last few days of any campaign when it is all about making sure your most reliable voters are going to actually go vote.

For the last few months, as we have covered the district knocking on doors, we have listened to voters' concerns, found out what issues are important to them and introduced them to Perry. Each exchange was documented into the database with a rating of the voter's support: 1-Strong Gershon, 2- Lean Gershon, 3- Undecided, 4- Lean Zeldin and 5- Strong Zeldin. For those voters who were leaning to Perry or undecided, we went back in hopes that we might persuade them.

But at GOTV time, we focus on the 1s and 2s, those that we already know are strong Gershon voters or leaning Gershon. And it is all about finding out what they might need to make sure they go vote next Tuesday. Do they know where their polling place is? Do they need a ride to the polls? Asking what time of day they are thinking of voting, especially because if they say later in the day, we can always give them another call on Election Day to make sure they voted.

This is the science behind canvassing. The doors we knocked on were not random. We did not spend time with die-hard Republicans and Trumpsters. For months, we focused on energizing Democrats and persuading those "persuadables." That focus changed today. The walk list was a little different and the canvassing script was different.

I had signed up for one shift out of the Riverhead office and another shift at the Quogue office. I put on my Blue Wave LI shirt, attached my Perry Gershon button to my jacket, had my bottle of water and some nuts in my bag, and drove to Riverhead, which is about 20 minutes away.

The office is on Main Street in Riverhead. This is the same street where we handed out flyers about Zeldin's record over the summer. Main Street reflected the ups and downs of all small towns today. The street is dotted with thriving small stores and restaurants housed in lovely renovated buildings while next door are empty, boarded-up buildings where the battle against the big box retailers and online sellers like Amazon has already been lost.

I pulled into the parking lot behind the campaign office. The sign said three-hour parking which I knew would be fine because I should be done long before that. I had also brought my laptop and headphones for phone banking just in case it was a heavy rain, since I do not canvas in the rain. But by the time I got to Riverhead, the rain had stopped.

Walking from the parking lot to Main Street, I turned a corner and quickly found the store front with all the Perry Gershon signs in the window. I walked in and was heartened by how crowded the office was. There were two people sitting at a table by the front window who were putting "Endorsed by Newsday" stickers on the new Perry palm cards. There was a crowd of about five people at the front counter learning about canvassing and how to use the MiniVAN app.

I signed in on the signup sheet on the counter. Most of the would-be canvassers were older, probably retired, which is probably why they could take time out in the middle of the day. They were dividing into pairs to get ready to go out. Another gentleman, also close to my age, walked in and asked about yard signs.

After they all left, I spoke with Jeanne Greco and Jason Berkenfeld, who were in charge at the office. I told them that I was there to canvas but I didn't like to drive so I asked if I could I be paired with a driver. I said I was happy to wait until someone arrived who would be a driver.

I told them a little about the book project and asked them if they were getting a lot of canvassers. Jeanne said that despite the bad weather they had been very busy on this first day of GOTV, surprising for a Friday afternoon. She showed me the new palm cards with the stickers.

While we were talking a tall young man with a baseball cap walked in, came up to the counter to sign in and told Jeanne that he was there to canvas. She asked him if he minded being the driver since she had a non-driver ready to go out. He said sure. Jeanne introduced us. His name is Frederic Sjoberg. They discussed what territory to give us, which walk list, and Frederic decided to put it on the MiniVAN app on his phone. We gathered up the palm cards as he put in the walk list number and pulled up the list on his phone. It was a large list, with a lot of homes, but not very far away. I told them I needed to be done by about 2:30 PM so I would have time to go home, get a bite to eat and then head over to the Quogue office for my second shift.

We walked out the front door and down Main Street to where Frederic's car was parked. We plotted out our route and while we got settled in the car, I told Frederic about the book project and asked if he minded speaking to me on the record. He said he was happy to. I asked Frederic where he was from since I could not place his accent. He told me he is from Finland, that he cannot vote yet since he is not a citizen, but his wife and children are, and that they live in Brooklyn but have a vacation home here on the East End that they come out to every weekend. He felt that the election is so important, because we need a check on Trump, that he felt inspired to knock on doors in our district, since his Brooklyn district is already represented by a Democrat. He said they had come out from Brooklyn last night, took the kids out of school for the day, so that he could spend today and the weekend helping to get Perry elected. I thanked him and told him that I found this remarkable, at a time when so many people in the country are apathetic, that he would help out in a district that isn't even his.

He was very skilled at navigating the roads, finding places to park the car, and using MiniVAN. The first few addresses were on a busy road so we parked on a smaller side street and then walked over. But all the addresses on our list had been converted to professional buildings. Not one of them was a residence. Clearly the list was wrong. We put down "moved" as the category but wondered why these would be on a GOTV list, when we are in theory going to people who have already been reached out to and marked as 1s or 2s?

The next house had a person who was voting for Zeldin, which made us even more suspicious of the list. At the next few houses no one was home, we left the palm card and my copies of the endorsements in the doorways, but before we went much further, I tried to call the Riverhead office to see if the list was given to us by mistake. It did not seem like a GOTV list.

While I was waiting to hear back from either Jeanne or Jason in the office, we kept going and our next addresses were in a neighborhood of small houses and a trailer park. We noticed that all the names on the list had a Slavic spelling. Frederic guessed they were Ukrainian. Turns out he had lived and worked in the Ukraine for a while and spoke fluent Ukrainian.

How serendipitous that was. Most of the residents in this neighborhood were home and almost all of them were more comfortable in Ukrainian than English. They were leaning Gershon but a few needed some convincing and many of them needed information about where their polling place is. Frederic being able to speak to them in their native language was incredibly valuable. One man stood out. He was home with his young daughter. He said his wife was at work but he worked from home. He spoke English but was clearly more comfortable speaking Ukrainian.

He said he didn't know much about Perry but he did not like Trump. We got the feeling that he may have voted for Trump in 2016 but no longer liked his policies or his rhetoric, particularly what he was now saying about getting rid of birthright citizenship. He was registered as Unaffiliated. Frederic spoke to him in Ukrainian, which I could not understand, but he told me afterwards that along with immigration, healthcare was very important to him. Frederic showed him the newspaper endorsements and explained that Zeldin is one of Trump's biggest supporters. He told Frederic that Perry had his vote and he asked for two palm cards, one for him and one for his wife.

We had a similar experience at a few other houses. When we turned a corner and saw the Ukrainian Church in the neighborhood, Frederic said that explained the heavily Ukrainian neighborhood. I told him how amazing that this was our walk list and he spoke their language but he informed me that he spoke seven languages, so there were a lot of neighborhoods that he would have been able to speak to residents in their native tongue.

We finished up the list and then headed back to the office, quite buoyed in spirits by our experience. There had been a few Zeldin supporters but all in all very positive. I told Frederic that this was my only day canvassing out of the Riverhead office but I hoped he would canvas all weekend because he was a natural and all those languages were an incredible plus.

The author and Frederic at the Riverhead campaign office

When I got home it was after 3:00 PM and by the time I had lunch, it was 3:30 PM and I was late for my second shift. I also realized that I was just too tired to go back out again. I contacted Jake and Joy to let them know and said I would be in Quogue tomorrow for the 12-3:00 PM shift. I then lay down on the couch and fell asleep. When I woke up it was dark outside the house and inside. As I walked around turning lights on, I knew that my plans to walk two shifts back to back was just not realistic.

Saturday, November 3rd
Hope vs. Fear
Election coverage on the news starkly highlighted that Americans are living in two completely different countries. The Democratic rallies, with guest speakers

such as President Obama and Oprah Winfrey, were filled with talk of hope, diversity and inclusivity. Trump rallies were all about the nation being under attack by an invasion from a dangerous caravan coming to the border that requires 15,000 troops to protect us and that any other story is fake news. One campaign was based on hope, the other based on fear.

Before 2016, I would have said that hope always wins out over fear. Now I was not so sure. Fear motivates, fear sells. The Kavanaugh hearings woke up the Republican base. No one seems confident anymore if there will even be a blue wave. There was talk that the Republicans could even maintain their majority in the House by one vote.

When Trump won my only antidote to despair was to stay focused on what I could do to resist. I do the same thing now. To suppress the panic, I kept my attention on GOTV. I knew I should be casting a much wider net for the book, like visiting more campaign offices, spending more time with Perry, interviewing more grassroots and Democratic Committee members, doing more research on the election. But I couldn't. The only thing I could do to keep from being swallowed by fear was to keep reaching out to voters. And that meant knocking on more doors.

Today I went to the Quogue office. I was paired up with Andrea, who I had just gone canvassing with a few days ago with Mike, and she was happy to drive. We were assigned a list in Westhampton. Andrea and I had both printed copies of the endorsement graphic as well as the *Newsday* endorsement and I had the new palm cards from Riverhead the day before.

It was overcast and windy but the rain had held off. After a short time, the sun came out, the sky was blue and Andrea joked that maybe this was a good omen for the election. At most of the houses, folks weren't home but we left the palm card and the endorsements, so even though we hadn't spoken with them, they would know that someone had cared enough to visit their homes. The new palm card had a lot of information about Election Day and hours of voting.

When people were home, the Democrats we spoke with assured us that they were voting for Perry. We followed the script and also asked what time they planned on going to the polls and if they needed a ride, and punched in that information into the app. Every person voting for Perry told us how important this election is, how important it was for them to vote. One woman, about my age, told me she looked forward to voting, she had waited two years to vote. That she was so angry. She thanked us for everything we were doing knocking on doors and speaking to voters. We shook her hand.

As we got towards the end of our list, we decided to split up, each taking a different side of the street in order to finish faster. I knocked on the door of a small house that was badly in need of a new coat of paint and had cardboard taped to half of the front window. A woman who looked to be in her seventies came to the door. I told her that I was a volunteer for the Perry Gershon campaign, the Democrat running for Congress in our district. She said, "Oh, I was watching the debate the other night and I think your guy is the one who wants to protect Medicare and Social Security."

I said, yes, he is and asked her if those issues were important to her. She said yes, that she depended on both of them. I gave her the palm card and told her about the endorsements. She looked down at the sheet. I mentioned how Perry would protect Social Security and Medicare as well as coverage for pre-existing conditions.

She stopped reading and looked up at me. She paused and then said she wasn't sure about Perry because she remembered that Perry wasn't good at border security. She remembered that Perry didn't support building the wall. She then went into a long tirade about the "caravan" and the danger of "those people" who come here illegally and are taking advantage of the services they aren't entitled to and their kids are using up all the resources in our schools and they don't behave like our kids did and then millions of them vote. As she told me these stories, she got very animated, her eyes widened, her hands gestured wildly. The more she talked, the louder and more agitated she became.

I was about to tell her that none of what she was ranting about was true but I held back because there was no point. I knew that nothing I said would make a difference. I thanked her for her time and then told her I had to go. As I started to walk away, she invited me in for a cup of tea. She said she had much more she wanted to tell me. I smiled, thanked her for her offer of tea but that I had many more houses to get to before it got dark. I did ask her to take a look at the materials I gave her and then I said goodbye.

I walked away and headed to the next house but the conversation stayed with me. The lies, the bigotry, the spewing of *Fox News* talking points, normally all of that would set off my anger. But what I felt afterwards was a profound sadness. I knew even then, at that moment, that this exchange was the essence for me of what this election was about. Here was a person who depended on a strong social safety net to survive and yet she quickly jettisoned protecting that lifeline as her primary voting issue because of the ginned-up fear of those "others" who, she has been told over and over again, were dangerous, undeserving and scamming the system.

It took us almost three hours but we finished the whole walk list of several streets, over 50 houses. That night, my experience with the woman in the small house with the cardboard on the broken window was hard to shake. It heightened my anxiety about the election, about the state of the country.

Conversely, weekend GOTV efforts over the last few weeks were encouraging, particularly in Brookhaven. Here are a few images posted on Facebook, including:

- A photo of the crowd of volunteers at Perry's Farmingville campaign office in Brookhaven;
- Rebecca Dolber, Patty Callan and Deb Dolber pitching in to help;
- And Roland Hoffmann and Patty Callan canvassing for Perry.

Today at the main office in Setauket, hundreds of people showed up, including busloads of students, to help GOTV. They were treated to a visit from former Brooklyn Congresswoman Elizabeth Holtzman, who spoke to the crowd about the importance of this election, before they all went out knocking on doors.

Sunday, November 4th
Hate Continues

On Zeldin's Facebook page he was imploring his supporters to vote so that the district had "results rather than resistance." Again, he referred to Perry as Park Avenue Perry and called his campaign a house of cards.

This was my response:

> <u>Barbara Weber-Floyd:</u> *Results? Let's talk about the GOP tax bill which is going to slam each of us with higher taxes when we file next April and lower our property values. You did not do one single thing to protect us from this tax increase when it was in committee and even voted for it to go to a vote on the floor. And it was designed to hit us after the election. And now that you and your profligate party have blown up the deficit by giving huge tax breaks to the 1%, you plan on coming after our Social Security.*

I then added that if Zeldin delivered results, why did every newspaper editorial board endorse Perry?

Our different grassroots groups' Twitter and Facebook pages were filled with photos and stories of everyone's canvassing experiences over the weekend. Here are two of my favorites.

Steven Kramer, Indivisible Northfork:
2600 calls for @perrygershon made so far by the GOTV volunteers at The Dark Horse phone bank here in Riverhead! So impressive to watch first time phone canvassers jump in w/ both feet & seasoned canvassers crush list after list. Y'all are an inspiration! Rock on friendlies!

Kathryn Szoka, PEER:
While canvassing this week, I've had several conversations with great folks who rarely vote. Initially, some weren't sure they'd go on Tuesday. - mostly because voting just didn't seem to make a difference in their lives. I get that. But standing face to face, discussing the importance of protecting healthcare, social justice, the environment; AND discussing the extreme positions of our CD1 rep & his closeness with DT; well - snap - they GET that. And, they are telling me they'll call friends to go to the polls! YES.
If you or anyone you know isn't sure they'll vote, no matter the reason, PM me. Let's chat. No judgment. You matter. What you think matters. I want to hear from you. I want you to know that YOUR vote is needed & it will make a difference. #AllTogether

I felt cautiously optimistic. And then I saw a message from Zeldin saying that Perry's supporters had defaced the signs. This brought the subject of the signs and the hate speech back into the news.

Perry held a press conference to address it.

Perry Gershon for Congress

Lee Zeldin, a Jew and a sitting US Congressman, is accusing my campaign of drawing a swastika on our own campaign signs for political advantage. I have been running for office for 18 months, and this is the lowest I have seen him go.

It is egregious for so many reasons, on both a personal and national level. My grandfather fought against the promoters of the swastika in World War II and helped in the liberation of Dachau. Anti-Semitic acts spiked 97% in New York last year. And just last weekend, 11 Jews were killed in the deadliest act on American Jewry our nation has ever seen. Our country needs leaders who will show zero tolerance for this behavior, even more so because our President repeatedly fails to condemn acts of intolerance and hatred.

> *What Lee Zeldin's campaign calls "shenanigans," I call a hate crime. I condemn this act, and all acts of hatred, whether it be towards me, my campaign, or my opponent. In the last week, my campaign has seen its signs defaced with the words "baby killer" and "gay lover", and now with a giant swastika, all on public display. These are not so much insults at me, but directed at all of the good people of NY-1. When Lee tells reporters he's been the longtime victim of Facebook "attacks" he never reported until now, he's attempting to manufacture equivalence by minimizing a hate crime. When he tells reporters I vandalized my own signs with a symbol that has been repugnant to generations in my family, that's obscene. The Suffolk County Police hate crimes unit is investigating the actual targeting of only one campaign, the abhorrent defacing of my signs.*

Seven synagogues in New York City were targeted with fires over the weekend. Yesterday, two women were shot and killed at a yoga class in Florida by a man who had posted virulent anti-women rhetoric. At the end of every day, I wrote down the same fear-filled question in my notes – what will become of this country if the GOP grip on power is still tightly clenched after Tuesday?

Monday, November 5th
Last Day of Door Knocking

As a rule, I do not canvass in the rain but today was the last day and I wasn't going to miss it. Lulu and Andrea and I went out together, with Andrea driving. It was a really tough list because it included Main Street in Westhampton Beach where you have apartments that are above the commercial buildings. They are hard to find, with staircases in the back leading up to the apartments. As the day progressed, the rain came down harder. We were getting soaked.

It was the usual routine – not home, left the palm card and endorsements. But a couple of memories stand out.

Lulu and I stood at the door of a man in his seventies, listed as Unaffiliated. We were dripping water on his welcome mat. We knocked and he came to the door. He was very friendly. He invited us in and we demurred, saying we have a lot of doors to knock on and we didn't want to get water all over his wood floors. I gave him my spiel how we were volunteers with the Perry Gershon campaign, the Democrat running for Congress, how crucial this election is and the election is tomorrow. I asked him if he had decided or made up his mind how he was going to vote.

He told us that, to be honest, he hadn't been paying much attention yet, that he's an Independent and he really makes up his mind at the end, but he would be interested in what I had to say about Perry. I told him a lot about Perry, we talked to him about all the endorsements and we gave him copies of all of our materials about Perry. He said he would read them. We asked him if he knew where his polling place was and he said he did.

And then he said, “But to be honest, the biggest recommendation for your guy is the fact that you are both out here soaking wet in the rain knocking on my door. He has my vote just for that!” We shook his hand and thanked him as we all laughed.

As we walked away, Lulu turned to me and said, “That is why you knock on doors, because somebody who maybe wouldn't have voted at all might now vote just because we spoke to him.”

They dropped me off at home when we were done, where I had an hour to take a hot shower and have a bite to eat before driving to Sharon’s to continue canvassing with her in Eastport. Today I was breaking my own rules about canvassing in the rain and trying to do two shifts in one day. But this was it. Tomorrow is Election Day.

Around this time, I got a text from Joy saying that the campaign was steering everyone towards phone banking, but if we wanted to do another walk list instead, we could. Another EEAN member, Pat Falk, met us at Sharon’s. I told them about Joy’s text and said, “Listen, whatever you want to both do, I will do, if you would prefer to phone bank, I will do that, but I really prefer knocking on doors.” They agreed. Pat and I left our cars at Sharon’s and then the three of us took off. I really liked canvassing with three, since the person driving the car could stay with the car and the two people knocking on doors could take each side of the street. It went much faster that way. I no longer felt afraid to knock on the door by myself. I had come a long way since that first time canvassing with Mike. Sharon, who was driving would stay in the car. I took the odd numbered side of the street and Pat took the even numbers. We had a very big list. I think there were 70 houses.

Most people were not home but for the people I spoke with it seemed to make a difference. I knocked on the door of one home and the woman who answered the door was about my age and not on our list. The person on my list was a 20-year-old who was a registered Democrat.

The woman who answered the door scowled at me but I was not deterred. I very politely asked for the person on my list. She said, "Well, that's my daughter" and it did not look like she was going to call her daughter to the door when the daughter walked up behind her. I shook her hand, told her who I was and why I was there, asking her if she had made up her mind who she was voting for.

She said, "You know, I really haven't, I haven't been paying attention." So, I told her about Perry, about the issues he supported and about all the endorsements. Meanwhile, the mother was standing behind her and glaring at me the whole time. But the daughter was very friendly and eager to speak with me about the election. She asked a lot of questions that I tried my best to answer and I left her with the whole packet of Perry's materials. She was particularly interested in the *Newsday* endorsement. She said she would read everything. She asked me for information on her polling place. I pulled that information up in MiniVAN and gave it to her. She thanked me and shook my hand.

I was chuckling to myself when I got back to the car and told Sharon and Pat the story and we all agreed that she might just vote for Perry just to piss off her mother!

We went to every house on our list until we got to a series of houses right on Montauk Highway. By then it was raining again and getting dark. We decided to skip these houses since it was too hard to park the car on the busy street and get to each house in the dark. We drove back to Sharon's and as we drove up, there was another car in her driveway. A woman named Bonnie got out and told us she was canvassing for Perry, which gave us all a good laugh. Sharon assured her that she and her husband, Doug, were voting for Perry and could mark them down as strong supporters of Perry. We asked her if she was going to come to The Dark Horse restaurant tomorrow for the watch party. She said she was thinking about it.

Bonnie left, as did Pat, who had to get home, but Sharon and I went out to get a bite to eat. We were both starving. We went to a little restaurant near her and had hamburgers. I got to really talk with her about her vacation in Peru, which sounded amazing and about how we're feeling about the race. We tried to discuss what EEAN might be doing after the election but neither of us could really think past tomorrow.

Before I left, Sharon and I decided we would go vote in the morning at our different polling places then go to Joy's for phone banking. Then meet up later at The Dark Horse for dinner. I told her that my sister Nanci was planning on joining us and then we were both going to Southampton for the watch party with the SHDems. We had heard that Perry might stop by The Dark Horse to say hello on his way to the campaign event in Hauppauge.

That night I thought about the women I worked with today - Sharon, Pat, Joy, Lulu, Andrea - and all the other women who have been part of this effort for two years in our district and around the country. Women like us, women who got mad, women who had enough.

On my answering machine, was a robo call with a message from the Zeldin campaign saying that Perry isn't honest enough to be our congressman because he is a liar. And that's the tenor of the Trump/Zeldin campaign. In addition, I heard from several people that some voters got a flyer in the mail today, designed to look like it came from Kate and the Women's Equality Party telling voters to cast their vote for Kate on that line. We knew this didn't come from Kate because Kate had repeatedly told her supporters to ignore her name on that line. Yes, she was listed on the ballot on this line because she had petitioned with the Women's Equality Party to be on their line if she won the primary and unfortunately the rules did not allow her to remove her name even though she didn't win the primary. Then here comes the Zeldin camp trying to exploit that with a dishonest mailer, another form of voter suppression. The word went out on all the different Facebook pages to ignore that mailer and to vote for Perry. Zeldin must be really worried about how close this election is going to be.

Before I went to bed, I saw an email from Nanci that she sent out to our friends and family.

> *I usually don't send political emails but I wanted all of you to know that tomorrow, Babs and I will be together to find out if all our marching and post card writing and, in Babs' case* ***endless*** *hours of work and energy pays off. I am cautiously optimistic that women and young voters are going to send a big message to the immoral leadership of not only the President but the entire Republican Party that has stood silently by and let him try to destroy all the values that our country stands for.*
>
> *I really think we will take the House. But if we should lose both the House and the Senate, I think we will come closer than a lot of people could imagine in places like Georgia and Texas...and Barbara and I will be disappointed but we are not going to crumble. We are committed to fighting even harder to get our country back in two years, a fight that starts on Wed. regardless of the outcome Tues. night.*

After we marched in DC two years ago, little Mackenzie (who went to the zoo with Aunt Mimi while Elyse, Vicky, Babs and I marched), had listened to us talking and listened to the television coverage after the march and then at one point in the evening, she picked up one of our signs and marched around the room chanting, "We're not gonna go away." We vowed to her and to all our children that day that we would keep fighting the good fight. We have and we will. But it would make it a lot easier if we could get the House tomorrow night!

To my sister who has been an inspiration to me, my girls, and I know to ALL of you, I can't thank you enough for all you have done to make a blue wave a good possibility to start washing away the ugliness that has taken hold of our country. We will either celebrate together tomorrow night or lean on each other to stay standing, but I will remain forever grateful that I got to share these last few years mobilized with you. You have lived up to the signs that Elyse made for our Women's March in DC quoting Michelle Obama in her last address as First Lady-

"Be Focused, Be Determined, Be Hopeful, Be Empowered"...You have done all of those things and with a passion that we rarely see in people today. So, remember, whatever happens tomorrow...we're not gonna go away!

Love,
Nanci

I was deeply touched by Nanci's email. We began this journey together and she reminded me of what it is all about. I sent this email back:

To my dearest sister,

You have made me cry and I cannot thank you enough for your beautiful words. I am so excited that we will be together tomorrow to attend two watch parties - first with the grassroots and then with the Southampton Democrats - and will hopefully also get to see Perry, our candidate, who has done such an incredible job. We started this journey together when we decided, just a few days after the election in 2016, that we would be at the first Women's March in D.C. and so I am grateful that we will be together to see the results of this almost two-year journey. And you are right, no matter what happens tomorrow, we will carry this fight forward on to 2020 and beyond... Oh, and everyone should wear blue tomorrow in honor of the blue wave that I believe in my heart is coming. It is just a question of how large a wave it will be.

Love,

Barbara

p.s. Now make sure you all go out and vote tomorrow!!!!

Chapter 21

Tuesday, November 6th – Election Day

"I think that each individual has to do their part. It takes one person, even just one. Look at Martin Luther King, and so many of the other great individuals that have contributed to the betterment of this country, even during turbulent times. We have to stay positive to keep ourselves going, because if we see no hope then there's no reason to press on. I always look towards positive change, because when I put myself in the position to see positive things happen, then I see positive things happening around me because of the energy I put out there."

Elena A. Rivera-Williams, SHDems Executive Committee

I woke up tired. I planned on going back out and either canvassing or phone banking at Joy's house. She was still going strong as a pop-up base of operations for the campaign. But I decided instead to make phone calls from home. I just didn't have enough energy left to go out. I told Sharon and Joy.

Using my computer, I was able to do the kind of phone banking where it only connects if someone answers the phone. These were all Democrats. They all told me they planned on voting. I suggested they vote early because we were anticipating long lines and because the rain was expected to get worse. I asked them if they needed a ride to the polls and if they knew where their polling place is. This was the election day script.

I went as long as I could until I was practically falling asleep at my desk. I knew that I had reached the end of my energy. I hoped a lot of other people picked up the slack because my body felt heavy, like lugging around lead. I was done.

I was seeing reports on Facebook from all of the different grassroots groups that turnout was high across the district. I even saw a post about some people who live in New York City and did not get their absentee ballots, so they took the Hampton Jitney out to the East End to vote. I read a story of one man in our district who was in Florida for the winter, didn't get his absentee ballot so he flew back today to cast his vote. I was not able to verify these anecdotes but they boosted my spirits nonetheless.

I understood someone being that motivated to cast their vote. This was the first time since November, 2016 that we could do more than protest. I was cautiously optimistic that there will be a blue wave.

There were so many times in the last couple months, particularly after the Kavanaugh vote, when I felt more doubt than confidence that the blue wave was coming. I worried how much Trump and Zeldin's phony caravan and fear-mongering and using the military at the border to emphasize that point, might awaken the GOP base to come out and vote. Coupled with all the voter suppression tactics and the gerrymandering then a blue wave could be thwarted.

But today, on Election Day, I believed in my heart that all the women who marched for the last two years, who organized, who joined huddles, who joined Democratic Committees, who made phone calls, who wrote postcards, who laid down in "die-ins" for the ACA and stood up for gun safety, would now march to the polls. I also believed that younger voters, awakened by Parkland, would march to the polls. And all the Democrats who sat home in 2016 and helped to elect Trump, would march to the polls.

I got dressed and went to the firehouse to vote. Both Eugene and Matt had voted by absentee ballot since they were both away. There were quite a few people there, far more than the primary, but no line. Of course, it was early in the day. I was voter number 174. Around the same time in the morning on primary day and I was number five.

When I voted in the morning, it was drizzling. But just as predicted, by the afternoon it became a downpour. The weather report said the entire eastern seaboard was hit with this storm. My anxiety spiked. Bad weather depresses turnout.

I got a text from Sharon who was at her polling place and she said the rain did not seem to be dampening turnout there. *"It's not hurting here. I'm sitting in my car watching people still coming in. I was #371. That is incredible. I think 40 voted all day in the primary."* And she included a picture of her smiling at her polling place.

Nanci was picking me up around 6:30 PM and we were going to The Dark Horse restaurant in Riverhead to join with EEAN and Indivisible North Fork for dinner. We heard there was even a chance that Perry would stop by. I could only imagine how exhausted and nervous he was feeling after this long journey.

Then Nanci and I were going to drive to Southampton to spend some time with the SHDems at their watch party at the Southampton Inn, where along with the news coverage of the national news we will have an in-house feed of our election in CD#1. We would then come back to my house to watch the national coverage. She was sleeping over though had to be up early for work but we would stay up and watch as much as we could, especially if it was good news. We had champagne ready.

I looked at my email and saw a message from my Dad. He had sent an email to his friends before Election Day, which he then shared with us today. I was so moved by it that I asked him if I could post it on Facebook. He said yes and I posted it across all the grassroots groups in CD#1:

> *I asked my Dad, Jack Weber, if I could share with all of you this email message for Election Day that he sent to many of his friends. He is a Democrat. Many of his friends are Republicans. He hopes it might sway some of them and he is praying tonight that we get a response from the country that is a loud and clear repudiation of hate that elects a Democratic Congress. Please feel free to share with your friends. It is from someone who served in the Navy during WWII and in the Korean War. He is and always has been my inspiration.*
>
> *"Guys. Our group is a mixture of R and D but I like to think we are all Americans and as such, perhaps you are just as worried about this country as I am. I lived through the 1930s and WW II, I watched anti-Semitism grow, not only in Germany but here as well. I watched and listened to the American/ German Bund, the America First, and yes Col. Charles Lindbergh, verbally supporting Hitler and now I see it returning again.*
>
> *Hatred of minorities is on the rise; hatred of Muslims, hatred of blacks, hatred of immigrants and yes hatred of Jews. We witnessed a torch lit march of a neo-Nazi group chanting "Jews will not replace us ". Now the death of Jews gathered in prayer in Pittsburgh and the murderer shouting "Jews must die". Where is this going? When will it stop? I said I was worried but I'm also mad and angry with many people.*

The rhetoric and hatred on both sides of the political spectrum must stop but it must begin with the president. He must set the example for all to follow. He has the biggest and most powerful pulpit in the world, not only to be the commander in chief but to be the healer in chief and make this country one again. Don't tell me how much he has done with the tax law, with the conservative judges he appointed, with his policies on trade. This country is drowning in hatred and as an American Jew of 94 years experience I can tell you it's getting worse and it MUST stop. Now.

I got that off my chest, if I don't see you sooner have a happy Thanksgiving with your family.
Jack"

So many of my Facebook friends responded and asked if they could share his words, that he inspired them and to please tell him thank you. I let him know and he was surprised at the response. I told him I was not. He is an inspiration to us and everybody who knows him.

Nanci picked me up and we headed to The Dark Horse. The rain had let up a bit, though was still worrisome that it was so heavy throughout the afternoon. We met Sharon in the parking lot and walked in together. For all the times I have phone banked and attended meetings in the conference room in the basement of the restaurant, I have never eaten here. Turned out they have a decent gluten free menu. Indivisible arranged a pre-fixe dinner for us which included one drink. We sat at a large table together: Rebecca, her Mom, Deb, her fiancé, Sarah, Syma, Sharon, Nanci and me along with Melinda from EEAN and Laura Venugopalan and Steven Kramer from Indivisible.

There was a television at the bar and we watched as a few results started coming in. We cheered as Democrats took a few House seats. I had been hoping to see Perry, but he wasn't able to stop by. We also would have loved to stay longer but we needed to head to Southampton so we had to leave before a lot of other Resisters arrived. Nanci drove us to Southampton, and it was slow going because it was a downpour again. I was glad we counseled voters to vote early because it was doubtful people were going out to vote now, an hour before the polls closed.

We got to Southampton after the polls closed. I introduced Nanci to Mike, Katey, Robin, Gordon, Jake and Joy, and later to Andi and Ron when they arrived, along with several other committee members.

We got drinks from the bar but my anxiety level was so high that I hardly touched it. We were watching the two screens, the television set above the bar with the national news on *MSNBC* and a large computer screen on the other side of the room that had the feed with the votes in CD#1 and CD#2. While both Zeldin and King were ahead, it was close. Since votes were still coming in, I tried to be hopeful.

Earlier in the evening, several key losses in the House, Senate and Governor's races had heightened my anxiety that we were going to fall short of a blue wave. But now, the news was projecting one Democratic House win after another. As the Democrats inched closer to taking control of the House, we could feel the excitement in the room building.

The author and her sister, Nanci Hennes, on Election Night.

Suddenly, as we were all mingling and talking, *MSNBC* announced that the Democrats had taken back the House. There it was, emblazoned across the television screen in a large, banner headline, "Democrats Take the House." Many races were too close or too early to call, but enough were completed that they could safely make this call.

A giant cheer erupted in this room. Nanci and I hugged each other. We were close to tears. A very happy roomful of Democrats hugged and took pictures with each other.

Happy Democrats Katey Moran, the author and Mike Anthony cheering the blue wave.

We were still hugging, applauding and celebrating this news and learning of the number of districts across the country that were still too close to call, many in deep red areas, when folks started pointing to the computer screen across the room. We walked over to get a closer look. As all eyes turned to this screen, the room grew quiet. Both Perry and Luiba had lost.

It had been very close in CD#2 and then the votes from the Nassau County part of that district came in and decided it for King. The margin for Perry looked to be a loss of about 6%. People said it will get closer when all the absentee ballots are counted but not enough for Perry to win. We heard that Perry had given his concession speech at the Hauppauge party and called Zeldin to concede. I was thinking of all the people I know, like Wendy, who are at the Hauppauge party and had to hear a concession speech.

Nanci and I decided at that point to drive back to my house to watch the returns of the national news. In the car we talked about the great import of the national news, of the Democrats taking back the House, of the new committee chairmen and women who will be Democrats, of the check now on Trump. I was reminded of what Perry told me when I interviewed him that if we won in this district but Democrats didn't take back the House, then there was no victory. I tried very hard to hold onto that.

We settled down in my living room and turned the television to *MSNBC*. We opened Nanci's bottle of pink champagne, the same bottle that had stayed shut in 2016, and toasted the Democratic win in the House. I served us an array of appetizers to go with our champagne. We talked about how different this was from two years ago. We stayed up very late celebrating and watching the coverage, even though Nanci had to wake up early to go to work. We sat close together on the couch. There were no adequate words to convey just what we were feeling. We kept repeating the headline of the night. "The Democrats take back the House." But underneath our relief were two nagging thoughts that slightly tempered our great joy: news reports that it wasn't a wave but more of a trickle and the fact that we were not able to carry Perry over the finish line.

PART IV
AFTER THE ELECTION

Chapter 22
The Blue Wave

> ***"Personally, it was difficult to maintain my enthusiasm after Election Day. I cannot speak for other members, but I struggled through November and December. Once 2019 rolled around, we started working on local GOTV efforts and on issues where we could accomplish things. On some level, recovering from the loss remains a work in process for me."***
> Steven Kramer, Indivisible North Fork

As I had hoped when I started this project in November, 2017, the headline after the 2018 midterm election was that this electoral success was powered by women. The day after the election on *The Last Word* on *MSNBC*, Lawrence O'Donnell said, "The Resistance won the House."[54] Michelle Goldberg, who often wrote about the Resistance, titled her column in *The New York Times* on November 10th, "The Resistance Strikes Back."[55]

And what was thought to be a small blue trickle on election night was revealed to be a tsunami as 2018 drew to a close. The turnout was the highest for a midterm election in four decades. As close races continued to be decided for the Democrats, it was clear that we had the blue wave we had been hoping for and that wave included deep red districts across the country, in places like California, Oklahoma, New Jersey and South Carolina.

Democrats took 40 seats in the House, won governorships and state legislature seats across the country and kept the damage in the Senate to the minimal amount. Here in New York, we now have a complete Democratic government. Issues we canvassed for here, such as election reform and single payer healthcare for New Yorkers, now have the chance to become law.

From all reports, it was women across the country, in suburban districts like mine, who never stopped fighting, starting with the Women's March and on to Election Day.

"It really was a blue wave. It wasn't that we just scraped by and took a few more seats. The size of the win expressed the dissatisfaction with Washington, with Trump and with the Republicans," said Andi.

Taking back the House was thrilling. It was the most important outcome from this election. It was the purpose of the Resistance. No longer will the House be a rubber stamp for Trump, obstructing justice to protect him. Those days are over.

I was also pleased to see the makeup of the Democratic win in the House, the number of women, the number of people of color, the diversity. Andy Kim, the founder of Rise Stronger, won in New Jersey. This tsunami gave us breathing room that we haven't had for two years.

Yet I was plagued with a feeling of lethargy. Like a lingering cold, I could not shake a sense of malaise.

The reason, I knew, was because Perry lost. How ironic, I thought, that I began this journey because of Trump but here I was despondent because of what happened in CD#1.

It hurt to not be part of the blue wave. Yes, we dramatically reduced the margin of Zeldin's victory compared to 2016 when he won by 16%. Once all the absentee ballots were counted, Zeldin's margin of victory was only 4%.

Congressional District 1 – Congressional Representative 2018

Election Districts: 473

Votes Cast: 270,006 out of 475,448 (56.79%)

CANDIDATE	PARTY	VOTES	SHARE
Zeldin, Lee M.	Republican	121,562	45.02%
	Conservative	14,284	5.29%
	Independence	2,693	1.00%
	Reform	488	0.18%
	TOTAL	139,027	51.49%
Gershon, Perry	Democratic	124,213	46.00%
	Working Families	3,778	1.40%
	TOTAL	127,991	47.40%
Browning, Kate M.	Women's Equality	2,988	1.11%

Source: Suffolk County Board of Elections[56]

In the local newspapers, including *Riverhead Local*, Zeldin was quoted from his victory speech on election night that his win was "results vs. resistance" and that with the election over, "our country needs to do a much better job uniting."[57]

After the divisive campaign he ran, insulting all of us who disagreed with the Trump agenda, refusing to hold a town hall or meet with us, lying about Perry, I found his calls for unity insulting.

I did travel with Sharon and Syma to a rally on November 8th in front of Zeldin's office that was part of a nationwide protest to protect the Mueller report. Perry was there and spoke to the crowd. We all cheered, for him, and for the Democrats taking back the House.

While the protest had been momentarily invigorating, for the rest of 2018, I found it hard to shake off the fog I was in. I dutifully attended meetings, doing what was required but I did not feel as hands-on or as enthusiastic as I had been before November 6th. My heart wasn't in it.

I spoke to others who were also feeling a bit withdrawn about politics. Maybe we were just very tired though this level of activist fatigue was certainly not true of everyone. I watched many others, like Sharon, eager to advocate for many of the New York State initiatives we now had a chance to pass with our all Democratic government, in particular the New York Health Act. Others continued to be out there on the front lines protesting Zeldin.

I had the added dilemma of trying to figure out how to end the book. While I had never known what 2018 would bring, in my dream scenario, the epilogue would be watching Perry being sworn in as our congressman as he took his place with the freshman class swept in on the blue wave. That ending fit in with my original title for the book, "Building the Blue Wave." Since that storybook finale was not to be, I had trouble figuring out not only a new title but a fitting ending for this two-year project.

I could have just stopped with the midterm election. That had been the plan. But after much thought, I decided to do some post-election reporting, analyzing our district and the election results. This analysis did not include the news of the day and I no longer kept a diary of what we were doing. For those reasons, this section is not chronological but is organized by the type of subject and the sources I interviewed. This reporting sought to bring closure to this story and to uncover lessons we could take forward into 2020.

Chapter 23

How to Flip the First

"I thought it would be difficult for Perry to win for one main reason - we are a parochial bunch out here in CD#1. When I first heard 'Park Avenue Perry,' I thought 'Ouch.' However, when I see that Congressional Democrats won in similar districts in the USA sharing similar demographics, social, and economic factors, I can't help but think we under performed. I can't imagine having more volunteers carrying a candidate's message, so it wasn't a lack of boots on the ground, and I don't think it was for lack of money. The message was the same as other successful Democrats - healthcare. So, what was it?"

Mike Anthony, SHDems

I reached out to my many sources including the primary candidates and Perry and asked for their insights into the midterm election. The following responses are representative of the answers I received.

Andrea Klausner, SHDems

"I have a couple of different thoughts on that. Obviously, there's the advantage for Zeldin of being an incumbent and having your name out there and having money behind you to get your message across. Also, Perry wasn't that strong coming out of the gate. Being a first-time political candidate there was a lot he needed to learn. He needed to learn how to be an effective public speaker, how to raise money, how to get his message across in his campaign, what his messages were. I thought he grew a lot during the campaign. I like Perry very much and if he runs again, I'm going to work hard for him."

David Posnett, R&R

"Perry was our best bet in 2018. He tried as hard as he possibly could, and given all his handicaps (carpetbagger, first time politician, etc.), he did okay. For 2020 I will see who runs for the Democrats. And I will pick the person who, in my view, has the best chances of winning. I will back any Democrat that comes out on top. I think it's premature to discard Perry. He may be our only viable choice."

Mike Anthony, SHDems

"Maybe Perry just wasn't that appealing a candidate, although I see him as a very good man, he didn't quite strike enough chords. More charisma needed, perhaps? Also, was his wealth off-putting? Was healthcare not the striking issue it was in other districts? Maybe his humanitarian approach to immigrants didn't play well in up-Island Townships. I don't know for sure, but I come back to my first point: Tim Bishop lived in Southampton for many years, his family goes back to early periods of Southampton, and he was a college provost and, most importantly, well known. Perry did better than his predecessor, Anna Throne-Holst, but both with similar problems, outsiderism. I hate to write this stuff, but this is what I come back to. I'm still thinking about this point, though, with Trump in the White House, we should have won. My hope, too, is that the Democrats perk up in Brookhaven."

Greg Haynes, Perry Gershon campaign staff

"The Brookhaven town GOP machine is right up there with anything you can find, probably the best run GOP machine anywhere; well-oiled machine and when they decide to mobilize, they go all out. We also had difficulties in Smithtown; there was a GOP voter advantage. And the third thing is that Zeldin ran a number of times before. His campaign had clear knowledge of who his supporters were, and they got better every time at identifying them and reaching out to them. We, on the other hand, ran a first-time candidate."

Dick Sheehan, SHDems

"I like Perry and I worked hard to get him elected after he won the primary. He ran a smart primary campaign and he outspent everybody, including Kate Browning, by a wide margin. He had deep pockets and I understand that he spent one million dollars of his own money in the primary. But I think Kate Browning would have done better than Perry in the general election for several reasons: she is from Brookhaven where there are more votes, her background is more appealing in Brookhaven, she had a proven track record and nobody could have called her a carpetbagger."

Eileen Duffy, SHDems and LVLZ

"I'm disappointed, but I think that Perry came really close and a lot more people were engaged because of things like Let's Visit Lee Zeldin. LVLZ helped to maintain the interest and outrage about what Zeldin was doing. But I do wish Perry had used that platform a lot more than he did when he was running."

Steven Kramer, Indivisible Northfork

"As a political novice (this was the first campaign I have interacted with) I was struck most by the lack of participation by our Riverhead Town Democratic Committee (DemCom). Other than our notable cross membership, we saw very little (any) participation from the members of the DemCom in our weekly GOTV efforts. The sense I get, the grassroots did a lot of heavy lifting, feet in the street efforts in conjunction with Perry's campaign, but the DemCom here was largely absent. To that end, I offer Southold Town as a case study, where close interaction between the grassroots, the DemCom and the Gershon campaign was a recipe to flip a known GOP stronghold. We were not able to translate that here in Riverhead or beyond into Brookhaven. To many DemCom members, I do not think they saw Perry as THEIR candidate."

Robin Long, SHDems

"You've got to understand, Perry went from being a human being to being a political person and you just can't make that transition on the congressional level. You can't do it. It's almost impossible to do. People think running for office is easy, it's not. You've got the clothes, the way you sit, the way you point, the way you talk, the way you eyeball somebody. I teach candidates you've got to learn how to look at people. You've got to touch them. You can't take somebody and turn them into a candidate that is going to beat a Republican incumbent overnight. People do not unseat incumbents unless there's a reason or unless the opposition is so overwhelming. Also, in this district, we have a tale of two towns, the east and the west and never the twain will meet. Perry was never able to establish a persona in the west. I love Perry very much, but I don't know if he can get the persona that's necessary to talk to the people west of Riverhead. I grew up with those people. I raised my children in those neighborhoods. They're very blue collar and they need a lot of interaction."

I reached out to all five of Perry's primary opponents for comments but only heard back from three. Included below are comments emailed to me by Brendon, David and Elaine

Brendon and David focused on changes they feel still need to be made within the Democratic Party.

Brendon Henry

"Midterm elections tend to have low turnout. This year the grassroots played a huge role in getting people active and generating historically high turnout. My loyalty has and will always be to the people. Being in a party doesn't define you, your actions do. I think the party is facing a key time for its growth and survival. It needs to be transparent, remove the old guard, and allow the new movements to grow. If we keep preaching about change, then strangling it at inception, while running the same old candidates, then the party should just give up elections now. America has always been a land that says if you can dream it, you can be it. The Democratic Party needs to be the party that not only says it, but believes it. Expecting people to fall in line and just vote party line is a disservice to citizens, we need candidates that inspire."

David Pechefsky

"In NY-1 lots of people worked incredibly hard to see a Democratic victory and Perry's campaign deserves credit for putting up a good fight. My view remains that the Democratic Party still needs to have a more consistent message about what it stands for and that to be successful both electorally and in achieving meaningful change we need to advance candidates unafraid to talk about economic inequality and the disastrous consequences of our foreign policy – morally and financially - on our democracy.

Nationally, the number of women and the diversity of the incoming Democratic members of Congress as well as wins in the statehouses make me feel hopeful. Whether the newcomers can shake things up and move the party away from its dominance by corporate donors to a more truly people-centered agenda remains to be seen.

One thing that is exciting is that several of my team members are running for local office in Brookhaven. I do think that CD-1 is ultimately won or lost in Brookhaven and for that reason your chances are best with a good Brookhaven candidate but the base needs to be built and more engagement at the lower levels is needed."

Elaine's email response was very detailed because it was based on a presentation about her experience as a candidate that she gave to a class of graduate students after the election. Much of her focus was on fundraising in the primary and the general election.

Elaine DiMasi

"My experience as a first-time candidate and scientist running for Congress was a terrific one, and I think one of the most valuable things I can do going forward is to share what I've learned. In late November 2018, I spoke to the Graduate Women in Science and Engineering at Stony Brook University about campaigns, political capital, and some of the huge differences between a science culture and a political culture.

Our NY CD-1 2018 Democratic primary and general election put some important questions to the test. How conservative is our district? How much of a difference does canvassing make? Our Democratic nominee was not distinguished by fundraising - he spent more money for the primary than he did to combat Rep. Zeldin, and a good bit less than generally recommended for the general election - but it certainly was notable for the grassroots canvassing effort.

Our canvassing was sufficient to reduce the gap against Rep. Zeldin, but not to win. In my opinion we were missing a truly talented, experienced politician with deep roots in the community and an ability to rally voters across the spectrum. Former Rep. Bishop did not keep his seat easily, and he needed to maintain all of his personal connections to progressives and conservatives alike to battle Rep. Zeldin when challenged. A Democrat can win this district if they are a terrific fundraiser ($4Million for the general election), terrifically talented and charismatic, and profoundly connected to the people who live and work here.

Had I been the nominee, our canvassers would have had a different experience. My story, of a scientist leaving the Laboratory to bring a problem-solving attitude to Congress during Trump times, was a non-partisan one that can be interpreted in a conservative as well as a progressive manner. Voters in the general election don't ask, "How will you beat Zeldin?" as the Democratic primary voters did. Their question is, "What have you done for me and what will you do for me?" We proved in this election that in the Democratic primary, it's money that counts.

If you make a graph of the votes obtained, versus dollars spent, for our election, DiMasi, Pechefsky, Viloria-Fisher and Browning's votes versus dollars spent fell along the same line. In other words, Browning raised twice as much as Viloria-Fisher, who raised twice as much as DiMasi. Browning earned twice as many votes as Viloria-Fisher, who earned twice as many as DiMasi. Pechefsky was a little below the line (similar funds to VFF and fewer votes), reflecting less strong connection to the district than DiMasi, Browning, and Viloria-Fisher. Gershon spent much more money and did not reap votes proportional - he "saturated" our primary voters.

The meaning of fundraising needs to be better understood. I under-raised my rollout goal by a factor of four: I wanted $100,000 of seed money and raised $22,000. Proportionately, I was underfunded at the primary: my goal was $400,000, and I had raised and spent $88,000. I earned 1300 votes, while I had been aiming for 4000-5000. This means that I underestimated my win number, since over 7000 votes would be needed to win - showing again that our canvassing had an effect to bring out more Democrats. Fundraising is a great test of political persuasion - if you have connections, if you can influence others, you can get their money, and that money will turn into votes in the Democratic primary. At the end of the process, my message versus Vivian's or Kate's was not important; but during the run-up to that point, our abilities and experience influenced our capacity to raise money - noting that money that you take from your own pocket works almost as well.

Though everyone "knows" how important funds are, I think the political ecosystem does not like to emphasize it unduly. Voters without deep pockets might not participate at all if they think it won't do any good. I would like activists as well as future hopefuls to take heart because in NY, some fund matching legislation may level the playing field. And there are always stories of terrific grassroots candidates to learn from. I want to emphasize that everyone who helped a candidate with fundraising and canvassing was making the process as democratic as possible. Those who remained neutral to protect their political capital or simply their "investment" contributed to the deepest pocket taking the election for sure. Note that in the NY01 general election, the non-Democrats want more from a candidate than name recognition. They want a connection and a story that resonates. I look forward to seeing a new candidate enter the field who has what it takes to win this race."

Perry and I started communicating about a month after the election to try to set up an interview but before we were able to schedule time together, Perry was the guest speaker at the J. P. Spata Southampton Democratic Club breakfast in December. First, he spoke about the campaign and then took questions from the audience. I recorded the meeting and asked Perry if I could include it in the book. He agreed. The transcript is lightly edited and condensed and reprinted here with Perry's permission.

Perry Gershon:
We got Zeldin's attention, he had to work very, very hard in order to retain the seat in a way he hasn't done before. When I was driving back from Hauppauge on election night, Lee called me and we had an interesting conversation because I never had a conversation where I saw the human side of him before. And he congratulated us for putting up a good effort and pointed out this is by far the closest election he's ever had, the first time he's really had to work for it and how impressed he was in the volunteerism that we have on our side. To me, this was the most important part of our campaign. We brought people out, people who had supported any of the seven democrats who were in the primary initially. Everybody got together to defeat Lee Zeldin. People believed in the cause and people sincerely wanted to help me get it done. I was really impressed with the effort and I have nothing to be sad about, other than the fact that I'm not going to be in Washington and Lee Zeldin is.

When we started, I thought if we could get 115,000 votes we'd win the election. I don't know what the final vote count is going to be, they're still counting, and the last I heard they'll have an announcement on Tuesday. But I suspect it'll be 125,000 plus. That's many more votes than anyone, winner or loser, ever received in a midterm election. Unfortunately, Zeldin got a few more votes; it'll be less than five percent, maybe as low as two percent. It was really, really close. We generated support in the district that the national party had kind of written off after Anna's loss two years ago. Anna lost by 17 points and as much as I hated to admit it, it was a struggle to get national attention.

I think going forward we are in a position where they'll find New York was a winnable district for Democrats. We showed them that. We must stay energized. We can't go back to fighting, and feuding. The Hillary-Bernie days are past us now. We were united in NY01. And we need to stay that way. If we want to win this vote we have to start making inroads to persuadable voters, crossover voters, I don't know what you want to call them, but this group of people that did not turn out for us. We got 125-135,000 votes, Zeldin got 135,000 votes. He energized people too and he energized people to be fearful of our message.

I think we accomplished a ton. I think we really showed Democrats can get united with grassroots efforts. We really didn't have that much help from the county party either. We just built a grassroots movement of people. We were organized in Southampton, in Riverhead, in Farmingville and Setauket and out of those four offices we had countless pop up offices and really were out canvassing and getting people's attention. In the end we were endorsed by every local newspaper that endorsed. That was a big deal, including the Independent who doesn't usually endorse the Democrat. *Newsday* and *The New York Times* were totally on board. We did a lot right and I think it's something that we just need to build on. I'm going to stop there and just take questions.

[AUDIENCE] Did the East Hampton summer home issue have an effect? It's very hard to know. When we called, our polls said people didn't really care. And when you look at his ads as a progression of his ads, he stopped talking about the Park Avenue idea. It was more I want to give healthcare to illegal immigrants and bankrupt Medicare and I'm lying about offshore oil investments. If I were to run again, I would be involved full time in everything. I'm here today, and I'm going to continue to be here throughout this district. We were in Bellport last night. And we'll spend more time in Smithtown and other parts of Brookhaven because that's where you have to go. I understand a little bit better and the truth is I hadn't lived out in East Hampton full-time for all that long. I lived part-time for decades. Now I'm living there full-time and time is on my side there.

[AUDIENCE] There are those who believe that Democrats need to link hands with the western part of the district in order to compete.
If there was a popular Democrat on the western side of the district, that would be the ideal candidate. The problem is there just isn't anybody right now. That's not to say no one could step up, it'd be great if someone stepped up who had a good following, charisma, the ability to raise money. Those are all the things you need in order to successfully run for office. You need to get people to believe in you. You need to have the energy to stay at it. It's very, very difficult to campaign and I was at it, day in day out, I took a break last December, but I did not take a day off from January until the election. So that's grueling and not everyone can do it. Someone, me or someone else, someone will emerge. There's a lot of good stuff going on in this district. There's a good feeling right now when the absentee ballots get announced, it'll be even closer and that will push it even further along.

[AUDIENCE] This is a big congressional district and you won, I think, every election district on the east end. How are the issues different on the Southfork than they are in Brookhaven and Smithtown? Are the issues different west of the district than they are in the eastern part of the district?
I think the issues are different when you are talking to Democrats versus when you are talking to non-Democrats, more so than the geographic. One thing that universally is on people's minds all through NY01 is the environment and Zeldin knew that, which is why he made up this story about how I invested in off-shore oil drilling. And he tried to tell a story that he was an environmentalist and denied his own track record. So, the environment is spread out everywhere. But I think after that, there's more interest in job growth, in building the economy on the other side of the canal. I think on this side the environment is an even stronger

issue. Immigration is the one that Democrats and Republicans have completely different points of view on. Quite frankly it's an issue that I care a lot about but I didn't advertise immigration as an issue on television because I didn't think it was going to be helpful for swaying the kinds of voters that I needed to sway. Zeldin took the fact that on July 4th I went to a rally in Sag Harbor against family separation and he said I went to an anti-ICE rally. And he convinced people that the purpose of that rally was anti-ICE and I was protesting America on July 4th. That was the big one that really got used against me.

[AUDIENCE] How much of an impact did the polling services, like Nate Silver, that had us at 15 to 1, have on the race?
It's actually a great question and it's something that I felt as I was trying to raise money and get people interested in the race. People would say, well there's Nate Silver, there's Cook, there's all the rating services. The problem is the services use public polling data and Nate Silver, more than the other, use prior election data. So, the 2016 vote is what drove Nate Silver's numbers more than anything else and Trump's victory here. I honestly believe that if the Kavanaugh hearing hadn't been controversial, if the Democrats had just let him get confirmed, we would have won here. I think that it energized the other side more than anything else in this election.

One of the things that I've realized as a candidate is that much more important than truth is “truthy;” if something sounds good, voters like it. I don't tell lies. I can't do that. It's not my personality but there were some things that I should have done in a more truthy way, if I had it to do over again. The fact that Zeldin didn't vote for the Trump tax plan doesn't absolve him of any responsibility. And I should have just been attack, attack, attack on that because that's an issue that I think could have moved people more on the other side of the canal. And we just didn't do enough about it. That's my one regret.

[AUDIENCE] I didn't understand why gun control didn’t resonate more. I realize the immigration thing kind of overwhelmed it but I was on a call with Zeldin about a year ago that I was asked to participate in and he's totally opposed to gun control and he speaks eloquently about it but he very plainly doesn't believe in any gun control. And I get that we’re in a bubble out here, I realize that, but I'm shocked every time I talk to somebody and think aren’t they concerned about children and gun violence in their schools?
Guns were probably the toughest issue that we grappled with. On the one hand I think a majority of the people in the district want to see better gun laws. And concealed carry reciprocity, which is Zeldin's pet issue in particular, really doesn't have a following. But having said that, there are a number of people who

are passionate about their right to have a gun, to own a gun and Zeldin effectively got them concerned that I wanted to take away their gun. It didn't matter what I said, where truth and fiction don't necessarily converge with one another, the more he made me out to be the anti-gun candidate it pushed people who might otherwise stay home to go out and vote for him. That was a fine line. As I said, I knew going in if we were going to win, it would be by driving our turnout up. We needed to get as many of our voters out as we could and hope his voters stayed home. The gun issue was one that rallied his voters.

Chapter 24

Not the Same NY01

"I think repetition works. And I don't just mean NY01, I mean all over the country. If we go after Republicans again on healthcare and just over and over and over again, drive home the point that Democrats are the ones that are going to protect your healthcare, Republicans are the ones that are going to take it away, then that message will work. In 41 districts, that message worked in 2018. And there's no reason why it can't work in other districts."

Tim Bishop, former NY01 Democratic Congressman

After hearing from everyone, I felt I needed one more interview to help put the midterm election in a more historical perspective. So, I reached out to the Democrat who knows more about winning elections in CD#1 than anyone, our former Congressman Tim Bishop. He not only won six elections and served the district from 2003-2015, but he ran against Zeldin twice, beating him in 2008 and losing to him in 2014, in a race that many saw as a precursor to the Trump era.

Tim has long-standing roots in Southampton, his family going back generations, and was associated with Southampton College, when it was part of Long Island University (LIU) for 29 years, serving as Provost for 16 of those years before he won his first election to Congress in 2002. Since 2015, he is the Visiting Professor and Director of the Center for Community Solutions at St. Joseph's College here on Long Island. According to his biography, in addition to teaching, he is a Senior Advisor at a Washington, D.C. government relations firm called Envision Strategies and is on the boards of the Suffolk County Water Authority, the New York State Environmental Facilities Corporation and Asta Financial Corporation.

The following is a lightly edited and condensed transcript of my on-the-record conversation with former Congressman Tim Bishop.

Let me start with this dynamic: Suffolk County is one of 206 counties nationwide that voted for Obama twice and then voted for Trump. I have a very hard time wrapping my head around that. Were you surprised at the

margin of Trump's win in 2016 or had you seen the seeds of this earlier in your 2014 race?
Yes, and yes. First, I was not surprised that Trump carried the county. I was surprised that he carried it by the margin by which he did. Yes, Obama carried Suffolk County twice but let's remember there is the Suffolk County of Babylon Town and Huntington Town and then there's Suffolk County of Brookhaven Town and the East End Towns. There are very few so called Democratic enclaves in NY01, in our part of Suffolk County. Brookhaven is a Republican town. If you look at the Town Board composition of Brookhaven, seven people, six of them are Republicans. Riverhead is a Republican town. Southold is a Republican town. Shelter Island is Democratic and Southampton right now is Democratic but historically has been Republican. And Smithtown in NY01 is absolutely hopeless for a Democrat. Obama got 36% of the vote. The more populated parts of Western Suffolk, Babylon and Huntington, not in NY01, they are much more Democratic, particularly Babylon.

So, when they say Suffolk County is a pivot county, and it's true, it's primarily those more Democratic parts that are not in NY01?
Obama carried NY01 by, I believe, a point, in 2012. I'm doing this from memory, you can look it up. He carried Suffolk by more. In 2014 the last year I was on the ballot, Andrew Cuomo lost NY01 by seven. So, one cannot generalize about NY01 and Suffolk County and think that they are identical. They're not. I was surprised, I'll say again, at the margin by which Trump carried NY01, by 12. That's a healthy margin and Zeldin beat Anna by I think 16.

Historically, is that a change for NY01? It is certainly a change from your first race in 2008.
I beat Lee Zeldin who was at the time just a kid, he had no resume whatsoever, I beat him 58 and a half to 41 and a half in 2008. Historically, my favorable ratings were somewhere in the high 60s to low 70s. And my unfavorables were somewhere in the high teens to low 20s, so in other words pretty good.

Congressional District 1 – Congressional Representative 2008
Election Districts: 460
Votes Cast: 277,628 out of 426,672 (65.07%)

CANDIDATE	PARTY	VOTES	SHARE
Bishop, Timothy H.	Democratic	141,727	51.05%
	Independence	12,919	4.65%
	Working Families	7,437	2.68%
	TOTAL	162,083	58.38%
Zeldin, Lee M.	Republican	100,036	36.03%
	Conservative	15,509	5.59%
	TOTAL	115,545	41.62%

Source: Suffolk County Board of Elections[58]

Obama gets elected in November of 2008. We poll in March 2009 and now my favorables are in the low 50s. I'm still the same guy, but in the course of four months, I went from having a plus/minus, a fav/unfav in my favor of about 40 points, 45 points to a fav/unfav in my favor of about 12 points or 15 points. What explains that? What explains that is the election of Barack Obama which inflamed people's resentments, their fears. Then we Democrats compounded that by our legislative agenda. First, the stimulus, which the Republicans did an excellent job of portraying as a giveaway to the American people, though the economy would have collapsed had we not passed it.

And TARP begins under Bush.
TARP and the stimulus are two separate things. So yes, first thing was TARP. TARP was bi-partisan. And it began under Bush and we basically saved him. Nancy Pelosi saved him because if it hadn't been for Nancy we wouldn't have been able to get it through the House. And now history has proven us right. TARP was absolutely the right thing to do. Barack Obama gets elected and the first month, Bush's last month in office, we lose 800,000 jobs. Obama inherits a deficit of $1.3 trillion. The economy is in free fall and we've got to do something. So, we have an $850 billion stimulus. Again, history has proven us right. Now if anything, history has proven that the stimulus was too small but at the time that number represented the absolute outside of what we could've gotten, and let's remember that it went through the House without a single Republican vote and I think we got three Republican votes in the Senate.

Right off the bat, we've got two major public policy positions that the opposition did an extremely effective job of demonizing. Unfairly, inaccurately, and shamelessly political but they did an excellent job of demonizing it. We then compound that by opening up with cap and trade and the Affordable Care Act. Again, we Democrats did a horrible job of messaging on both. So, you've got four major public policy areas and one of which, cap and trade, crashed and burned. The other three were enacted into law with hardly any Republican support, in particular the Affordable Care Act. And again, history's proven us right. It was the right thing to do. So, you take all of that and all of a sudden, a district where a left of center Democrat, like myself, representing a district with 25,000 or 30,000 more Republicans than Democrats can get elected with almost 59% of the vote. Earlier in 2006, I got 62%. So you take that district, and now all of a sudden, it's back to being a 50/50 district in terms of how people vote. Is there one isolating factor? Probably not but each one was a building block. So, the district where Lee Zeldin ran against Tim Bishop in 2014, was a vastly different district than the one where Lee Zeldin ran against Tim Bishop in 2008.

Because of this energized Republican base?
Let us also remember that in 2006 it is the height of the hugely unpopular Iraq War. The Bush Administration compounded the Iraq war with the debacle of Katrina. We had all the manifestations of a failed presidency. And so, 2006 was a great year for Democrats. 2008 was a great year for Democrats. Now all of a sudden, we're in charge. But people are still unhappy, and so what do people do? They take it out on the party that's in charge. 2010 was a disaster for Democrats, we recovered slightly in 2012, and then 2014 was a second disaster for Democrats.

2014 was also terribly low voter turnout, particularly on the Democratic side.
In NY01 in particular, yes. And I think that's something that's instructive. In terms of Democratic candidates, the turnout in 2018 for a mid-year election was quite high relative to historical norms.

It was the highest midterm election turnout in four decades. And our turnout in NY01 was higher than the national.
That's right. We need to go to school on that. The Democratic candidate still lost. And so what that means is the notion that someone like AOC (Rep. Alexandria Ocasio-Cortez) could come out and run in NY01 and work her magic here is nonsense. The notion that a Democrat can win in NY01 by simply energizing the Democratic base and turning them out is a fallacy. In order to win here a Democratic candidate must, must, must have crossover appeal. During the primary of 2018 and I didn't publicly back anyone, but I was quite disturbed by the candidacies of some people.

You thought they were too far to the left?
I once said to David Pechefsky, 'How are you going to win with this platform?' And he said, 'I'm going to turn out Democratic votes.' And I said, 'Do you really think there are enough of them.' He said, 'Yes.' Guess what? There aren't. And I think that's instructive. NY01 became a different district on or about December of 2008 and it then progressed even further to the right.

Let me ask you about immigration. Over and over again when I was knocking on doors speaking to voters I kept hearing about the caravan. I document an episode in the book where I'm talking to a woman in a low-income area in a house that's in a terrible state of disrepair. She's my age, a senior citizen. She's registered as Unaffiliated. And when we first started talking she said, 'Oh yeah. I read about Perry and he supports Social Security and Medicare" which she depended on and so she started out saying that she was voting for Perry. Then she moved to talking about the caravan, of "those people" getting benefits they don't deserve, and then she said she couldn't cast her vote for Perry.
Immigration is an issue that has ebbed and flowed in NY01. When I ran the first time in 2002 it was a fairly prominent issue. In 2004 it wasn't that prominent. In 2006 I ran against a guy who made immigration his set piece issue. The open border thing, nobody was talking about open borders. That is a Trump fiction. I supported comprehensive immigration reform. He presented it as amnesty. Same in 2008. There used to be a guy that stood outside of the 7-11 in Southampton every single morning, waving an American flag with a giant sign that said, 'Round them up and send them back.'

This was in 2007?
I'm told he was out there for years, starting in 2006 through 2009 and that he was paid to be there, off the books by the way, by some contractor who felt that he was losing out on jobs to contractors who employed undocumented workers. I don't know if that's true but I've heard it from at least ten different people. On Saturdays a whole collection of anti-immigration people would gather there. Rain, snow, it didn't matter, they were out there with their signs every Saturday morning. In the early days of his campaign against me in 2008, Zeldin joined them. So he tried to make that an issue. It then began to fade from prominence. I beat him by 16 or 18 points, so it didn't really affect the outcome of the election. 2010 immigration is not an issue at all. 2012, it was not an issue at all. And even, I saw polling in the summer of 2013 that said that 60% of our district supported DACA and a path to earned legalization as part of comprehensive immigration reform. Then we had the first wave, spring of 2014, we had the first wave of migrant children, unaccompanied minor children arriving at the border. Do you remember this?

Yes, I do.

And it was presented in a way that was spectacularly dishonest. The reality is these were kids arriving at the border finding a border protection agent and saying, 'Please help me.' But there were tens of thousands of them. They weren't detained the way they are now. They were taken, processed and then sent to family elsewhere in the country. Because of the immigrant population that we have, a fair number of them found their way to Long Island. All of sudden we have school districts complaining about an influx of these immigrant children with lots of needs and how do we accommodate them. Then we also had tax activists saying, 'look at what the cost of these people are doing to our schools. I can't afford to pay any more than I'm already paying.' And people are taxed a lot for school. It became an issue. That was in part what drove the majority for Zeldin in 2014, though not the only thing.

I think principally, 2014 for me and other members of Congress was a referendum on Obama. The previous cycle, 2012, one of my best friends, a guy named Ben Chandler (D), lost to Andy Barr (R- Kentucky's 6th District). Ben didn't have a chance. It was all about Obama. And in 2014, I don't think I ran a great race. This is not false modesty. I think we made mistakes. But I think if I had James Carville running my campaign, and I was as great a campaigner as Bill Clinton, I think I still would've lost.

Last summer, there was an article in Politico analyzing why Long Island still loves Trump. It really was all about immigration. It mentions the 2014 race and Zeldin's focus on immigration.

I'll never forget this. I've been so wrong about so much about Trump. He did a robo call for Zeldin in the election of 2014 and I remember thinking, 'Thank you so much Lee Zeldin. Is there a more reviled man in American than Donald Trump? So, great, you want him on your side, fabulous.' I couldn't have been more wrong. Yes, Zeldin did a very effective job of heightening the fear associated with immigration. And I am a firm believer, I can't prove this, but whenever people go to the polls and fear is one of the emotions upper most in their mind, more than not, they're going to pull the Republican lever not the Democratic lever. They're going to support the daddy party not the mommy party.

Perry got very, very close; four percent is a dramatic change. But I just felt that we never had an answer to the fear-mongering. We have answers that are rational and logical but they don't address the fear.

One of the things I learned, and this was classic Democrats, was when I mounted an argument on any issue that was rooted in fact and logic and reason and experience, if that argument didn't carry the day, I did not then have a plan B. If the truth doesn't carry the day, I don't know what to do. I think that's a big problem for Democrats. But I don't believe the immigration issue was dispositive in this district. I think we did not do as much on the most vulnerable area for Republicans, healthcare, I think if there is any one reason why Lee Zeldin got 51% and Perry Gershon got 47, that's it.

One of the things I hate about politics is that in order for a challenger to win, the challenger must convince the electorate that the incumbent deserves to be fired. You do not convince the electorate that the incumbent deserves to be fired by rising above the fray or putting out this spectacularly well-developed policy agenda. Because the other guy can say, "Hey, I'm doing that. That's all great but I'm doing the job." You have to convince people that the guy is not doing the job. Or the job he is doing is antithetical to the interests of the people he was elected to represent. We did not do that in 2016 or 2018. Zeldin did it to me effectively in 2014. I did it to Felix Grucci in 2002. People ask why are our politics so ugly? That's at the very core of it.

Do you think we could have done a better job focusing on the tax bill?
No, in 2018 we couldn't because people had not yet felt the impact and it took too long to explain. We blue states got hosed on the tax bill and Lee Zeldin, who we sent to Washington to be a part of the majority to deliver policies that benefited the people that he represented, he voted for it before he voted against it. That should not have been enough to inoculate him. His party let us down. Big time. But it hadn't hit people yet. Now I think we can.

In higher income places like Smithtown, where they've now been hit very hard, could that make the difference in 2020?
Not in Smithtown, no. I think Smithtown is a lost cause. I think it was 2006, I got 62% of the vote but I think I barely carried Smithtown. 51.1% or something like that. Every other cycle I got clobbered. And the way I always looked at the race in terms of the big picture is whatever I didn't get in Smithtown I had to make up and then some in the five East End towns. And then the race was won or lost in Brookhaven.

How did you do it in Brookhaven?
I got two pieces of advice from former members of Congress when I first got elected. One was from Tom Downing (former NY02 Democratic Congressman) about Suffolk County politics. He said to me, 'Go to everything. If there's an event, be there.' And the second was from George Hochbrueckner (former NY01 Democratic Congressman) who said, 'Make sure that your constituent service is at the highest possible level.' And so I focused on both of those things. For 12 years I worked, for the most part, seven days a week, 80, 90 hours a week. And

I had a constituent service staff that I would put up against any staff in the country.

I have heard that about your constituent services. In fact, Robin Long said to me that when you sat with constituents, they felt like they were the only person in that room and that you were present in the district, attending all the events, the firehouses. But how do you do that as a challenger, how you do constituent services?
You don't. It's hard. You have to impeach the constituent service that the incumbent has done. You have to get some collection of people who will be willing to speak for the record. And this is not specific to Zeldin. This is to any incumbent. I went to see Congressman X and he let me down. And then you have another person say I went to see Congressman X, had the exact same experience. Staff was rude, you know. You have to impeach the service.

Zeldin's office is horribly rude to those of us in the other party. I've called his office so many times and they are nasty, they call us names. But he does not behave that way with his supporters. I've been to some of his events. I get the feeling his constituent services for his supporters are quite good. But I want to go back to looking at 2014 which was historically low voter turnout. I think only 39% of the electorate voted here in 2014. And that brings up a question for me, why would people who supported you in the past just not vote at all?
I don't know. It certainly wasn't for lack of effort trying to get them out. I mean we worked so hard for months. I don't know whether it was complacency, thinking 'he doesn't need my vote' or whether it was 'I've soured on him.'

Congressional District 1 – Congressional Representative 2014

Election Districts: 473
Votes Cast: 172,757 out of 442,772 (39.02%)

CANDIDATE	PARTY	VOTES	SHARE
Zeldin, Lee M.	Republican	77,062	44.61%
	Conservative	16,972	9.82%
	TOTAL	94,035	54.43%
Bishop, Timothy H.	Democratic	68,387	39.59%
	Working Families	5,457	3.16%
	Independence	4,878	2.82%
	TOTAL	78,722	45.57%

Source: Suffolk County Board of Elections [59]

There was also a smear campaign against you by Zeldin. I remember the robo calls.

Yes. The campaign was ugly. Millions of dollars from super PACS were spent against me. But that was the case in 2010 and 2012. I think it had more to do with being an off year, the Obama presidency is winding down. There was fear and anger associated with this latest influx of immigrants. The economy was doing okay but still jobs were an issue. There's a couple of different ways a member of Congress can approach his or her job. One is to try to be a national player, like AOC. Another is to pick your spots in terms of policy. And another is to focus on using the power and the pockets of the federal government to help deal with local issues. That was the path that I took. I did it for a couple of reasons. One, is that for eight of the 12 years I was in office I was in the minority and it's awfully hard to have a policy footprint when you're in the minority. And two, I focused on the areas where I was highly regarded on both sides of the aisle, such as higher education policy, environmental policy, water policy, shoreline protection, things like that. And I focused on constituent service and I viewed the elected officials that represented all of my district as a team. And I focused on being a contributing member of that team because my theory was that the vast majority of the people we represented didn't care whether we had an R or a D after our names. They just wanted somebody to be sympathetic to the issues that they had and to try to help them. I was happy to do that. That approach will carry the day, I think, in a high turnout election. It would not carry the day in a low turnout election. A low turnout election turns on snippets of information. One of the great tragedies of our democracy is that way, way too many of our voters are at a minimum, under-informed if not simply not informed at all.

I saw a statistic recently that said more people get their news from *Fox News* and right- wing media than all the other news outlets combined.

Certainly, pluralities of people get their news from *Fox* and right-wing media.

How do you break through that? And was that true when you were first running?

No, it was certainly not true in 2002 or 2004 or 2006. But in 2008 it was prominent and 2010 it was hugely prominent. I can remember laughing about this, though it wasn't all that funny. We used to know what had been the subject of Glenn Beck's show every night by coming in and turning on the answering machine in our office in the morning. There would be scores of messages left. What is the Congressman doing about fill in the blank? What is the Congressman's position on this issue, just to let him know we're coming to get him. And sure enough, that was the subject of the Glenn Beck show that previous evening. That was a new phenomenon in 2010. And it hasn't gone away.

What do you think we need to do in NY01 to beat Zeldin in 2020?
One, we need a candidate with crossover appeal. 2018 in my opinion showed that you do not win NY01 simply by juicing Democratic turnout. You need a candidate that has crossover appeal that can do very well with that large block of so-called blank voters in NY01 and you have to peel off at least 20% of Republicans. It's just the law of large numbers. So that's one. And two, we have to recognize what issues are playing with people and I really don't care what the polling says. I know polling says guns play well. But healthcare is in my opinion the greatest vulnerability for Republicans. It's going to become even more so with this case in the 5th Circuit Court. Our argument has to be: 'Say all you want about constitutionality and government takeover of healthcare, but guess what? Twenty million of our fellow citizens have healthcare who wouldn't otherwise have it because of the ACA and 50, 60 million Americans have access to cheaper healthcare even with pre-existing conditions because of the ACA. Now an insurance company can't refuse to insure someone like in the past because of having a pre-existing condition.'

We have to personalize that story in NY01 and hold accountable the people who think that taking away healthcare is okay. Lee Zeldin voted for a healthcare plan that would have resulted in 25 million fewer Americans having healthcare insurance than is currently the case. That's not a freebie. That's something that people have to be held accountable for.

Zeldin had the gall at the debates to say that he supported protection for pre-existing conditions.
Every Republican said that and it was spectacularly dishonest. They said it because there were some bills that under the most obscure conditions, pre-existing conditions would have been covered. But there were bills, two that were voted on in the House, three that were voted on in the Senate, and all five of them eliminated protections for pre-existing conditions. That's unassailable. And Lee Zeldin voted for the two in the House and Lindsey Graham voted for the three in the Senate. To now say, everybody supports pre-existing conditions? Come on. If that's the case then you don't vote for a piece of legislation that doesn't support it. The one that was the classic, was this guy Josh Hawley (R Senator-Missouri), I mean he was one of the attorneys general who filed this court challenge, who signed onto the case that would've eliminated pre-existing conditions protections and he then runs a campaign in which he said he supported them. How you get that kind of chutzpah is beyond me.

Chapter 25

How Goes the Grassroots?

"If you think of us all on a giant bicycle and we are all paddling at the same time and then somebody gets really tired and they pull their feet off and it's okay because everybody else is still paddling. We are still going. We can still do this. Everybody just needs to sometimes take a minute."

Patricia Callan, EEAN

With a better understanding of the midterm election results and our district, I then turned to the grassroots. I wanted to know how these groups were faring in the post-election world of 2019. So much of our focus had been on the blue wave. How were we all doing in 2019?

By January, my own post-election malaise had lifted but I still felt lethargic about activism. It certainly didn't help that the country was mired in the longest government shutdown in history. The month felt long and cold and my chronically sore wrists did not help my mood. I wore braces all the time and had to limit how long I could work at my computer to minimize the pain.

I was even ambivalent about attending the 2019 Women's March. I didn't purchase T-shirts for us or make any plans to go. It seemed like too much effort to drag myself to D.C. Was I just tired? Had Trump finally worn me down? Or were the controversies swirling around the March this year, especially these accusations of anti-Semitism and the splintering into two marches, the reasons for my lack of enthusiasm to participate?

Nanci was more motivated than I was. In the end, we decided to go to D.C. and Nanci, Vicky, Elyse and I would carry our 2017 posters. As we got closer, a sense of excitement slowly crept in and I began to look forward to it. Maybe getting out and marching would help reconnect me to the mission. But then we were forced to cancel our trip due to predictions of very bad weather on Sunday, when we would be driving back to New York. I heard from people who went that while the crowd was much smaller than the two previous years, it was still a large gathering and the people who went found it inspiring.

EEAN meetings continued and I continued to attend, despite my ambivalence. In those first meetings in 2019, we discussed what to do about the drop in our membership and what things we could do to bring people back. We also discussed ways to restructure the group, both on the leadership level and for the general membership. Of the leadership, we were all still here but we were all tired. This small core tended to do all the work. We needed to change that.

Rebecca and Sharon were working on how we could restructure the group to make it more efficient and to try to spread the work around. They consulted with Sarah Reeske, the Albany organizer for Indivisible New York. She offered guidance on how to better organize our group so that we can be more effective going forward. Part of that reorganization involved leadership members having specific jobs – public relations contact, photographer, Facebook coordinator, etc. – so that we knew with each event who would be taking charge of these jobs. Sarah suggested we write up a Standard Operating Procedure (SOP) for each job so that if the person in charge was unavailable, then any other member could take over and the ball would not be dropped. Instead of organizing by subject matter, which we had been doing, we would be organized by actions that needed to be done to move our core mission of educating the public forward. I volunteered to be the PR contact and worked on creating my SOP for that job.

"The meeting with Sarah Reeske from Indivisible came at exactly the right time," said Rebecca. "It makes sense that we are not the only group experiencing organizational challenges and I was encouraged to see that Indivisible is investing resources to help with this. We all have a lot of passion but organizing is strategic and requires thoughtful planning. I know we'll be maximizing our time with her moving forward to make sure we are setting the group, and the movement as a whole, up for success."

We also decided that along with helping to get the local 2019 Democratic candidates elected, we would advocate for the New York State initiatives, particularly the New York Health Act. And we stayed involved with local issues here on the East End, like supporting a Gay Pride Parade in Patchogue where we handed out rainbow colored ribbons with EEAN stamped on them.

While we may not have had the energy or numbers we had in 2017 and 2018, we slowly found our footing in 2019. I emailed the grassroots groups I had been in contact with the last two years to see if their experience was similar to EEAN. Of those who responded, they reported that their groups were intact and active. Some had smaller memberships, others did not.

"I don't think there has been any drop in R&R participation," said David Posnett of Resist and Replace. "We were wise to cut our meetings from weekly to monthly, and to take a breather so therefore there was no 'burnout.' Our meetings are attended as much as ever. We have great speakers and attendees.

Many of us have chosen to focus on an issue. Personally, for me it will be climate change and healthcare. It's different for each of us and that makes it interesting."

"After the 2018 election, it was kind of like, everybody just kind of quieted down for a while," said Eileen, referring to the activity on LVLZ. "But by the spring everyone's okay. Also, it makes me feel a lot better that Zeldin's now in the minority. He can't do as much damage and he's not going to be on TV as much."

I reached out to Ilse to see how they were doing in their district, District 15, in Lakeland, Polk County, Florida. Their Democratic candidate had also lost and also by a smaller margin than in 2016. Democratic Congressional candidate Kristen Carlson lost by 56.96% to 42.89% in 2018, a margin of over 14% but in 2016, the Republican won 61.39% to 38.61%, an almost 23% margin.[60]

She sent me a detailed update of how her group was doing after the election. Their level of activism in a heavily GOP district continued to be inspiring.

> *"We have lost about 75 members in the past two years and our monthly meetings average 45-65 people. Unlike Kathie and Rich, we did not have a focused mission. Our meetings have speakers on state and local issues and present a social setting for Democrats to meet. At one of our meetings, I spoke about the protesters outside a women's clinic and asked that someone join me the next day for a counter protest. A couple of our younger members grabbed on to the idea and the passion has surprised me. Our leadership has started an escort program at a Women's Center to counteract the anti-choice protesters that yell and scream at young women as they enter the clinic. The clinic has welcomed us and on that first day asked me, 'Where have you guys been all these years?' In fact, last month the RepubliCONs bought the building next to the clinic and opened a FAKE clinic that offers no real medical information and offers 'help' if a woman does not terminate her pregnancy. This project alone has served to re-energize our group. We have weekly schedules of volunteers that we publish on a private Facebook site. TAKEAWAY from this is that volunteers expect specific tasks on passionate issues and we need to provide leaders who are willing to organize each project.*
>
> *We also have had several projects where we register voters. A monthly First Friday is manned by a group from our club that hands out candy, information about Democrats in the county, and registers voters. Although it is only once a month, we have had a hard time*

> *manning the tent. It's a large event filled with people who are looking for giveaways (yes, they bring bags like trick or treat!). Hot, dusty and often confrontational. Lots of angry Trumpers attend. That said, we have managed to register about ten voters a month. Incremental, but important in this red county. The club also will pitch a tent and table at any other public event in Lakeland. In this way, we are slowly announcing the presence of Democrats in a RepubliCON-ruled county. We have also attended the MLK parades that take place in our African-American neighborhood and many of us have joined the local NAACP. At the Gay Pride event, we pitch our tent and banners. At the Garden Show, we pitch our tent. You get the idea. We wear our blue DWCL shirts and just show up to announce our presence.*
>
> *On a personal note, my husband Frank and I spend almost six months a year at our lake house in PA. I have been able to delegate the CALL GIRLS (phone committee that reminds about meetings and other issues such as poster parties, canvassing etc.) and the Welcoming and Refreshments (that I did alone) to committees who are doing a spectacular job. We've had a few health issues and have stepped away from major leadership and physical roles. Frank and I contribute HEAVILY to the DEC of Polk County and are constantly called on by candidates. At this time in our lives, at 72 and 76, writing checks, making suggestions, attending meetings and phone calls are our major contributions."*

To understand how people were feeling about the movement on a more personal level, I sat down with my grassroots focus group, the leadership ladies of EEAN, for a final group interview.

It was the end of March. It had taken some doing, but we finally found a date that everyone was available to attend. As I waited for them to arrive, I put out cheese, crackers, fruit, corn chips and salsa on my dining room table. I set out wine glasses, plates and napkins. My refrigerator was stocked with white wine and beer.

I thought about the last time, almost a year ago, that we sat at this table, the leadership ladies of EEAN, for our first group interview. It seemed like a lifetime ago, at the beginning of this project and early in the primary. In preparation for this interview, I went back and read the first group interview. So much has happened since then. Like bookends, these conversations marked the journey we have all been on together. Luckily Patty was able to attend this time.

After everyone arrived, we caught up a little bit with each other. We celebrated Rebecca's wedding to Sarah, which was last month. From the pictures she posted on Facebook, it looked like a very joyous affair and she and Sarah both looked beautiful in their white outfits. Syma told us about the road trip that she and Lloyd took, just the two of them, driving down south. She said Lloyd is unchanged in his love for Trump which is still hard for her to cope with but he is very good to her and the trip helped them to reconnect and leave politics aside. Sharon told us about her vacation in Florida, in the sunshine. Wendy filled us in on some health problems that her family is dealing with. Cindy discussed what was going on at work. And I updated everyone on where I was with the book.

Below is a lightly edited and condensed transcript of our conversation.

In going back and editing the book, and looking at what I was feeling right after the 2017 Women's March, I got a certain pang of sadness that I'm not feeling what I felt then. I don't know whether it comes from becoming more hardened or exhaustion.

Syma: I would suggest something else. Part of what has quieted my fervor has been the infighting within our own party, and I think that has offended me or hurt me or disappointed me and affected me more. I don't feel the same enthusiasm working with my fellow Democrats as I'm feeling in our own group. I am particularly talking about the other group that we work with in the Democratic group, the SPC, and what's happening within the Democratic Committee and the hostility from last fall.

Wendy: In Southampton?

Syma: Yes. One of the things that made me feel so positive was what we had done and what we had accomplished together and it feels as though it's all falling apart and crumbling. So that's in our party, and it's happening nationally in many places. That's what I think, robbed me.

Cindy: I think there is stuff going on, but the whole Democrats in disarray is like a really popular media storyline, and the Democrats are way more unified nationally than they are split up. I just think it's really popular for them to turn it into the Democrats are going to eat their own, and we need to resist that.

Wendy: Like you were saying about the media. I hate to agree with Trump on anything, but the media does like the sound bite.

Cindy: You're not agreeing with Trump when you say that. When Trump says fake news, he's talking about pretending that something that the media, I mean the media has its issues, but they are not going out and trying to report things that are false. They might interpret it wrong, but they'll put the emphasis on it. He's talking about a different thing. Don't let them get away with that.

Patricia: And now with all the different candidates and how varied they all are. I mean, we have all different kinds of candidates coming out and now everybody's fighting over that.

Wendy: Yeah, but at the core, they agree. They will never vote against women's reproductive rights. They will never vote against the environment and climate change. They will never vote against gun control.

Patricia: I know, basically they are on the same page on most of the issues, but I'm talking about the infighting. I see it in the groups with the Bernie people and Tulsi Gabbard's people. Kamala Harris, and Elizabeth Warren, they are all biting at each other. It's like, "people just support your person, you don't have to bite at the other person."

Wendy: But that's on social media, which we can't let that dictate…

Patricia: But it's very powerful. That's how people get their information. When I see all that fighting that makes me distressed because I'm thinking why are we fighting amongst ourselves? I mean we are trying to pull together and beat this guy and be the party of 2020.

Like Syma, I used to look forward to the SPC meetings. I thought we achieved something important there. I still look forward to our meetings but there are times lately where it all starts to feel like a burden. I think, "I don't want to make this list of phone calls. I really don't want to do this."

Sharon: Barb, you better not tell me that!

Barbara: I won't, I'm sorry. Not your events!

Patricia: It's because it's stressful.

Sharon: We had 23 pretty enthusiastic people at Roland's house last week.

Wendy: It's getting out and talking and connecting.

Sharon: It's being positive about what we did and what we are going to do going forward.

What do you take from these two years, what we've learned as a group or what you've learned personally, now into 2020?

Wendy: That we don't stop.

Patricia: We don't stop, and I think that we're strong for each other because we each support each other. I mean, if one of us is down we all rally and we do really pick each other up.

Sharon: We started something amazing that has never been done before, and we did it.

Patricia: We are still doing it.

Sharon: People all over the United States started this Resistance, and it's powerful.

Patricia: I don't think it's over. Sometimes, like when you go on a diet and then you're losing weight and then all of a sudden you plateau for a little bit? Maybe you're on a little plateau for a minute.

Wendy: A lot of what we're trying to do is something you can't do, some of its generational. Like, we need a change in the voting system. You can't do that instantly. Some of the things that are so important to do, the reference I keep thinking about is women's suffrage. So many people who fought hard for that but then didn't live to see it.

Rebecca: Susan B. Anthony didn't live to see it.

Wendy: And part of the reason is that the people in power aren't the ones who are trying to make the change. How do you make the change when you have no power?

Barbara: Do you think this movement, like that one, can sustain itself?

Patricia: I think for two more years, yes.

Rebecca: Of course, and I think that it's going to become less of a Resistance and more of a way of life, which is the whole point. The way that we were living was not sustainable in every single way. Not even just politically. Everything was being looked over. People aren't paying attention to civics, to the political process. They were going through their lives and not participating in democracy. That was not sustainable. The Resistance was born out of immediacy and Trump didn't just come out of nowhere. This is all connected. So the Resistance is not going to necessarily be resisting, it's going to change and it's going to have to morph into a way of being in order for our democracy to sustain itself.

Cindy: The alternative is that we won't have a democracy.

Syma: That's what keeps me from giving up. Basically, it is the feeling that the vast majority of the country doesn't pay any attention at all so if we who are paying attention stop, then we are essentially saying that democracy is over.

Rebecca: Can I just say, don't look at it as giving up, you just have to take a break. Because this needs to be forever.

Patricia: That's what I was saying, we have maybe hit a plateau right now. Everybody just needs to coast for a minute.

Rebecca: If you stop coming to meetings for a little while, you just take your time. You don't come to a few meetings, but you are going to come back. You have to rejuvenate.

Wendy: And you are going to vote all the time.

What do you envision EEAN doing for the 2020 campaign?

Sharon: We've got 2019 first. And with New York State, we have a chance to really do things. We really do. We have all these groups that are working on everything, and we can make a difference, and that's where our energy has to go. We can't get numb about it.

Wendy: And we really have to concentrate on 2019, because nothing breeds success like success. If we can get a couple of people on town councils and turn things around here, that will lay the groundwork for 2020. So, we can't overlook the election this year.

Rebecca: As to 2020, again, the group won't endorse, but if anybody wants to work for Perry's campaign or anyone else's campaign, we would encourage them to do it.

Syma: It seems to me that I'm hearing a lot more about grassroots activity in Brookhaven town than before.

Wendy: EJ Lopez is doing a great job bringing people out, Latinos and others, and he's active in the Brookhaven Action Network. There are a few people that really are energized and they are trying to reach out and do things, and there are some new committee people that are getting out there, but always more people are needed. Always.

Rebecca: I would like to see other groups continue putting on these educational forums and active participation in events like the postcards. I'd like to see less talking, more doing and just encouraging people to stay informed and to stay involved. At first, we were doing a lot of meetings where people were getting together and we were talking about everything on a week to week basis, but not only do I not think it's necessary, I think it's actually-

Wendy: Counterproductive?

Rebecca: Yes. People just talk.

Cindy: The thing about talking is it is not doing. And talking amongst yourselves is definitely not doing something.

Wendy: Like from the beginning with the Brookhaven Democratic Party when there was a lot of pushback, and I said they are the same as we are and let's see who lasts and look at this core group of active people because it's very, very hard to get people to stay in for the long haul and do the tedious grinding work of getting people on the ballot, getting people elected. It really is. It's not for everybody. My whole life being interested in politics, especially as a woman, I can turn people off in two seconds like that.

Patricia: I'm doing that now. And I'm new in politics because I really didn't care before.

Sharon: Now we have this big event coming April 2nd. That's one of our initiatives, and then in May we have Lisa Votino speaking about her experiences going to the border and working with people seeking asylum.

Rebecca: I think we should rebrand what we call them. I don't think we should call them general membership meetings.

Cindy: I agree with you.

Rebecca: I think it should be educational forums.

There are studies that focus on one of the greatest challenges in modern society today, which has left people feeling alienated and ripe for things like white nationalism, is a lack of community. A lack of feeling they are connected to a community. I thought in many ways that's what the Resistance is for many of us, this feeling of being connected to the community. So, I guess my question is, do you think we can keep that going?

Syma: I think one of the things we have to think about is making our community educational forums a little bit more social so that after the speech is over, if we are serving cookies or ice cream, something, then people can stay around and talk to each other and get to know each other a little bit. I think that's the thing that's missing, that community feeling.

Cindy: After the event has an advantage because then we can talk. Or you can invite whoever the speaker is to stick around. I think you're right, that's a good idea Syma.

Rebecca: Patchogue has been a place that has events for the Resistance. So maybe if we alternated between Patchogue and Riverhead, because The Dark Horse Restaurant is a great place but if we also partner with People Power Patchogue like we do with Invisible North Fork, we could rotate our forums for both east and west.

Cindy: One of the things we've learned to do differently instead of sending a representative to a big steering committee where there's 20 different groups is instead forming alliances with specific groups for specific events.

Syma: We did pull off a couple of very good educational programs.

Rebecca: We did. I feel like it's just so much easier to be nimble when you are working with fewer people. I mean, the truth is when I work with Sharon and we are on the phone, we just get so much done. It's not by committee. And I know that you lose something with that when it's not with the bigger group, but I want to find a better balance.

I like that word, nimble. Yes, if we can be more nimble, more flexible. That is a really great idea. Every group seems to have a core group of doers, like Steven Kramer at Indivisible North Fork and Kathryn Szoka at PEER. So rather than connecting to 20 groups, we connect with the doers in very specific groups.

Rebecca: It felt like when you took the representatives from each group in that CD1 committee and you put them all in the same room, there was this power struggle, which I can't get down with. I love sharing power.

When we had the first group interview, we talked a lot about what being part of this Resistance meant to each of you personally, what it gave you personally. Is that the same or has it changed?

Group: Changed.

Syma: For me initially it was an escape. It gave me a place to talk about democracy and Democrats when at home I couldn't do that, and where I felt very captive. It was very much a freeing experience, and in the process, it helps me learn and evaluate better so that my husband and I can come to an understanding. He was always handling it better than I was. He was always more gracious, more understanding, more willing to listen to the different news stations than I ever was, but I became a little more willing to be flexible also, and I became more flexible in our communication so that it got better as a result of being around EEAN. Having a place to come and blow off steam rather than directing it at him. So anyways, it's been a nice feature in my marriage.

Barbara: We saved your marriage.

Wendy: That is good, I don't know if I could top it.

Patricia: I mean, actually I had broken up because of the whole election and we spent a year and nine months apart, and now that we are back together.

Barbara: Really?

Patricia: Yes, since September and he's like a different person. We spent a year and nine months apart, now it's like I'm learning about this new person because, first of all he's watching *CNN* and *MSNBC* and *BBC*. All these things, before he was only watching *Fox* and he listened to his parents and his dad is a Republican. That was all that he knew. Then I was gone for a long time, and I don't know what happened but when I came back it was like time stood still in his house. I walked in, and I'm like really? There are still pictures of me on the wall, really?

Barbara: Did he approach you, Patty, to get back together?

Patricia: Actually, we bumped into each other and then he asked me to go have drinks, and I was like seriously? Are we going to kill each other?

Barbara: Have you told him how deeply hurt you were?

Patricia: I told him when it happened two years ago. You know me, I don't mince words. I said some foul words and emails and phone calls but then that was it. Then I found you guys, and I channeled all my energy into Resistance and trying to make a difference and putting my money where my mouth is and to my rescue dog. Good old Foxy. Then, I didn't pay attention to him for a long time, and now he's got a different perspective. I think he sees things differently. I mean, he hasn't changed his party affiliation or anything, but the fact that he doesn't have *Fox News* on all the time or tries to force me to watch it. It was almost the opposite. Now he will not put any of that on because he knows and he doesn't want to engage in any of those arguments that he enjoyed previously. He doesn't want to have any of those arguments, so we don't. We don't talk much about politics, but I know that he's been watching. He'll make little comments here and there. Oh, you probably liked that that happened. I go, oh actually I do. That's the end of it. And we have a stronger, nicer relationship now because I think he realizes that I'm not going to stand around. I had a life in between there, and he knows about this group through other people who said good things about us.

Rebecca: You just reminded me, I had lunch with Cindy Morris the other day, and she was the one that was talking to Dave Calone, and Dave Calone went to her and said I'm thinking about running, who do I need to talk to? She said as it pertains to the Resistance, there are two groups. She said go to Resist & Replace if you want money, and go to East End Action Network if you want to get something done.

Barbara: Yay EEAN!

Rebecca: She goes, "that group knows how to mobilize and get things done."

Patricia: We are getting it out there because people are talking about us now.

Syma: Yeah, a lot of people know. I'll say something about EEAN and people say, I know what that is.

Rebecca: The same things are true for me. I found camaraderie, and I was really active in college, and I feel that coming back to activism has been awesome and something I've been craving. I think what's changed is that I've learned personally how to set better boundaries. I think the reason that I got sick last year was because I had no idea that I wasn't managing stress. I thought I was managing stress because I don't get nervous, I can speak in front of people and I just sort of equated that with being fine, but I think I was internalizing a lot, and taking on other people's stuff. Not just from this group, but from my whole entire life. This has really helped me realize that I need to manage my stress better, I need to have better boundaries with people. I thought I was really doing it well, but I don't think I was. I earlier said to Barbara when Trump got elected, I felt like a somatic physical change. I felt radicalized.

Patricia: There was a physical change. It was a nauseating feeling.

Rebecca: Something happened. Something happened to me.

Patricia: Your gut role.

Rebecca: And it changed my body chemistry, changed my mind. I don't think I put enough emphasis on that. I don't think I gave it the attention that it deserved.

Patricia: Well, look at how many things he's threatened for your way of life. It's terrible. He shouldn't have that control.

Rebecca: No, he shouldn't. Also, the other thing that this has taught me is that I have to live my life. I feel like I'm in a different osition than a lot of people in the Resistance in that, I'm just married.

Patricia: You're not retired.

Rebecca: I'm not retired. I work, I run my own business, and I was giving so much, and I have to really focus on my life because my life hasn't really been lived totally. All this stuff happens in order for you to learn this, so it's all good.

Patricia: Well sometimes it is really hard, learning to balance it. You have to balance it. Even me with my mom, now I feel, she's pretty much stable in a place so we know she's okay, but when you don't have that, and you guys have all different issues going on underneath, it's so hard to put that away and say all right, so we have to write postcards, and we have to go to Zeldin's office, I have to make a sign. There has to be a balance.

Rebecca: We want so much as women, too. We want to do everything.

Patricia: We have to.

Rebecca: I always want to do everything, and then there's this guilt when you're not.

Wendy: I don't think I've ever learned to balance it. I'm not a balanced person. I may appear as one, but I've never learned how to properly balance. I bore the hell out of my own family by constantly saying, "Do you know what happened today?" I mean, this is before Trump.

Patricia: But that's what I like about you. You always know what's happening.

Wendy: Yeah, but you still want to turn this off sometimes.

Patricia: Yes, that would be nice.

But maybe in a way being a part of this movement gives an outlet for all of that. So that's it has some place to go.

Wendy: It has and it hasn't. About shutting things off, that's the human condition. It's just I'm always at the food pantry, I'm always feeling I have to do more. I have to do things for people, what can I do? I spent three hours at the library with an immigrant family getting them all cards. I always feel like I don't do enough, I need to do more and I do a fair amount.

Patricia: You do a lot.

Wendy: I do a fair amount, and I wish that I could just say to myself sometimes okay that was enough.

Rebecca: You have to change the belief in your head because it also has meaning when you're not doing something.

Wendy: That I have to always produce something.

Cindy: Then you can start not listening to it, but you've got to figure out what the belief is.

Rebecca: Well just ask yourself if it's true. You don't want to go to the food pantry that night, well does that mean that you're not a dedicated person? Of course not. It means you don't want to go to the food pantry that night, plain and simple.

Wendy: At least you deserve to be tired. The other day I was there from 9:00 AM until 7:30 PM at night with one hour off because I had to do deliveries, but no, I could never not go.

Rebecca: But do you get something from it?

Wendy: I do. I love going, I love doing things.

Cindy: For me, I'm not sure what to say. I don't know what I was expecting except it's probably the same thing that was true then and now is that the group is the thing I enjoy out of all this. These groups become important and we really do support each other, and that's a big deal. In terms of working on stuff, that's a matter of thinking that I have to because I don't want the country that we are going towards. If we don't, who will?

Sharon: I feel good about everything. I try to focus, and there's all this other stuff, but I try to focus on one thing that I think is important. Because in the beginning I was everywhere-

Wendy: And that makes it much harder.

Sharon: Rebecca has helped me not be everywhere, but it's important to just pick one thing or three things and get something accomplished and focus on it. I just really enjoy what I'm doing. I'm retired, but I tell people the Resistance is my new job. The dining room table is covered with magic markers, flyers and postcards and I love it. I will keep doing it, though I have been thinking that after 2020 when Trump is out of the office, then maybe all these little groups, maybe we try to consolidate all of the Indivisible groups and have an East End Indivisible instead of all these little groups. And that's how we continue on after this election so we can still do as much as we want to do, but you would have a more collective group. I don't know; that's just something I think about. We don't want to lose this because it's going to be a way of life.

Wendy: I don't think of it as Resistance, I just think of it as what it is.

Cindy: You know it's interesting you say that because that was the name we started with, but we are not resisting as much as we were in the beginning. It's not like when we were out there protesting the Muslim ban. We are doing more-

Wendy: Building.

Cindy: Yeah.

Wendy: It's just not the way I think of it now. I don't think of protest as being our main tool.

I was struck in our first interview how much being a woman was a big part of having gotten involved from the very beginning. I think all of us said it wasn't even so much Hillary losing, it was Trump winning. If she had been beaten by, I think that was a quote, "a more traditional Republican," we probably wouldn't be doing this, but it was the idea that this misogynistic, disgusting human being who had no business being president defeated the first possible woman president. Is still connected to being a woman?

Cindy: For me it was never about being a woman.

Patricia: I think it was for me, and now I think it's more so because of all the attacks on women.

Wendy: Yeah, and I think about reproductive rights. I know it sounds mean, but I'm done with all white men. Like enough already, I am done.

Sharon: Remember that picture of all those white men at the table in Washington, D.C. when they decided to vote on women's reproductive health?

Wendy: The whole identity politics, I want to shut up about identity politics. The only way there are such things as identity politics is if we all can see that somehow white men are unbiased, and have a clear perspective that has no identity. I'm like, are you kidding me? No. You have an identity as much as a white woman or a black woman. We all come to it with our different life experiences of perspective. So, the whole identity politics that they were throwing around in the beginning, I was like are you kidding me?

Cindy: And we are seeing a repeat now in terms of the way they are treating the women candidates. 'Oh, she's not likable.' Elizabeth Warren was likable until she was running. She was very rational and they thought she was charismatic until she was running.

Rebecca: You're not surprised though, right?

Wendy: No.

Rebecca: I'm not surprised. When I say that it's very much about being a woman, it's not for me about reproductive rights or my physicality, it's the way men have not served us. It has gotten us into this mess. What I understand is that there needs to be a huge shift towards the feminine in order to correct this garbage. Because it serves no one including men, and what they don't understand, or what they will come to learn I should say, is that the way of women, the divine feminine, is going to be a better way for everyone.

Wendy: Everyone.

Syma: Here's the difference. Women see the world as inclusive, and we can and will work to address their issues as well. They only see their issues and exclude ours.

Cindy: Yes. It's not working for them either.

Syma: That's right, they don't know.

Rebecca: Some, maybe.

Cindy: Like the fact that we still don't have childcare. The same issues we all dealt with when our kids were little. They made a childcare center at work and at some point, they closed it around the time from when my son was two.

Wendy: On the way here, I was listening to a NASA report about a woman who is supposed to do a spacewalk. Hundreds of men have made spacewalks, only 13 women. NASA, in a budget cut, got rid of the smaller spacesuits.

Rebecca: There was supposed to be an all-woman team.

Wendy: Those are the things where even if I have become "woke" as to being female, the system ends up being a roadblock.

All the data from the midterm election shows that it was women like us, who started with the Women's March, joined the Resistance, then got out in their districts knocking on doors, that powered the blue wave, particularly in the suburbs. Do you think that will be the same thing in 2020?

Rebecca: Yes, because I think everything is moving towards that.

Syma: The ones around the fringe are going to fall in and fall out as they have been doing all along, but I think a lot of the core people will still be there, and the people who became core people who weren't before.

Rebecca: And we'll take more in. As we lose, we'll gain.

Barbara: We have as many members as we had?

Rebecca: We have more.

Wendy: Do people ever drop off?

Rebecca: Yes, people unsubscribe from the newsletter every week.

Wendy: Oh, do they?

Rebecca: They do. But look at the new generation of kids that have been affected by gun violence, who are now going to be powering this movement, and people like me who are going to be voting and are going to be having children. This is like the long game. We have a baby, and my baby is going to be a warrior from day one. There's going to be no mistake that this child has a duty to give back. They might not, but I do think that more people will start to instill that in the next generation because it's going to be necessary. They are going to need that.

Patricia: They are going to need that fighting spirit for themselves even for climate change and all the things that we are screwing up for them.

Rebecca: There are so many challenges. I can't help but think that things like town halls will come back, civic groups will come back. I don't know. Maybe I'm an optimist.

I love that. You're more optimistic than pessimistic. Let's go around. Optimistic or pessimistic?

Patricia: Optimistic.

Sharon: Optimistic definitely.

Rebecca: Optimistic.

Wendy: Optimistic. We wouldn't be here doing what we do if we weren't.

Cindy: I don't know. Probably more optimistic. I have deep pessimism sometimes but overall you have to keep going. I think things always go back and forth, but my parents were involved with Henry Wallace. It's not like this is the first social movement.

Rebecca: And I understand that. I also understand that it's a pendulum and that it could and probably will get a lot worse. I think he will win in 2020. But it's not the end of the world.

Sharon: That would be the end of the world for me.

Rebecca: What do you mean?

Sharon: I don't know I think I would be psycho, jump off the bridge if he wins again.

Patricia: Seriously. If he wins again I'm going to move. I'm going to Canada.

Rebecca: I think if the election was held tomorrow he would win.

Syma: Well, I don't know how to answer that. I am both. I don't know. From moment to moment sometimes that seems to change. In truth, the burden seems heavier. The phone calls seem harder. Going out and knocking on doors seems harder. How much of that is a function of my own age and how much is a function of disappointment or wanting something that I can't see happening, wanting Trump to have to pay some price. Nothing is happening to him. So that's a part of it, but I'm struggling with that issue.

Rebecca: Can I say one more thing though? In terms of it being hard, I just can't help but feel gratitude for what I have and the privilege that I have being white, and living in a community that's very stable, having friends. There are people in this world who really struggle on a daily basis just to survive. So as hard as it is, as hard as it can be, we are so lucky, and I just have to keep that perspective every time it feels like it's too much.

Cindy: In terms of optimism and pessimism, I mean, I don't know whether Trump will win. I think it's definitely a danger assuming he won't, it's very stupid. I don't mean that to be judgmental.

Wendy: We are not assuming, we are just hoping.

Cindy: The problem is, the way in which I'm pessimistic is there are so many structural problems. The fact that they have the Supreme Court, that gerrymandering will be allowed…

Rebecca: Our cybersecurity, social media has not been addressed.

Cindy: All of that, but even more than that we don't have a democracy. We have the Electoral College which doesn't represent the majority of the people.

Patricia: Mitch McConnell blocking the crap out of everybody.

Cindy: So even after 2020, where do we go?

Rebecca: Right. It's scary but it's the long game.

Chapter 26
The SHDems

"It's not a matter of being afraid of a primary. It's a matter of what's right. Why would you think that the rules don't apply to you as a progressive? No, the rules are there for everybody. That's the only thing that keeps us from anarchy, because otherwise, if the rules don't exist, the majority is going to walk all over the minority. The rules are there to protect you, not for you to abuse."

Robin Long, SHDems

I next turned my attention to the SHDems. How was the committee doing? Were the tensions as acute as in 2018 or had we, as an organization, found ways to put them behind us as we faced an important local election in 2019?

The year started with new initiatives to address the "need for more transparency and democracy" with a subcommittee working on a new handbook for members, spearheaded by Second Vice Chair Andi Klausner and a new organizing structure with ED reps reporting to zone leaders who reported to regional coordinators.

I hoped the work on the new handbook and this more open structure might help to put some of the discontent behind us. But as I sat in my first zone meeting, a member sitting next to me muttered anti-Gordon statements under her breath throughout the meeting. It took all my restraint to not walk out. I did not attend a second zone meeting.

Periodically I asked myself if I wanted to stay on the SHDems. I was aware that it did not have the same feeling of community for me as EEAN. But I thought of Mike, Gordon, Robin, Andi, Lulu, Joy, Katey, George, Jorge and all of the other members I worked with and decided to stick it out a while longer. It was a privilege to represent the Democratic Party in our township. I didn't want to give up on that yet.

The primary job of the committee, finding, supporting and electing Democrats, continued. Since the 2017 election, Southampton Township had passed new legislation on a wide range of issues, from public health to transportation and the environment. Especially exciting was new affordable housing being built and expanded public transportation. With the 2019 election, we needed to keep

Democrats in office so we could build on these successes. Our message for the 2019 election was "Democrats Deliver."

The committee had to scramble a bit to adjust to a new election schedule but it was for a good reason. New York State finally enacted election reform. Bottled up for years by the GOP and the IDC, the new progressive Democratic state government had finally given New York what so many other states have had for years, in-person early voting, an issue that Democratic Committees and grassroots groups had been actively advocating. It would begin with this fall's local election.

Because of the new early voting, the SHDems executive committee had a shortened schedule to find and interview candidates and then present them to the entire membership for a vote. Under the new rules we had approved last year, any other member could request to be considered at the general membership meeting even if they had not been selected by the executive committee.

The meeting to vote on the recommended candidates was held in February, earlier than usual, and I missed it because I was out of town. But I heard from SHDems who were there that the slate of candidates the executive committee had put forward was approved. No one else requested consideration.

The Southampton Town Council consists of four seats plus the supervisor. In the 2017 election Democrats attained a supermajority by putting three Democrats on the Council and retaining the supervisor seat. Democrat Jay Schneiderman was up for reelection as supervisor and Democrat John Bouvier for councilman. Because the Town Council terms are for four years, Democrats Julie Lofstad and Tommy John Schiavoni, who were elected in 2017, were not up for reelection this year.

The one Republican on the Town Council, Christine Preston Scalera, chose not to run for reelection making it an open seat with no incumbent. The executive committee selected Craig Catalanotto, who was active in several local civic associations, and the SHDems voted for him to be the other endorsed candidate to run.

The Southampton Trustee Board has five members who serve two-year terms so all members are up for reelection this year. This Board oversees all issues having to do with the waterways. The SHDems nominating convention approved endorsing four Trustee candidates: Bill Pell and Ann Welker, who were both up for reelection, as well as Eileen Duffy and David Mayer. Eileen had interviewed with the executive committee to be a Town Council candidate but was selected to be the Trustee candidate instead. A fifth candidate, Andrew Brosnan, was later added to the slate.

These endorsed candidates were on our official petition, in addition to Democrats who had been voted on at the meeting and running for other offices. Along with the petitions, the Democratic Committee printed up palm cards with all the candidates' photos and biographies. We had to hurry, because of the shortened schedule, to get all the signatures needed to get their names on the ballot for the fall election. I never thought I would be canvassing with snow on the ground but we did and Lulu and I got all of our signatures done in early March.

And so despite the friction that still existed, the business of our political committee continued. It was clear that some of the tension had dissipated, though complaints from the different sides of the divide continued to be heard. There also continued to be a lack of cohesiveness within the executive committee.

I really had no comment on most of it. I wasn't on the executive committee, nor did I want to be. I just wished there was more congeniality and more trust. It would make the work easier. It felt like divisions had hardened and we weren't all speaking the same language. For those members who wanted more say in how candidates were chosen, they were still unhappy despite the new resolution that allowed hats to be thrown in the nominating ring outside the executive committee.

I sensed the majority of the membership was more aligned with where I was. I did not want more input into the selection of candidates. What I wanted was an efficient, viable search committee that would do the vetting, make suggestions to an executive committee that members trusted who could then present candidates to the general membership for a vote. But that was not what we had.

Still, despite the consistent grumblings, we got the work of the committee done. We had a slate of candidates, we got signatures to get them on the ballot and we would work in the fall to get out the vote for them. I would not have called the SHDems a cohesive organization but it was also not dysfunctional. We had more registered Democrats than Republicans in Southampton Township, we had a supermajority on a Town Board that was doing great work for the community and we had full committee membership. Not that long ago all of these would have seemed like a pipe dream. So, given it was now time for me to turn away from reporting and instead complete the final writing and editing for the book, this would have to be the answer to the question of how the SHDems were doing since the midterm election.

But sometime in March, I got word that something was amiss with our petition process. Lulu and I had already completed gathering our signatures. I got a call from a member of EEAN asking if I knew why there was a petition circulating with Eileen's name for Town Council. Wasn't she the endorsed candidate for Trustee? I said yes, as far as I knew. Then why was there a petition with her name for Town Council? I was told that this petition looked just like ours, with the Democratic slate of candidates but instead of Craig's name for Town Council it had Eileen's. I had no answer but, to be honest, I was busy writing the book and didn't pay much attention.

Even as the first articles began to appear in the local newspapers in early April, I kept the story at arm's length. Looking back, I wish I had interviewed the principal people involved in the controversy as it was happening but I didn't. Of course, I had no way of knowing back in April that it would continue past the spring and end up decided in the courts in the summer.

Apparently what happened was that Eileen, with the support of a small number of SHDems (many who had been part of the anti-Gordon faction) and LVLZ members, had decided to run for Town Council, even though she was not the endorsed candidate, even though she had accepted the position to be the endorsed candidate for Trustee and even though we had collected all of our signatures on petitions that listed her as running for Trustee. This was prompted by their belief that Craig was not progressive enough and did not deserve to be the endorsed candidate. She created her own petitions, collected her own signatures and was now looking to force a primary for Town Council since there would be three Democrats running for only two spots. The primary would be in June. Their goal with the primary was to eliminate Craig and replace him with Eileen, who they perceived as the true progressive.

Needless to say it was a mess and it poured gasoline on the kindling of ongoing discontent. It was like the chairmanship challenge but on steroids and much more public because the situation garnered quite a bit of attention in our local press. With LVLZ openly supporting Eileen, the SHDems internal tensions now extended out into the grassroots. With accusations being thrown back and forth in dueling letters to the editor and on social media, it got overheated.

The argument from Eileen and her supporters was, "This is democracy in action and why were SHDems afraid of a primary?" Whenever I was asked that question, my answer was always the same, "Isn't Eileen breaking the rules of our committee? Didn't she accept the position of Trustee?" I worried that the signatures we had worked so hard to collect might be invalidated because she was running for another position. If that happened, would it throw all of our Democrats off the ballot?

But it turned out to be simple. There are very specific election laws that address the legality of just such a situation and given that, this would end up being decided in court. When I heard that, I reached out to Eileen, as a friend, and encouraged her to drop her petitions. I did not think she could win in court and I feared what the experience would cost her both in legal fees and reputation. I was not able to persuade her.

The case was brought by George Lynch, our treasurer, which is why the case is entitled Lynch vs. Duffy. As it made its way through the courts, because Eileen kept appealing, at each level the court ruled in George's favor and invalidated Eileen's petitions on the basis that she violated two statutes of election law. One that you cannot run for two positions at the same time and two, that she included names on her petition without asking permission of those people.

Once the Court of Appeals ruled on May 29th, it was done. The decision ended with the following sentence:

> "Here, Duffy affirmatively altered an existing designating petition containing other names by substituting her own name in place of the name of a candidate who had [*3] been endorsed by the committee. Moreover, under the circumstances of this case, the problem of misleading voters was compounded by the simultaneous circulation of two designating petitions designating Duffy for two separate public offices (see *Matter of Lutfy v Gangemi*, 35 NY2d at 182; cf. *Matter of D'Angelo v Maloney*, 164 AD3d 1078)."[61]

In conversation with Robin over the summer, I asked her about the Lynch vs. Duffy case. She was still angry at having been forced to go through the time and expense of a court case because of Eileen's actions. She had also been personally attacked by some of Eileen's supporters, one going so far as to call her "a Stalinistic sock puppet" for opposing Eileen's petitions.

"I was threatened with, 'if you knock Eileen off the ballot, the left is going to come and get you.' And I said, 'Well good. Could they take me on vacation? I'm really tired.' The response was, 'You wait to see. The left is going to explode.' And I said, "They're not going to explode for Eileen Duffy, and they're not going to explode if I've done the right thing."

At the September SHDems meeting, which I attended, Robin patiently explained the applicable election laws and why the cases were decided in George's favor. It was important for the members to understand the law and why George had challenged Eileen's petitions in court. It was clear, at least from the members in attendance at this meeting, that the number of people who were supporting this primary challenge was small. The vast majority of the committee was vocally angry. There was no explosion on the left.

The truth was if Eileen had created honest petitions – either a petition with just her name on it or had asked and received permission to put other candidates' names on her petition - and if she had withdrawn her name for Trustee before gathering signatures or had never accepted the Trustee nomination in the first place, she would have been well within her rights to run as an outsider and force a primary. Those are the rules. In fact, other Democrats did just that with the Trustee race, forcing a Democratic primary in June. Even after the primary, candidates continued to run on other ballot lines. The Trustee race became a free-for-all with ten names on the ballot for the five spots.

I spoke with George at the fall SHDems meeting and asked him to email me a comment about the case for the book. I sent messages to Eileen asking her the same. I could see from the postings on LVLZ that she continued to actively administer the Facebook site, taking the fight to Zeldin as well as advocating for Democratic initiatives such as early voting. But she did not respond to my requests for a comment.

George emailed me the following comment:

> *"As the named petitioner in Lynch v. Duffy, I affirm that the suit's purpose was not to block a primary election, or to favor one candidate over another, or to frustrate any imagined majority. The only aim of this lawsuit was to protect democracy, which requires the observance of certain rules. Without these rules, we would have chaos, not democracy.*
>
> *Eileen Duffy accepted the Southampton Democratic Party's nomination for Town Trustee, but then changed her mind and circulated petitions naming her as a candidate for Town Council. These petitions contained the names of other candidates without their knowledge or consent.*
>
> *Ms. Duffy thus broke two simple rules: First, you can't run for two different offices at once because that confuses the voters. Second, you can't name other candidates on your petition, claiming their support without their consent, because that misleads the voters.*

That's all there was to the lawsuit. These aren't complicated, legalistic restrictions; these are plain rules based on ordinary common sense, such as anyone laying down the rules would impose. Three courts – the trial court, the Appellate Division, and the Court of Appeals in Albany – ruled that Eileen Duffy's behavior constitutes fraud on the voters and declared all her petitions invalid.

Some contend that the party leadership prevented a free election, but that's not what happened here. What happened is that we enforced the rules and made our democracy work."

For me, the entire affair – the refusal to support the endorsed candidate because of a perception that this person is not progressive enough and defying the rules because of a belief that the ends justify the means - was a chilling reminder of the 2016 campaign, the result of which gave us the election of Donald Trump. It remains to be seen going into 2020 whether or not the left-wing of the Democratic Party is more interested in making a statement about purity than in defeating Republican policies.

"I think Democrats have to learn the same lesson over and over - don't let the good become the enemy of the best," said Mike Anthony. "Lay it all out on the line for our nominated Democrats, whether it's your favorite or not. Our worst candidates are better than 99% of Republicans."

I wondered if the divisions in our committee are a microcosm of the divisions within the national Democratic Party. Robin did not think so.

"It isn't a microcosm, and I'll tell you why," she said. "There is no philosophical difference between their positions and ours. This is individual people with egos who feel that they are better suited or better whatever or better-better, but it's not like in the national where you have philosophical differences between Bernie Sanders and Kamala Harris and Cory Booker, and there are differences in a lot of what they believe in. They are slight, but there are differences. But in our district, these people have not argued that we are philosophically not correct. I have yet to find where the differences are. We're on the same page when it comes to water. Let's talk about what local does. When you get down to local issues and you ask them, 'Where's the differences?' there are none, so that's why I don't find it to be a microcosm. I find this to be a lot of people who feel entitled to run the coop, and when they don't win by the rules, they go off the track and out on their own."

I wasn't sure. I did see glimmers of the same tension on the national stage. I think Elaine DiMasi summed it up well in an email to me about these divisions and the dangers they pose to the cohesion of the Democratic Party.

"Regarding divisions across the spectrum of the left, they are real. Opposing political parties, like the Greens, are the Democrats' opponents," wrote Elaine. "What part of 'opposition' is so hard to understand? Progressives that support Democratic Socialism may or may not want to identify with the Democrats."

I tried to tune out all the noise. I hoped others would do the same. The stakes were too high to do otherwise. I took a break one day from finishing the book and went out knocking on doors. I wanted to remind Democratic voters about the great work our elected officials have been doing and about the quality and substance of all of our candidates. Just like old times, Mike picked me up and together we walked up and down streets in Hampton Bays, speaking to voters and handing out campaign materials. We would not know until November if the chaos and rift in the committee negatively impacted our chances in the general election.

Chapter 27

The Big Picture

"Some national commentators have talked about this as a movement, which is logical, but I don't use that language because it is much more complicated than a movement. That's true even within a group like Indivisible, which has a national headquarters that likes to use that language of 'our movement' and project an image of a relatively-unified ideological agenda. What I see on the ground, though, is far more dispersed and ideologically diverse than a movement. Is that diversity a problem? As a historian, I look at the big picture and in the long run, I actually think that many of the same things that make this a difficult experience, like what you're experiencing at the Democratic Committee, go hand-in-hand with the things that make it likely to last and likely to institute changes that have the potential to be more impactful."

Lara Putnam, Professor and Chair of the Department of History at the University of Pittsburgh

To finish the post-election reporting and add closure to the midterm election, I wanted to better understand this progressive movement I had been a part of as well as well as the relationship of the grassroots to the Democratic Party. In my own district, I had witnessed the highs (the creation of the SPC) and the lows (Lynch vs. Duffy) of that relationship. Were these tensions typical or unusual for the country as a whole?

To gain insights on these big picture questions, to get a broader 30,000 feet view of the work we had been doing, I reached out to Professor Lara Putnam, historian at the University of Pittsburgh who has been studying the Resistance since its inception. I had discovered Professor Putnam through a 2018 article published in Democracy Journal entitled "Middle America Reboots Democracy."[62]

She and Professor Theda Skocpol of Harvard University are studying the anti-Trump grassroots groups in districts similar to mine. They and others have a book coming out in January 2020 based on this research called *Upending American Politics* (Oxford University Press).[63]

In August, Professor Putnam and I spoke over the phone and below is a lightly edited and condensed transcript of our conversation.

I found your article fascinating because it described the activism I've been doing the last two years. In "Middle America Reboots Democracy", you mentioned that a lot of the local Democratic Committees were not embracing the grassroots. Here in Southampton Township it was different. We created a steering committee of both the Democratic Committee and the grassroots. We found this infrastructure helpful in 2017 and I would like to think it contributed to a successful local election that year. So, I wanted to ask if in your research looking at these other districts, if you found other examples of that kind of coordination?

I think that there are a wide variety of local experiences, and there are also some really clear patterns. I have written about this on-line for the American Communities Project: one article about Pennsylvania (Political Organizing Has Been Intense Since 2016. What Could It Mean for 2020?[64]) and one about national trends (Grassroots Blossom Across America, Reshaping Country's Political Geography[65]).

The American Communities Project looks at patterns among counties so that we can sort of move away from thinking in red state-blue state absolutes, and instead think about different kinds of places. Suffolk County in the classification system used by the American Communities Project, is what they call an urban suburb. More educated and somewhat racially and economically diverse. And then I'm sure if you dive into Suffolk County, there are parts that look more exurban, maybe a little more rural, a little homogeneous and then other parts are more, you know, sort of denser, and a little more diverse in form.

Yes.

We've seen in these urban suburbs and exurbs, these are the areas where the connections between the local Democratic Party and the new grassroots have come together most smoothly and most consistently. So, actually, your experience is very typical and kind of emblematic of the kind of pattern that we see having happened in the urban suburb and in the more exurban areas. Some of the urban suburbs, the ones that are closest to big cities, traditionally already have a pretty upscale but liberal local, political panorama, but others that were farther away from the big cities, more rural, more conservative district, had more conservative local politics. And from those areas, there tended to be a lot of similarity and connections between the people who were already serving for the local Democratic Committee, who were maybe few and far between but, were engaged local residents, and so, when the new grassroots emerged, the people who were taking the lead in those new grassroots group, already had a lot of informal connections or potential connections, to those other people who were the existing local Democratic Party insiders in these places.

Because it's not like you had the big city patronage machine. It's not like you had some large-scale Democratic hierarchy built in the heyday of, say, industrial union organizing that had its own logic. So, in areas like yours, the urban suburbs and exurbs, there tends to be a lot of information flow and connection and mutual understanding, that's helped local Democratic Party structures and the new grassroots figure out how to work together.

So, on some level, it depended on the characteristics of the district or the county, whether the local Democratic Party began to work well with the grassroots?
Exactly. Because you can sort of contrast the experience you are describing in your township with, let's say, a place like Queens, where you have a local Democratic Party machine in the city, and they have their stakeholders who have an interest in maintaining firm control. Whether that reflects material benefits or ideological commitments or personal ties, the bottom line is there's an old school Democratic machine and when the new grassroots emerge, they don't necessarily share an ideological vision of where our country should be going. They don't necessarily share a diagnosis of what's most important. That group, that Democratic machine doesn't necessarily have any interest in opening their doors if that means they risk seeing their own power begin to crumble. So, in big city areas you have a different conflict around whether the local Democratic Party hierarchy are going to make room for the new energies and new possibilities, such as grassroots, because to do so can be a real threat to some types of stakeholders.

In contrast, in more suburban and exurban areas—like in the area where you are, it sounds like—there tends to be a different dynamic, with more openness and synergies.

That's very interesting. I hadn't thought that the nature of the area might dictate whether or not the Democratic Party opened the door to the grassroots. While it was effective in 2017, when we moved to the midterm election, we experienced more fracturing. Your article came out before the midterm election. In your continued research, are you seeing examples of tensions and divisions, like the Bernie/Hillary split, in 2018?
I'm curious to hear more from you about how this sort of expressed itself. Was it fractious during the primaries because people had different kinds of ideas about which kind of Democrats could possibly win in NY01?

Yes, I would say that's what started it. We had six Democrats running in the primary and they ran the gamut from what were considered very progressive to more centrist, and I think as people attached themselves to some of the candidates, that's really where we started to see the fracturing. Particularly within the Democratic Committee meetings, it became much more divisive which gives me a lot of concern for 2020.
I'm taking notes on this as well because this is so interesting to me. It really does reflect some very similar patterns that we are seeing elsewhere. In the kind of districts that saw an Obama/Trump swing, people generally do have different analyses of what kind of Democrat could win. This means that among people working to revitalize local Democratic politics, things can be really conflicted: because people genuinely have very sincere and very different ideas about what is the route for Democrats to win there. And because it's the kind of district where there's very genuinely not a single answer to that question.

And so, I think part of what ends up being experienced by people, is a pulling in opposite directions, that is at some level rooted in the kind of district you are in, which maybe has parts that are those upscale suburbs and other parts where you have a population that is less economically secure, less highly educated, people who are more traditional lunch-pail Democrats and have been thinking that today's Democratic Party may not be for them. Often, these are counties that would be classified not as urban suburbs but as middle suburbs: somewhat less well-off, less pervasively college-educated, more union-heavy. In places like that, the new grassroots often include some people who feel pretty strongly like "Bernie would've won" and "we've got to offer a more radical vision of making a society more equal and that's the only way we're going to get to win" and then you've got other people who say "that doesn't sound right to me, that's not why I'm here." Part of what those positions reflect is that genuinely there are different possible alternative routes for the Democratic Party.

And so then, the challenge for organizers is to not feel that we need to convince each other because at some times, we're both right. Instead the goal can be to focus on how we build local structures of dialogue so we can function. On some things we're just going to agree to disagree and maybe just choose not to have that set of arguments.

If you've been successful in building a local structure within which people can engage even when they have different, heartfelt analyses of what's going on, and different preferences and different policy priorities, then your challenge is not to overcome and end those differences, but to sustain a system that is capable of encompassing different views.

That is such wise advice. I'm trying to think of how we could try and apply that. It has saddened me that we started out creating this infrastructure and working so well together and having such success in 2017. Now this steering committee, the Southampton Progressive Caucus, has tensions within it from these different factions which have turned into such a lack of trust with each other that I don't think we can get everyone together in a room. But I want to switch gears a bit and look beyond my township, to the congressional district. For all our tremendous organizing and grassroots work, we were not able to flip our district. We came close. Our GOP congressman won by 16 points in 2016 and he only won by 4 in 2018.
Wow.

It was a dramatic difference but it wasn't enough and I think that has exacerbated these divisions. There are people who say, "If the more progressive candidate had been the nominee, it would have energized Democrats." On the other side, there are people who say, "Yeah, but so many of you ultra-progressives didn't work for the nominee because you didn't consider him progressive enough." It's hardened the divisions. In reading your last piece, you seem much more optimistic about 2020 than I am at this point in terms of how the grassroots, the anti-Trump movement, is going to impact the 2020 election, maybe because I see our anti-Trump movement as more divided.
This is why I think it's important to think about what is happening not in terms of a movement but rather in terms of a new kind of engagement, one that encompasses a pretty wide range of ideologies and a wide range of analyses of what's going on and what has brought participants into action in the same place, kind of together and kind of not together. Then the question does not have to be how can we all get on the same page: which is good, because I don't think that's going to happen, and it's not going to happen for different reasons in different places.

If it were the case that it is a single movement with a single ideology and everyone has to get on board or not participate, then that's pretty limited how many people it can involve, and how much impact it can have.

But if we think of it in terms of an ecosystem and in terms of infrastructure, we can recognize that there is fundamental and encompassing change under way. We've got an ecosystem growing in which a whole lot more energy has been added into the local politics. Yes, there's a lot more tension, but there's also a lot more people who met up, started doing things, and met other people. So, the challenge is not to all agree, but to find ways to make the infrastructure sustainable and effective. You don't need to be pushing everyone to be the same.

Rather, the question is, are you allowing people to engage in different ways that are, despite their differences, building momentum toward the much broader common goal of civic engagement and the rebuilding of a healthier political life.

There are going to be some places where goals coincide and others where it is more conflictive. The local Democratic Committee place is one place where, you know, people get elected and then decisions need to be made. So, by definition that is sometimes going to be more conflictive. But it's actually super healthy for the open conflict to exist, because if everyone is convinced they are being heard, then no one's saying, "I'm going to take my marbles and go home." No one is saying, "The Council vote was rigged against me and all my people are leaving." People are just saying, "Wow, that was really frustrating, I needed cooling off time." But if they're sticking with it, then that's actually a really fruitful place for that conflict to be happening: even if it doesn't feel good.

It doesn't feel good but you are right because at the same time nobody has left.

So that's great. You should all congratulate yourselves. That's awesome! You are part of a structure where people are sticking it out and care enough to argue, and at least are in a face-to-face relationship, and are in agreement that this is an enterprise worth arguing through. On some things you're going to disagree and vote and you're stuck with the results, but you have other things you are going to continue to collaborate on. This is part of what's healthy about an ecosystem in which you have, let's say, different groups. Different groups can bring different things, in terms of the activities that they're doing. Maybe some groups are all about canvassing for the local candidate. Other groups are maybe doing postcards, other groups are doing a letter to the editor campaign. The groups are also different in terms of the degree to which they choose activities that do or don't require ideologically uniformity.

So, if we are writing and canvassing together for a local D.A. candidate, we can decide we don't need to be in complete agreement about whether you support Medicare for All or not. For the local D.A. we're going to find that basic adequate overlap for action, and we're going to work together, and on other things we're not. And so that's what can make you, if you step back and watch the bigger picture, in the long haul more effective. It's important that people find some places where they can be involved in meaningful action together, even as there are other places, like those uncomfortable, local Party committee meetings, where people have agreed to kind of argue it out.

It is also possible over time, having occasions for joint action that don't require a lot of ideological consensus, can help make those difficult arguments a little less fraught and a little more fruitful. Activities where people from different groups with different views come together, like a protest, can help create informal cross-cutting ties between people who are usually on different sides of debates. So, you come to know that when you need a bunch of people to show up and speak out about X and Y, you know that you can rely on them. Even though you also know that there are other things that you really, really disagree on. Maybe you don't even like the way you disagree, you don't like the terms that they use but that's okay because it's a genuine disagreement, it is a heart-felt disagreement, and you're still finding ways that you can have informal structure that has you working in the same broad area of local regional politics and arguing when you have to argue.

Because you also have some of these cross-cutting moments together, that are face-to-face engagements so you do not just attack each other on Facebook, and over time you're going to find your way into that space when you can start rebuilding a little trust.

That really captures my experience and many others I have interviewed. We came to the grassroots after Trump's election, we went to the Women's March, we created our huddle, and maybe because it wasn't about electoral politics, it wasn't even about the Democratic Party, we came together and formed a community, so we didn't feel so alone. But the local politics and the Democratic Committee do not have that same feeling of community.
Totally understand. On the one hand, the goal is to create an ecosystem in which everyone, you and everyone else who wants to be involved, has some spaces with a social network where it is reinforcing a common mission, where you adore each other, and you're working together, and you're on the same page. But you also need to have some spaces with some agreed upon structures and rules and transparency that are going to bring you and your network of people into a space of dialogue—and even sometimes uncomfortable dialogue—with people who are coming from a very different place. The Democratic Committee is now playing that role for you, just like Democratic Committees are now in many places. These have become places where people actually argue about things that matter: or argue about really small procedural details or local disputes that are part of these broader issues. And it's a productive place to be having those arguments.

I agree though right now I'm not sure yet whether those arguments are productive because there is a danger that we're going to lose seats on the Town Council this year because of events that resulted from this fracturing. We want to be this big tent, but I'm afraid it could end up being

counter-productive where we end up losing some of the gains we've made because of actions that stemmed from these disagreements.
It is entirely possible that if those fractures and disagreements move into, "I'm definitely not going to support so-and-so even though that's what the committee has voted on or is endorsing," yes, things break down. On the other hand, and it's not that I want to be to be Pollyanna-ish about this, but however it plays out, people can learn from that. If there is a really heartbreaking loss at the local level, maybe that's a necessary part of the learning process. Each one of us individually and in our groups need to engage in serious thinking about what can work and what can change and what can happen. And we make choices, and see how they play out, and we learn from it. As long as that learning seems to grow then it remains productive, even when sometimes, you know, there are painful fights and also sometimes there are maybe losses that could have been avoided.

Grassroots democracy carries that risk. When lots of people with different ideas are given a genuine stake, sometimes that's going to end up with sub-optimal outcomes. But my own sense is that on balance, that's still a healthier system than one with fewer people fully vested in trying.

It is encouraging for me to hear that. Which leads into another question. Do you see what we've been creating the last two years, this infrastructure, as something sustainable post-Trump?
Absolutely. I think there's no question that if you look back at the recent history of the Right, it was energized local networks very similar to these that have fueled the sustained rise of the Republican Party. If you look back at what laid the ground work for the Tea Party, if you look back at the rise of the religious right, the places where you could see that rise first was in local school board races. It happened in places all across the country where some people on the right who felt their values were challenged and felt like their country was going in the wrong direction, became super energized and very focused and did an extremely effective job of mobilizing their social networks, including networks of people who were home schooling their kids and so on, and mobilized those networks for political impact in elections.

And then that didn't die down once people got elected to those school boards because, the story in political organizing is always more- the more you do, the more you're capable of doing more. And so that movement of local engagement became the seed bed of a whole bunch of people who then went onto to run for town council or county legislature. And those conservative networks and connections that were built were then able, in the wake of Barack Obama's election, to make this huge jump forward as a whole bunch of people who thought that Barack Obama's election did not fit with their vision of what they wanted. When they stepped forward, they didn't step forward into nothing, they were stepping into local Republican ecosystems that were already pretty vibrant and engaged because of this local, connective work that people on the religious right had been doing.

After 2009 it wasn't just about school boards and town councils, they flipped state house seats, they flipped congressional districts. At that point they also had more resources pouring in from national Republican funders, but it was never just about those external resources. Rather, you had this genuinely powerful combination of new people stepping into an infrastructure that was there for that use, and channeling that emotion into electoral action.

And in all these years, there was nothing like it on the left. Quite the contrary. It was the absolute opposite.

I feel like I was one of those people responsible for not creating that infrastructure. I was part of OFA, I went to Pennsylvania, New York's sister state to campaign for Obama and then he won and I went back to my life. I was one of those people who didn't even know who my town council members were.

There are so many stories like yours. It's so striking to me how often post-'16 grassroots leaders have this same backstory of involvement in the first Obama campaign. I recently co-authored an op-ed in the *Washington Post* that spelled out just how many people got involved in that Obama campaign and then how that surge of involvement disappeared. And it disappeared because it never occurred to people from the bottom up, nor leaders from the top down, that people should, in the wake of Obama's election, still run for their local county races, their local Democratic committees.

I also think a big part of it was the economic collapse, the Great Recession. Suddenly many of us were fighting for our livelihoods and to hold on to our homes so that put a real damper on activism. But also, I never got a call from anyone at OFA saying, "I met you knocking on doors in Pennsylvania, come join the Democratic Committee."

Exactly. And just stop and think about it now, in your role as group organizer: if you had a list of people who had done something in the electoral campaign that just took off, you know, two months ago, you'd be calling all of those people to get them to a meeting, right?

Oh, absolutely! OFA must have had a list. Did they just not share it with local groups?

That's literally what happened. OFA got involved in this debate between people who wanted the list of everything that OFA had created. Some people wanted to turn that over to the DNC, who were going to own it as a super list and as a potential donor list, and other people wanted to hold it and keep it as property of the Obama campaign. But, essentially, they treated it as a database of potential donors, rather than as a human ecosystem. No one suggested, let's help people run for local Democratic Committee spots, or let's get some people start organizing the community around X and Y. This was not on the radar screen. And meanwhile in 2009, the folks who were organizing Tea Party groups were finding every available form of organizing and meeting each other at protests and they were following up with each other—and nothing similar was happening on the left. And on a very basic level, that's led to exactly where we are today in terms of the balance of state house legislatures, in terms of who controlled the 2010 redistricting process or the redistricting after the 2010 census and so on.

We weren't successful in the congressional district but we were more successful on the state level and in turn we have seen this year, a whole range of progressive legislation that we've been waiting in New York for decades to have, like early voting. So, yes, I really see that difference, locally and state-wise, exactly what you're talking about.
What you are describing is this big interconnected system, and, exactly, there are lots of different threads. So, taking control of the state legislature not only impacts a lot of very important legislative policies, but also has implications for things like redistricting that in turn have implications for things like national politics.

Part of why I think it's actually productive and a good thing that what's happening on the center-to-left today isn't a centralized movement with highly coordinated agenda-setting and prioritization, is that for people with groups like yours, you've got a lot of different potential priorities. You are focusing on township politics, regional politics, flipping a state legislature seat, the congressional district: and it turns out there are lots of synergies between them. You're building the personal connections so that the next time that there's an active presidential election going on, you've got a broader range of people to call on and they have a broader range of experience of what voters might be thinking on Long Island and so on. So, the fact that everyone doesn't have to be on exactly the same page in terms of political priorities in order to be working on a concrete task is helping groups like yours across the country build local capacity. And that's a really good thing, a real advantage.

You're really helping me to see there is a much bigger picture beyond just the congressional race and to look at this ecosystem we have created, which

didn't exist before, which will hopefully go on past the Trump years, past the congressional race.
And once there is a Democratic candidate, their campaign is going to be so much better off because the local infrastructure will be there, the infrastructure that wasn't there before. And you will have people who are engaged and who actually do know each other, with social networks of people with different views. Being able to mobilize and engage with those different viewpoints is going to make the next congressional candidate more effective, is going to make the next presidential candidate and their campaign more effective. But if the only people you are interacting with and building connections to are people who have just your same vision, it would mean that you're not getting out, you're not reaching out broadly enough to the full range of potential Democrats you need to reach. So, in some sense, within a county, the more people are arguing in the Democratic meetings, the better I think that that county is doing in terms of pulling in the full range of potential Democrats in that place.

That's an optimistic view which I fervently hope is correct. My last question is where do you see this whole ecosystem playing out if, God forbid, Trump is reelected in 2020?
To me, part of the reason I think it's so important that so many groups like your own have gotten involved in local-level politics and state-level politics, is if Trump is reelected, with the radical remaking of the federal judiciary, which has already been speeding along for the last three years, it's just going to accelerate and a whole bunch of things that people have come to rely on as basic fundamental rights supported by America's courts will be threatened. And so, there's going to be a huge shift towards state legislatures as the critical battlegrounds. The state legislatures are already super important but the difference that state laws will make on real lives under a potential second Trump administration would be massive.

I know how emotionally devastating another Trump victory would be for everyone doing the work that you are, but my prediction would be that people who have the experience of working together in local and state-level politics, those people would just pour even more energy into state-level initiatives, as they should.

And again, that's one of the advantages of the fact that this pattern of engagement has grown organically in place after place, with local groups learning more and then figuring out what else they need to know. So, the very nature of having grown organically from the real grassroots up has meant that people have an increasingly sophisticated and detailed understanding of how local and state-level politics work in their region and why it matters.

Speaking with Professor Putnam was enlightening for me. I looked forward to reading her chapters in the book co-edited by Theda Skocpol and Caroline Tervo, when it comes out in January.

My conversation with Professor Putnam brought back the memories of how we founded the SPC. At that time, I thought it would be an important conduit between the Democratic Party and the grassroots, a key player in this new ecosystem that she described. But it has been dormant in 2019. I knew it would not be easy to put the broken parts of this group back together. After all, LVLZ was a founding grassroots member. But it felt too sad to me to just throw it away. I sent an email to the group with an update on the book and mentioned Professor Putnam's analysis:

> *The last section of my book includes a conversation I had with a historian who has been studying the anti-Trump movement. According to her research, our experiences in both creating the SPC and the subsequent tensions we have experienced relating to the 2018 election and what the direction should be for the Democratic Party are not unusual for our kind of suburban district. And in fact, can be a sign of strength. Her data shows that the anti-Trump groups that have experienced often severe push/pulls about policy can, if they can agree to disagree and respect the other side's point of view, emerge stronger and more effective at transforming their districts. Her assessment for the reason for this is that they are not trapped in their own ideological bubble but instead have learned how to listen to and tolerate multiple points of views and by so doing have a greater ability to reach and persuade the voters in their districts.*
>
> *I would like to believe that she is correct. Her evaluation gives me some hope that we can find a way to come back together for the battle that is going to be 2020, in our district and in the presidential race.*

Syma emailed me back to say it was a "spectacular" email and thanked me for sharing it. Robin and I spoke in person. Despite her disappointments over what had transpired with both the chairmanship challenge and the court cases, she was not averse to seeing if we could move forward with the SPC but first we would need much discussion about which grassroots groups would be included. She told me she would always be happy to work with EEAN and PEER. Speaking to Andi, she agreed. She also suggested returning to what we had done best in 2018, which was hosting forums and debates for the candidates.

I did not hear back from anyone else. But it was a beginning.

Chapter 28

The 2020 Election Begins

"As for me, my life has always been about defying expectations. To do things that people said were impossible or improbable. When I'm down, I rebound. I get back up and I come out fighting."

Perry Gershon speaking at the announcement that he is running again in 2020

Five months after the midterm election, while I was busy conducting my post-election analysis, I got an email from Perry inviting me to an event where he was going to announce he is running again next year. I asked him if I could cover it for the book and he agreed. Here, I thought, is the fitting final chapter for this saga. With the midterm election in the rearview mirror, we now look straight ahead to the 2020 race. So, on April 3rd, I traveled with Wendy and Cindy to a restaurant in Brookhaven for the kick off of Perry's campaign.

Wendy had been involved for months with Perry's "kitchen cabinet" and in the car, she explained to us why she was all in for his 2020 campaign.

"When I was asked if I would be willing to join a group of active volunteers from Perry's 2018 campaign to provide him with feedback and advice to further strengthen his candidacy for a second run in 2020, I immediately said yes for a number of reasons," she said.

"First, I believe that with a presidential election in 2020, CD1 cannot afford to have a candidate starting from scratch without name recognition. Perry Gershon started with none in his first race and through persistence and a well-funded campaign managed to make his name known to the majority of voters in CD1. Secondly, while working closely with Perry and his staff in 2018, I came to admire his work ethic, his knowledge and willingness to learn what he didn't know, his ability to grasp complex issues, and his thoughtful assessment of what issues affected CD1 residents and how best to address them. Lastly, he's a good, decent, honest man, perhaps "old-fashioned" values, but do those ever really go out of style? I know if he's successful and becomes our representative, Perry will work hard every day to do the best for each and every resident of our district, trying to make their lives fairer, healthier, and with expanded opportunities for all."

We got there very early to help set up, though there wasn't much for us to do, a lot of other Perry supporters were already taking care of the preparations. The restaurant had a large, open room in the back with a small stage in front and a sound system. When we arrived, musicians were practicing on the stage and testing out the sound system. A few people were putting up Perry signs around the room.

As more people arrived, it was like a reunion for many of Perry's staff. I saw Dan and other people I recognized from the campaign. We said hello to Perry's son, Logan, who was helping with the sound system as well as Perry's wife, Lisa, when she arrived. Some people ordered lunch, sitting and eating at a row of tables alongside the wall in the large room. Wendy and Cindy sat down for lunch.

Dick Sheehan and his wife, Carolyn, arrived and we talked a bit about what was happening with the SHDems. Dick and I joined at the same time, in fact we were introduced at the same general meeting and we shared the same focus – the grave threat to the country posed by Trump and Trumpism. We both had little patience for the small, divisive group of SHDems that kept making every meeting so contentious. Dick has taken on even more responsibility with the committee since he is now a regional coordinator.

As we were talking, several people came up and said hello to me, remembering me from the EEAN postcard parties and candidate forums. They already knew Wendy and Cindy and I introduced them to Dick and Carolyn. There was a festive mood in the room.

Perry arrived to great applause. He made the rounds of the room, greeting supporters. When he came over to where we were standing, we hugged and talked briefly about the book. He told me he was glad I was going to finish the book; I had mentioned to him right after the election that I wasn't sure what I was going to do with the project. We agreed that his announcement about running again was a nice ending to our story.

As it got closer to 2:00 PM, the room became more crowded. There were trays of appetizers being passed around by waiters and people went to the bar to get drinks. There were several children running around and the sound of one baby crying. Music was playing.

I stood towards the back of the room, away from the speakers, because it was a little too loud for me and I found a shelf to lean on so that I could take notes and have a place to position my phone in order to record the announcement.

Perry was introduced by Pat Halpin, a Democratic politician I didn't know. I learned he had been the Suffolk County Executive. In his introduction, he said, "Perry you have to run again, because we need you. We need someone who's going to fight."

Halpin was a natural politician. In his remarks, he spoke without notes and walked around the stage, making eye contact with the audience. He had an ease that Perry just doesn't have, even though I know how hard he has worked at getting better at this.

By the time Perry took the stage, the crowd was applauding and chanting Perry's name.

He spoke for about 15 minutes, talking about the different issues that are important to the district, such as climate change, immigration, the opioid crisis and the economy and how Zeldin did not address the needs of the district. He also commented on the Democratic Party and zeroed in on healthcare, which was the key focus for the campaign last year.

"As Democrats, we're a big tent party. We've got a mix of ideals and visions to guide us, but there are certain things that tie us together. We believe in the rule of law. We believe in equality and we believe in social justice. As a party, we stand for universal healthcare, because healthcare is a right, not a privilege."

He talked about the inroads we made in 2018, laying the foundation and infrastructure for going forward and the importance of the Democrats taking back the House. He introduced the great candidates running in Brookhaven this year and welcomed the local Democratic Committee chairs who were there, like Gordon.

He pointed to the success we had turning out the Democratic vote in Southampton and East Hampton. He encouraged everyone to work hard in 2019 for all the candidates running this year, including Steve Bellone, who is up for reelection as County Executive.

He reminded everyone what was at stake by listing Zeldin's votes in Congress. He emphasized how much we are being hurt by the tax law and outlined the ongoing horror that is the Trump administration. He told us that these are the reasons he is running again in 2020.

"I fought hard for my family, for myself, and now I want to fight hard for the people here on Long Island. And you know what? Failure is not an acceptable answer, and that's why I'm going to be running again in 2020."

There were loud cheers from the crowd. He was joined on stage by several family members, including Lisa, Logan and his parents, who I recognized from his television advertisements. While the musicians played, the crowd clapped and chanted "Perry, Perry, Perry!" Campaign staffers walked around with clipboards getting names and email addresses.

And just like that, the 2020 race to oust Zeldin began.

Within days, the campaign posted a fundraising link and a picture from the Saturday announcement .[66]

DEFEATING LEE ZELDIN IN 2020

It doesn't take an outsider to see the old ways, the divisive Lee Zeldin and Donald Trump ways, just aren't working – not for Long Island families, not for America.
That's why, this weekend, I kicked off my campaign for Congress, and why I'm asking for your support.

<u>Please donate $5 today and let's get this campaign going together.</u>

> It was great to be joined by over 200 supporters, including elected officials and town Democratic chairs. With your support, we will turn NY-1 blue again and unseat Lee Zeldin in November 2020. Thanks to all that came, to my family for joining me on stage, and to former County Executive Pat Halpin for his wonderful introduction and words of encouragement.
>
> Our nation has too many pressing issues for us to stand for any more of the Lee Zeldin and Donald Trump agenda.
>
> **Prosperity for all families. Climate change. The gun violence epidemic. These are just a few of the issues that we must address before it's too late.**
>
> The road to 2020 is going to be tough. The entrenched Washington D.C. special interests that bankroll Lee Zeldin aren't going to let him go down without a big fight.
>
> **Your grassroots support had us knocking on the door to victory in 2018. And it will put us over the top in 2020. Donate today to kick off this campaign.**
>
> **I look forward to walking the road to 2020 with you. We have a lot of work ahead of us. And I know we're up to the challenge.**
>
> Onward,
> **Perry**
> Posted on April 7, 2019.

Unlike in the early part of the primary last year when we could not get coverage from the local newspapers, everyone covered his announcement. Such is the advantage of having run last year and now having name recognition in the district.

Some of the articles mentioned other candidates who might run, including Nancy Goroff, chair of the chemistry department at Stony Brook University. (Later in the summer, she formally announced her candidacy, confirming that she will indeed be running in the primary. Her website is "Goroff for Congress."[67]

Right after Perry's announcement, I turned to my sources and asked them what they thought about Perry running again. Their answers ranged from negative to non-committal to supportive.

Dick Sheehan, SHDems

"As to 2020, I am hopeful but truly afraid that Zeldin and Trump could very well win again in 2020. We Democrats are shooting ourselves in the foot in so many ways. I am concerned that the progressive wing of our party may result in (a) the wrong nominee for POTUS & (b) that we may end up NOT united at the end of the nominating process. I fear that Perry is not the right candidate for all of CD1. He's strong out here in the Hamptons but he doesn't play well in the western part of our congressional district. I wish that I had a more optimistic viewpoint but this is my unvarnished opinion."

Andi Klausner, SHDems

"Even though he didn't win last year he got closer than anyone has and we have to remember that Lee Zeldin had the name recognition and was the incumbent so it was hard. And Perry was learning, he was a newcomer to the political process. I think he's grown a lot. I think his chances this time will be better."

Robin Long, SHDems

"We have got to change the dialogue. You can't change the voter. You can't change the prejudice. You can't change the inbred anti-Semitism. You're going to fight that, you're not changing that. But we can change the dialogue to a winning dialogue and that is, 'Your family is not going to exist if the finances in this country continue the way they're going.' Morality means nothing to people. But money does. We might need a candidate from a union, a fireman, a cop, a policeman, somebody from the military. Or we need to tune Perry up to better address these issues."

Steven Kramer, Indivisible Northfork

"A lot of folks in the grassroots are hoping for a unicorn candidate that can magically beat Zeldin. They forget Perry narrowed the gap from 16% to 4%, not by magic, but through hard work, diligence and engaging the grassroots. If he can manage in the next year to build bridges with the Democratic Party and strengthen his efforts with the grassroots such that ALL forces (at peak strength) are pulling together in 2020, there is no reason he should not be able to win the seat. I do not see any other candidate with the necessary name recognition, grassroots

AND Democratic Committee buy in or existing campaign infrastructure to make that happen."

Wendy Turkington, EEAN

"It would be great if we had somebody from Brookhaven, but nobody has stepped up. He's permanently living in East Hampton now, he is a resident, not just a summertime person, and he's doing his homework. Those kitchen cabinets he created gave him a great deal of feedback."

Syma Gerard, EEAN

"I'm finding his dedication interesting, and his willingness to work and change and learn, I think that's really interesting. He's staying out here, and now getting to know a lot of people out here."

We were not the only ones already looking ahead to the next race against Zeldin. The different political sites that analyze House races had also started projecting the 2020 races. They all still listed the district as Republican for 2020, ranging from lean Republican to likely Republican. Despite our narrowing the gap in 2018, it did not change their view that Zeldin had the advantage.

The DCCC announced their list of targeted GOP districts for 2020 and NY01 was on the list. Then the RNC identified the eight most vulnerable GOP members and Zeldin was on that list. It mentioned that he only won reelection last year by a margin of 4%. I found it gratifying that both sides of the aisle viewed him as vulnerable.

After Perry announced, I reached out to Congressman Zeldin's press office to request an interview. Using their online form, I explained that I was publishing a book about the Resistance and the midterm election and was requesting a comment from him about facing Perry again in 2020. I also wanted to ask about the rumors in the press that he might follow some other GOP congressmen who have announced retirement rather than run next year. I did not receive a response.

We never did get a chance to sit down for our follow-up interview, but I emailed Perry a list of questions and he emailed me back his answers.

The responses I have heard from Democrats about your running again run the gamut from not happy to ecstatic. Clearly those who are thrilled need no convincing to support your candidacy. But what do you say to voters, who are not happy you are running again, and are assigning some responsibility to the 2018 loss to your campaign, that will convince them to give you their support?

The 2018 results should speak for themselves. Democratic turnout was at its highest level ever in a midterm election, and we brought a 16% deficit down to a more modest 4%, likely 3% if the third-party candidate had not been on the ballot. And we were successful without help from D.C. Our campaign learned much from the 2018 cycle and can apply those lessons in 2020. It will require much hard work, but I have a known name throughout the entire district now, which gives me a big advantage in challenging Zeldin.

You have stayed in the public eye since that election, wisely building on that name recognition. What other advantages do you bring to 2020 because you ran against Zeldin in 2018?
I developed a feel from 2018 of issues that motivate voters in NY-1, and the issues that do not move voters in this district. I am confident our campaign will demonstrate an ability to learn from its mistakes. I am very focused now on spending time with the groups that did not turn out for me – specifically the less politically active.

Is that the lesson learned from 2018, to focus on the groups that did not turn out for you?
It takes a lot of effort and time to become known in all corners of the district, but that is necessary if we are to beat Lee Zeldin.

Looking at the FEC filings, the long primary cost you a lot, leaving you not as much funding for the general election as Zeldin had. I have also heard he got a large influx of outside money. How do you prevent another primary fight leaving you short of funding come the general election?
That is an impossible question to answer in a democracy. One cannot prohibit other challengers from running in a primary. However, I can and will do the best job possible to demonstrate that I am the Democrat most likely to defeat Lee Zeldin.

***The New York Times* mentioned that Zeldin might be another GOP congressman who will retire rather than run again in 2020. You know him better than anyone, having run against him last year. Do you have a sense that he will retire rather than run?**
I would be very surprised if Zeldin were to retire. I am sure he dislikes being in the minority and can see the writing on the wall that his party is unlikely to take the House back in 2020. But he has raised over $1 million, most of it from corporations and PAC's. Zeldin is already selling his soul to special interests, so he will owe it to them to run again. I will not take any corporate PAC money, and I am here to represent the needs of NY-1.

There are growing concerns that the Democratic presidential candidates are creating a circular firing squad which would open the door to a Trump reelection. Where do you assess the presidential primary race at this point?
Too soon to tell. However, every one of our Democrats running for president would do a far better job for America than Trump has.

Nationally and within our district, there are disagreements among Democrats of how far to the left the party should go and what wins elections, centrist Democratic policies or more liberal policies. What do you think is the best answer to that question to win in NY01?
I believe in broad appeal. The Democratic nominee, or quite frankly every elected official, is there to represent everyone. Those who voted for him or her and those who did not.

It seemed to me that one of the hardest things in 2018 running against Zeldin was how to counter his blatant dishonesty, such as his claim that he supported protections for pre-existing conditions. Democrats don't seem to do a good job coming up with answers to the GOP lies. What will you do differently this time to push back against the GOP alternate reality?
We need to be vociferous in calling out the lies as soon as the statements are made. And to use every medium available to us.

Do you think healthcare will still be the number one issue in 2020?
Yes, especially its role in the general theme of the affordability of living on Long Island.

No matter how hard we tried when we were talking to voters, we could not communicate the negative impact the GOP tax bill was going to have on our district. Now that many of us have had to endure the higher tax bill this past April, do you think that the tax bill will resonate more with voters than it did last year?
Absolutely. Lee Zeldin voted for the first version of the tax bill, H Con Res 71 on October 5, 2017. He may have changed his mind along the way, but his first vote made the tax bill possible, and Zeldin cannot deny responsibility. Long Islanders were hurt badly when they paid their taxes last April, and memories are long. The number one issue I heard from people all summer is that taxes are too high – well the GOP tax plan is the reason things got worse.

Fear and immigration were also key issues nationally and in our district. I heard a lot about the caravan while out canvassing. How should Democrats address people's fears on this issue and at the same time expose the racism that is inherent in the Trump/Zeldin fear-mongering?

We need immigration reform. Democrats should not deny that fact, and I don't. The Senate passed bipartisan reform in 2013, and that needs to be a model for what we can do. But cruelty, family separation and many of Trump's tactics are completely un-American.

Do you think the 2020 race will essentially be a referendum on Trump? And does that help you or hurt you in our district, which went so big for Trump in 2016?
I believe Trump is in the process of self-destruction. It's a long process, but it unfolds daily. The tariffs are causing destruction in our markets and hurting real people, farmers and consumers. Ultimately, I see that as Trump's demise.

The anti-Trump grassroots groups in our district, groups like EEAN, LVLZ and PEER, certainly helped get out the vote in 2018. How big a role do you see their involvement in the 2020 race and do you think there are ways they can be more effective than they were in 2018?
The grassroots role was critical and must be repeated if we are to win in 2020. I hope our campaign and the grassroots organizations can integrate even more next year. The joint effort was one of the things I took pride in during the campaign. Even Zeldin saw its effects.

Epilogue

As I was finishing this manuscript, the Ukraine scandal erupted. Trump is now facing impeachment. For me, he has deserved to be impeached for a long time; for the abuse of power and obstruction of justice outlined in the Mueller report, for violating the emoluments clause, for being an unindicted co-conspirator in the Michael Cohen case. The integrity of the Constitution demands it. But if he is not convicted in the Senate, which is the likely outcome, does this embolden his base, making it "Kavanaugh and the caravan" writ large? And what would the impact be on Zeldin, one of Trump's biggest supporters?

I thought seriously about continuing this project through 2020. But as intriguing as that is, I decided to end the book as I planned. It is not that these new questions aren't important. They are. But they are not really part of this story, the story of the rise of the women of the Resistance. They are a different story, part of another book for another time.

This story ends as it began, with an election.

On November 5th, 2019, Matt and I walked up the steps of our local firehouse to vote. Eugene had already mailed back his absentee ballot weeks ago. It was Matt's first time voting on Election Day since the disastrous 2016 election. He voted by absentee ballot for 2017 and 2018 because he was away at graduate school. Finished with school and temporarily living at home as he determines his next step, he was able to join me in voting in person this year. We joked that our voting together brought my project full circle from three years ago.

That night, Mike Anthony and Dick Sheehan picked me up to attend the SHDems watch party. As before, there were two large screens in the room, one turned to national news and one to our local Southampton Township races. There were a lot of cheers that night. In national news, we cheered that a Democrat had won the governorship in Kentucky and that Democrats took control of their state legislature in Virginia. Just like in 2018, in both Kentucky and Virginia, it appeared that Democratic surges in the suburbs made all the difference.

The cheers were even louder when the local returns came in. All of our Democratic elected officials won reelection by very large margins. It wasn't even close. Craig didn't win - a Republican retained that Town Council seat – but the Democrats still maintained their supermajority and even picked up a Trustee seat. It was a great relief that the chaos from earlier in the year did not appear to be a factor in the election.

(In some post-election news: right before Thanksgiving and the publication of this book, Bridget Fleming who had easily won reelection as our representative to the Suffolk County Legislature, sent out an email announcing her decision to run in 2020 to oppose Lee Zeldin for Congress. She will be a formidable candidate, squaring off against Perry and Nancy Goroff in the primary.)

Looking at the 2019 election results, there was much to be happy about. Still, there were red flags.

First, Democrats did not fare as well in other townships here in CD#1 as in Southampton. That was not a good sign for next year's congressional race. Second, though we don't have the final numbers yet, turnout locally appeared to be low, closer to 2015 numbers than 2017. Third, people who worked on the campaigns reported a dramatic drop in volunteer participation in comparison to the last two elections which certainly made GOTV harder. And fourth, many committee members were either absent from the 2019 election process or working against the endorsed candidates. In fact, the Democrat who won a Trustee seat was not the endorsed candidate. The divisions within the committee continued. As happy as we all were watching the election results, the celebration was smaller than the last two I attended.

We have come a long way since the 2016 election and in almost every way, 2019 was a good year for Democrats. But if we are going to be successful in 2020, if we are to power the second blue wave, then the red flags need to be resolved.

Impeachment and the 2020 election, these are tough battles ahead. The burden is heavier when we are not united. To reclaim and rebuild our democracy, we must first work at reconciliation. The mistrust within the Democratic Party has to stop. Trump is exhausting and dispiriting but so is Democratic divisiveness. They both depress turnout and encourage voter apathy.

President Obama told us in 2008, "We are the change we seek." There is no savior coming to do it for us. It is up to us to protect the rule of law and foster the policies this country needs. Healthcare, gun reform, climate change, income inequality, student debt, wage stagnation, social justice; time is running out.

It isn't easy and a big tent is messy. But we are one Resistance, grassroots and Democratic Party, two halves of the same whole. If we nurture our progressive ecosystem together, for the long haul, we can create a country that works for everyone.

To all of you who have been part of this journey, from the Women's March to today, I implore you to not lose heart and not give up. Each of you is needed for the fight ahead. I know you are tired. So am I. I know at times you feel discouraged. So do I. I know some days you would like to just tune it all out. So would I.

But I ask you to remember how you felt when you first donned your pink pussy hat and marched down Pennsylvania Avenue, chanting "This is what democracy looks like" and "We're not going to go away." Remember why you marched, why you joined a huddle, why you made phone calls, why you knocked on doors, why you wrote postcards. Remind yourself who it was for – for our country, for women, for our children and for us. We are an important part of that equation. For me, without this movement, I would have consigned myself to the darkness. Instead, activism and the friends I have made ushered in the light.

And so, the work goes on.

One day, in late September, Wendy picked me up and we headed to The Dark Horse Restaurant in Riverhead where EEAN was participating with Indivisible Northfork for their Action Wednesday. This was part of our being "nimble," joining with another group whose mission aligned with ours. The action this day involved writing postcards and stuffing envelopes with flyers to inform voters about the schedule for the new in-person early voting here on the East End.

Wendy and I talked in the car on the way there. It felt good to reconnect. So busy finishing the book, I had not been to a meeting in months. When we got to the restaurant, we walked in to this large room, a now familiar place, the site of so many grassroots events since 2017. Late afternoon sunlight streamed in from the wall of windows on one side. Seated at tables were members of Indivisible Northfork and EEAN. Patty and Cindy weren't able to get away from work in time to make it but the rest of the leadership ladies were there. Everyone looked up when we walked in and smiled and waved. We smiled and waved back.

We asked if we should work on postcards or flyers and were told the postcards were done so we should focus on the flyers. Wendy and I picked up a pile of the flyers and envelopes then headed to a nearby table. We found two empty seats. I took off my jacket, sat down at the table and put my purse on the floor beside me. Before getting started, I paused for a minute and looked around the room, taking it all in. At a nearby table, I heard Syma laugh in response to a story that Sharon was telling her. Next to me, Wendy was catching up with an Indivisible Northfork member at our table. At the front of the room, Rebecca and Steven Kramer were standing over a calendar and planning the next event. Across from us, Nancy Rose was stacking up boxes filled with the completed postcards and envelopes that were ready to mail.

I smiled. Then I picked up a flyer and neatly fit it into the envelope.

Index

A

B

C

D

T

U

V

W

X

Y

Z

Footnotes

Part I – Looking Back at the Beginning: 2017

Chapter 2: Finding My Way and Joining a Huddle

[1] New York State Legislative Task Force on Demographic Research and Reapportionment, "2012 Congressional Maps - Congressional District 1," *New York State Legislative Task Force on Demographic Research and Reapportionment*, 2012, www.latfor.state.ny.us/ (accessed Dec. 3, 2019).

[2] U.S. Census Bureau, et al, "My Congressional District 116th Congress," *U.S. Census Bureau*, 2018, www.census.gov/mycd/?st=36&cd=01 (accessed Dec. 3, 2019); U.S. Census Bureau (2018), *American Community Survey 1-year estimates*, Retrieved from *Census Reporter Profile page for Congressional District 1, NY*, https://censusreporter.org/profiles/50000US3601-congressional-district-1-ny/ (accessed Nov. 30, 2019).

[3] Suffolk County Board of Elections, "Final Results of General Election on Tuesday, November 8, 2016, President and Vice President," *Election Night Tally*, Nov. 8, 2016, apps2.suffolkcountyny.gov/boe/eleres/16ge/default.htm (accessed Nov. 30, 2019).

[4] ---, "Final Results of General Election on Tuesday, November 8, 2016, Representative in Congress, 1st Congressional District." *Election Night Tally*, Nov. 8, 2016, apps2.suffolkcountyny.gov/boe/eleres/16ge/default.htm (accessed 30 Nov. 2019).

[5] Barbara Weber-Floyd, Letter, *The Southampton Press,* Eastern ed. A:10, Feb. 23, 2017, http://digital.olivesoftware.com/Olive/APA/Southampton/#panel=document (accessed Nov. 30, 2019).

Chapter 3: Rebecca Dolber – The Outsider

[6] *Rebecca Dolber/R.E.D.*, 2019, http://www.rebeccadolber.com/ (accessed Nov. 30, 2019).

[7] Susan Hodara, "COMMUNITIES; Irvington Bans V-Word in Play's Ads," *The New York Times,* March 3, 2002,

https://www.nytimes.com/2002/03/03/nyregion/communities-irvington-bans-v-word-in-play-s-ads.html (accessed Nov. 30, 2019).

Chapter 4: The Democratic Party

[8] *JP Spata Southampton Town Democratic Club*, 2019, https://www.shdemclub.com/ (accessed Nov. 30, 2019)

Chapter 5: Robin Long – The Party Insider

[9] James Barron, "Tangled Strands: Anatomy of the New York City Scandal," *The New York Times*, March 23, 1983, https://www.nytimes.com/1987/03/23/nyregion/tangled-strands-anatomy-of-the-new-york-city-scandal.html (accessed Nov. 30, 2019).

Chapter 7: Andrea Klausner – Career Activist

[10] Andrea Klausner, "Bio - This Woman's Work," *This Woman's Work*, 2019, www.thiswomansworkk.com/ (accessed Dec. 3, 2019).

Chapter 8: The Rest of 2017

[11] Barbara Weber-Floyd, Letter, *The Southampton Press*, Western ed. A:10, March 9, 2017, http://digital.olivesoftware.com/Olive/APA/Southampton/#panel=document (accessed Nov. 30, 2019)

[12] *Tax March*, 2019, https://taxmarch.org/ (accessed Nov. 30, 2019)

[13] Oliver Willis, "GOP Rep (Zeldin) brushes off town hall mom pleading for help for her heroin-addicted son," *Resist and Replace*, April 29, 2017, https://resistancesuffolk.blog/2017/04/29/gop-rep-zeldin-brushes-off-town-hall-mom-pleading-for-help-for-her-heroin-addicted-son/ (accessed Nov. 30, 2019)

[14] Robert Pear and Thomas Kaplan, "Senate Rejects Slimmed-Down Obamacare Repeal as McCain Votes No," *The New York Times*, July 27, 2017, https://www.nytimes.com/2017/07/27/us/politics/obamacare-partial-repeal-senate-republicans-revolt.html (accessed Nov. 30, 2019)

---

[15] Amanda Bernocco, "Democrats Sweep in Southampton Town Elections," *27east,* Nov. 9, 2017, http://www.27east.com/news/article.cfm/General-Interest-Southampton/539218/Democrats-Sweep-In-Southampton-Town-Elections (accessed Nov. 30, 2019)

[16] James Hohmann, "The Daily 202: Anti-Trump backlash fuels a Democratic sweep in Virginia and elections across the country," *The Washington Post*, Nov. 8, 2017, https://www.washingtonpost.com/news/powerpost/paloma/daily-202/2017/11/08/daily-202-anti-trump-backlash-fuels-a-democratic-sweep-in-virginia-and-elections-across-the-country/5a023fd230fb0468e76541b3/ (accessed Dec. 2, 2019)

Part II – Getting to Work: January 2018 – August 2018
Chapter 11: February 2018

[17] "Rep. Zeldin Hosts Pizza and Policy Town Hall in Westhampton Beach," *Congressman Lee Zeldin Representing New York's First District*, Feb. 13, 2018, https://zeldin.house.gov/media-center/press-releases/rep-zeldin-hosts-pizza-and-policy-town-hall-westhampton-beach
(accessed Nov. 30, 2019).

[18] Lisa Finn, "Hundreds Protest Outside Zeldin's Office, Demand Action On Guns," *Patch*, Feb. 21, 2018, https://patch.com/new-york/patchogue/hundreds-protest-gun-violence-outside-zeldins-office (accessed Nov. 30, 2019)

[19] Kate Riga, "Six Democrats Campaign For Chance to Challenge U.S. Representative Lee Zeldin In November," *27east*, Feb. 20, 2018, http://www.27east.com/news/article.cfm/East-End/548047/Six-Democrats-Continue-To-Campaign-For-Representative-Lee-Zeldins-Seat-Foreshadowing-A-Competitive-Primary (accessed Nov. 30, 2019)

Chapter 13: April 2018

[20] Avery Anapol, "Dems flip New York state seat that Republicans have held for four decades," *The Hill*, April 24, 2018, https://thehill.com/homenews/campaign/384746-dems-flip-new-york-state-seat-that-republicans-have-held-for-three-decades (accessed Nov. 30, 2019)

Chapter 14: May 2018

[21] East End Action Network, editor, "Southampton Progressive Caucus Democratic Primary Debate #1 – May 5th, 2018," *YouTube,* May 10, 2018, https://www.youtube.com/watch?v=Au0SNCFmBAM (accessed Dec. 1, 2019).

[22] Michael Bamberger, et al., "First Golfer: Donald Trump's relationship with golf has never been more complicated," *Golf,* Aug. 1, 2017, https://www.golf.com/tour-news/2017/08/01/president-donald-trump-relationship-golf-more-complicated-now (accessed Dec. 1, 2019).

[23] Rick Murphy, "Paul Davis Does Pechefsky," *The Independent*, May 15, 2018, https://indyeastend.com/news-opinion/south-fork/paul-davis-does-pechefsky/ (accessed Dec. 1, 2019).

[24] *Solidarity Sundays*, https://www.solidaritysundays.org/ (accessed Dec. 1, 2019).

[25] *Vote Like A Mother*, https://votelikeamother.org/ (accessed Dec. 1, 2019).

[26] *Take Action Suffolk County*, https://www.takeactionsuffolk.org/ (accessed Dec. 1, 2019).

[27] David Freedlander, "Why Long Island Still Loves Trump," *Politico Magazine*, May 23, 2018, https://www.politico.com/magazine/story/2018/05/23/donald-trump-ms-13-long-island-218417 (accessed Dec. 1, 2019).

[28] Christopher Peterson, "Congressional Review Act Reversal of CFPB Auto Lending Guidance Would Be Bad for Consumers, Bad for the Country," *Consumer Federation of America*, April 17, 2018, https://consumerfed.org/press_release/congressional-review-act-reversal-of-cfpb-auto-lending-guidance-would-be-bad-for-consumers-bad-for-the-country/ (accessed Dec. 1, 2019).

Chapter 15: June 2018

[29] Carol Polsky, "Progressive groups looking toward LI congressional primaries," *Newsday*, June 10, 2018, https://www.newsday.com/long-

island/politics/democrats-progressives-local-elections-1.18852728?pts=893559 (accessed Dec. 2, 2019).

[30] Suffolk County Board of Elections, "Final Results of Federal Primary on Tuesday, June 26, 2018," *Election Night Tally*, June 26, 2018, apps2.suffolkcountyny.gov/boe/eleres/18pf/default.htm (accessed Dec. 1, 2019).

[31] "With primaries over, LI congressional campaigns heat up," *News12 Long Island*, June 28, 2018, http://longisland.news12.com/story/38537377/with-primaries-over-li-congressional-campaigns-heat-up (accessed Dec. 1, 2019)

Chapter 16: July 2018

[32] Jill Filipovic, "Trump's worst enemy: Middle-aged moms," *CNN,* July 3, 2018, https://www.cnn.com/2018/07/03/opinions/trump-worst-enemy-middle-aged-moms-filipovic/index.html (accessed Dec. 1, 2019).

Chapter 17: August 2018

[33] Greg Wehner, "Trump Makes A Quick Stop," *The Southampton Press*, Western ed. A:1+, August 23, 2018, https://www.27east.com/search-archive/?type=current (accessed Dec. 1, 2019).

[34] Christopher Walsh, "Zeldin Takes Pass on Forum," *The East Hampton Star*, Aug. 23, 2018, https://www.easthamptonstar.com/archive/zeldin-takes-pass-forum (accessed Dec. 1, 2019).

[35] Nancy Lofholm, "Pathbreaking transgender attorney Danyel Joffe's work led to Colorado law compensating people wrongly convicted of crimes," *The Colorado Sun*, Aug. 24, 2018, https://coloradosun.com/2018/08/24/danyel-joffe-obituary/ (accessed Dec. 1, 2019).

Chapter 18: September 2018

[36] Bob Woodward, *Fear: Trump in the White House*, (New York: Simon & Schuster, 2018).

[37] Anonymous, "I Am Part of the Resistance Inside the Trump Administration," *The New York Times,* Sept. 5, 2018, https://www.nytimes.com/2018/09/05/opinion/trump-white-house-anonymous-resistance.html?rref=collection%2Fsectioncollection%2Fopinion&action=click&contentCollection=opinion®ion=rank&module=package&version=highlights&contentPlacement=6&pgtype=sectionfront (accessed Dec. 1, 2019).

[38] Charlie Savage, "Leaked Kavanaugh Documents Discuss Abortion and Affirmative Action," *The New York Times*, Sept. 6, 2018, https://www.nytimes.com/2018/09/06/us/politics/kavanaugh-leaked-documents.html?action=click&module=Top%20Stories&pgtype=Homepage (accessed Dec. 1, 2019).

[39] Lulu Bouvier, "Luluknits – About Us," *Luluknits*, luknits.com (accessed Dec. 1, 2019).

[40] T.E. McMorrow, "Zeldin and Gershon Square Off," *The Independent*, Sept. 11, 2018, https://indyeastend.com/news-opinion/south-fork/zeldin-and-gershon-square-off/ (accessed Dec. 1, 2019).

Part III - Race to the Finish: October to November 2018

Chapter 19: October 2018

[41] *The Setauket Neighborhood House*, http://www.setauketneighborhoodhouse.com/ (accessed Dec. 1, 2019).

[42] Jack Bryan, editor, *Active Measures*, https://www.activemeasures.com/ (accessed Dec. 1, 2019).

[43] Lisa W. Foderaro, "Will Too Much Love From Trump Be a Bad Thing for a Long Island Congressman?" *The New York Times*, Oct. 15, 2018, https://www.nytimes.com/2018/10/15/nyregion/lee-zeldin-trump-support.html?rref=collection%2Fsectioncollection%2Fnyregion&action=click&contentCollection=nyregion®ion=rank&module=package&version=highlights&contentPlacement=5&pgtype=sectionfront (accessed Dec. 1, 2019).

[44] U.S. Census Bureau, "QuickFacts Southampton town, Suffolk County, New York; Brookhaven town, Suffolk County, New York," *U.S. Census Bureau*, 2018, www.census.gov/quickfacts/fact/table/southamptontownsuffolkcountynewyork,brookhaventownsuffolkcountynewyork/PST045218 (accessed Dec. 2, 2019); U.S. Census Bureau, et al, "My Congressional District 116th Congress," *U.S. Census Bureau*, 2018, www.census.gov/mycd/?st=36&cd=01 (accessed Dec. 3, 2019); New York State Board of Elections, "NYS Voter Enrollment by Congressional District, Party Affiliation and Status," *2019 Enrollment by Election District/New York State Board of Elections*, 2019, www.elections.ny.gov/EnrollmentCD.html (accessed Dec. 2, 2019).

[45] The Editorial Board, "New York Times Endorses Antonio Delgado, Liuba Grechen Shirley, Perry Gershon, Anthony Brindisi, Tom Malinowski and Mikie Sherrill," *The New York Times*, Oct. 20, 2018, https://www.nytimes.com/2018/10/20/opinion/sunday/endorsements-house-congress-new-york-jersey.html (accessed Dec. 2, 2019).

[46] Justin Wise, "GOP lawmaker sends voters incorrect absentee ballot info," *The Hill*, Oct. 23, 2018, https://thehill.com/homenews/campaign/412768-gop-lawmaker-sends-mailer-to-voters-with-incorrect-absentee-ballot-info (accessed Dec. 2, 2019).

[47] Khorri Atkinson, "Republican congressman admits to sending inaccurate absentee ballot info," *Axios*, Oct. 23, 2018, https://www.axios.com/zeldin-voters-inaccurate-absentee-ballot-4bbb7cf1-03f1-42b4-adb5-932113385b8c.html (accessed Dec. 2, 2019).

[48] Rachel Maddow, "DOJ charged Russian woman, TRANSCRIPT: 10/22/2018, The Rachel Maddow Show," *MSNBC,* Oct. 22, 2018, www.msnbc.com/transcripts/rachel-maddow-show/2018-10-22 (accessed Dec. 2, 2019).

[49] Campbell Robertson, et al., "Quiet Day at a Pittsburgh Synagogue Became a Battle to Survive," *The New York Times*, Oct. 28, 2018, https://www.nytimes.com/2018/10/28/us/pittsburgh-synagogue-

shooting.html?action=click&module=Spotlight&pgtype=Homepage (accessed Dec. 2, 2019).

[50] The Editorial Board, "Perry Gershon to represent 1st Congressional District," *Newsday*, Oct. 28, 2018, https://www.newsday.com/opinion/editorial/perry-gershon-to-represent-1st-congressional-district-1.22504848?fbclid=IwAR2RNU4lCCLTqm5qpvi02cOD-vAVoeFuMmi97FMbnARw9BfidLTS7NzhXCY (accessed Dec. 2, 2019). Reprinted by license permission.

[51] "Gershon on defaced campaign signs: This is just pure hate," *News12 Long Island*, Oct. 30, 2018, http://longisland.news12.com/story/39381918/perry-gershon-campaign-signs-defaced-with-anti-gay-language?fbclid=IwAR2Jqs0Nyj3F9HRpVzCkcdqoaTJSpkH2wZ1C3zSxZUp43RZgheiXZJef8lo (accessed Dec. 2, 2019).

[52] Hampton Bays Union Free School District, editor, "Congressional Debate: Perry Gershon and Lee Zeldin," *YouTube,* Oct. 29, 2018, https://www.youtube.com/watch?v=L_-PCF4ckso&feature=youtu.be&fbclid=IwAR3PD5yu1FrrRWgOFztQe89gAwxkV7h8Wrk_6cKinsC_PRQ0VjpGNJMBAPk (accessed Dec. 2, 2019).

[53] Denise Civiletti, "Zeldin and Gershon go head-to-head in first public debate in the race for NY-01," *Riverhead Local*, Oct. 30, 2018, https://riverheadlocal.com/2018/10/30/zeldin-and-gershon-go-head-to-head-in-first-public-debate-of-the-race-for-ny-01/ (accessed Dec. 2, 2019).

Part IV- After the Election

Chapter 22: The Blue Wave

[54] Lawrence O'Donnell, "Trump fires Sessions, TRANSCRIPT: 11/7/2018, The Last Word with Lawrence O'Donnell," *MSNBC*, Nov. 7, 2018, http://www.msnbc.com/transcripts/the-last-word/2018-11-07 (accessed Dec. 2, 2019)

[55] Michelle Goldberg, "The Resistance Strikes Back, Two years of progressive organizing built the blue wave," *The New York Times*, Nov. 10, 2018,

https://www.nytimes.com/2018/11/10/opinion/sunday/democrats-resistance-women-georgia-trump.html (accessed Dec. 2, 2019).

[56] Suffolk County Board of Elections, "Final Results of General Election on Tuesday, November 6, 2018, Representative in Congress, 1st Congressional District ," *Election Night Tally*, Nov. 6, 2018, apps2.suffolkcountyny.gov/boe/eleres/18ge/default.htm (accessed Dec. 2, 2019).

[57] Denise Civiletti and Maria Piedrabuena, "Zeldin scores decisive victory over Gershon for U.S. Congress," *Riverhead Local*, Nov. 6, 2018, https://riverheadlocal.com/2018/11/06/zeldin-scores-decisive-victory-over-gershon-for-u-s-congress/ (accessed Dec. 2, 2019).

Chapter 24: Not the Same NY01

[58] Suffolk County Board of Elections, "Final Results of General Election on Tuesday, November 4, 2008, Representative in Congress, 1st Congressional District," *Election Night Tally*, Nov. 4, 2008, apps2.suffolkcountyny.gov/boe/eleres/08ge/default.htm (accessed Dec. 2, 2019).

[59] ---, "Final Results of General Election on Tuesday, November 4, 2014, Representative in Congress, 1st Congressional District," *Election Night Tally*, Nov. 4, 2014, apps2.suffolkcountyny.gov/boe/eleres/14ge/default.htm (accessed Dec. 2, 2019).

Chapter 25: How Goes the Grassroots?

[60] Office of the Supervisor of Elections, Polk County Florida, "Summary Results - Election Night/2018 General Election," *Lori Edwards, Polk County Supervisor of Elections*, June 5, 2019, enr.electionsfl.org/POL/Summary/1805/ (accessed 2 Dec. 2019).

Chapter 26: The SHDems

[61] United States, SUPREME COURT OF THE STATE OF NEW YORK Appellate Division, Second Judicial Department, *Lynch v. Duffy*, Docket no. 04168, May 29, 2019, *Justia U.S. Law*, https://law.justia.com/cases/new-york/appellate-division-second-department/2019/2019-04931.html (accessed Dec. 2, 2019).

Chapter 27: The Big Picture

[62] Lara Putnam and Theda Skocpol, "Middle America Reboots Democracy," *Democracy: A Journal of Ideas*, Feb. 20, 2018, https://democracyjournal.org/arguments/middle-america-reboots-democracy/ (accessed Dec. 2, 2019).

[63] Theda Skocpol and Caroline Tervo, editors, "Upending American Politics," *Oxford University Press*, 2020, https://global.oup.com/academic/product/upending-american-politics-9780190083533 (accessed Dec. 2, 2019).

[64] Lara Putnam, "Suburbs, Political Organizing Has Been Intense Since 2016. What Could It Mean for 2020?" *American Communities Project*, Aug. 6, 2019, https://www.americancommunities.org/in-pennsylvanias-exurbs-and-urban-suburbs-political-organizing-has-been-intense-since-2016-what-could-it-mean-for-2020/ (accessed Dec. 2, 2019).

[65] Lara Putnam and Gabriel Perez-Putnam, "Grassroots Blossom Across America, Reshaping Country's Political Geography," *American Communities Project*, Sept. 13, 2019, https://www.americancommunities.org/grassroots-blossom-across-america-reshaping-countrys-political-geography/ (accessed Dec. 2, 2019).

Chapter 29: The 2020 Election Begins

[66] "Defeating Lee Zeldin in 2020," *Perry Gershon for Congress 2020*, April 7, 2019, https://www.perrygershon.com/2019/04/07/defeating-lee-zeldin-2020/ (accessed Dec. 2, 2019).

[67] *Nancy Goroff for Congress*, 2019, https://www.goroffforcongress.com/ (accessed Dec. 2, 2019).

Works Cited

Anapol, Avery. "Dems flip New York state seat that Republicans have held for nearly four decades." *The Hill*, Capitol Hill Publishing, a subsidiary of News Communications, 24 Apr. 2018, thehill.com/homenews/campaign/384746-dems-flip-new-york-state-seat-that-republicans-have-held-for-three-decades. Accessed 30 Nov. 2019.

Anonymous. "I Am Part of the Resistance Inside the Trump Administration." *The New York Times*, The New York Times Company, 5 Sept. 2018, www.nytimes.com/2018/09/05/opinion/trump-white-house-anonymous-resistance.html?rref=collection%2Fsectioncollection%2Fopinion&action=click&contentCollection=opinion®ion=rank&module=package&version=highlights&contentPlacement=6&pgtype=sectionfront. Accessed 1 Dec. 2019.

Atkinson, Khorri. "Republican congressman admits to sending inaccurate absentee ballot info." *Axios*, Axios Media, 23 Oct. 2018, www.axios.com/zeldin-voters-inaccurate-absentee-ballot-4bbb7cf1-03f1-42b4-adb5-932113385b8c.html. Accessed 2 Dec. 2019.

Bamberger, Michael, et al. "First Golfer: Donald Trump's relationship with golf has never been more complicated." *Golf*, EB Golf Media, 1 Aug. 2017, www.golf.com/tour-news/2017/08/01/president-donald-trump-relationship-golf-more-complicated-now. Accessed 1 Dec. 2019.

Barron, James. "Tangled Strands: Anatomy of the New York City Scandal." *The New York Times*, The New York Times Company, 23 Mar. 1983, www.nytimes.com/1987/03/23/nyregion/tangled-strands-anatomy-of-the-new-york-city-scandal.html. Accessed 30 Nov. 2019.

Bernocco, Amanda. "Democrats Sweep In Southampton Town Elections." *27east*, The Press News Group, 9 Nov. 2017, www.27east.com/news/article.cfm/General-Interest-Southampton/539218/Democrats-Sweep-In-Southampton-Town-Elections. Accessed 30 Nov. 2019.

Bouvier, Lulu. "Luluknits - About Us." *Luluknits*, 2014, luknits.com/. Accessed 1 Dec. 2019.

Bryan, Jack, editor. *Active Measures*. Super LTD, 2018, www.activemeasures.com/. Accessed 1 Dec. 2019.

Civiletti, Denise. "Zeldin and Gershon go head-to-head in first public debate in the race for NY-01." *Riverhead Local*, East End Local Media , 30 Oct. 2018, riverheadlocal.com/2018/10/30/zeldin-and-gershon-go-head-to-head-in-first-public-debate-of-the-race-for-ny-01/. Accessed 2 Dec. 2019.

Civiletti, Denise, and Maria Piedrabuena. "Zeldin scores decisive victory over Gershon for U.S. Congress." *Riverhead Local*, East End Local Media, 6 Nov. 2018, riverheadlocal.com/2018/11/06/zeldin-scores-decisive-victory-over-gershon-for-u-s-congress/. Accessed 2 Dec. 2019.

"Defeating Lee Zeldin in 2020." *Perry Gershon for Congress 2020*, Perry Gershon for Congress, 7 Apr. 2019, www.perrygershon.com/2019/04/07/defeating-lee-zeldin-2020/. Accessed 2 Dec. 2019.

East End Action Network, editor. "Southampton Progressive Caucus Democratic Primary Debate #1 - May 5th, 2018." *YouTube*, 10 May 2018, www.youtube.com/watch?v=Au0SNCFmBAM. Accessed 1 Dec. 2019.

The Editorial Board. "New York Times Endorses Antonio Delgado, Liuba Grechen Shirley, Perry Gershon, Anthony Brindisi, Tom Malinowski and Mikie Sherrill." *The New York Times*, The New York Times Company, 20 Oct. 2018, www.nytimes.com/2018/10/20/opinion/sunday/endorsements-house-congress-new-york-jersey.html. Accessed 2 Dec. 2019.

---, editor. "Perry Gershon to represent 1st Congressional District." *Newsday*, 28 Oct. 2018, www.newsday.com/opinion/editorial/perry-gershon-to-represent-1st-congressional-district-1.22504848?fbclid=IwAR2RNU4lCCLTqm5qpvi02cOD-vAVoeFuMmi97FMbnARw9BfidLTS7NzhXCY. Accessed 2 Dec. 2019.

Filipovic, Jill. "Trump's worst enemy: Middle-aged moms." *CNN*, Turner Broadcasting System, 3 July 2018, www.cnn.com/2018/07/03/opinions/trump-worst-enemy-middle-aged-moms-filipovic/index.html. Accessed 1 Dec. 2019.

Finn, Lisa. "Hundreds Protest Outside Zeldin's Office, Demand Action On Guns." *Patch*, Patch Media, 21 Feb. 2018, patch.com/new-york/patchogue/hundreds-protest-gun-violence-outside-zeldins-office. Accessed 30 Nov. 2019.

Foderaro, Lisa W. "Will Too Much Love From Trump Be a Bad Thing for a Long Island Congressman?" *The New York Times*, The New York

Times Company, 15 Oct. 2018, www.nytimes.com/2018/10/15/nyregion/lee-zeldin-trump-support.html?rref=collection%2Fsectioncollection%2Fnyregion&action=click&contentCollection=nyregion®ion=rank&module=package&version=highlights&contentPlacement=5&pgtype=sectionfront. Accessed 1 Dec. 2019.

Freedlander, David. "Why Long Island Still Loves Trump." *Politico Magazine*, Politico, 23 May 2018, www.politico.com/magazine/story/2018/05/23/donald-trump-ms-13-long-island-218417. Accessed 1 Dec. 2019.

"Gershon on defaced campaign signs: This is just pure hate." *News12 Long Island*, News12 Interactive, 30 Oct. 2018, longisland.news12.com/story/39381918/perry-gershon-campaign-signs-defaced-with-anti-gay-language?fbclid=IwAR2Jqs0Nyj3F9HRpVzCkcdqoaTJSpkH2wZ1C3zSxZUp43RZgheiXZJef8lo. Accessed 2 Dec. 2019.

Goldberg, Michelle. "The Resistance Strikes Back, Two years of progressive organizing built the blue wave." *The New York Times*, The New York Times Company, 10 Nov. 2018, www.nytimes.com/2018/11/10/opinion/sunday/democrats-resistance-women-georgia-trump.html. Accessed 2 Dec. 2019.

Hampton Bays Union Free School District, editor. "Congressional Debate: Perry Gershon and Lee Zeldin." *YouTube*, 29 Oct. 2018, www.youtube.com/watch?v=L_-PCF4ckso&feature=youtu.be&fbclid=IwAR3PD5yu1FrrRWgOFztQe89gAwxkV7h8Wrk_6cKinsC_PRQ0VjpGNJMBAPk. Accessed 2 Dec. 2019.

Hodara, Susan. "COMMUNITIES; Irvington Bans V-Word in Play's Ads." *The New York Times*, The New York Times Company, 3 Mar. 2002, www.nytimes.com/2002/03/03/nyregion/communities-irvington-bans-v-word-in-play-s-ads.html. Accessed 30 Nov. 2019.

Hohmann, James. "The Daily 202: Anti-Trump backlash fuels a Democratic sweep in Virginia and elections across the country." *The Washington Post*, 8 Nov. 2017, www.washingtonpost.com/news/powerpost/paloma/daily-202/2017/11/08/daily-202-anti-trump-backlash-fuels-a-democratic-sweep-in-virginia-and-elections-across-the-country/5a023fd230fb0468e76541b3/. Accessed 2 Dec. 2019.

JP SPATA Southampton Town Democratic Club. , 2019, https://www.shdemclub.com/. Accessed 30 Nov. 2019.

Klausner, Andrea. "Bio - This Woman's Work." *This Woman's Work*, 2019, www.thiswomansworkk.com/. Accessed 3 Dec. 2019.

Lofholm, Nancy. "Pathbreaking transgender attorney Danyel Joffe's work led to Colorado law compensating people wrongly convicted of crimes." *The Colorado Sun*, 24 Aug. 2018, coloradosun.com/2018/08/24/danyel-joffe-obituary/. Accessed 1 Dec. 2019.

Maddow, Rachel. "DOJ charged Russian woman. TRANSCRIPT: 10/22/2018, The Rachel Maddow Show." *MSNBC*, NBC Universal, 22 Oct. 2018, www.msnbc.com/transcripts/rachel-maddow-show/2018-10-22. Accessed 2 Dec. 2019.

McMorrow, T. E. "Zeldin And Gershon Square Off." *The Independent*, 11 Sept. 2018, indyeastend.com/news-opinion/south-fork/zeldin-and-gershon-square-off/. Accessed 1 Dec. 2019.

Murphy, Rick. "Paul Davis Does Pechefsky." *The Independent*, 15 May 2018, indyeastend.com/news-opinion/south-fork/paul-davis-does-pechefsky/. Accessed 1 Dec. 2019.

Nancy Goroff for Congress. Goroff for Congress, 2019, www.goroffforcongress.com/. Accessed 2 Dec. 2019.

New York State Board of Elections. "NYS Voter Enrollment by Congressional District, Party Affiliation and Status." *2019 Enrollment by Election District/New York State Board of Elections*, 2019, www.elections.ny.gov/EnrollmentCD.html. Accessed 2 Dec. 2019.

New York State Legislative Task Force on Demographic Research and Reapportionment. "2012 Congressional Maps - Congressional District 1 ." *New York State Legislative Task Force on Demographic Research and Reapportionment* , 2012, www.latfor.state.ny.us/. Accessed 3 Dec. 2019. Map.

O'Donnell, Lawrence. "Trump fires Sessions. TRANSCRIPT: 11/7/2018, The Last Word w Lawrence O'Donnell." *MSNBC*, NBC Universal, 7 Nov. 2018, www.msnbc.com/transcripts/the-last-word/2018-11-07. Accessed 2 Dec. 2019.

Office of the Supervisor of Elections, Polk County Florida. "Summary Results - Election Night/2018 General Election." *Lori Edwards, Polk County Supervisor of Elections*, 5 June 2019, enr.electionsfl.org/POL/Summary/1805/. Accessed 2 Dec. 2019.

Pear, Robert, and Thomas Kaplan. "Senate Rejects Slimmed-Down Obamacare Repeal as McCain Votes No." *The New York Times*, The New York

Times Company, 27 July 2017, www.nytimes.com/2017/07/27/us/politics/obamacare-partial-repeal-senate-republicans-revolt.html. Accessed 30 Nov. 2019.

Peterson, Christopher. "Congressional Review Act Reversal of CFPB Auto Lending Guidance Would Be Bad for Consumers, Bad for the Country." *Consumer Federation of America*, 17 Apr. 2018, consumerfed.org/press_release/congressional-review-act-reversal-of-cfpb-auto-lending-guidance-would-be-bad-for-consumers-bad-for-the-country/. Accessed 1 Dec. 2019.

Polsky, Carol. "Progressive groups looking toward LI congressional primaries." *Newsday*, 10 June 2018, www.newsday.com/long-island/politics/democrats-progressives-local-elections-1.18852728. Accessed 2 Dec. 2019.

Putnam, Lara. "Suburbs, Political Organizing Has Been Intense Since 2016. What Could It Mean for 2020?" *American Communities Project*, 6 Aug. 2019, www.americancommunities.org/in-pennsylvanias-exurbs-and-urban-suburbs-political-organizing-has-been-intense-since-2016-what-could-it-mean-for-2020/. Accessed 2 Dec. 2019.

Putnam, Lara, and Gabriel Perez-Putnam. "Grassroots Blossom Across America, Reshaping Country's Political Geography." *American Communities Project*, 13 Sept. 2019, www.americancommunities.org/grassroots-blossom-across-america-reshaping-countrys-political-geography/. Accessed 2 Dec. 2019.

Putnam, Lara, and Theda Skocpol. "Middle America Reboots Democracy." *Democracy: A Journal of Ideas*, 20 Feb. 2018, democracyjournal.org/arguments/middle-america-reboots-democracy/. Accessed 2 Dec. 2019.

Rebecca Dolber/R.E.D. 2019, www.rebeccadolber.com/. Accessed 30 Nov. 2019.

"Rep. Zeldin Hosts Pizza and Policy Town Hall in Westhampton Beach." *Congressman Lee Zeldin Representing New York's First District*, U.S. Federal Government, 13 Feb. 2018, zeldin.house.gov/media-center/press-releases/rep-zeldin-hosts-pizza-and-policy-town-hall-westhampton-beach. Accessed 30 Nov. 2019.

Riga, Kate. "Six Democrats Campaign For Chance To Challenge U.S. Representative Lee Zeldin In November." *27east*, The Press News Group, 20 Feb. 2018, www.27east.com/news/article.cfm/East-End/548047/Six-Democrats-Continue-To-Campaign-For-

Representative-Lee-Zeldins-Seat-Foreshadowing-A-Competitive-Primary. Accessed 30 Nov. 2019.

Robertson, Campbell, et al. "Quiet Day at a Pittsburgh Synagogue Became a Battle to Survive." *The New York Times*, The New York Times Company, 28 Oct. 2018, www.nytimes.com/2018/10/28/us/pittsburgh-synagogue-shooting.html?action=click&module=Spotlight&pgtype=Homepage. Accessed 2 Dec. 2019.

Savage, Charlie. "Leaked Kavanaugh Documents Discuss Abortion and Affirmative Action." *The New York Times*, The New York Times Company, 6 Sept. 2018, www.nytimes.com/2018/09/06/us/politics/kavanaugh-leaked-documents.html?action=click&module=Top%20Stories&pgtype=Homepage. Accessed 1 Dec. 2019.

The Setauket Neighborhood House. Setauket Neighborhood Association, www.setauketneighborhoodhouse.com/. Accessed 1 Dec. 2019.

Skocpol, Theda, and Caroline Tervo, editors. "Upending American Politics." *Oxford University Press*, 2020, global.oup.com/academic/product/upending-american-politics-9780190083533. Accessed 2 Dec. 2019.

Solidarity Sundays. 2017, www.solidaritysundays.org/. Accessed 1 Dec. 2019.

Suffolk County Board of Elections. "Final Results of Federal Primary on Tuesday, June 26, 2018." *Election Night Tally*, Suffolk County Government, 26 June 2018, apps2.suffolkcountyny.gov/boe/eleres/18pf/default.htm. Accessed 1 Dec. 2019.

---. "Final Results of General Election on Tuesday, November 8, 2016, President and Vice President." *Election Night Tally*, Suffolk County Government, 8 Nov. 2016, apps2.suffolkcountyny.gov/boe/eleres/16ge/default.htm. Accessed 30 Nov. 2019.

---. "Final Results of General Election on Tuesday, November 8, 2016, Representative in Congress, 1st Congressional District." *Election Night Tally*, Suffolk County Government, 8 Nov. 2016, apps2.suffolkcountyny.gov/boe/eleres/16ge/default.htm. Accessed 30 Nov. 2019.

---. "Final Results of General Election on Tuesday, November 4, 2008, Representative in Congress, 1st Congressional District." *Election Night Tally*, Suffolk County Government, 4 Nov. 2008, apps2.suffolkcountyny.gov/boe/eleres/08ge/default.htm. Accessed 2 Dec. 2019.

---. "Final Results of General Election on Tuesday, November 4, 2014, Representative in Congress, 1st Congressional District." *Election Night Tally*, Suffolk County Government, 4 Nov. 2014, apps2.suffolkcountyny.gov/boe/eleres/14ge/default.htm. Accessed 2 Dec. 2019.

---. "Final Results of General Election on Tuesday, November 6, 2018, Representative in Congress, 1st Congressional District ." *Election Night Tally*, Suffolk County Government, 6 Nov. 2018, apps2.suffolkcountyny.gov/boe/eleres/18ge/default.htm. Accessed 2 Dec. 2019.

Take Action Suffolk County. 2017, www.takeactionsuffolk.org/. Accessed 1 Dec. 2019.

Tax March. 2019, taxmarch.org/. Accessed 30 Nov. 2019.

U.S. Census Bureau (2018). *American Community Survey 1-year estimates.* Retrieved from *Census Reporter Profile page for Congressional District 1, NY* <http://censusreporter.org/profiles/50000US3601-congressional-district-1-ny/>

United States, SUPREME COURT OF THE STATE OF NEW YORK Appellate Division, Second Judicial Department. *Lynch v. Duffy*. Docket no. 04168, 29 May 2019. *Justia U.S. Law*, Justia, law.justia.com/cases/new-york/appellate-division-second-department/2019/2019-04931.html. Accessed 2 Dec. 2019.

U.S. Census Bureau. "QuickFacts Southampton town, Suffolk County, New York; Brookhaven town, Suffolk County, New York." *United States Census Bureau*, U.S. Department of Commerce, 2018, www.census.gov/quickfacts/fact/table/southamptontownsuffolkcountynewyork,brookhaventownsuffolkcountynewyork/PST045218. Accessed 2 Dec. 2019.

U.S. Census Bureau, et al. "My Congressional District 116th Congress." *U.S. Census Bureau*, U.S. Department of Commerce, 2018, www.census.gov/mycd/?st=36&cd=01. Accessed 3 Dec. 2019.

Vote Like A Mother. Like A Mother, 2018, votelikeamother.org/. Accessed 1 Dec. 2019.

Walsh, Christopher. "Zeldin Takes Pass on Forum." *The East Hampton Star*, 23 Aug. 2018, www.easthamptonstar.com/archive/zeldin-takes-pass-forum. Accessed 1 Dec. 2019.

Weber-Floyd, Barbara. Letter. *The Southampton Press*, Eastern ed., 23 Feb. 2017, sec. A, p. 10. *27east*, digital.olivesoftware.com/Olive/APA/Southampton/#panel=document. Accessed 30 Nov. 2019.

---. Letter. *The Southampton Press*, Western ed., 9 Mar. 2017, sec. A, p. 10. *27east*, digital.olivesoftware.com/Olive/APA/Southampton/#panel=document. Accessed 30 Nov. 2019.

Wehner, Greg. "Trump Makes A Quick Stop." *The Southampton Press*, Western ed., 23 Aug. 2018, sec. A, pp. 1+. *27east*, www.27east.com/search-archive/?type=current . Accessed 1 Dec. 2019.

Willis, Oliver. "GOP Rep [Zeldin] brushes off town hall mom pleading for help for her heroin-addicted son." *Resist and Replace*, David Posnett, 29 Apr. 2017, resistancesuffolk.blog/2017/04/29/gop-rep-zeldin-brushes-off-town-hall-mom-pleading-for-help-for-her-heroin-addicted-son/. Accessed 30 Nov. 2019.

Wise, Justin. "GOP lawmaker sends voters incorrect absentee ballot info." *The Hill*, Capitol Hill Publishing, a subsidiary of News Communications, 23 Oct. 2018, thehill.com/homenews/campaign/412768-gop-lawmaker-sends-mailer-to-voters-with-incorrect-absentee-ballot-info. Accessed 2 Dec. 2019.

"With primaries over, LI congressional campaigns heat up." *News12 Long Island*, News12 Interactive, 28 June 2018, longisland.news12.com/story/38537377/with-primaries-over-li-congressional-campaigns-heat-up. Accessed 1 Dec. 2019.

Woodward, Bob. *Fear: Trump in the White House*. New York, Simon & Schuster, 2018.

Made in the USA
Monee, IL
28 March 2020